EDUCATION
A Conceptual and Empirical Approach

EDUCATION
A Conceptual
and Empirical Approach

Mary Alice White

Teachers College, Columbia University

Jan Duker

Teachers College, Columbia University

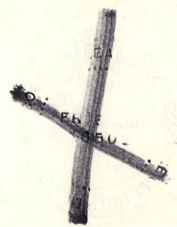

HOLT, RINEHART AND WINSTON
New York   Chicago   San Francisco   Atlanta
Dallas   Montreal   Toronto   London   Sydney

Copyright © 1973 by Holt, Rinehart and Winston, Inc.
All rights reserved
Library of Congress Catalog Card Number: 73-52
ISBN: 0-03-080209-1
Printed in the United States of America
3 4 5 6   038   9 8 7 6 5 4 3 2 1

Cover: Red-figured painting on kylix, detail, *Instruction in Music and Grammar in an Attic School.*
State Museum, Berlin.

Preface

The title of this book reflects our purpose, which is to introduce the student to a particular approach to the study of education. We believe that the conceptual and empirical approach described and exemplified here provides a particularly useful framework for accomplishing two major goals: (1) to assist the student in thinking analytically about different models of education and their goals, how schools attempt to reach them, and how the goals are related to the characteristics of the society that established the schools; and (2) to help the student learn to evaluate the evidence in debates about education, to know what qualifies as acceptable evidence, and to look critically in the light of this evidence at the claims of proponents of various approaches to education.

The conceptual tool we have chosen is that of the educational model. We have described and analyzed some of the important historical and theoretical models of schooling to help the student focus on the implicit and explicit goals of any educational system he may study. These models are discussed in Section 1. They have been selected partly for the contrast in goals which they offer, and partly for their clarity as models in developing a conceptual approach. We have attempted to present the essential elements of each model in a form that parallels other models so the student can compare and contrast them. For example, he can compare the Athenian model of schooling to the Chinese model and the contemporary American models without being overwhelmed by masses of detailed information. Although we hope to broaden the student's historical perspective about schooling, our primary aim is to help him learn and practice a way of thinking about schools in which he can conceptualize a model of schooling, examine how the society affects the model, and evaluate the role of schools in enabling a society to accomplish its goals.

The empirical approach to educational evidence is stressed in Section 2. Selected educational models are evaluated against the relevant educational evidence as the student is introduced to some of the important issues in such evaluation. The emphasis is on the nature of empirical evidence and how it can be used to evaluate what works in education.

The two tools of conceptual and empirical analyses are brought together in Section 3 and employed to discuss some of the current issues in learning, teaching, curriculum, and schooling. In discussing the issues, we attempt to exemplify an approach that emphasizes conceptual and empirical factors. Although we hope to avoid partisan views, we do not hope to present conclusive answers in areas as complex and much debated as some of those discussed. After reading our book, however, we hope that students will be more skillful in reaching valid conclusions about educational issues by asking the relevant questions, looking for the appropriate evidence, and basing their conclusions on the evidence rather than on faith, preconceptions, or claims of advocates.

The readings for each section have been selected to illustrate the conceptual and empirical issues under discussion in the text. The range of topics covered is as broad as the time span, but each reading has been included for its value in increasing the ability of the student to think rigorously and systematically about educational issues.

The approach developed in this book has been taught several times as an introductory course. The instructor may find it helpful to provide students with guided opportunities for practicing conceptual and empirical techniques. In our experience, students of education, whether beginners or experienced teachers, have enjoyed learning how to collect educational evidence in live classrooms; for example, learning to make observations in classrooms or to collect evidence regarding a particular aspect of their own teaching. They have found the acquisition of these skills an exciting way to study education as human behavior.

We are indebted to many colleagues at our respective universities for providing an atmosphere in which conceptual and empirical approaches to education could flourish. We are especially indebted to the educational thinking of Robert Schaefer of Teachers College and Marcia Edwards of the University of Minnesota. We are pleased to acknowledge our gratitude to John Mulhern and to Katy Kimball for their help in the preparation of this book.

Rye, New York   MARY ALICE WHITE
January 1973   JAN DUKER

Contents

Models of Education

Historical Models of Education

The essential factor in the organization of a living state, the world is coming to realize, is the organization of an education.
—H. G. Wells, *The Outline of History*, vol. 2, p. 579.

KOU K'AI-TCHE,
The Instructress in the Palace.
The British Museum, London.

A basic assumption of this book is that rational and systematic analysis of educational goals and evidence is essential if we are to behave intelligently about education. We will be concerning ourselves primarily with three basic questions about education:

1. What is education expected to achieve?
2. By what yardstick is it to be measured?
3. According to what evidence is it to be evaluated?

Competing goals are present today. Some groups want more and more traditional achievement; some want more positive interpersonal relationships. Others contend that schools not only should educate more and more pupils, but that they should educate according to a set of values that some term "humanistic." It is not merely means that are under examination, but the ends as well.

Analyzing Educational Goals

Where do we begin our analysis? We begin with the goals of education. Unless we can be quite clear about what we want a system of schooling to do, we can never maintain a useful discussion. In reviewing a book, one of the rules is that the reviewer should evaluate the book in terms of what the writer was trying to accomplish. And so it is with schooling systems. They are designed in complex ways to accomplish certain objectives. What point is there in arguing that School A does not produce talented writers if School A has been organized to produce graduates who can compete in the economy with a high school diploma, or to produce pupils who can get into a certain range of four-year colleges, or to keep pupils in the

building without harm to each other for six hours a day? Often the objectives of a school system are vague, even contradictory, a compromise between what one force in society wants the system to do versus what another wants it to do, but the objectives are there, implicitly if not explicitly.

What are some common goals for our current school system? What does the man in the street expect the United States schooling system to accomplish—the blue-collar worker who has bought his own home recently, the government employee, the postal clerk, the garage mechanic, the insurance salesman, the saleslady, the high school student—what do they want schooling to accomplish? We almost forgot to ask what the scholars want from schools, probably because they are a drop in the bucket in voting power, although a big drop in the process that makes certain decisions.

Here is a sample of what one group of people said they wanted our public school system to do (White, 1970). This broad array of goals was produced by thirty university students, a relatively homogeneous group. Think what a more extensive survey might produce!

G To increase a person's income
  To help him go up the ladder occupationally and socially
E To help him handle everyday problems like contracts, the law, and payments, his money and property
  To teach him the story of his country
  To teach him to be patriotic and loyal to this country
E To teach him to read and write well
  To teach him to do arithmetic well
  To teach him how to be a good citizen
  To teach him how to be responsible in a democracy
E To teach him to stay out of trouble such as crime, jails, and drugs
  To teach him how to understand life around him
  To teach him the classics and various fields
E To teach him new knowledge and new ways of gaining knowledge
  To teach him not to mess up the environment
  To teach him good health habits
  To teach him about the human race
E To teach him how to analyze issues and to think critically
  To teach him to think conceptually
  To develop in him a love for learning
  To teach him how to be a life-long learner
  To give every pupil the same educational opportunity
  To give every pupil the same educational achievement
  To teach him a certain outlook on life
  To teach him a certain philosophic or religious point of view, or to strengthen it
  To teach him how to be a political participator
  To teach him English, spoken and written

To teach him a certain level of literacy
To increase the supply of certain skills needed for our nation
To supply manpower for military defense
To provide leadership in certain areas

How could we deal with such a mixture of goals in a systematic way? One way would be to look at them from the perspective of history, searching for relationships between certain educational goals and the particular kind of society in which they arose. This might give us some clues as to what is happening now in our society, and it might enable us to make some predictions.

We might also look at the kinds of evidence people accept as determining whether or not a system is accomplishing a particular goal. If the educational goal were maximal literacy, then measuring the percentage of people over a certain age who can read at a specified level might be a reasonable procedure. But suppose that the educational goal were to produce a certain kind of character. The Spartan model of education, which will be discussed below, proposed to do just that: to produce a Spartan character. How would we know if the schools were succeeding? We might compare the percent of Spartan warriors who surrendered in one battle with the percent who had surrendered in previous battles, but such figures would be rather hard to obtain. If an important military loss occurred, and if there were charges, accurate or not, that the loss was due to a lack of bravery on the part of Spartan soldiers, then we would predict that the Spartan school system would come under immediate attack and that a change in leadership would be likely. Could we predict what those reforms would be? We could predict that such a school system would be changed in those ways that people viewed as likely to produce better and braver soldiers: probably more military content in the curriculum, more strenuous training, more emphasis on patriotism and bravery, more followership training, more awards for bravery, more rigorous endurance tests, less scholarly learning, more retired generals appointed to important posts with the school, and fewer scholars who could not model courage in battle.

Let us begin a short historical trip during which we are going to ask these two questions:

1. What educational goals arose in what kind of society?
2. What evidence would have been acceptable to measure progress toward such goals?

This trip will provide much evidence on the relationship between the goals of society and the goals of education.

Historical Models of Schooling
A School System for an Empire

Unlike many historical trips through education, we will start not in Athens, but in China, because China's educational model may have begun earlier and because it has received much less attention in the West. We will rely heavily on several sources for this account (Hu, 1962; Latourette, 1938; Li, 1965; MacNair, 1946; Myers, 1960).

The fifth to the third century B.C. was a period of chaos in China, the era of the Contending States. The society had been one in which there were essentially two classes, that of the nobility, and that of the vast peasantry with few rights. The eldest son of the nobility was educated at court, while district boarding schools educated the younger sons of the noble class. The intellectuals of that time taught in these district boarding schools, or at court, or set up wandering schools as did Confucius (551– 479 B.C.). While these schools were being set up in China, perhaps the first boarding schools anywhere, Greece was beginning its Golden Age.

Confucius, the most revered figure in Chinese history, was a social reformer who was frustrated in his ambition to be appointed to an important administrative post. In his time, China was a divided country in which rulers of the various states warred among themselves and subjected their people to excessive taxes and forced labor. Confucius and the followers who gathered about him traveled throughout the states and attempted to persuade the ruling feudal lords to carry out a variety of social reforms. The teaching of Confucius was intensely moral. The goal for the individual was to become a superior man, a man of perfect virtue. The goals for society were a harmonious family, a well-ordered state, and a peaceful world.

Confucius's teaching method was one of informal conversation with his students. He accepted students from poor families, thus breaking the monopoly which the rulers had on control of the techniques of government. Some of his students reached positions of authority and influence. The Confucian school was nearly wiped out during the Ch'in dictatorship (221– 206 B.C.); however, Confucianism became the state doctrine in 136 B.C. during the succeeding Han dynasty (202 B.C.–A.D. 220). Twelve years later a national university was established. Departments were formed around the classics, which soon became the required texts in all subjects, and selection of good officials eventually became dependent on knowledge of them.

When Confucius set up his school, he was influenced by the immediate past, which had been anarchical, so it is not surprising that one of his major educational goals was to bring about order to establish a moral base. He started by defining terms, much as the analytic philosophers of the twentieth century have done. At this very early point in educational history, we might note a possible connection between an educational system that puts high emphasis upon bringing order into the forefront, and a preceding period of turbulence within society. We might think that it is no coincidence, for example, that Russell thought it important to define terms and to bring more precision to bear upon philosophy in the period following World War I.

In the district boarding schools in early Chinese history, the curriculum consisted of intricate etiquette, rites, and ceremonies as the major subjects, followed by dancing, music, archery, charioteering, writing, and arithmetic. What does such a curriculum tell us about the educational objectives? We would conjecture that this was a school system designed for training younger sons of the noble class who might inherit the family title, and therefore needed to know how to behave around the court where such rites were a very important part of life. The rites served to bind together people of a certain class through their own in-group ceremonies, which kept them in close personal touch with each other, and permitted them to share power in some sort of organized way. As Hookham (1970, p. 25) points out, formally ordered relationships have special value in times of upheaval: "These observances, which may strike us as empty formalities, appeared significant and valuable in times when social relationships were dissolving and when established authority was being challenged at all levels of society. . . ." We might guess that dancing and music were important parts of the leisure time of court life, that writing and arithmetic played some sort of functional role in the lives of the nobility, and that archery and chariot driving were handy things to know in time of war.

In the schools that followed the teachings of Confucius, rites had the same important position within the curriculum, followed by music and literature. And what was left out? The omissions suggest a somewhat different emphasis in educational goals, which did not include the training of warriors.

We will now take considerable liberties with the history of China in order to emphasize some relationships between educational objectives and social conditions. The first empire was established in China in 221 B.C. It was probably the first national state of such size in the world. The supreme school of thought at that time was the Legalist school which held that the law of the state was supreme. From this view came its name, "Legalist," meaning one who was a specialist in the law. This particular philosophy obviously was compatible with the concurrent development of a unified empire. The first emperor of China, Shih Huang-Ti (222–210

B.C.), must have been a remarkable man. In his rather short reign, he abolished feudalism and established an imperial government by which the governors of the thirty-six administrative provinces were appointed. He put the Great Wall around China's boundaries. In order to eliminate local leadership, he moved the aristocracy bodily from the provinces to the national capital. And then he burned the books.

If a ruler wanted to build a large, unified, centralized empire in China at a time when it was ruled by many feudal lords with competing regional loyalties, he might well bring all these competitors into the capitol where they would lose their local and regional power. He might collect military weapons, melt them down, and cast them into bells and statues. One can understand building the Great Wall to keep the empire in and the enemies out. But why did Shih Huang-Ti order the burning of the books? By burning those books that belonged to private people, the emperor was ensuring the destruction of a basis for comparing his outlook on life with any other, or for disputing his views on the basis of any recorded authority. He was putting all knowledge in the hands of his own centralized government. Li (1965, p. 101) describes the motivation as follows: "Shih Huang-Ti and his advisers concluded that if different schools of thought were allowed to contend and criticisms of government policies were left unchecked, they would soon become seeds of dissension and discontent which in turn might weaken government control over its subjects, induce revolts, and eventually break up the empire." Some books of a technical nature were exempt from burning, as was an authorized version of history.

This very energetic emperor died in 210 B.C. He was said to be the most hated emperor of China. The policy of antiintellectualism won him the enmity of the country's intellectual leadership, who had great respect and much local power. When revolts developed and spread, the intellectuals joined the rebels and hastened the decline of this dynasty. As Li comments, "and ever since few historians have had much good to say about China's first totalitarian regime" (p. 101). His son succeeded him as emperor, but was killed in a revolt in 207 B.C. After several years of warfare, a peasant, Liu Pang, fought his way to rule. He became first emperor of the Han Dynasty (202 B.C.–A.D. 220), one of the longest and greatest in the country's history.

The rise of a scholarly class.   Inevitably there were changes in the schools during the Han Dynasty. What would we predict? Philosophy and literature were revived, books were restored and copied, memories of scholars were recorded. The first act, educationally, was to retrieve the lost information. The Legalist school of thought waned and the Confucian school of thought came back to power, perhaps because they were the only scholars still alive, and few scholars had survived. They also knew the rites. Knowledge of traditional rites in any society is ordinarily very important, particularly when they are in danger of being lost, as when the books were burned. (Imagine, if you can, that all the books, movies, TV tapes, tape recordings, cassettes, and every other means of recording information were destroyed overnight in our country! Imagine how all of us would feel when we realized that we had lost our recorded past. The most important people in our society would suddenly be those who still remembered, those who knew what it was like before, those who remembered knowledge and could tell us.)

In the early years of the Han dynasty, no single school of philosophical thought prevailed. In 140 B.C., Emperor Wu-Ti (140–87 B.C.) came into power. He favored the adherents of Confucianism, and eventually appointed a descendant of Confucius superintendent of public instruction. Under Wu-Ti's reign, the Confucians became the dominant scholarly class in China. This scholarly class, highly esteemed and influential, became an important part of Chinese life for centuries. Entry into the scholarly class could be gained on the basis of merit rather than through birth alone. The Confucian scholars brought continuity with the past and influenced education and government in China into the twentieth century.

In 124 B.C., Emperor Wu-Ti founded the first system of state schools and examinations, apparently one of the first such systems anywhere in the world. It grew into a huge civil service system that lasted until 1905. When our public school systems are criticized for being archaic, unchanging, and much too bound to the past, we might remind ourselves that the past is not very long ago in our country. In fact, our current educational system in many respects is not older than seventy-five years. Yet in China a national examination system lasted over *two thousand years.*

The Chinese model of education perhaps represents the longest human experience with education, and for that reason alone would be a model from which we can learn. As a model, it produced the earliest organized national system of education whose aim was to educate a selected civilian population for government service. Significantly, the Chinese governmental structure as early as the fourth or fifth century B.C. was placed in the hands of civilians who were to be admitted to this governing class on the basis of tested competence, and not through inheritance. Because the aim of the educational model was to produce a high level of civil servants, the educational system was government controlled and centrally administered.

In the Chinese model, a scholarship class was equated with a governing class. It was no doubt among the first educational models to equate the two. Scholarship was seen as the appropriate criterion for governing. In traditional China, as Hu (1962) points out, there was no hereditary aristocracy based on birth, religion, or wealth. Hu describes the preeminence of education as follows: "Throughout the ages, the Confucian ideal of leaving the reins of government and social control in the hands of the morally superior or educated members of the society persisted, thus making traditional Chinese society, at least in theory, an open one, the sole criterion for upward mobility being proved ability through education" (p. 7). The elevation of the scholarly class also provided for cultural unity and the transmission of culture, but it is very important to note that this model assumes that scholarship is the relevant criterion for choosing people for positions in government. The scholarly class was given the highest status, it had the tested knowledge of a highly selected group, and it had power. When we discuss Plato's model of education, we might remember that the Chinese model was the first to put knowledge and power together. The scholarly class had access to mobility on the basis of merit. Mobility did occur, even though it might require that an entire family put its resources together to educate a bright young man, but the rewards were proportionately high. Under Emperor Wu-Ti, a national university was established in China in 125 B.C., and by the second century A.D. there were some 30,000 students enrolled.

In China, there were three levels of examination quite similar to what we have now at the bachelor's, master's, and doctorate levels. The bachelor level was called "flowering talent," the master's level "promoted man," and the doctorate "advanced scholar." It is said that the examinations were strict, that they were very fair, and that no identification was used. Candidates were isolated for several days in their cells. The rate of suicide was probably very high because quotas were set and no more than 1 percent passed the examinations at the various levels. Passing the examinations was a tremendous honor to the person, his family, and his community. Candidates could retake the examination as many times as they liked. It is said that grandsons and grandfathers would occasionally sit together for the examinations. MacNair (1946, pp. 7–14) has given a detailed description of this examination system.

Examinations as the goals of education.   During the T'ang dynasty (A.D. 618–907), the examination system became greatly elaborated. Candidates could compete for a wide variety of degrees and had a choice of topics: classics, mathematics, calligraphy, Taoist studies, and for the army, tests of skill in martial exercises, As Latourette (1938) comments, however, "degrees taken in the classics appear to have been the most highly esteemed. Any radical departure from established theories would scarcely commend itself to the bureaucrats who read the papers" (pp. 216–217).

As time went by, the examinations in the Chinese system became more and more narrowly based and inflexible. They stressed minute knowledge of the classics, chiefly Confucian literature and philosophy. Eventually only essays were required, to be done in various classical styles. Originality was not encouraged. As broad education was no longer tested, it was dropped from the curricular goals, and in time, all mathematics was eliminated.

Eventually the examination *became* the goal of education. This is a very important point, one likely to happen when examinations become critical entry points for mobility in a class structure. As the examination became more narrow, education itself became more narrow. When this happens, we see a circular educational model, one in which students go to school to learn how to pass an examination, which determines admission to the next educational level, where they prepare to pass the next examination, and so forth.

One reason for describing the Chinese model and examination system at length is that they provide an interesting historical example of the lack of realistic performance criteria to permit the use of *criterion-referenced measures*. There is a good deal of talk among educational specialists today about the need to think differently about standardized achievement tests. These achievement tests are *norm-referenced measures*, which measure how well a person does compared to some group whose performance serves as the norm or standard. Let us assume that you are teaching a sixth grade class. Sally reads at grade level 6.6, which means that she reads at the level of average students six months along in the sixth grade. If she took this test in the second month of the school year, she would be reading about four months above the national median (6.6 less 6.2). What we are measuring is how well Sally does compared with the group on which the test was standardized. The yardstick is the median, the performance level above and below which 50 percent of the sixth grade in the national sample performed at a certain point in time. If you are interested in how an average pupil is doing, this may be quite a good measure. The median defines the midpoint, so that half of the nation's pupils are going to be below the median just by definition. In our big cities, more than half of the pupils measure below the median. By choosing the median, we are by definition assigning half of the pupils in the nation to a position below the norm. This is difficult for many parents to understand. In the public view, it sounds as though half of the pupils are doing badly, which is not necessarily the case.

Criterion-referenced measurement, on the other hand, requires that the criterion used to measure progress should be a performance criterion established ahead of time, preferably stated in precise behavioral terms. If what we want to know is how well Sally can do arithmetic, we may get only a part of the picture when we compare Sally with the national median.

We may want to give Sally some tests of arithmetic to see what she can do, and what she cannot do, having stipulated ahead of time the precise operations that we want her to accomplish by the end of sixth grade. In this approach, we focus on determining arithmetical operations Sally can perform, not on how she compares with other sixth graders.

In the Chinese system, the ability to write an essay in a particular classical style does not seem to have very much to do with the ability to function as a government official. Presumably, the ability to write a pleasant and even elegant letter is a nice asset, but a criterion-referenced measure would select from among the scholarship class those people, for example, who could handle satisfactorily (to be defined) the complaints of thirty citizens with 90 percent success (to be defined) within forty-eight hours. Today we hear of rudeness and inefficiency in many service occupations. If the criterion for hiring clerks in our service businesses is a high school diploma, then we may have a criterion that bears little relationship to the quality of the service to be rendered. A much better test might be, for example, to determine how well the clerk clerks. Can he do the necessary tasks quickly and pleasantly? Can he handle customer complaints, add up purchases, wrap parcels, make change, and write out charge slips? This would be an example of criterion-referenced measurement, for how the clerk is to perform on the job is detailed precisely. Applicants are then tested for their ability to carry out the tasks required.

Let us remember criterion-referenced measurement because we want to come back to it quite often as an important technique. When measurement by examination does not have reference to some stated criterion of performance, the examination may become irrelevant. Education in such cases is tied to the examination, and then education may become the servant of an irrelevant examination.

Change in the system.   In China, the national educational system and examination system lasted until 1905, when China found herself somewhat disturbed by the advances of western civilization, and particularly disturbed by the advances in Japan. As a result, there was a demand for a radical change in the educational system. The old examination system was abolished and a new educational system was initiated with a grade division of 6–4–4 in two tracks, one academic and one technical or practical, very much like our western model. Between 1895 and 1925, Christianity expanded markedly in China. Latourette (1938, p. 481) reports the following data for numbers of Protestant missionaries in China: 1889–1300; 1905–3500; 1910–5000; 1925–8000. Roman Catholic missionaries, although fewer in number, showed a comparable increase. Missionaries often built schools, which was one source of western influence on education.

Another was the great student migration that occurred after 1900 when thousands of Chinese students studied abroad. Many went to Japan and Europe, but many also came to the United States. One historian has commented, "In some respects, between 1895 and 1933 the mental life of China moved farther from its old moorings than that of the West had done between the thirteenth and the twentieth century" (Latourette, p. 487).

By 1937, prior to Communist control of China, it was reported that 43 percent of Chinese school age youths were enrolled in school; in the 1960s, under Communist control, it was claimed that 94 percent were enrolled. What is not clear is who was being counted as school age, or what kind of schooling they were enrolled in. Nevertheless, it is quite obvious that Chinese Communists, like their ancestors, have a strong stake in widespread education. In 1958, the vice-premier of the state council and chief propagandist of the Communist party in China, Lu Ting-Yi, made this statement about the role of education in that type of government: "Socialist education is inconceivable without Communist party leadership. Socialist education is one of the powerful weapons for transforming the old and building the new society" (See Readings: Section 1, for full text). This may be one type of educational model for a totalitarian state, and we notice two things about it: one, that education must be run by the party, and two, education is an instrument for the transformation of society. If the aim is to transform society, it is essential that education reach everyone in some form. If the aim is to transform society in the name of any political theory, then it is important to model the schools in the desired political form.

In June 1966, during the Cultural Revolution, it was announced that all regular schooling would be suspended to permit the formulation of new and ideologically purer criteria for student admission (Dorrill, in Robinson, p. 94). This announcement was the culmination of the purging of academic officials at all educational levels. "Work teams" sent to the schools by party committees had provided the major mechanisms for carrying out the purge at the local level. The universities in China reopened in 1970 after four years of being closed. The Chinese universities were reopened to peasants, admitted to study a selected curriculum, who apparently received preference in admission over scholars and those in the upper classes. What would we predict about the curriculum of these universities? The universities were opened for the study of engineering and other vocational training. In Aristotle's terms, this education would be an illiberal one.

In summary, before 1905, the Chinese model had three characteristics: one, it was designed to produce officials for government service; second, it was based on scholarship for selection purposes; and third, selection was done through examined competence. We will term this model that of the *tested scholarly officialdom model*, meaning it used testing, that scholarship was the ingredient, and that its purpose was to create government officials.

The Athenian Model of Schooling

There are several different models of schooling identified with Greece. The earliest model was based on Homer, a model that Marrou (1956) has termed "Homeric chivalry"; there was the Spartan model which we shall discuss later; the Athenian model of the fifth century B.C.; Plato's and Aristotle's model; the educational changes carried out by the Sophists; the model proposed by Isocrates; and finally, the classical model which derived from all these sources and which we associate with the Hellenistic Era in history. It is beyond the purpose of this book to deal with each of these. For the purpose of conceptualizing, however, we shall deal mainly with the Athenian model of the fifth century B.C. and urge the reader to pursue the others through the references at the end of this chapter.

We can be sure from the outset that the Athenian model of schooling will be different from the model that prevailed in China. Athens was a relatively tiny city-state, cut off by mountains and a rugged coastline from other areas of what we now call Greece. By contrast, China was early accessible through its navigable rivers and had a more easily traveled land mass. An empire was geographically possible in China in 221 B.C., whereas the largest administrative unit to flourish in Greece at the same time was that of the city-state.

In the beginning of the fifth century B.C., Athenian education was theoretically open to all its citizens; but since education was a private arrangement between a tutor and the pupil's father, which required both money and three or four years of leisure, the students were largely aristocratic. The purpose of this type of schooling was to educate selected young men in those leadership characteristics related to their handling of power and responsibility as the ruling group of the city-state. The curriculum included virtue as defined at that time, aesthetics, military prowess and bravery, physical skill, and the in-group social skills of music and art, much like the skills of court etiquette in China. Even music had a direct relationship to leadership functions, at least according to Russell's report: "Music, though it could play its part in courtship, existed primarily to promote courage in battle—a purpose to which, according to Plato, it ought to be confined by law" (Russell, in Gross, 1971, p. 5). Selected social skills probably served much the same purpose in Athens as they did in China, bonding the select and ruling group, helping it to maintain its own close and smooth ties, and regularizing the system of power so as to prevent its dissolution by internecine fighting among the ruling group.

These schools and gymnasia, whether by conscious intent or not, provided the city-state with a continuity of leadership that had the desired attributes as defined by that leadership. The accounts handed down to us suggest that among those admitted to the schools, the more able were likely to rise to prominence either through physical and military skills, or through the skills of reason or aesthetics. It would be well to remember that the glories of Athens at that time were possible largely because it was an economically viable slave state, where the free and prosperous men had leisure to talk, to pursue ideas, to train their young men who were not hard at work during their youth, and where the Sophists and others had the time to argue what an education should be about. Athens was one of the first places, perhaps the *first* place in Western Civilization, that had a large group of literate people with the leisure to use their minds freely on topics of greater importance than the next meal, the next foraging expedition, the next harvest, or the next battle. It is interesting to wonder whether the same intellectual flowering would have taken place had this same leisure been available to another culture at an earlier time.

The Athenian model of the fifth century selected sons of free men who were trained to take on the responsibilities of the government. This model emphasized intelligent management and the use of the mind in such skills as logic, argumentation, debate, and dialogue. It emphasized virtue, belief in the good man, and belief in the good life. What was new was enjoyment of life. Aesthetics and the use of leisure were highly prized, to be used in an enjoyable, refined, and cultured way. Loyalty to the city and state was also stressed. This Athenian model could be termed that of the "good and noble guardians."

Later, in the fifth century A.D., many changes occurred in this model, one of which involved a continuous debate as to whether education should be democratic or reserved for the aristocracy. As the military aspect of schooling diminished, the role of sports and participation in them by all citizens, who were going to the gymnasia daily by the end of the century, increased. Apparently this democratization of the gymnasia led to the concept of schooling for all citizens, for it was sometime in this fifth century that the first formal school was founded in Athens, although private tutors and their classes continued to exist.

Democratic schooling was opposed by Plato and Aristotle, as well as others, who distinguished between a "liberal" education—that intended for the free man, from the word "liber" meaning free—and an "illiberal" education—that intended to train the slave in manual tasks and household chores. The liberal education that they espoused was for the sons of the aristocracy. (Plato's ideal school would have admitted girls.) The principle which we accept without question, namely, that everyone in our country is entitled to an education, was a principle that many Athenians rejected.

Plato and Aristotle were not the only Greeks to influence the development of education. As early as 600 B.C., Sappho was headmistress of a remarkable school for girls on the island of Lesbos. This school offered an education as advanced as was available to men at that time. While we are all familiar with Plato's ideas about an ideal school for the very select, we should also remember that Isocrates was equally eloquent about an education for all citizens. According to Marrou (1956), it was Isocrates who was the prime educator of Greece in the fourth century B.C., and it was he, not Plato, who was the major influence in developing what we call classical education. Where Plato sought perfect knowledge, Isocrates supported the most nearly right solution. Isocrates has been described as having a "middle-of-the-road, common-sense attitude" toward knowledge and the possibility of learning absolute truth (Proussis, 1965, p. 65). Isocrates wrote that "likely conjecture about useful things is far preferable to exact knowledge of the useless, and that to be a little superior in important things is of greater worth than to be pre-eminent in petty things that are without value for living" (Quoted in Proussis, p. 66).

The Spartan Model of Education

The Spartans had quite a different model of education. Spartans were a minority in their geographical area, and maintained political control by being very efficient soldiers, well able to defend their frontiers. The Spartan educational goals were military competence, courage, obedience, and physical fitness. At the age of seven, each son was taken away from his family and put into training that lasted until he was eighteen. It was extremely rigorous training, organized by packs, with one boy as the leader. They underwent tests of endurance, and fighting instincts that would be useful for guiding an efficient military unit were encouraged. The curriculum put little emphasis on reading, except they may have read, or had read to them, Homeric poems about war. There was little poetry or other arts, except marching songs and a military type of dancing. The only surprise in this military model is that girls were also educated. They lived at home but otherwise had very similar training, especially in physical fitness. Girls were also trained for motherhood and child care. Why did the Spartan model include girls? One possible reason is that the Spartans were a minority, and they needed to utilize everybody in their community. Girls were important as a source of added manpower and of healthy babies. Babies who were not healthy were left to die to avoid the costs of bringing them up.

An interesting question to raise in this context is how many years passed from the time of Sparta before girls were again educated on an equal basis? It was not until 1850, or about 2000 years later, that the English universities opened to women, not on an equal basis, but at least there was access. In Lutheran and Calvinistic areas, girls attended school with boys in the sixteenth century; female academies opened their doors in the seventeenth and eighteenth centuries. In the United States, Oberlin admitted girls in the 1830s, and Mt. Holyoke was founded during this same period.

The Spartan model was certainly military, and if we add the word, "state," it would give emphasis to the devotion to the state that this model stressed. So we might term the Spartan education a *state military model* in which every able body was needed for imminent battle and would give his life obediently to the state.

The Western Liberal Arts Model

Adler and Mayer (1958) have stated that there has been one model of education in the western world, beginning in Greece and lasting some twenty-five centuries. This statement should make us pause. Of course, there were variations in the model as they point out, but essentially it was the same model, what we are going to call the *western liberal arts model* to make sure that we keep in mind constantly that this is a western model. (One reason for introducing the Chinese model first was so we would not be parochial in our educational views.)

There were three major characteristics of that western liberal arts model as it existed over time. First, the model was intended to school the few, the privileged group, not the many. Until 1850, schooling was never applied to the majority, to the many, and certainly not to all. Second, its basic concern was "to prepare the leisured few for the learned and holy vocations, and later, for the highest ranks of commerce and government," as Adler and Mayer note. Clearly this model prepared the advantaged for the select occupations and positions of their time. Third, the aim of the model, as far as content was concerned, was to mold a good man into service to society. The assumption was that education would make him a good man, and that he, in turn, should render service to society. The curriculum reflected the importance of leisure. "In a world where nearly all the labor was done by slaves, the students were members of that minority destined by birth or fortune, usually by both, to live a life of leisure" (Adler and Mayer, 1958). A point often forgotten in educational debates about the western liberal arts model is that it was intended only for the advantaged class. Their use of leisure time had a very important influence upon the curriculum. This model was not originally intended for ordinary people, or for a society such as ours, but was developed in a society where the work was performed by slaves, and in agricultural and industrial societies, by peasants and workers.

The situation is very different in the United States today. Out of over 200 million people, 60 million are involved in education in some way—as pupils, teachers, or administrators. Education is the single biggest industry in our country with almost 3 million teachers, over 7 million college students, and annual expenditures of about 65 billion dollars (*Education Supplement, Saturday Review*, October 18, 1969). We should try to keep such figures in mind when we begin to compare educational models. However bad or good one may think the United States educational system is, the magnitude of it is staggering. We forget that it is a relatively new idea that everybody should go to school. As of 1969, 98.9 percent of the children in the United States between the ages of seven and thirteen were enrolled in school (*Statistical Abstract of the United States*, 1970). Historically, this is an incredible percentage.

The curriculum of the western liberal arts model included grammar; logic, which contained within it debate; rhetoric, the art of persuasion and lawmaking (a very important talent if people were to be educated to be officials and to serve the state); geometry; geography; natural history; astronomy; arithmetic; and music. These were the liberal arts that prepared a free man for a life of public service and for intellectual and aesthetic activity. To be in public life, he needed grammar as he needed to be able to write well. He needed logic, which included speaking well and persuasively. Since he needed to know something about the world around him, he needed geography, geometry, natural history, and astronomy. He needed arithmetic for public office and for managing his personal life; and he needed music for his leisure. Over the centuries, the definition of service has changed. The classical model emphasized service to the state, whereas the medieval version emphasized service to God.

The basic western liberal arts model and the Chinese model have lasted over twenty-five centuries. Why have these educational models been so durable? Things do not last that long without serving important purposes. Did the conditions in which these two models thrived remain essentially unchanged so that there was no need for another model, or were these models answering some stable or basic needs that persisted through change? Perhaps education is one of those things about which we are naturally conservative for a variety of reasons as Stephens (1967) has suggested. In the minds of many people, the western liberal arts model is one they take for granted as being best. It symbolizes a good education. It is a quality education, the kind of education identified with cultured people. Technical schooling or non-liberal arts schooling does not have these associations with status.

The curriculum in the western liberal arts model was the same for everyone, presumably because the people who were admitted represented a small, homogeneous group. No productive skills were included, nor was technical or vocational education as we use these terms today. Advanced education was also assumed to be liberal in nature, which meant that advanced education was for the learned professions. Some of the related assumptions of this model, as Adler and Mayer pointed out, were: (1) the pursuit of knowledge was to be lifelong, (2) the teacher himself was viewed as a lifelong learner (we need to remember that this western liberal arts model did not prevail in our country in its early days when the typical teacher was an itinerant who was poorly paid and lowly viewed), and (3) learning required scholarly research if it was to be advanced (this was thought to occur best in a community of scholars where ideas could be shared). It was in this model that the notions of scholarship and of a community of scholars first emerged.

The model makes considerable sense if the objective is to educate the few who are going to carry responsibility in government and public life and are going to use their leisure in the worthiest possible manner. This means they would need to be educated for it. These few would have the chance for lifelong pursuit of knowledge, rather than training for a job. The teachers of these few also could pursue learning in a lifelong pattern within a community of scholars where each needed to talk to others to advance knowledge. In those days, it was somewhat easier to be a master in one's field, and that field could be a good deal broader than it is today. Today we are swamped with information, some of it useful, but the problem is that we have to read it all to locate the useful. The community of scholars was a special community for learning in its historical context. The few who had the necessary money, time, and position, were able to achieve a learning culture which many academic people would find very appealing. The question arises as to whether this type of learning community is an appropriate model for the twentieth-century American system. The answer depends on our goals. If we want learning to take place on a lifelong basis, it may be a very appropriate model.

The English Public School Model

The English public school model, which originated in the fifteenth or sixteenth century, is a variant of the western liberal arts model. Its outstanding nineteenth century spokesman was Thomas Arnold (1795–1842), the father of Matthew Arnold. He was headmaster at Rugby, a leading English public school. (The word "public" meant private in our terms.) According to Russell (1926), the aim of such schools was to educate aristocratic pupils for positions of authority and power throughout the empire. The product was a character that was energetic, stoical, physically fit, and possessed high standards of rectitude and a sense of mission. If we were asked to invent an educational system to produce leaders who would have authority and power in an empire, we probably could do no better. It is too bad the Romans did not think of it. Russell (1926) concludes that what was lacking was intellect, as intellect might have caused doubt, and also some kinder qualities that might have interfered with certain assumptions of an empire. But he agrees that it was an excellent model for a permanent aristocracy.

If we analyze the English public school model a little more carefully, we see that it has many features of the Spartan model. It trains for fitness, energy, stoicism, and high standards of behavior. It also contains much of the Athenian model with emphasis on moral integrity and a sense of mission translated into service to the empire. A sense of mission seems necessary for running an empire. One has to believe that the empire should exist, that this way of life is superior to that of the colonials, or the system would collapse The Athenian model had a very conscious sense of responsibility for political management. The English model demanded duty to the state, written as empire, so the basic ingredients were service to the empire and aristocracy. We shall term the English model the *aristocratic empire model*.

There are many similarities between the English and the Chinese models. However, let us note some differences. The Chinese selected competitively an aristocracy of scholars to run their country; England chose its aristocratic sons and trained them to run the empire. The Chinese preferred intellect, the British preferred character. Both systems had their defects. The Chinese scholars got so minutely scholarly that they became irrelevant. The British character's defect is symbolized by the novel and movie, *The Bridge Over the River Kwai*, where the colonel behaved with high standards of rectitude, great courage, and stoicism, enduring all kinds of physical hardship, without ever asking himself why he was building the bridge or whether it would serve the enemy.

We have now looked at the Chinese, the Spartan, the Athenian, and the British school models. The last two are variations on the western liberal arts model, a model designed for a society that had three special characteristics (Adler and Mayer, 1958). It was designed for a society that was undemocratic, nonindustrial, and prescientific. These sound like broad generalizations, but the more we look at educational models, the more we may be impressed with the fact that there is a clear division between those models of the preindustrial and prescientific era, and those that came after. And there was still a further division between those that were intended for the few as compared with those that were shaped to fit a democracy.

The American Model

Let us turn now to the American model as it was conceived historically. In the Colonial Period before our Revolution, education was a part of the charter granted by the king to those who came to the colonies and was controlled by the colonial government. A very important point historically is that education was carried out in a variety of churches. The curriculum stressed literacy and religion.

In New England, a clear concern for education resulted in laws for public education being passed, but not implemented. New England shaped an educational model of a public school system that eventually had these characteristics: (1) the state could require parents to educate their children, (2) the state could require communities to establish schools, (3) public funds could be used to pay for such schools, and (4) public authorities would have the direct and final authority over these schools. Let us reflect a moment here. "The state could require parents to educate their children." When had that ever happened before? Never, except perhaps in Sparta. "The state could require communities to establish schools." That had rarely happened before. "Public funds could be used to pay for such schools." Perhaps the Chinese model did, but it was an exception too. "Public authorities would have the direct and final authority over these schools." Imagine making education compulsory! The state could tell parents what they must do with their children! The state could require communities to establish schools! We take quite for granted a school system that in its conception and development was so unique. The model of schooling that came out of New England was a revolutionary model.

Schools grew in the United States during the eighteenth century in response to three conditions, as Cremin (1970) points out. First, there was a rise in economic growth with considerable social mobility, so schools became a very appropriate vehicle for going up the ladder. Second, there were many competing religious sects, each of which established its own schools in order to persuade more people. Ideas, outlooks, and philosophies competed, and there were many different ways to be educated. Third, schooling was important because of an increasing interest and participation in public affairs for which the medium was reading. One could argue that had television been around in those days, the big growth in literary and schooling might not have occurred.

Cremin points out that there was a premium on literacy. The society of revolutionary America may have achieved the highest intensity of public interest and participation in politics that any western society had achieved to that date. Probably colonial America was a unique society because of two conditions: social mobility was readily possible and there was freedom to think as one wished. As there were competing and alternative educational systems available, it must have been an intoxicating educational time. The liquor was literacy and this made the difference. It was a society in which education worked for people, as it got them the things they wanted in an expanding economy, in a society in which they experienced at the same time both economic and intellectual freedom.

To go further, we would hypothesize that the real revolution in the United States was not our war with England, but the educational system we developed, and that this unique model of schooling, more than any other single factor or single institution, helped to build our society. de Tocqueville (in Mayer and Lerner, 1966, p. 38) published his observations in 1835 after an extended trip to this country where he said: "But it is the provisions for public education which, from the very first, throws into clearest relief the originality of American civilization." He reported, with what must have been some astonishment, that schools were established in each community and were run by municipal officials who saw to it that the children attended school and who were empowered to fine the parents if they did not. He found this incredible, and it was. Later he commented on the lack of distinguished writers, poets, and scientists in America, implying that our cultural products were not up to that of the continent, but that many skills were present throughout our society. He remarked (p. 277) that if a visitor's attention "is concentrated on the learned, he will be astonished on how few they are; but, if he counts the uneducated, he will think the Americans the most enlightened people in the world." Later in describing those who go to the frontier, de Tocqueville creates this marvelous image:

> As soon as the pioneer reaches his place of refuge, he hastily fells a few trees and builds a log cabin in the forest. Nothing could look more wretched than these isolated dwellings. The traveler approaching one toward evening sees the hearth fire flicker through the chinks in the walls, and at night, when the wind rises, he hears the roof of boughs shake to and fro in the midst of the great forest trees. Who would not suppose that this poor hut shelters some crude and ignorant folk? But one should not assume any connection between the pioneer and the place that shelters him. All his surroundings are primitive and wild, but he is the product of eighteen centuries of labor and experience. He wears the clothes and talks the language of a town; he is aware of the past, curious about the future, and ready to argue about the present; he is a very civilized man prepared for a time to face life in the forest plunging into the wilderness of the New World with his Bible, ax, and newspapers (p. 279).

If we have been imagining all this time that those of our forebearers who came over during the Colonial Period were uneducated crude folk, we may have to change our opinion. They may have arrived uneducated and crude, but they became literate quite fast. They did read newspapers, and they did engage in political controversy. Our tradition of reading newspapers and of being engaged in controversy over public affairs is an extremely strong tradition, not one invented in the last ten years. We should retain this image of our pioneers going out with a Bible, ax, and newspapers. In other accounts there are references again and again to newspapers arriving in the mail because the people wanted to know what was going on.

A critical assumption of the American educational model was that since political power was to be held in the hands of the common man through his vote, education of the common man therefore was essential in order for him to exercise his political power intelligently. Most accounts of American education stress that universal suffrage meant universal education, but there is one notable gap. If it is true that we developed universal education because we wanted the voters to be educated, the theory does not apply to women. Women achieved education long before they achieved the vote in 1920. American women have had potentially a more generous education, and more access to it, than women anywhere in the world. But they have not always done so well with it. The proportion of women in higher education has been declining until recently in our country, compared with other advanced countries. In the 1950s and 1960s, the rate of women who entered graduate school and completed their degrees was lower than it had been in the 1920s and 1930s, and well behind Russia, France, England, and Germany.

The American model further stipulated that most education would have to be public. The model was to be a public model supported by public funds and controlled by public authority. Education would have to be mandatory because it was in everybody's interest to be educated. Such education was to serve the public interest, especially education for citizenship. Education was not to be parochial or unduly influenced by any one group. If we accept the democratic premise and build a model of a school system to serve it, the model must be public, and must represent all the things that go into the making up of the public. It cannot be partisan in its curriculum or teaching.

Education, in this model, becomes the business of the citizenry. Therefore, in this model, education becomes a basic part of the political process, subject to most of the pressures and conflicts that exist in the Congress or in state legislatures. When a model of schooling is designed for a democracy, by definition a political model of schooling evolves. It could be said that we have used schooling to change our society, as Communist China has done, but that we have different goals in mind. We require that our citizens be educated, that they be informed, and that they are taught participation in our democracy. Because our model is responsive to the public, and is run by public authority, it will have active political pressures put upon it.

Public debate over education in such a model would be more widespread, more active, and continuously more explosive than in any other model we have examined. This is a point worth noting: the democratic model of schooling will engender more debate and controversy of a political nature than any other model developed so far. The select university of the fourteenth century was educating a very few people who probably did not have major differences in points of view about their educational model, nor did they have to share their schooling with a high percentage of other people.

This model of American education, as it was conceived of historically and as it has developed, has two major characteristics: it was education for democracy, and it was a universal model. We will term it the *democratic universal educational model.*

To what extent this model has succeeded will be one of our major concerns. This leaves us with big questions. Which educational model is best suited to a democratic society that is also scientific and either industrial or postindustrial? What model would fit a nondemocratic, scientific, and industrial society? Is it possible to take the western liberal arts model, designed for the few, and make it work as a model for the masses? Is it appropriate? Do we need a new model of universal schooling designed for a technological society, postindustrial, perhaps, and scientific, but struggling with the issues of the quality of human life? If the United States is going to educate everybody, as it already is, should the model turn out one kind of character? Russell (1926) makes a very important argument that before you can educate, you need to describe the kind of character you want. If we are going to educate everybody in the country, what do we want the product to be?

REFERENCES

Adler, M. J., & Mayer, M. *The Revolution in Education.* Chicago: University of Chicago Press, 1958, 14–34.

Cremin, L. A. *American Education: The Colonial Experience, 1607–1783.* New York: Harper & Row, 1970.

de Tocqueville, A. *Democracy in America.* J. P. Mayer & M. Lerner (Eds.) New York: Harper & Row, 1966, 38–39, 277–280.

Education Supplement, Saturday Review. October 18, 1969.

Hookham, H. *A Short History of China.* New York: St. Martin's Press, 1970.

Hu, Chang-Tu (Ed.) *Chinese Education under Communism.* Classics in Education No. 7. New York: Teachers College Press, 1962.

Latourette, K. S. *The Chinese: Their History and Culture.* New York: Macmillan, 1938.

Li, Dun J. *The Ageless Chinese: A History.* New York: Scribner, 1965.

MacNair, H. F. (Ed.) *China.* Berkeley: University of California Press, 1946.

Marrou, H. I. *A History of Education in Antiquity.* New York: Sheed & Ward, 1956.

Myers, E. D. *Education in the Perspective of History.* New York: Harper & Row, 1960.

Proussis, C. M. The Orator: Isocrates. In P. Nash, A. Kazamias, & H. Perkinson (Eds.) *The Educated Man: Studies in the History of Educational Thought.* New York: Wiley, 1965, 54–76.

Robinson, T. W. (Ed.) *The Cultural Revolution in China.* Berkeley: University of California Press, 1971.

Russell, B. *Education and the Good Life.* New York: Boni & Liveright, 1926.

Russell, B. The role of individuality. In R. Gross & P. Osterman (Eds.) *Individualism.* New York: Dell Publishing, 1971, 3–14.

Schrag, P. *Saturday Review.* September 19, 1970, 68–69.

Statistical Abstract of the United States: 1970 (91st annual edition). Washington, D. C.; U. S. Bureau of the Census, 1970.

Stephens, J. M. *The Process of Schooling.* New York: Holt, Rinehart and Winston, 1967.

White, M. A. *Informal Survey of Goals for Schools.* 1970 (unpublished).

Red-figured painting on kylix, *Instruction in Music and Grammar in an Attic School*.
State Museum, Berlin.

Theoretical Models of Education

To an extent characteristic of no other institution, save that of the state itself, the school has power to modify the social order.
— John Dewey, *Moral Principles in Education*, p. v.

In the previous chapter, we reviewed selected historical models of education and analyzed some of their characteristics. Now we will turn to some theoretical models of education with the hope that we can make some fruitful comparisons.

Plato

Plato's model was primarily concerned with virtue, the good life, and the good man. Plato wrote: "Education produces good men and good men act nobly." We might interpret the model as one aimed at producing good men on the grounds that good men make a good society (Hamilton, 1957). Among the characteristics of this theoretical model were, first, that community life was to be paramount so that the child would be educated to be loyal to the state rather than to his parents, and, second, that the educational community would be opened only to the citizens of Athens. At the age of twenty, members of this governing class were to be divided into two types. The practical type would be directed into military service whereas the wise type would be retained for another ten years of additional scholarly study. Another selection was to be made from this already select pool of wise scholars when they were thirty years of age. Those chosen at age thirty studied philosophy for five years, and then had an extended internship in public affairs. At the age of fifty, these graduates were to become the guardians of the good and the state, the veritable elite. It is interesting to note that Plato's plan was to include women on the same educational levels as men, which was quite radical for the time.

The emphasis on the importance of community life in overcoming parental control recurs frequently in models of education even today. The kibbutz in Israel is a contemporary example. In Plato's model, education served to shape young people for service to whatever end the governing group had in mind, which could be service to the state or loyalty to a point of view or a certain doctrine.

It would be difficult to implement Plato's model in a democracy such as ours because of its implications about a governing class and because it required that people be selected on such subjective traits as wisdom. As an educational model for selecting and training judicious people to govern the state, however, it is an imaginative one, and in many ways, a rational one. In certain respects it is a criterion-referenced model in that people are selected for their early evidence of wisdom, and then trained to develop more wisdom through study and experience. It would be hard to find a more reasonable model if one wished to create a society run by wise guardians. From the democratic point of view, however, it is hard to accept the notion that people should be selected on the basis of ability rather than by popular vote. Plato's model is characterized by virtue as well as by selection of people from the governing class, so that we might name this model that of the *good and noble guardians*.

Rousseau

Rousseau (1911) had several revolutionary notions about education, most of them related to his concern for children as unique people. (See Rousseau in Readings: Section 1.) We forget that children have been regarded historically as something of a drawback unless they were economically or politically useful in a hereditary line where property and power were passed through offspring. Other than that, children have been regarded as a burden, and as imperfect images of adults. In the United States today, the pendulum has gone to the other extreme, one in which children are not only respected but at times given a special place of privilege and affection in comparison to what other societies have done historically. Our preoccupation with children can be demonstrated in the legislation that has been passed on their behalf since the beginning of the twentieth century. Politicians have remarked that almost anything will pass if it is for the benefit of children. Provisions for special education tend to be passed when a lobby of parents crowd the state house since no politician hoping for reelection is likely to vote against a measure which will benefit children, particularly children with a handicap. Legislation creating such programs as Head Start, Follow Through, and Aid to Dependent Children are examples of this concern for children. It is interesting to speculate whether our attitude toward children will change as children become less and less desirable in an overpopulated world. We might find a reversal in values occurring as children become not only less desirable from the point of view of the planet, but even a threat to the survival of those now living.

Rousseau was a radical in his day because he advocated the view that children were something other than miniature, incompetent adults. He argued instead that children were people in their own right, with their own characteristics. His educational model was based on this major assumption. Two outstanding characteristics of Rousseau's model of education were respect for the child and his rights, and adherence to the aim of helping the child to develop naturally. Rousseau's assumption here, of course, was that the child is naturally good. In Rousseau's model, education was based on the study of the child himself. This is the first time we see this emphasis in these selected educational models. It is a radical notion that children are worth studying because they should be educated in ways different from adults, or that education should be based on the study of the person whom you are trying to teach. This is a beginning of a scientific attitude in the sense that observation in education is stressed, much as one would use it in a natural history.

This emphasis of Rousseau's on basing education on a study of its learners gave rise to innovators like Montessori who devised a curriculum based on observation of how children learn. In Rousseau's model, the teacher moves out of the role of didactic disciplinarian and becomes a consultant to the learning child, much as Montessori's teachers become consultants to the child. Rousseau also emphasized the importance of early childhood learning: "As soon as the child begins to take notice, what is shown him must be carefully chosen" (p. 30). "In the dawn of life, when memory and imagination have not begun to function, the child only attends to what affects its senses. His sense experiences are the raw material of thought; they should, therefore, be presented to him in fitting order, so that memory may at a future time present them in the same order to his understanding. . . ." (p. 31). Rousseau, like Quintilian, Comenius, and Locke, stressed the importance of early learning, and of the sequence of sensory input (Castle, 1962). These were also stressed at a later date in Piaget's theories about stages of intellectual development and the importance of early sensory experiences.

The major educational aim of Rousseau's model was to help children to develop naturally, the assumption being that naturalness is a good state. In order to reach this aim, Rousseau's educational methods included giving children more real liberty and less power. This concept is somewhat difficult to understand. He believed that wickedness came from weakness, and that children did not naturally love power but were taught by experience to love it. He recommended the use of guided choices and did not maintain that children should be left to do whatever they wished. How this was to be done is not entirely clear from the examples he gives, but Rousseau's intent is clear that the child's experiences should be carefully guided toward the educational goal.

To treat children in a humane and respectful manner was indeed revolutionary because the practices at the time were often cruel and without compassion or respect for the ways in which children learned. In evaluating Rousseau's model, the basic assumption of whether children develop naturally into the kinds of people society wants them to be must be weighed. Are children naturally good, or are they naturally bad, born with original sin? Or are they born naturally neutral? A basic philosophical stance in most educational models is its view of the innate nature of the child in a moral, ethical, or religious sense. If a model assumes that children are born with sin, or as part animalistic, or without an ethical nature, or without a developed conscience, then the educational model is very likely to imply that one of its objectives is to correct this state of affairs by changing the child's nature. This has usually been the assumption behind religious schools, sometimes pursued with missionary zeal. Plato argued that it was the aim of education to produce good men, but he also gave weight to innate disposition by selecting those who were wise at the age of twenty, implying that part of that wisdom was an innate trait as well as one that was developed through experience or education.

Christianity has assumed that children are born with original sin. Judaism has taken a somewhat neutral stance about children's innate character. Rousseau was one of the first major educators to argue that children were born naturally good and that it was the wrong experience that made their natures evil. (Jesus often referred to children as being good or innocent.)

One of the current debates about American schools is that they have a negative impact on children and often demean them. Many critics view the schools as harming children, whose nature they view as naturally a good deal better, a good deal kinder, a good deal more open to learning than the schools seem to assume. No one has charged that our school system has made evil children out of what were naturally good children, although some statements have implied that schools have increased the negative attitudes of some groups of children, or have increased certain undesirable characteristics such as hostility, resentment, delinquency, or a negative attitude toward future learning. Were Rousseau alive today, he might be arguing that our schools have not helped children to develop naturally, or given adequate respect to them, or made sufficient study of the children whom they are trying to teach.

The model of education that Rousseau espoused might be termed, the *natural child model*, with the understanding that naturalness is equated with goodness in his model.

Gambetta

Some ten years before Gambetta spoke about education in 1880, France had lost the Franco–Prussian War, and many of its industrial areas in the north, to Germany. It had been a humiliating defeat followed by an economic recession and political confusion. This setting is important background for understanding the model that Gambetta was proposing. Gambetta himself had been a member of the radical party, one that favored republicanism over monarchy. He was in and out of public office from the period 1870 to 1880, one of his out-of-favor periods including a successful escape from besieged Paris in a balloon. Gambetta's ultimate objective was the revival of the French nation to its former levels of power, grandeur, and genius. Gambetta's model of education interests us because it may be representative of educational models during serious national stress (See Gambetta in Readings: Section 1).

Gambetta (1906) said that it is essential for ". . . superior classes to elevate and emancipate this people of workers, who hold in reserve a force still virgin but able to develop inexhaustible treasures of activity and aptitude. We must learn and then teach the peasant what he owes to Society and what he has the right to ask of her" (p. 197). Specifically, ". . . each man should be intelligent, trained not only to think, read, and reason, but made able to act and fight. . . . We must push to the front education. Otherwise we only make a success of letters, but do not create a bulwark of patriots" (p. 198). Gambetta attributed the loss of the war and two of France's provinces to the inferior physical and moral condition of the nation. To cure this sickness he called for ". . . an education as complete from base to summit as is known to human intelligence. Naturally, merit must be recognized, aptitude awakened and approved, and honest and impartial judges freely chosen by their fellow citizens, deciding publicly in such a way that merit alone shall open the door" (p. 199).

What did Gambetta want education to achieve? He wanted a restoration of a superior moral and physical condition in order to restore France to power, a restoration that would require maximum use of her population's resources. Peasants would be a source of supply for ability as well as a source for patriotic soldiers who would not be in such inferior condition as to lose another war. Patriotism clearly is a major aim of this model. Note, however, his emphasis on a fair system, where merit alone will open the door. Here we see the republican influence rejecting the favoritism of class in the past, and supporting the important notion of educational equality and opportunity.

Gambetta and his ideas in education have not held a large place in the history of education, but his model has some important implications for us. Is it like any other model we have examined? It is like the Spartan model in its emphasis upon physical skill and patriotism. But Gambetta also refers to a nineteenth-century theme, the need for developing science and industry, which reminds us again of the national setting in which France had lost areas of great industrial potential. Gambetta apparently feared that Germany might surpass France in its scientific and industrial applications, a fear that proved very accurate. We might define Gambetta's model as a *national revival model with a republican emphasis.*

We might speculate that a model very much like this could appear under two conditions that existed when Gambetta was speaking. One condition might be when a country has lost an important objective, such as a major war; and another, when a country is behind technologically and economically and needs an increased pool of educated talent in order to catch up. This model would have to arise after 1850 because it is linked to scientific advances and is well attuned to the potential of an industrialized society. But we might expect to find this model where these two conditions occurred simultaneously in history, for example, in Japan in 1945, and we may see it emerge again.

Huxley

T. H. Huxley, an eminent British biologist, gave a speech at the opening of Sir Josiah Mason's College in Birmingham, England in 1880. (It is interesting to note that Huxley's speech was delivered in the same year as that of Gambetta.) The setting in which he spoke is again a significant one because this college apparently was being founded to meet some technological needs in an industrial part of England. Huxley's views were strongly influenced by the revolution in scientific thinking that Darwin's theory had touched off. In this particular speech, a dedication, Huxley (1888) argues that the object of the institution is "to promote the prosperity of the manufacturers and the industry of the country." In Huxley's model, we have an excellent example of an educational model consciously shaped by both industrial and scientific forces. We can anticipate that his model therefore is going to be radically different from the western liberal arts model which had existed for twenty-five centuries (See Huxley in Readings: Section 1).

What did Huxley advocate? First, he opposed the liberal western model, as we had anticipated. In this speech, he debated with Matthew Arnold, son of the headmaster of Rugby, Thomas Arnold, the merits of the traditional schooling which Arnold symbolized, as compared with the new model which Huxley was advocating. Huxley opposed the western model because he said it would waste the time of the student scientist and because the scientific model of schooling is superior in achieving culture. This is a type of debating one-upmanship in which he was responding to the snob appeal of culture, much as though he had said one could not be a real gentleman unless one understood science. C. P. Snow (1959) in current times has made a somewhat similar observation about the breach in knowledge between the scientist and the liberal arts graduate.

Huxley made a strong case for a scientific curriculum, stressing the scientific revolution, the importance of the Darwinian leap, and the need for education to adapt itself to a revolution in thinking and knowing about its own world. His argument that the scientific model was a better way to achieve culture, however, is not so forcefully sustained. Huxley does not make clear what his product would look like for he does not define the kind of man that would emerge from his education. He simply says that it is time that we educate people in the new scientific outlook, for ". . . there is one feature of the present state of the civilized world which separates it more widely from the Renascence than the Renascence was separated from the Middle Ages." This marvelous statement makes clear the quantum leap in knowledge, epitomized by Darwin's theory, that has so radically changed our world and our models of education. As Huxley quite rightly pointed out, the scientific and industrial knowledge that emerged after 1850 not only shaped the daily lives of all people within its influence and formed the basis for economic prosperity for millions, but man's whole theory of life depended upon this new knowledge as it threw into question all the basic beliefs that had existed for twenty-five centuries.

This separation in thinking is more vast than we realize when we see how it has changed the human institution that had been unchanged for twenty-five centuries. Here is Huxley opening a new college, and quite properly enthusiastic and optimistic about science, which on the one hand increases man's intellectual understanding of the universe and daily life, but on the other hand, leads to the type of prosperity Birmingham represented in an industrial-scientific society. Huxley's speech could not have been given twenty years or two centuries earlier. The chasm was that great. In our present time, it is easy for us to forget that Darwin's revolution is only a little over one hundred years old, and yet, because of Darwin, we are as far away from the Renaissance as the Renaissance was from the Middle Ages. We shall characterize the Huxley model as the *scientific industrial model*.

Russell

Bertrand Russell not only writes with style, but he is one philosopher who uses behavioral objectives. He says that a model for education cannot be designed without prescribing the kind of person the model is to produce (See Russell in Readings: Section 1). Russell (1926) selects for his model four characteristics: (1) vitality, which implies interest in life, leading to a sane objectivity about it; (2) courage, because it enables one to face situations without fear, and therefore unselfishly; (3) sensitiveness, meaning an appropriate emotionality and a capacity for abstract sympathy for people and situations that have not been experienced directly; and (4) intelligence, so that one can be knowledgeable and curious for new knowledge. Russell selects these four major characteristics for his model because he believes men and women with such characteristics would produce a good society and a good life. He says, "education is the key to the New World." We might remember that he said this in 1926.

Russell's model differs in that he is explicit about the traits that he thinks make up the good person. He is concerned with educating people who will be world citizens, who can feel for other people without knowing them firsthand, and who are vitally engaged in life and its problems but can be so engaged intelligently and objectively.

Is his character description a good one for today's society almost fifty years later? Many might argue that it is. Did Russell hit the nail on the head fifty years ago in his selection of these particular four traits? Will a fifth trait, some kind of self-control or self-discipline, be necessary? Perhaps it is going to be increasingly important for us to monitor our behavior in terms of its effects upon others in areas such as crowding, pollution, overpopulation, and the need for rational planning, which will mean giving up some individual freedoms. We might predict that the American character may go through severe strain in making such changes, because traditionally it has been a character that was free to do as it pleased in a land that was large and rich in resources. As these conditions change, the need for self-control and the acceptance of outside control may become paramount. We might hypothesize not only that such changes would require a revolution in values, but that they might require a new kind of educational model. We might term Russell's model that of the *universally desirable character.*

Dewey

In his chapter on the aims of education, Dewey undertakes four basic definitions. First, the aim of education is defined as the continued capacity for educational growth for all. Second, such a model of education requires a democracy if it is to be for all. Third, the aim of education must come from within the educational process since no aim should be imposed from without. Fourth, to act with an aim is to act intelligently (See Dewey in Readings: Section 1).

Dewey (1964) defines his criteria for good aims. Aims must stem from existing conditions and should arise through foresight, acting intelligently, and weighing alternatives. This he calls in some passages, "experimentalism." The aims must be flexible, that is, capable of being altered to meet circumstances. They must always represent a freeing of the activities, which means doing something with the object since the object itself is not the goal. The doing, in turn, leads to continuing the activity successfully, so activity may go on and not end. "Every means is a temporary end until we have attained it. Every end becomes a means of carrying activity further as soon as it is achieved." The fluidity of Dewey's definitions of means and ends is a difficult one for most readers.

In still a later section, Dewey defines aims applied to education, utilizing the above criteria:

1. Aims must be developed from the actual conditions, from the pupils. We notice here a parallel with Rousseau. Dewey especially espouses aims that are developed from children's instincts and acquired habits, with emphasis upon the individuality of children.
2. The educational aim must be flexible and adaptable to existing conditions.
3. The aim should be a broad survey of present activities. "What a plurality of hypotheses does for the scientific investigation, a plurality of stated aims may do for the instructor" (p. 110).

This third definition of educational aims again interchanges ends and means, which seem somewhat to dissolve into each other.

When Dewey stated his enthusiasm for a plurality of hypotheses, perhaps he meant that the intelligent teacher would keep an eye on all the activities of the classroom and be alert to developing an aim out of what the children were doing. As stated in the quotation above, however, Dewey's enthusiasm for a plurality of hypotheses runs counter to scientific methodology as it is generally practiced in education today. By choosing multiple aims, by making the aims flexible and changeable, and by adapting the aims to local conditions, Dewey was opposing several major principles of educational research that are accepted today.

Dewey's position may be a responsive one, but it makes for enormous difficulty in trying to find out what works in education. In the Head Start program, for example, it was common practice for the aim to be flexible, to be adapted to local conditions, and to be as varied and as broadly defined as improving nutrition, increasing socialization, and building better vocabularies. Under these somewhat diffuse Deweyan aims, the outcome was very difficult to measure. The evidence (Westinghouse Learning Corporation–Ohio University, 1969) suggests that the Head Start program, as a whole, did not increase children's ability to succeed in school as measured some two to three years later. Had the aims of Head Start been more restricted, such as, for example, to nutrition, and had nutrition been carefully measured over a two- or three-year period, an effect might have been seen in the increased health of those children attending Head Start. This would have been possible only if an aim had been selected, carefully defined, and pursued quite consistently to see what the results would be.

The example of Head Start illustrates the importance of careful design in measuring the effects of an educational program. Certain criteria are commonly held to be essential if we are to find out what works. First, the aim must be clearly stated from the outset by the developer, and not altered or modified by those who use it. Second, it must be applied either in a standard controlled way in all situations, or else varied systematically according to some previous design that is adhered to throughout. Third, exploring one preselected testable hypothesis is usually viewed as the aim of the investigation, although we can use experimental designs that employ many variables to see how they interact.

Dewey's aims are stressed because they highlight some of the major issues today in trying to assess what works in education. From the point of view of investigators concerned with educational measurement today, behavioral objectives and criterion-referenced norms are considered highly desirable. Dewey's lack of scientific rigor in stating his aims and how they would be measured may have contributed substantially to the reputation of his progressive education followers as being muddle-headed. If a teacher cannot tell when she is achieving the stated aims of an educational program, she is likely to interpret those aims in whatever way she understands or is comfortable with. Dewey really conceived of teachers as inventing their own aims and changing them. He could not see himself as stating aims from outside because that would have contradicted his democratic beliefs. Dewey perhaps intended that teachers themselves should be intelligent experimenters who could relate their aims to the observations they made in the classroom, and who would have the fullest possible conception of future achievement so as to maximize alternatives. This might be a Deweyan definition of creative teaching.

This leaves us in a dilemma. On one hand, most of us might agree with Dewey that teachers need to be intelligent and spontaneous, to use observation for changing their aims, and to employ the fullest possible conception of future achievement for each child in the classroom. This is exciting teaching. It is hopeful teaching. It is democratic teaching in Dewey's sense. On the other hand, we also need the evidence to determine whether or not a particular educational program really achieves this or that aim. To have dependable evidence means abiding by some commonly accepted rules of research investigation so that other people will accept such evidence.

There is a basic value conflict here. If we propose an educational program, we cannot be democratic about its application or measurement if we want to find out whether or not it achieves its stated goals. Experiments are not democratic processes. They are quite autocratic in design, rigorous in methodology if they are good, and should not be changed by votes. Perhaps Dewey was not aware of this dilemma, but had he been, he might well have been appalled at the conflict between his democratic values and the need for scientific methodology. In opting for democratic values, a choice with which one can agree from the point of view of ideals, Dewey might have missed a scientific ideal in not finding out if his educational model would work. In doing so, he missed a great chance to find out what his model of education could have done, which would have been possible had he been willing to be a little less democratic about the aims, methodology, and measurement. Here we see then the first conflict in a modern model of education, a conflict between science and democracy. We will define Dewey's model as the *continuous democratic experimental model*.

ten Hoor

ten Hoor, a philosopher in an American university, outlined an educational model in 1953 which he termed *education for privacy* (See ten Hoor in Readings: Section 1). ten Hoor stated four aspects of his model, each aimed at self-improvement: (1) a philosophical orientation to the cosmos; (2) a steady vision of the good life; (3) a serenity of the emotions and of the spirit; and (4) the ability to live entertainingly with oneself, which involves the appreciation and practice of the fine arts.

Does this model seem familiar to us? It is the model, as ten Hoor pointed out, of that half of the western liberal model aimed at the cultivation of oneself. The other half of that model, education for public service, when put together with the cultivation of oneself, represents the whole goal of a liberal education. So here is a modern proponent for the cultivation of oneself in a period when others have been crying for education for social reform, social action, or relevance. He delineates the drawbacks of the social participation model, including exposure to those who wish to save others by imposing their own notions upon them. In the years that have passed since this article was written, we have become increasingly aware that the desire to reform the world, no matter how idealistic, can mean the imposition of values on others, sometimes through aggression and intolerance for any other point of view.

To the extent that the western liberal arts model committed itself to the cultivation of oneself, to living entertainingly with oneself through the fine arts, it implied a value system which did not require the imposition of one set of values upon others. Here the object was to learn to enjoy oneself, to increase one's talents, to appreciate fine arts, but there was no one taste that was to be imposed upon people who held a different view. If we choose a model of education for social reform, or for any form of idealism, we will have to deal with the problem that such a model will involve a set of values to be propagated. If so, what happens to the notions of democracy, of the freedom to hold whatever values one wants? This problem is present even in Plato's model, no matter how ideal it seemed. The great and wise guardians in Plato's model were presumably going to impose their notions of what was good upon the government and on the people whom they governed. This should give one pause since in a democracy, the ultimate wisdom is thought to be in the heads of the people.

ten Hoor's model was derived historically from the western liberal arts model which was intended to serve the highly select population of pupils from aristocratic backgrounds who had leisure that they needed to learn to use wisely. If we ask ourselves whether this model fits our present society, we might say that it does not, because it does not appear to fit a democratic society in which everyone goes to school, nor does it have a contemporary scientific or industrial look to it. On further thought, education for privacy may become a reality when universal prolonged education is available to all; when and if our society becomes stabilized in terms of both population and economy; when growth will no longer be a consuming passion, but stability may become more the rule. Then again we may espouse education for each person to live entertainingly with himself. When we have reached a society for all, or almost all, of the kind that was open to the few in the western liberal arts model, education for privacy could become the public education model.

REFERENCES

Castle, E. B. *Educating the Good Man: Moral Education in Christian Times*. New York: Collier Books, 1962.
Dewey, J. Aims in education. *Democracy in Education*. New York: Macmillan, 1964, 100–110.
Gambetta, L. Education for the peasantry in France. In W. J. Bryan (Ed.), *The World's Famous Orations*. Vol. 7. New York: Funk & Wagnalls, 1906, 58–60.
Hamilton, E. *The Echo of Greece*. New York: Norton, 1957.
Huxley, T. H. Science and culture. In *Science and Culture*. New York: D. Appleton, 1888, 7–30.

Plato. See The politics of Aristotle.

Rousseau, J. J. *Émile*. New York: Dutton, 1911, 29–35.

Russell, B. The aims of education. *Education and the Good Life*. New York: Boni & Liveright, 1926, 47–83.

Snow, C. P. *The Two Cultures and the Scientific Revolution*. New York: Cambridge, 1959.

ten Hoor, M. Education for privacy. *The American Scholar*, Winter 1953–54, **23**, 27–42.

The politics of Aristotle. Translated by B. Lowell, *The World's Great Classics*, Vol. 17. New York: The Colonial Press, 1900, Book VIII, 196–204.

Westinghouse Learning Corporation—Ohio University. *The Impact of Head Start*. Clearinghouse for Federal Scientific and Technical Information, 1969.

Readings
Section 1: Models of Education

To be ignorant of what occurred before you is to remain always a child. For what is the worth of human life, unless it is woven into the life of our ancestors by the records of history?

—Cicero

READINGS: SECTION 1

Ting-Yi, L. Education must be combined with productive labor. In Chang-Tu Hu (Ed.), *Chinese Education under Communism*, Classics in Education No. 7. New York: Teachers College Press, 1962, 115–128.

Rousseau, J. J. *Émile*. New York: Dutton, 1911, 29–35.

Gambetta, L. Education for the peasantry in France. In W. J. Bryan (Ed.), *The World's Famous Orations*, Vol. 7. New York: Funk & Wagnalls, 1906, 196–199.

Huxley, T. H. Science and culture. Address delivered at the opening of Sir Josiah Mason's College at Birmingham, 1880. In *Science and Culture*. New York: D. Appleton, 1888, 7–30.

Russell, B. The aims of education. In *Education and the Good Life*. New York: Boni & Liveright, 1926, 47–83.

Dewey, J. Aims in education. In *Democracy and Education*. New York: Macmillan, 1964, 100–110.

ten Hoor, M. Education for privacy. *The American Scholar*, Winter 1953–54, *23*, 27–42.

EDUCATION MUST BE COMBINED WITH PRODUCTIVE LABOR

Lu Ting-Yi

Editors' note: The following excerpt is from an article by Lu Ting-Yi written when the author was head of the Propaganda Department of the Central Committee of the Chinese Communist party and vice-premier of the State Council. This excerpt is from the English translation of this article published in 1958 by the Foreign Language Press, Peking. The reader should note that this educational policy statement was made prior to the Cultural Revolution and may shed some light on the educational issues of that revolution. This excerpt appeared in *Chinese Education under Communism*, edited by Chang-Tu Hu, Teachers College Press, 1962, and is reprinted by permission of the editor.

. . . In the final analysis, the debate on education that has been going on in recent years boils down to the question of "what is all-round development." Marxists believe in "producing fully developed human beings" and in achieving this through education. It is well that our educationalists often talk about all-round development. Yet there are differences of principle in the interpretation of all-round development. Judging by our country's experience in education in the past nine years, although the bourgeois pedagogues do not directly and openly oppose all-round development and even appear to "support the principle actively," yet they interpret it one-sidedly as meaning education through learning of extensive book knowledge. They do not hold with students studying politics and participating in productive labor. In fact they vulgarize the idea of all-round development and equate it with the bourgeois educational line which rears "know-alls."

We Communists interpret all-round development in an entirely different way. The essence of all-round development is that the students should acquire comparatively broader knowledge, become versatile people capable of "going over in sequence from one branch of production to another, depending on the requirements of society or their own inclinations" (F. Engels: *Principles of Communism*). We maintain that civilians should take up military service and retired military men go back to production. We maintain that cadres should participate in physical labor and productive workers in administration. All these propositions are already being put into practice gradually. Measures such as these which involve both the division of labor and change of work conform to the needs of society. They are more reasonable than the division of labor under the capitalist system. They not only increase production but enable the state to carry out reasonable readjustment of the productive forces when this becomes socially necessary, without causing social upheaval.

Our leap forward in industry and agriculture is already giving rise to the problem of the partial transfer of producers to other branches of production when what they are making grows in output to the point where it meets the current maximum demands of the people and there is even a surplus. Without such transfer there would be failure to meet the demands of the people, to develop the productive forces of society continuously and raise the people's living standards continuously. Our educational and other relevant spheres of work must prepare the ground for such transfers. Education should enable the students to acquire broad knowledge. But how broad depends on concrete objective and subjective conditions. In the future, when communist society is fully consolidated, developed and mature, men will be trained in many kinds of work and be able to undertake many professions while specializing in selected fields. This is what we aim at. We must march to this goal.

In our country's present conditions, we can train people to do many kinds of work, but cannot yet train "people to be capable of undertaking any profession." The essence of all-round development is also that the knowledge imparted to the students must be not one-sided and fragmentary, but comparatively complete knowledge. This requires that education should serve politics and be combined with productive labor. Speaking of his ideal of education in the future, Karl Marx referred to "an education that will, in the case of every child over a given age, combine productive labor with instruction and gymnastics, not only as one of the methods of adding to the efficiency of production, but as the only method of producing fully developed human beings" (*Capital*, volume I). That is, he urged that students acquire comparatively complete knowledge and be able to engage not only in mental labor but manual labor as well. Book knowledge alone, however broad, is still partial and incomplete. People with extensive book knowledge alone and without experience of practical work are only what the bourgeoisie call "know-alls." They are not what we regard as people of all-round development. Physical development must be sound. In addition, a communist spirit and style and collective heroism should be inculcated in childhood. This is the moral education of our day. Both are linked with the development of intellectual education. Both are related to manual work and therefore the principle of combining education with labor is unshakable.

In brief, the all-round development we stand for is this: Students should be enabled to acquire comparatively complete, broader knowledge, grow up physically fit, and acquire communist morals. In his "On the Correct Handling of Contradictions Among the People," Comrade Mao Tse-tung said: "Our educational policy must enable everyone who gets an education to develop morally, intellectually, and physically and become a cultured, socialist-minded worker." This is our educational principle of all-round development. "A cultured, socialist-minded worker" is a man who is both politically conscious and educated. He is able to understand both mental and manual work. He is what we regard as developed in an all-round way, both politically and professionally qualified. He is a worker-intellectual and an intellectual-worker.

We insist on the educational principle of all-round development. We consider that the only method to train human beings in all-round development is to educate them to serve working-class politics and combine education with productive labor. We say the only method, because there is no other way to achieve this aim. Bourgeois pedagogues do not agree. They consider the only method to train people to have what they call "all-round development" is to read books and learn by rote. They are absolutely against students learning politics and, in particular, students becoming laborers. According to our educational principle of all-round development, we can and must rely on the masses to run education. According to the bourgeois educational principle of so-called "all-round development," they can rely only on experts to run education; they cannot rely on the masses. According to our educational principle of all-round development, education must be under the leadership of the Communist Party. According to the bourgeois educational principle of so-called "all-round development," education can only be led by experts; it does not need the leadership of the Communist Party as the Communist Party is "a layman." From this we see that different interpretations of all-round development lead to different and even opposite conclusions. That is why we say that the debate on education in recent years ultimately boils down to the question of "what is all-round development." This is essentially a struggle between proletarian and bourgeois educational ideas. . . .

The chief mistake or defect in our educational work has been the divorce of education from productive labor. The policy of combining education with productive labor was put forward by our Party early in 1934. Comrade Mao Tse-tung already then said: "What is the general policy for the Soviet culture and education? It is to educate the broad masses of the toiling people in the spirit of communism, to make culture and education serve the revolutionary war and the class struggle, to combine education with labor, and to enable the broad masses of the Chinese people to enjoy civilization and happiness." In 1954 when the period of economic rehabilitation was over and the First Five-Year Plan was already in operation, the Central Committee of the Party raised the question of adding productive labor to the curricula of the schools. But the proposal encountered obstruction and was not carried through at that time. The Central Committee of the Party repeatedly stressed its policy that education must be combined with productive labor—at the national conference on propaganda work in March 1957, in the editorial of *Renmin Ribao (People's Daily)* on April 8 of the same year, and at the Nanning meeting in January 1958. It is only now that this policy of the Party has been carried out on a nationwide scale. Education must serve politics, must be combined with productive labor, and must be led by the Party— these three things are interrelated. Education divorced from productive labor is bound to lead, to a degree, to the neglect of politics and of Party leadership in educational work, thus divorcing education from the realities of our country and eventually causing right deviationist and doctrinaire mistakes. . . .

The cultural revolution is to enable all 600 million Chinese people, except for those who are incapable, to do productive work and to study. This means to make the masses of our workers and peasants intellectuals as well and our intellectuals laborers too. Only when the masses of the workers and peasants and the intellectuals alike develop along the line of making up what they lack is it possible to change thoroughly the irrational legacy of the old society and eradicate the backwardness of each, i.e., eliminate the cultural deficiency of the masses of workers and peasants and eliminate the bourgeois thinking of the intellectuals. This is, therefore, a very far-reaching revolution which demands that education must serve working-class politics, that is be combined with productive labor. . . .

Our socialist construction demands the utmost effort and consistent pressing ahead; it demands building the country industriously and thriftily; it also demands technique and culture and the training of large numbers of socialist-minded and professionally proficient technicians in conformity with the principle of achieving greater, faster, better, and more economical results. These needs of socialist construction also demand the combination of education with productive labor. . . .

Because the principle of combining education with productive labor is beginning to go into operation, with schools setting up their own factories and farms, and factories and agricultural cooperatives establishing their own schools on a large scale, the phenomenon of students who are at the same time workers and peasants and of workers and peasants who are students at the same time is beginning to appear. This, too, has the embryo of communist society. It can be imagined that when China enters into communism, our basic social organizations will be many communist communes. With few exceptions, each basic unit will have workers, peasants, traders, students, and militia. In the field of education, each basic unit will have its own primary and secondary schools and institutions of higher learning; at the same time everybody will have the time to acquire education as both laborer and intellectual. . . .

To the bourgeois educationalists it seems impossible to get greater, faster, better, and more economical results in education. But the tremendous growth in educational work can make it develop with greater, faster, better, and more economical results. The combination of education with labor, making education an activity that is warmly welcomed by the workers and peasants, is an important way of arousing mass initiative in the setting up of schools. The principles of running schools by applying the mass line under Communist Party leadership are: First, to combine unity with diversity. The purpose of the training is unified, that is, to train socialist-minded, educated workers; but the schools can be run by the central or local authorities, factories and mines, enterprises and agricultural co-operatives, and the forms the schools can take are varied. They may be full-time, or part-work part-study, or spare-time schools; they may collect fees or be free of charge. As production grows further and working hours can be shortened, the present spare-time schools will be similar to part-work part-study schools. When production develops considerably and public accumulation rises greatly, the schools that now charge fees will similarly become free.

Second, to combine the spreading of education widely with the raising of educational levels. The level of education must be raised on the basis of popularization and popularization must be so guided as to raise the level of education. Some of the full-time, the part-work part-study, and the spare-time schools undertake the task of raising educational levels at the same time as education is being spread extensively through part-work part-study and spare-time courses. . . .

Third, to combine over-all planning with decentralization, to bring into play the initiative of both the various central government departments and the local authorities, guided by the Party committees, to develop education as fast as possible and enable this development to benefit, not hamper, the growth of production.

Fourth, to apply the mass line in the political, administrative, pedagogic, and research work in the schools. In all such work, it is necessary, guided by the Party committees, to adopt the method of open and free airing of views, and *tatsepao* and the method of the "three combinations" (for instance, in working out teaching plans and programs, the method can be adopted of combining the efforts of the teachers and the students under the leadership of the Party committee, and so on), and to establish democratic relations of equality—changing the old irrational relations—between the teachers and the students. Experience shows that remarkable achievements have been made where these methods have been adopted.

A struggle has to be waged before the combination of education with labor is effected, and this struggle will be a protracted one. Why? Because this is a revolution upsetting old traditions in educational work that have persisted for thousands of years. The principle of divorcing mental from manual labor has dominated educational work for thousands of years. All the exploiting classes in history have adhered firmly to this principle. More than two thousand years ago, Confucius took a stand against combining education with productive labor. He condemned Fan Chih[1] who "requested to be taught husbandry" and "requested to be taught gardening" as a "small man." Mencius opposed Hsu Hsing, saying: "Those who labor with their minds govern others; those who labor with their strength are governed by others. Those who are governed by others support them; those who govern others are supported by them. This is a principle universally recognized." On this point, bourgeois pedagogues are in full accord with Confucius and Mencius. Originally, education was linked with productive labor, but was separated in class society: now the link will be reforged. . . .

We must realize that to carry the combination of education with productive labor into effect means a fight with the old traditions that have persisted for thousands of years. Without the communist style of toppling down the old idols, burying doctrinairism, and daring to think, speak, and do, without the creative spirit of combining the universal truths of Marxism with the concrete realities of our country, we cannot succeed. Today, in our educational work, vigorous efforts are being made to pull down the outdated and set up the new. Bourgeois and doctrinaire ideas are being broken down and new, Marxist educational theories, systems and methods, curricula and school systems suited to our country are being created. This educational revolution has solid economic foundations. The Marxist doctrine of historical materialism teaches that the superstructure must conform to the economic base. The political system is superstructure, the concentrated expression of economic life. Education comes into the category of ideology and is also superstructure; it serves politics. Class society which has existed for thousands of years has had ownership by slave-owners, landlords, or capitalists as its economic base. The political systems that conform to these types of education that serve these dictatorships are those of the slave-owners, the landlords, and the bourgeoisie. These types of education differ from each other, but all have this in common, that education is divorced from productive labor, mental from manual labor, and manual labor and laborers are despised. The divorce of mental from manual labor is needed by all the exploiting classes, including the bourgeoisie. . . .

[1] The *Analects* record a conversation between Fan Chih, disciple of Confucius, and Confucius. Fan Chih said that he wanted to learn farming; Confucius said that he was not so good a teacher as the peasant. Fan Chih said that he wanted to learn how to plant vegetables; Confucius said that he was not so good a teacher as the kitchen-garden keeper. After Fan Chih had left Confucius told his other disciples that Fan Chih was a man with no great ambition. This conversation shows that Confucius had a contempt for productive labor and that he was against the combination of education with production.

ÉMILE

Jean-Jacques Rousseau

As I said before, man's education begins at birth; before he can speak or understand he is learning. Experience precedes instruction; when he recognises his nurse he has learnt much. The knowledge of the most ignorant man would surprise us if we had followed his course from birth to the present time. If all human knowledge were divided into two parts, one common to all, the other peculiar to the learned, the latter would seem very small compared with the former. But we scarcely heed this general experience, because it is acquired before the age of reason. Moreover, knowledge only attracts attention by its rarity, as in algebraic equations common factors count for nothing. Even animals learn much. They have senses and must learn to use them; they have needs, they must learn to satisfy them; they must learn to eat, walk, or fly. Quadrupeds which can stand on their feet from the first cannot walk for all that; from their first attempts it is clear that they lack confidence. Canaries who escape from their cage are unable to fly, having never used their wings. Living and feeling creatures are always learning. If plants could walk they would need senses and knowledge, else their species would die out. The child's first mental experiences are purely affective, he is only aware of pleasure and pain; it takes him a long time to acquire the definite sensations which show him things outside himself, but before these things present and withdraw themselves, so to speak, from his sight, taking size and shape for him, the recurrence of emotional experiences is beginning to subject the child to the rule of habit. You see his eyes constantly follow the light, and if the light comes from the side the eyes turn towards it, so that one must be careful to turn his head towards the light lest he should squint. He must also be accustomed from the first to the dark, or he will cry if he misses the light. Food and sleep, too, exactly measured, become necessary at regular intervals, and soon desire is no longer the effect of need, but of habit, or rather habit adds a fresh need to those of nature. You must be on your guard against this.

The only habit the child should be allowed to contract is that of having no habits; let him be carried on either arm, let him be accustomed to offer either hand, to use one or other indifferently; let him not want to eat, sleep, or do anything at fixed hours, nor be unable to be left alone by day or night. Prepare the way for his control of his liberty and the use of his strength by leaving his body its natural habit, by making him capable of lasting self-control, of doing all that he wills when his will is formed.

From *Émile* by Jean-Jacques Rousseau. Everyman's Library Edition. New York: E. P. Dutton, 1911, pp. 29–35.

As soon as the child begins to take notice, what is shown him must be carefully chosen. The natural man is interested in all new things. He feels so feeble that he fears the unknown: the habit of seeing fresh things without ill effects destroys this fear. Children brought up in clean houses where there are no spiders are afraid of spiders, and this fear often lasts through life. I never saw peasants, man, woman, or child, afraid of spiders.

Since the mere choice of things shown him may make the child timid or brave, why should not his education begin before he can speak or understand? I would have him accustomed to see fresh things, ugly, repulsive, and strange beasts, but little by little, and far off till he is used to them, and till having seen others handle them he handles them himself. If in childhood he sees toads, snakes, and crayfish, he will not be afraid of any animal when he is grown up. Those who are continually seeing terrible things think nothing of them.

All children are afraid of masks. I begin by showing Emile a mask with a pleasant face, then some one puts this mask before his face; I begin to laugh, they all laugh too, and the child with them. By degrees I accustom him to less pleasing masks, and at last hideous ones. If I have arranged my stages skillfully, far from being afraid of the last mask, he will laugh at it as he did at the first. After that I am not afraid of people frightening him with masks.

When Hector bids farewell to Andromache, the young Astyanax, startled by the nodding plumes on the helmet, does not know his father; he flings himself weeping upon his nurse's bosom and wins from his mother a smile mingled with tears. What must be done to stay this terror? Just what Hector did; put the helmet on the ground and caress the child. In a calmer moment one would do more; one would go up to the helmet, play with the plumes, let the child feel them; at last the nurse would take the helmet and place it laughingly on her own head, if indeed a woman's hand dare touch the armour of Hector.

If Emile must get used to the sound of a gun, I first fire a pistol with a small charge. He is delighted with this sudden flash, this sort of lightning; I repeat the process with more powder; gradually I add a small charge without a wad, then a larger; in the end I accustom him to the sound of a gun, to fireworks, cannon, and the most terrible explosions.

I have observed that children are rarely afraid of thunder unless the peals are really terrible and actually hurt the ear, otherwise this fear only comes to them when they know that thunder sometimes hurts or kills. When reason begins to cause fear, let use reassure them. By slow and careful stages man and child learn to fear nothing.

In the dawn of life, when memory and imagination have not begun to function, the child only attends to what affects its senses. His sense experiences are the raw material of thought; they should, therefore, be presented to him in fitting order, so that memory may at a future time present them in the same order to his understanding; but as he only attends to his sensations it is enough, at first, to show him clearly the connection between these sensations and the things which cause them. He wants to touch and handle everything; do not check these movements which teach him invaluable lessons. Thus he learns to perceive the heat, cold, hardness, softness, weight, or lightness of bodies, to judge their size and shape and all their physical properties, by looking, feeling,[1] listening, and, above all, by comparing sight and touch, by judging with the eye what sensation they would cause to his hand.

It is only by movement that we learn the difference between self and not self; it is only by our own movements that we gain the idea of space. The child has not this idea, so he stretches out his hand to seize the object within his reach or that which is a hundred paces from him. You take this as a sign of tyranny, an attempt to bid the thing draw near, or to bid you bring it. Nothing of the kind, it is merely that the object first seen in his brain, then before his eyes, now seems close to his arms, and he has no idea of space beyond his reach. Be careful, therefore, to take him about, to move him from place to place, and to let him perceive the change in his surroundings, so as to teach him to judge of distances.

When he begins to perceive distances then you must change your plan, and only carry him when you please, not when he pleases; for as soon as he is no longer deceived by his senses, there is another motive for his effort. This change is remarkable and calls for explanation.

The discomfort caused by real needs is shown by signs, when the help of others is required. Hence the cries of children; they often cry; it must be so. Since they are only conscious of feelings, when those feelings are pleasant they enjoy them in silence; when they are painful they say so in their own way and demand relief. Now when they are awake they can scarcely be in a state of indifference; either they are asleep or else they are feeling something.

All our languages are the result of art. It has long been a subject of inquiry whether there ever was a natural language common to all; no doubt there is, and it is the language of children before they begin to speak. This language is inarticulate, but it has tone, stress, and meaning. The use of our own language has led us to neglect it so far as to forget it altogether. Let us study children and we shall soon learn it afresh from them. Nurses can teach us this language; they understand all their nurslings

[1] Of all the senses that of smell is the latest to develop in children; up to two or three years of age they appear to be insensible of pleasant or unpleasant odours; in this respect they are as indifferent or rather as insensible as many animals.

say to them, they answer them, and keep up long conversations with them; and though they use words, these words are quite useless. It is not the hearing of the word, but its accompanying intonation that is understood.

To the language of intonation is added the no less forcible language of gesture. The child uses, not its weak hands, but its face. The amount of expression in these undeveloped faces is extraordinary; their features change from one moment to another with incredible speed. You see smiles, desires, terror, come and go like lightning; every time the face seems different. The muscles of the face are undoubtedly more mobile than our own. On the other hand the eyes are almost expressionless. Such must be the sort of signs they use at an age when their only needs are those of the body. Grimaces are the sign of sensation, the glance expresses sentiment.

As man's first state is one of want and weakness, his first sounds are cries and tears. The child feels his needs and cannot satisfy them, he begs for help by his cries. Is he hungry or thirsty? there are tears; is he too cold or too hot? more tears; he needs movement and is kept quiet, more tears; he wants to sleep and is disturbed, he weeps. The less comfortable he is, the more he demands change. He has only one language because he has, so to say, only one kind of discomfort. In the imperfect state of his sense organs he does not distinguish their several impressions; all ills produce one feeling of sorrow.

These tears, which you think so little worthy of your attention, give rise to the first relation between man and his environment; here is forged the first link in the long chain of social order.

When the child cries he is uneasy, he feels some need which he cannot satisfy; you watch him, seek this need, find it, and satisfy it. If you can neither find it nor satisfy it, the tears continue and become tiresome. The child is petted to quiet him, he is rocked or sung to sleep; if he is obstinate, the nurse becomes impatient and threatens him; cruel nurses sometimes strike him. What strange lessons for him at his first entrance into life!

I shall never forget seeing one of these troublesome crying children thus beaten by his nurse. He was silent at once. I thought he was frightened, and said to myself, "This will be a servile being from whom nothing can be got but by harshness." I was wrong, the poor wretch was choking with rage, he could not breathe, he was black in the face. A moment later there were bitter cries, every sign of the anger, rage, and despair of this age was in his tones. I thought he would die. Had I doubted the innate sense of justice and injustice in man's heart, this one instance would have convinced me. I am sure that a drop of boiling liquid falling by chance on that child's hand would have hurt him less than that blow, slight in itself, but clearly given with the intention of hurting him.

This tendency to anger, vexation, and rage needs great care. Boerhaave thinks that most of the diseases of children are of the nature of convulsions, because the head being larger in proportion and the nervous system more extensive than in adults, they are more liable to nervous irritation. Take the greatest care to remove from them any servants who tease, annoy, or vex them. They are a hundredfold more dangerous and more fatal than fresh air and changing seasons. When children only experience resistance in things and never in the will of man, they do not become rebellious or passionate, and their health is better. This is one reason why the children of the poor, who are freer and more independent, are generally less frail and weakly, more vigorous than those who are supposed to be better brought up by being constantly thwarted; but you must always remember that it is one thing to refrain from thwarting them, but quite another to obey them. The child's first tears are prayers, beware lest they become commands; he begins by asking for aid, he ends by demanding service. Thus from his own weakness, the source of his first consciousness of dependence, springs the later idea of rule and tyranny; but as this idea is aroused rather by his needs than by our services, we begin to see moral results whose causes are not in nature; thus we see how important it is, even at the earliest age, to discern the secret meaning of the gesture or cry.

When the child tries to seize something without speaking, he thinks he can reach the object, for he does not rightly judge its distance; when he cries and stretches out his hands he no longer misjudges the distance, he bids the object approach, or orders you to bring it to him. In the first case bring it to him slowly; in the second do not even seem to hear his cries. The more he cries the less you should heed him. He must learn in good time not to give commands to men, for he is not their master, nor to things, for they cannot hear him. Thus when he child wants something you mean to give him, it is better to carry him to it rather than to bring the thing to him. From this he will draw a conclusion suited to his age, and there is no other way of suggesting it to him.

The Abbé Saint-Pierre calls men big children; one might also call children little men. These statements are true, but they require explanation. But when Hobbes calls the wicked a strong child, his statement is contradicted by facts. All wickedness comes from weakness. The child is only naughty because he is weak; make him strong and he will be good; if we could do everything we should never do wrong. Of all the attributes of the Almighty, goodness is that which it would be hardest to dissociate from our conception of Him. All nations who have acknowledged a good and an evil power, have always regarded the evil as inferior to the good; otherwise their opinion would have been absurd. Compare this with the creed of the Savoyard clergyman later on in this book.

Reason alone teaches us to know good and evil. Therefore conscience, which makes us love the one and hate the other, though it is independent of reason, cannot develop without it. Before the age of reason we do good or ill without knowing it, and there is no morality in our actions, although there is sometimes in our feeling with regard to other people's actions in relation to ourselves. A child wants to overturn everything he sees. He breaks and smashes everything he can reach; he seizes a bird as he seizes a stone, and strangles it without knowing what he is about.

Why so? In the first place philosophy will account for this by inbred sin, man's pride, love of power, selfishness, spite; perhaps it will say in addition to this that the child's consciousness of his own weakness makes him eager to use his strength, to convince himself of it. But watch that broken down old man reduced in the downward course of life to the weakness of a child; not only is he quiet and peaceful, he would have all about him quiet and peaceful too; the least change disturbs and troubles him, he would like to see universal calm. How is it possible that similar feebleness and similar passions should produce such different effects in age and in infancy, if the original cause were not different? And where can we find this difference in cause except in the bodily condition of the two. The active principle, common to both, is growing in one case and declining in the other; it is being formed in the one and destroyed in the other; one is moving towards life, the other towards death. The failing activity of the old man is centered in his heart, the child's overflowing activity spreads abroad. He feels, if we may say so, strong enough to give life to all about him. To make or to destroy, it is all one to him; change is what he seeks, and all change involves action. If he seems to enjoy destructive activity it is only that it takes time to make things and very little time to break them, so that the work of destruction accords better with his eagerness.

While the Author of nature has given children this activity, He takes care that it shall do little harm by giving them small power to use it. But as soon as they can think of people as tools to be used, they use them to carry out their wishes and to supplement their own weakness. This is how they become tiresome, masterful, imperious, naughty, and unmanageable; a development which does not spring from a natural love of power, but one which has been taught them, for it does not need much experience to realise how pleasant it is to set others to work and to move the world by a word.

As the child grows it gains strength and becomes less restless and unquiet and more independent. Soul and body become better balanced and nature no longer asks for more movement than is required for self-preservation. But the love of power does not die with the need that aroused it; power arouses and flatters self-love, and habit strengthens it; thus caprice follows upon need, and the first seeds of prejudice and obstinacy are sown.

First Maxim.—Far from being too strong, children are not strong enough for all the claims of nature. Give them full use of such strength as they have; they will not abuse it.

Second Maxim.—Help them and supply the experience and strength they lack whenever the need is of the body.

Third Maxim.—In the help you give them confine yourself to what is really needful, without granting anything to caprice or unreason; for they will not be tormented by caprice if you do not call it into existence, seeing it is no part of nature.

Fourth Maxim.—Study carefully their speech and gestures, so that at an age when they are incapable of deceit you may discriminate between those desires which come from nature and those which spring from perversity.

The spirit of these rules is to give children more real liberty and less power, to let them do more for themselves and demand less of others; so that by teaching them from the first to confine their wishes within the limits of their powers they will scarcely feel the want of whatever is not in their power.

EDUCATION FOR THE PEASANTRY IN FRANCE

Léon Gambetta

The peasantry is intellectually several centuries behind the enlightened and educated classes in this country. The distance between them and us is immense. We have received a classical or scientific education—even the imperfect one of our day. We have learned to read our history, to speak our language, while (a cruel thing to say) so many of our countrymen can only babble! Ah! that peasant, bound as he is to the tillage of the soil, who bravely carries the burden of his day, with no other consolation than that of leaving to his children the paternal fields, perhaps increased an acre in extent; all his passions, joys, and fears concentrated in the fate of his patrimony. Of the external world, of the society in which he lives, he apprehends only legends and rumors. He is the prey of the cunning and fraudulent. He strikes, without knowing it, the bosom of the revolution, his benefactress; he gives loyally his taxes and his blood to a society for which he feels fear as much as respect. But there his role ends, and if you speak to him of principles, he knows nothing of them.

It is to the peasantry, then, that we must address ourselves. We must raise and instruct them. Epithets which partizans have bandied of "rurality" and "rural chamber" must not become the cause of injustice. It is to be wished that there were a "rural chamber" in the profound and true sense of the term; for it is not with hobble-de-hoys that a "rural chamber" can be made, but with enlightened and free peasants who are able to represent themselves. Instead of becoming a cause of raillery, this reproach of a "rural chamber" should be a tribute rendered to the progress of the civilization of the masses. This new social force should be utilized for the general welfare.

Unfortunately we have not yet reached that point. Progress will be denied us as long as the French democracy fail to demonstrate that if we would remake our country, if we would bring back her grandeur, her power, and her genius, it is of vital interest to her superior classes to elevate and emancipate this people of workers, who hold in reserve a force still

Gambetta, L. Education for the peasantry in France. In W. J. Bryan (Ed.) *The World's Famous Orations*. New York: Funk & Wagnalls, 1906, vol. 7, 196–199.

[1] Born in 1838, died in 1882; elected to the Corps Legislatif in 1869; after Sedan aided in the proclamation of the Republic, becoming Minister of the Interior; aided in organizing the national defenses, and escaped from Paris in a balloon while the city was invested by the Germans, acquiring almost a dictator's position until the capitulation of Paris; President of the Chamber of Deputies in 1879, and Prime Minister in 1881.

virgin but able to develop inexhaustible treasures of activity and aptitude. We must learn and then teach the peasant what he owes to Society and what he has the right to ask of her.

On the day when it shall be well understood that we have no grander or more pressing work; that we should put aside and postpone all other reforms; that we have but one task—the instruction of the people, the diffusion of education, the encouragement of science—on that day a great step will have been taken in your regeneration. But our action needs to be a double one, that it may bear upon the body as well as the mind. To be exact, each man should be intelligent, trained not only to think, read, and reason, but made able to act and fight. Everywhere beside the teacher we should place the gymnast and the soldier, to the end that our children, our soldiers, our fellow citizens, may be able to hold a sword, to carry a gun on a long march, to sleep under the canopy of the stars, to support valiantly all the hardships demanded of a patriot. We must push to the front education. Otherwise we only make a success of letters, but do not create a bulwark of patriots.

Yes, gentlemen, if you had to submit to the supreme agony of seeing the France of Kléber and Hoche lose her two most patriotic provinces, those best embodying at once the military, commercial, industrial, and democratic spirit, we could blame only our inferior physical and moral condition. To-day the interests of the country command us to speak no imprudent words, to close our lips, to sink our resentments to the bottom of our hearts, in order to take up the grand work of national regeneration, to devote to it all the time necessary, in order that it may become a lasting work. If it need ten years, if it need twenty years, then we must devote to it ten or twenty years. But we must begin at once, that each year may see the advancing life of a new generation, strong, intelligent, as much in love with science as with the Fatherland, having in their hearts the double sentiment that he serves his country well only when he serves it with his reason and his arm.

We have been educated in a rough school. We must therefore cure ourselves of the vanity which has caused us so many disasters. We must realize conscientiously where our responsibility exists, and, seeing the remedy, sacrifice all to the object to be attained—to remake and reconstitute France! For that, nothing should be accounted too good, and we shall ask nothing before this. The first demand must be for an education as complete from base to summit as is known to human intelligence. Naturally, merit must be recognized, aptitude awakened and approved, and honest and impartial judges freely chosen by their fellow citizens, deciding publicly in such a way that merit alone shall open the door. Reject as authors of mischief those who have put words in the place of action; all those who have put favoritism in the place of merit; all those who have made the profession of arms not a means for the protection of France, but a means of serving the caprices of a master, and sometimes of becoming accomplices in his crimes.

SCIENCE AND CULTURE

Thomas Henry Huxley

I hold very strongly by two convictions:—The first is, that neither the discipline nor the subject-matter of classical education is of such direct value to the student of physical science as to justify the expenditure of valuable time upon either; and the second is, that for the purpose of attaining real culture, an exclusively scientific education is at least as effectual as an exclusively literary education.

I need hardly point out to you that these opinions, especially the latter, are diametrically opposed to those of the great majority of educated Englishmen, influenced as they are by school and university traditions. In their belief, culture is obtainable only by a liberal education; and a liberal education is synonymous, not merely with education and instruction in literature, but in one particular form of literature, namely, that of Greek and Roman antiquity. They hold that the man who has learned Latin and Greek, however little, is educated; while he who is versed in other branches of knowledge, however deeply, is a more or less respectable specialist, not admissible into the cultured caste. The stamp of the educated man, the University degree, is not for him.

I am too well acquainted with the generous catholicity of spirit, the true sympathy with scientific thought, which pervades the writings of our chief apostle of culture, to identify him with these opinions; and yet one may cull from one and another of those epistles to the Philistines, which so much delight all who do not answer to that name, sentences which lend them some support.

Mr. Arnold tells us that the meaning of culture is "to know the best that has been thought and said in the world." It is the criticism of life contained in literature. That criticism regards "Europe as being, for intellectual and spiritual purposes, one great confederation, bound to a joint action and working to a common result; and whose members have, for their common outfit, a knowledge of Greek, Roman, and Eastern antiquity, and of one another. Special, local, and temporary advantages being put out of account, that modern nation will in the intellectual and spiritual sphere make most progress, which most thoroughly carries out this programme. And what is that but saying that we too, all of us, as individuals, the more thoroughly we carry it out, shall make the more progress?"

We have here to deal with two distinct propositions. The first, that a

Huxley, T. H. Science and Culture. Address delivered at the opening of Sir Josiah Mason's College at Birmingham, 1880. In *Science and Culture*. New York: D. Appleton & Co., 1888, 7–30.

criticism of life is the essence of culture; the second, that literature contains the materials which suffice for the construction of such a criticism.

I think that we must all assent to the first proposition. For culture certainly means something quite different from learning or technical skill. It implies the possession of an ideal, and the habit of critically estimating the value of things by comparison with a theoretic standard. Perfect culture should supply a complete theory of life, based upon a clear knowledge alike of its possibilities and of its limitations.

But we may agree to all this, and yet strongly dissent from the assumption that literature alone is competent to supply this knowledge. After having learnt all that Greek, Roman, and Eastern antiquity have thought and said, and all that modern literatures have to tell us, it is not self-evident that we have laid a sufficiently broad and deep foundation for that criticism of life which constitutes culture.

Indeed, to any one acquainted with the scope of physical science, it is not at all evident. Considering progress only in the "intellectual and spiritual sphere," I find myself wholly unable to admit that either nations or individuals will really advance, if their common outfit draws nothing from the stores of physical science. I should say that an army, without weapons of precision and with no particular base of operations, might more hopefully enter upon a campaign on the Rhine, than a man, devoid of a knowledge of what physical science has done in the last century, upon a criticism of life.

When a biologist meets with an anomaly, he instinctively turns to the study of development to clear it up. The rationale of contradictory opinions may with equal confidence be sought in history.

It is, happily, no new thing that Englishmen should employ their wealth in building and endowing institutions for educational purposes. But, five or six hundred years ago, deeds of foundation expressed or implied conditions as nearly as possible contrary to those which have been thought expedient by Sir Josiah Mason. That is to say, physical science was practically ignored, while a certain literary training was enjoined as a means to the acquirement of knowledge which was essentially theological.

The reason of this singular contradiction between the actions of men alike animated by a strong and disinterested desire to promote the welfare of their fellows, is easily discovered.

At that time, in fact, if any one desired knowledge beyond such as could be obtained by his own observation, or by common conversation, his first necessity was to learn the Latin language, inasmuch as all the higher knowledge of the western world was contained in works written in that language. Hence, Latin grammar, with logic and rhetoric, studied through Latin, were the fundamentals of education. With respect to the substance of the knowledge imparted through this channel, the Jewish and Christian Scriptures, as interpreted and supplemented by the Romish Church, were held to contain a complete and infallibly true body of information.

Theological dicta were, to the thinkers of those days, that which the axioms and definitions of Euclid are to the geometers of these. The business of the philosophers of the middle ages was to deduce, from the data furnished by the theologians, conclusions in accordance with ecclesiastical decrees. They were allowed the high privilege of showing, by logical process, how and why that which the Church said was true, must be true. And if their demonstrations fell short of or exceeded this limit, the Church was maternally ready to check their aberrations—if need were, by the help of the secular arm. Between the two, our ancestors were furnished with a compact and complete criticism of life. They were told how the world began and how it would end; they learned that all material existence was but a base and insignificant blot upon the fair face of the spiritual world, and that nature was, to all intents and purposes, the playground of the devil; they learned that the earth is the centre of the visible universe, and that man is the cynosure of things terrestrial; and more especially was it inculcated that the course of nature had no fixed order, but that it could be, and constantly was, altered by the agency of innumerable spiritual beings, good and bad, according as they were moved by the deeds and prayers of men. The sum and substance of the whole doctrine was to produce the conviction that the only thing really worth knowing in this world was how to secure that place in a better which, under certain conditions, the Church promised.

Our ancestors had a living belief in this theory of life, and acted upon it in their dealings with education, as in all other matters. Culture meant saintliness—after the fashion of the saints of those days; the education that led to it was, of necessity, theological; and the way to theology lay through Latin.

That the study of nature—further than was requisite for the satisfaction of everyday wants—should have any bearing on human life was far from the thoughts of men thus trained. Indeed, as nature had been cursed for man's sake, it was an obvious conclusion that those who meddled with nature were likely to come into pretty close contact with Satan. And, if any born scientific investigator followed his instincts, he might safely reckon upon earning the reputation, and probably upon suffering the fate, of a sorcerer.

Had the western world been left to itself in Chinese isolation, there is no saying how long this state of things might have endured. But, happily, it was not left to itself. Even earlier than the thirteenth century, the development of Moorish civilization in Spain and the great movement of the

Crusades had introduced the leaven which, from that day to this, has never ceased to work. At first, through the intermediation of Arabic translations, afterwards by the study of the originals, the western nations of Europe became acquainted with the writings of the ancient philosophers and poets, and, in time, with the whole of the vast literature of antiquity.

Whatever there was of high intellectual aspiration or dominant capacity in Italy, France, Germany, and England, spent itself for centuries in taking possession of the rich inheritance left by the dead civilizations of Greece and Rome. Marvelously aided by the invention of printing, classical learning spread and flourished. Those who possessed it prided themselves on having attained the highest culture then within the reach of mankind.

And justly. For, saving Dante on his solitary pinnacle, there was no figure in modern literature, at the time of the Renascence, to compare with the men of antiquity; there was no art to compete with their sculpture; there was no physical science but that which Greece had created. Above all, there was no other example of perfect intellectual freedom—of the unhesitating acceptance of reason as the sole guide to truth and the supreme arbiter of conduct.

The new learning necessarily soon exerted a profound influence upon education. The language of the monks and schoolmen seemed little better than gibberish to scholars fresh from Vergil and Cicero, and the study of Latin was placed upon a new foundation. Moreover, Latin itself ceased to afford the sole key to knowledge. The student who sought the highest thought of antiquity found only a second-hand reflection of it in Roman literature, and turned his face to the full light of the Greeks. And after a battle, not altogether dissimilar to that which is at present being fought over the teaching of physical science, the study of Greek was recognized as an essential element of all higher education.

Thus the Humanists, as they were called, won the day; and the great reform which they effected was of incalculable service to mankind. But the Nemesis of all reformers is finality; and the reformers of education, like those of religion, fell into the profound, however common, error of mistaking the beginning for the end of the work of reformation.

The representatives of the Humanists, in the nineteenth century, take their stand upon classical education as the sole avenue to culture, as firmly as if we were still in the age of Renascence. Yet, surely, the present intellectual relations of the modern and the ancient worlds are profoundly different from those which obtained three centuries ago. Leaving aside the existence of a great and characteristically modern literature, of modern painting, and, especially, of modern music, there is one feature of the present state of the civilized world which separates it more widely from the Renascence than the Renascence was separated from the middle ages.

This distinctive character of our own times lies in the vast and constantly increasing part which is played by natural knowledge. Not only is our daily life shaped by it, not only does the prosperity of millions of men depend upon it, but our whole theory of life has long been influenced, consciously or unconsciously, by the general conceptions of the universe which have been forced upon us by physical science.

In fact, the most elementary acquaintance with the results of scientific investigation shows us that they offer a broad and striking contradiction to the opinion so implicitly credited and taught in the middle ages.

The notions of the beginning and the end of the world entertained by our forefathers are no longer credible. It is very certain that the earth is not the chief body in the material universe, and that the world is not subordinated to man's use. It is even more certain that nature is the expression of a definite order with which nothing interferes, and that the chief business of mankind is to learn that order and to govern themselves accordingly. Moreover this scientific "criticism of life" presents itself to us with different credentials from any other. It appeals not to authority, not to what anybody may have thought or said, but to nature. It admits that all our interpretations of natural fact are more or less imperfect and symbolic, and bids the learner seek for truth not among words but among things. It warns us that the assertion which outstrips evidence is not only a blunder but a crime.

The purely classical education advocated by the representatives of the Humanists in our day gives no inkling of all this. A man may be a better scholar than Erasmus, and know no more of the chief causes of the present intellectual fermentation than Erasmus did. Scholarly and pious persons, worthy of all respect, favour us with allocutions upon the sadness of the antagonism of science to their mediaeval way of thinking, which betray an ignorance of the first principles of scientific investigation, an incapacity for understanding what a man of science means by veracity, and an unconsciousness of the weight of established scientific truths, which is almost comical.

There is no great force in the *tu quoque* argument, or else the advocates of scientific education might fairly enough retort upon the modern Humanists that they may be learned specialists, but that they possess no such sound foundation for a criticism of life as deserves the name of culture. And, indeed, if we were disposed to be cruel, we might urge that the Humanists have brought this reproach upon themselves, not because they are too full of the spirit of the ancient Greek, but because they lack it.

The period of the Renascence is commonly called that of the "Revival of Letters," as if the influences then brought to bear upon the mind of Western

Europe had been wholly exhausted in the field of literature. I think it is very commonly forgotten that the revival of science, effected by the same agency, although less conspicuous, was not less momentous.

In fact, the few and scattered students of nature of that day picked up the clue to her secrets exactly as it fell from the hands of the Greeks a thousand years before. The foundations of mathematics were so well laid by them that our children learn their geometry from a book written for the schools of Alexandria two thousand years ago. Modern astronomy is the natural continuation and development of the work of Hipparchus and of Ptolemy; modern physics of that of Democritus and of Archimedes; it was long before modern biological science outgrew the knowledge bequeathed to us by Aristotle, by Theophrastus, and by Galen.

We cannot know all the best thoughts and sayings of the Greeks unless we know what they thought about natural phenomena. We cannot fully apprehend their criticism of life unless we understand the extent to which that criticism was affected by scientific conceptions. We falsely pretend to be the inheritors of their culture unless we are penetrated, as the best minds among them were, with an unhesitating faith that the free employment of reason, in accordance with scientific method, is the sole method of reaching truth.

Thus I venture to think that the pretensions of our modern Humanists to the possession of the monopoly of culture and to the exclusive inheritance of the spirit of antiquity must be abated, if not abandoned. But I should be very sorry that anything I have said should be taken to imply a desire on my part to depreciate the value of a classical education, as it might be and as it sometimes is. The native capacities of mankind vary no less than their opportunities; and while culture is one, the road by which one man may best reach it is widely different from that which is most advantageous to another. Again, while scientific education is yet inchoate and tentative, classical education is thoroughly well organized upon the practical experience of generations of teachers. So that, given ample time for learning and destination for ordinary life, or for a literary career, I do not think that a young Englishman in search of culture can do better than follow the course usually marked out for him, supplementing its deficiencies by his own efforts.

But for those who mean to make science their serious occupation, or who intend to follow the profession of medicine, or who have to enter early upon the business of life—for all these, in my opinion, classical education is a mistake; and it is for this reason that I am glad to see "mere literary education and instruction" shut out from the curriculum of Sir Josiah Mason's College, seeing that its inclusion would probably lead to the introduction of the ordinary smattering of Latin and Greek.

Nevertheless, I am the last person to question the importance of genuine literary education, or to suppose that intellectual culture can be complete without it. An exclusively scientific training will bring about a mental twist as surely as an exclusively literary training. The value of the cargo does not compensate for a ship's being out of trim; and I should be very sorry to think that the Scientific College would turn out none but lop-sided men.

There is no need, however, that such a catastrophe should happen. Instruction in English, French, and German is provided, and thus the three greatest literatures of the modern world are made accessible to the student. French and German, and especially the latter language, are absolutely indispensable to those who desire full knowledge in any department of science. But even supposing that the knowledge of these languages acquired is not more than sufficient for purely scientific purposes, every Englishman has, in his native tongue, an almost perfect instrument of literary expression; and, in his own literature, models of every kind of literary excellence. If an Englishman cannot get literary culture out of his Bible, his Shakespeare, his Milton, neither, in my belief, will the profoundest study of Homer and Sophocles, Vergil and Horace, give it to him.

Thus, since the constitution of the College makes sufficient provision for literary as well as for scientific education, and since artistic instruction is also contemplated, it seems to me that a fairly complete culture is offered to all who are willing to take advantage of it.

But I am not sure that at this point the "practical" man, scotched but not slain, may ask what all this talk about culture has to do with an Institution, the object of which is defined to be "to promote the prosperity of the manufactures and the industry of the country." He may suggest that what is wanted for this end is not culture, not even a purely scientific discipline, but simply a knowledge of applied science.

I often wish that this phrase, "applied science," had never been invented. For it suggests that there is a sort of scientific knowledge of direct practical use, which can be studied apart from another sort of scientific knowledge, which is of no practical utility, and which is termed "pure science." But there is no more complete fallacy than this. What people call applied science is nothing but the application of pure science to particular classes of problems. It consists of deductions from those general principles, established by reasoning and observation, which constitute pure science. No one can safely make these deductions until he has a firm grasp of the principles; and he can obtain that grasp only by personal experience of the operations of observation and of reasoning on which they are founded.

Almost all the processes employed in the arts and manufactures fall within the range either of physics or of chemistry. In order to improve them, one must thoroughly understand them; and no one has a chance of really understanding them unless he has obtained that mastery of principles and that habit of dealing with facts, which is given by long-continued and well-directed purely scientific training in the physical and the chemical laboratory. So that there really is no question as to the necessity of purely scientific discipline, even if the work of the College were limited by the narrowest interpretation of its stated aims.

And, as to the desirableness of a wider culture than that yielded by science alone, it is to be recollected that the improvement of manufacturing processes is only one of the conditions which contribute to the prosperity of industry. Industry is a means and not an end; and mankind work only to get something which they want. What that something is depends partly on their innate, and partly on their acquired, desires.

If the wealth resulting from prosperous industry is to be spent upon the gratification of unworthy desires, if the increasing perfection of manufacturing processes is to be accompanied by an increasing debasement of those who carry them on, I do not see the good of industry and prosperity.

Now it is perfectly true that men's views of what is desirable depend upon their characters, and that the innate proclivities to which we give that name are not touched by any amount of instruction. But it does not follow that even mere intellectual education may not, to an indefinite extent, modify the practical manifestation of the characters of men in their actions, by supplying them with motives unknown to the ignorant. A pleasure-loving character will have pleasure of some sort; but, if you give him the choice, he may prefer pleasures which do not degrade him to those which do. And this choice is offered to every man who possesses in literary or artistic culture a never-failing source of pleasures, which are neither withered by age, nor staled by custom, nor embittered in the recollection by the pangs of self-reproach. . . .

THE AIMS OF EDUCATION

Bertrand Russell

Before considering how to educate, it is well to be clear as to the sort of result which we wish to achieve. Dr. Arnold wanted "humbleness of mind," a quality not possessed by Aristotle's "magnanimous man." Nietzsche's ideal is not that of Christianity. No more is Kant's: for while Christ enjoins love, Kant teaches that no action of which love is the motive can be truly virtuous. And even people who agree as to the ingredients of a good character may differ as to their relative importance. One man will emphasize courage, another learning, another kindliness, and another rectitude. One man, like the elder Brutus, will put duty to the State above family affection; another, like Confucius, will put family affection first. All these divergences will produce differences as to education. We must have some conception of the kind of person we wish to produce, before we can have any definite opinion as to the education which we consider best.

Of course an educator may be foolish, in the sense that he produces results other than those at which he was aiming. Uriah Heep was the outcome of lessons in humility at a Charity School, which had had an effect quite different from what was intended. But in the main the ablest educators have been fairly successful. Take as examples the Chinese literati, the modern Japanese, the Jesuits, Dr. Arnold, and the men who direct the policy of the American public schools. All these, in their various ways, have been highly successful. The results aimed at in the different cases were utterly different, but in the main the results were achieved. It may be worth while to spend a few moments on these different systems, before attempting to decide what we should ourselves regard as the aims which education should have in view.

Traditional Chinese education was, in some respects, very similar to that of Athens in its best days. Athenian boys were made to learn Homer by heart from beginning to end; Chinese boys were made to learn the Confucian classics with similar thoroughness. Athenians were taught a kind of reverence for the gods which consisted in outward observances, and placed no barrier in the way of free intellectual speculation. Similarly the Chinese were taught certain rites connected with ancestor-worship, but were by no means obliged to have the beliefs which the rites would seem to imply. An easy and elegant scepticism was the attitude expected of an educated adult: anything might be discussed, but it was a trifle vulgar to reach very positive conclusions. Opinions should be such as could be discussed pleasantly at dinner, not such as men would fight for. Carlyle calls Plato "a lordly Athenian gentleman, very much at his ease in Zion." This characteristic of being "at his ease in Zion" is also found in Chinese sages, and is, as a rule, absent from the sages produced by Christian civilizations, except when, like Goethe, they have deeply imbibed the spirit of Hellenism. The Athenians and the Chinese alike wished to enjoy life, and had a conception of enjoyment which was refined by an exquisite sense of beauty.

There were, however, great differences between the two civilizations, owing to the fact that, broadly speaking, the Greeks were energetic and the Chinese were lazy. The Greeks devoted their energies to art and science and mutual extermination, in all of which they achieved unprecedented success. Politics and patriotism afforded practical outlets for Greek energy: when a politician was ousted, he led a band of exiles to attack his native city. When a Chinese official was disgraced, he retired to the hills and wrote poems on the pleasures of country life. Accordingly the Greek civilization destroyed itself, but the Chinese civilization could only be destroyed from without. These differences, however, seem not wholly attributable to education, since Confucianism in Japan never produced the indolent cultured scepticism which characterized the Chinese literati, except in the Kyoto nobility, who formed a kind of Faubourg Saint Germain.

Chinese education produced stability and art; it failed to produce progress or science. Perhaps this may be taken as what is to be expected of scepticism. Passionate beliefs produce either progress or disaster, not stability. Science, even when it attacks traditional beliefs, has beliefs of its own, and can scarcely flourish in an atmosphere of literary scepticism. In a pugnacious world which has been unified by modern inventions, energy is needed for national self-preservation. And without science, democracy is impossible: the Chinese civilization was confined to the small percentage of educated men, and the Greek civilization was based on slavery. For these reasons, the traditional education of China is not suited to the modern world, and has been abandoned by the Chinese themselves. Cultivated eighteenth-century gentlemen, who in some respects resembled Chinese literati, have become impossible for the same reasons.

Modern Japan affords the clearest illustration of a tendency which is prominent among all the Great Powers—the tendency to make national greatness the supreme purpose of education. The aim of Japanese education is to produce citizens who shall be devoted to the State through the training of their passions, and useful to it through the knowledge they have acquired. I cannot sufficiently praise the skill with which this double purpose has been pursued. Ever since the advent of Commodore Perry's squadron, the Japanese have been in a situation in which self-preservation was very difficult; their success affords a justification of their methods, unless we are to hold that self-preservation itself may be culpable. But only a desperate situation could have justified their educational methods, which would have been culpable in any nation not in imminent peril. The Shinto religion, which must not be called in question even by university professors, involves history which is just as dubious as Genesis; the Dayton trial pales into insignificance beside the theological tyranny in Japan. There is an equal ethical tyranny: nationalism, filial piety, Mikado-worship, etc., must not be called in question, and therefore many kinds of progress are scarcely possible. The great danger of a cast-iron system of this sort is that it may provoke revolution as the sole method of progress. This danger is real, though not immediate, and is largely caused by the educational system.

We have thus in modern Japan a defect opposite to that of ancient China. Whereas the Chinese literati were too sceptical and lazy, the products of Japanese education are likely to be too dogmatic and energetic. Neither acquiescence in scepticism nor acquiescence in dogma is what education should produce. What it should produce is a belief that knowledge is attainable in a measure, though with difficulty; that much of what passes for knowledge at any given time is likely to be more or less mistaken, but that the mistakes can be rectified by care and industry. In acting upon our beliefs, we should be very cautious where a small error would mean disaster; nevertheless it is upon our beliefs that we must act. This state of mind is rather difficult: it requires a high degree of intellectual culture without emotional atrophy. But though difficult it is not impossible; it is in fact the scientific temper. Knowledge, like other good things, is difficult, but not impossible; the dogmatist forgets the difficulty, the sceptic denies the possibility. Both are mistaken, and their errors, when wide-spread, produce social disaster.

The Jesuits, like the modern Japanese, made the mistake of subordinating education to the welfare of an institution—in their case, the Catholic Church. They were not concerned primarily with the good of the particular pupil, but with making him a means to the good of the Church. If we accept their theology, we cannot blame them: to save souls from hell is more important than any merely terrestrial concern, and is only to be achieved by the Catholic Church. But those who do not accept this dogma will judge Jesuit education by its results. These results, it is true, were sometimes quite as undesired as Uriah Heep: Voltaire was a product of Jesuit methods. But on the whole, and for a long time, the intended results were achieved: the counter-reformation, and the collapse of Protestantism in France, must be largely attributed to Jesuit efforts. To achieve these ends, they made art sentimental, thought superficial, and morals loose; in the end, the French Revolution was needed to sweep away the harm that they had done. In education, their crime was that they were not actuated by love of their pupils, but by ulterior ends.

Dr. Arnold's system, which has remained in force in English public schools to the present day, had another defect, namely that it was aristocratic. The aim was to train men for positions of authority and power, whether at home or in distant parts of the empire. An aristocracy, if it is to survive, needs certain virtues; these were to be imparted at school. The product was to be energetic, stoical, physically fit, possessed of certain unalterable beliefs, with high standards of rectitude, and convinced that it had an important mission in the world. To a surprising extent, these results were achieved. Intellect was sacrificed to them, because intellect might produce doubt. Sympathy was sacrificed, because it might interfere with governing "inferior" races or classes. Kindliness was sacrificed for the sake of toughness; imagination, for the sake of firmness. In an unchanging world, the result might have been a permanent aristocracy, possessing the merits and defects of the Spartans. But aristocracy is out of date, and subject populations will no longer obey even the most wise and virtuous rulers. The rulers are driven into brutality, and brutality further encourages revolt. The complexity of the modern world increasingly requires intelligence, and Dr. Arnold sacrificed intelligence to "virtue." The battle of Waterloo may have been won on the playing-fields of Eton, but the British Empire is being lost there. The modern world needs a different type, with more imaginative sympathy, more intellectual suppleness, less belief in bulldog courage and more belief in technical knowledge. The administrator of the future must be the servant of free citizens, not the benevolent ruler of admiring subjects. The aristocratic tradition embedded in British higher education is its bane. Perhaps this tradition can be eliminated gradually; perhaps the older educational institutions will be found incapable of adapting themselves. As to that, I do not venture an opinion.

The American public schools achieve successfully a task never before attempted on a large scale: the task of transforming a heterogeneous selection of mankind into a homogeneous nation. This is done so ably, and is on the whole such a beneficent work, that on the balance great praise is due to those who accomplish it. But America, like Japan, is placed in a peculiar situation, and what the special circumstances justify is not necessarily an ideal to be followed everywhere and always. America has had certain advantages and certain difficulties. Among the advantages were: a higher standard of wealth; freedom from the danger of defeat in war;

comparative absence of cramping traditions inherited from the Middle Ages. Immigrants found in America a generally diffused sentiment of democracy and an advanced stage of industrial technique. These, I think, are the two chief reasons why almost all of them came to admire America more than their native countries. But actual immigrants, as a rule, retain a dual patriotism: in European struggles they continue to take passionately the side of the nation to which they originally belonged. Their children, on the contrary, lose all loyalty to the country from which their parents have come, and become merely and simply Americans. The attitude of the parents is attributable to the general merits of America; that of the children is very largely determined by their school education. It is only the contribution of the school that concerns us.

In so far as the school can rely upon the genuine merits of America, there is no need to associate the teaching of American patriotism with the inculcation of false standards. But where the Old World is superior to the New, it becomes necessary to instil a contempt for genuine excellences. The intellectual level in Western Europe and the artistic level in Eastern Europe are, on the whole, higher than in America. Throughout Western Europe, except in Spain and Portugal, there is less theological super-stition than in America. In almost all European countries the individual is less subject to herd domination than in America: his inner freedom is greater even where his political freedom is less. In these respects, the American public schools do harm. The harm is essential to the teaching of an exclusive American patriotism. The harm, as with the Japanese and the Jesuits, comes from regarding the pupils as means to an end, not as ends in themselves. The teacher should love his children better than his State or his Church; otherwise he is not an ideal teacher.

When I say that pupils should be regarded as ends, not as means, I may be met by the retort that, after all, everybody is more important as a means than as an end. What a man is as an end perishes when he dies; what he produces as a means continues to the end of time. We cannot deny this, but we can deny the consequences deduced from it. A man's importance as a means may be for good or for evil; the remote effects of human actions are so uncertain that a wise man will tend to dismiss them from his calculations. Broadly speaking, good men have good effects, and bad men bad effects. This, of course, is not an invariable law of nature. A bad man may murder a tyrant because he has committed crimes which the tyrant intends to punish; the effects of his act may be good, though he and his act are bad. Nevertheless, as a broad general rule, a community of men and women who are intrinsically excellent will have better effects than one composed of people who are ignorant and malevolent. Apart from such considerations, children and young people feel instinctively the difference between those who genuinely wish them well and those who regard them merely as raw material for some scheme. Neither character nor intelligence will develop as well or as freely where the teacher is deficient in love; and love of this kind consists essentially in *feeling* the child as an end. We all have this feeling about ourselves: we desire good things for ourselves without first demanding a proof that some great purpose will be furthered by our obtaining them. Every ordinarily affectionate parent feels the same sort of thing about his or her children. Parents want their children to grow, to be strong, and healthy, to do well at school, and so on, in just the same way in which they want things for themselves; no effort of self-denial and no abstract principle of justice is involved in taking trouble about such matters. This parental instinct is not always strictly confined to one's own children. In its diffused form, it must exist in anyone who is to be a good teacher of little boys and girls. As the pupils grow older, it grows less important. But only those who possess it can be trusted to draw up schemes of education. Those who regard it as one of the purposes of male education to produce men willing to kill and be killed for frivolous reasons are clearly deficient in diffused parental feeling; yet they control education in all civilized countries except Denmark and China.

But it is not enough that the educator should love the young; it is necessary also that he should have a right conception of human excellence. Cats teach their kittens to catch mice and play with them; militarists do likewise with the human young. The cat loves the kitten, but not the mouse; the militarist may love his own son, but not the sons of his country's enemies. Even those who love all mankind may err through a wrong conception of the good life. I shall try, therefore, before going any further, to give an idea of what I consider excellent in men and women, quite without regard to practicality, or to the educational methods by which it might be brought into being. Such a picture will help us afterwards, when we come to consider the details of education; we shall know the direction in which we wish to move.

We must first make a distinction: some qualities are desirable in a certain proportion of mankind, others are desirable universally. We want artists, but we also want men of science. We want great administrators, but we also want ploughmen and millers and bakers. The qualities which produce a man of great eminence in some one direction are often such as might be undesirable if they were universal. Shelley describes the day's work of a poet as follows:

> He will watch from dawn to gloom
> The lake-reflected sun illume

> The honey-bees in the ivy bloom,
> Nor heed nor see what things they be.

These habits are praiseworthy in a poet, but not—shall we say—in a post-man. We cannot therefore frame our education with a view to giving every one the temperament of a poet. But some characteristics are universally desirable, and it is these alone that I shall consider at this stage.

I make no distinction whatever between male and female excellence. A certain amount of occupational training is desirable for a woman who is to have the care of babies, but that only involves the same sort of difference as there is between a farmer and a miller. It is in no degree fundamental, and does not demand consideration at our present level.

I will take four characteristics which seem to me jointly to form the basis of an ideal character: vitality, courage, sensitiveness, and intelligence. I do not suggest that this list is complete, but I think it carries us a good way. Moreover I firmly believe that, by proper physical, emotional and intellectual care of the young, these qualities could all be made very common. I shall consider each in turn.

Vitality is rather a physiological than a mental characteristic; it is presumably always present where there is perfect health, but it tends to ebb with advancing years, and gradually dwindles to nothing in old age. In vigorous children it quickly rises to a maximum before they reach school age, and then tends to be diminished by education. Where it exists, there is pleasure in feeling alive, quite apart from any specific pleasant circumstance. It heightens pleasures and diminishes pains. It makes it easy to take an interest in whatever occurs, and thus promotes objectivity, which is an essential of sanity. Human beings are prone to become absorbed in themselves, unable to be interested in what they see and hear or in anything outside their own skins. This is a great misfortune to themselves, since it entails at best boredom and at worst melancholia; it is also a fatal barrier to usefulness, except in very exceptional cases. Vitality promotes interest in the outside world; it also promotes the power of hard work. Moreover it is a safeguard against envy, because it makes one's own existence pleasant. As envy is one of the great sources of human misery, this is a very important merit in vitality. Many bad qualities are of course compatible with vitality—for example, those of a healthy tiger. And many of the best qualities are compatible with its absence: Newton and Locke, for example, had very little. Both these men, however, had irritabilities and envies from which better health would have set them free. Probably the whole of Newton's controversy with Leibniz, which ruined English mathematics for over a hundred years, would have been avoided if Newton had been robust and able to enjoy ordinary pleasures. In spite of its limitations, therefore, I reckon vitality among the qualities which it is important that all men should possess.

Courage—the second quality on our list—has several forms, and all of them are complex. Absence of fear is one thing, and the power of controlling fear is another. And absence of fear, in turn, is one thing when the fear is rational, another when it is irrational. Absence of irrational fear is clearly good; so is the power of controlling fear. But absence of rational fear is a matter as to which debate is possible. However, I shall postpone this question until I have said something about the other forms of courage.

Irrational fear plays an extraordinarily large part in the instinctive emotional life of most people. In its pathological forms, as persecution mania, anxiety complex, or what not, it is treated by alienists. But in milder forms it is common among those who are considered sane. It may be a general feeling that there are dangers about, more correctly termed "anxiety," or a specific dread of things that are not dangerous, such as mice or spiders.[1] It used to be supposed that many fears were instinctive, but this is now questioned by most investigators. There are apparently a few instinctive fears—for instance, of loud noises—but the great majority arise either from experience or from suggestion. Fear of the dark, for example, seems to be entirely due to suggestion. Most vertebrates, there is reason to think, do not feel instinctive fear of their natural enemies, but catch this emotion from their elders. When human beings bring them up by hand, the fears usual among the species are found to be absent. But fear is exceedingly infectious: children catch it from their elders even when their elders are not aware of having shown it. Timidity in mothers or nurses is very quickly imitated by children through suggestion. Hitherto, men have thought it attractive in women to be full of irrational terrors, because it gave men a chance to seem protective without incurring any real danger. But the sons of these men have acquired the terrors from their mothers, and have had to be afterwards trained to regain a courage which they need never have lost if their fathers had not desired to despise their mothers. The harm that has been done by the subjection of women is incalculable; this matter of fear affords only one incidental illustration.

I am not at the moment discussing the methods by which fear and anxiety may be minimized; that is a matter which I shall consider later. There is, however, one question which arises at this stage, namely: can we be content to deal with fear by means of repression, or must we find some more radical cure? Traditionally, aristocracies have been trained not to show fear, while subject nations, classes, and sexes have been encouraged

[1] On fear and anxiety in childhood, see *e.g.* William Stern, "Psychology of Early Childhood," Chap. XXXV. (Henry Holt, 1924).

to remain cowardly. The test of courage has been crudely behavioristic: a man must not run away in battle; he must be proficient in "manly" sports; he must retain self-command in fires, shipwrecks, earthquakes, etc. He must not merely do the right thing, but he must avoid turning pale, or trembling, or gasping for breath, or giving any other easily observed sign of fear. All this I regard as of great importance: I should wish to see courage cultivated in all nations, in all classes, and in both sexes. But when the method adopted is repressive, it entails the evils always associated with that practice. Shame and disgrace have always been potent weapons in producing the appearance of courage; but in fact they merely cause a conflict of terrors, in which it is hoped that the dread of public condemnation will be the stronger. "Always speak the truth except when something frightens you" was a maxim taught to me in childhood. I cannot admit the exception. Fear should be overcome not only in action, but in feeling; and not only in conscious feeling, but in the unconscious as well. The purely external victory over fear, which satisfies the aristocratic code, leaves the impulse operative underground, and produces evil twisted reactions which are not recognized as the offspring of terror. I am not thinking of "shell shock," in which the connection with fear is obvious. I am thinking rather of the whole system of oppression and cruelty by which dominant castes seek to retain their ascendancy. When recently in Shanghai a British officer ordered a number of unarmed Chinese students to be shot in the back without warning, he was obviously actuated by terror just as much as a soldier who runs away in battle. But military aristocracies are not sufficiently intelligent to trace such actions to their psychological source; they regard them rather as showing firmness and a proper spirit.

From the point of view of psychology and physiology, fear and rage are closely analogous emotions: the man who feels rage is not possessed of the highest kind of courage. The cruelty invariably displayed in suppressing negro insurrections, communist rebellions, and other threats to aristocracy, is an offshoot of cowardice, and deserves the same contempt as is bestowed upon the more obvious forms of that vice. I believe that it is possible so to educate ordinary men and women, that they shall be able to live without fear. Hitherto, only a few heroes and saints have achieved such a life; but what they have done others could do if they were shown the way.

For the kind of courage which does not consist in repression, a number of factors must be combined. To begin with the humblest: health and vitality are very helpful, though not indispensable. Practice and skill in dangerous situations are very desirable. But when we come to consider, not courage in this and that respect, but universal courage, something more fundamental is wanted. What is wanted is a combination of self-respect with an impersonal outlook on life. To begin with self-respect: some men live from within, while others are mere mirrors of what is felt and said by their neighbours. The latter can never have true courage: they must have admiration, and are haunted by the fear of losing it. The teaching of "humility," which used to be thought desirable, was the means of producing a perverted form of this same vice. "Humility" suppressed self-respect, but not the desire for the respect of others; it merely made nominal self-abasement the means of acquiring credit. Thus it produced hypocrisy and falsification of instinct. Children were taught unreasoning submission, and proceeded to exact it when they grew up; it was said that only those who have learned to obey know how to command. What I suggest is that no one should learn how to obey, and no one should attempt to command. I do not mean, of course, that there should not be leaders in co-operative enterprises; but their authority should be like that of a captain of a football team, which is suffered voluntarily in order to achieve a common purpose. Our purposes should be our own, not the result of external authority; and our purposes should never be forcibly imposed upon others. This is what I mean when I say no one should command and no one should obey.

There is one thing more required for the highest courage, and that is what I called just now an impersonal outlook on life. The man whose hopes and fears are all centered upon himself can hardly view death with equanimity, since it extinguishes his whole emotional universe. Here, again, we are met by a tradition urging the cheap and easy way of repression: the saint must learn to renounce Self, must mortify the flesh and forego instinctive joys. This can be done, but its consequences are bad. Having renounced pleasure for himself, the ascetic saint renounces it for others also, which is easier. Envy persists underground, and leads him to the view that suffering is ennobling, and may therefore be legitimately inflicted. Hence arises a complete inversion of values: what is good is thought bad, and what is bad is thought good. The source of all the harm is that the good life has been sought in obedience to a negative imperative, not in broadening and developing natural desires and instincts. There are certain things in human nature which take up beyond Self without effort. The commonest of these is love, more particularly parental love, which in some is so generalized as to embrace the whole human race. Another is knowledge. There is no reason to suppose that Galileo was particularly benevolent, yet he lived for an end which was not defeated by his death. Another is art. But in fact every interest in something outside a man's own body makes his life to that degree impersonal. For this reason, paradoxical as it may seem, a man of wide and vivid interests finds less difficulty in leaving life than is experienced by some miserable hypochondriac whose interests are bounded by his own ailments. Thus the perfection of courage is found in the man of many interests, who *feels* his ego to be but a small part of the world, not through despising himself, but through valuing much that is not himself. This can hardly happen except where instinct is free and intelligence is active. From the union of the two grows a comprehensiveness of outlook unknown both to the voluptuary and to the ascetic; and to such an outlook personal death appears a trivial matter. Such courage is positive and instinctive, not negative and repressive. It is courage in this positive sense that I regard as one of the major ingredients in a perfect character.

Sensitiveness, the third quality in our list, is in a sense a corrective of mere courage. Courageous behaviour is easier for a man who fails to apprehend dangers, but such courage may often be foolish. We cannot regard as satisfactory any way of acting which is dependent upon ignorance or forgetfulness: the fullest possible knowledge and realization are an essential part of what is desirable. The cognitive aspect, however, comes under the head of intelligence; sensitiveness, in the sense in which I am using the term, belongs to the emotions. A purely theoretical definition would be that a person is emotionally sensitive when many stimuli produce emotions in him; but taken thus broadly the quality is not necessarily a good one. If sensitiveness is to be good, the emotional reaction must be in some sense *appropriate*: mere intensity is not what is needed. The quality I have in mind is that of being affected pleasurably or the reverse by many things, and by the right things. What are the right things, I shall try to explain. The first step, which most children take at the age of about five months, is to pass beyond mere pleasures of sensation, such as food and warmth, to the pleasure of social approbation. This pleasure, as soon as it has arisen, develops very rapidly: every child loves praise and hates blame. Usually the wish to be thought well of remains one of the dominant motives throughout life. It is certainly very valuable as a stimulus to pleasant behaviour, and as a restraint upon impulses of greed. If we were wiser in our admirations, it might be much more valuable. But so long as the most admired heroes are those who have killed the greatest number of people, love of admiration cannot alone be adequate to the good life.

The next stage in the development of a desirable form of sensitiveness is sympathy. There is a purely physical sympathy: a very young child will cry because a brother or sister is crying. This, I suppose, affords the basis for the further developments. The two enlargements that are needed are: first, to feel sympathy even when the sufferer is not an object of special affection; secondly, to feel it when the suffering is merely known to be occurring, not sensibly present. The second of these enlargements depends mainly upon intelligence. It may only go so far as sympathy with suffering which is portrayed vividly and touchingly, as in a good novel; it may, on the other hand, go so far as to enable a man to be moved emotionally by statistics. This capacity for abstract sympathy is as rare as it is important. Almost everybody is deeply affected when some one he loves suffers from cancer. Most people are moved when they see the sufferings of unknown patients in hospitals. Yet when they read that the death-rate from cancer is such-and-such, they are as a rule only moved to momentary personal fear lest they or some one dear to them should acquire the disease. The same is true of war: people think it dreadful when their son or brother is mutilated, but they do not think it a million times as dreadful that a million people should be mutilated. A man who is full of kindliness in all personal dealings may derive his income from incitement to war or from the torture of children in "backward" countries. All these familiar phenomena are due to the fact that sympathy is not stirred, in most people, by a merely abstract stimulus. A large proportion of the evils in the modern world would cease if this could be remedied. Science has greatly increased our power of affecting the lives of distant people, without increasing our sympathy for them. Suppose you are a shareholder in a company which manufactures cotton in Shanghai. You may be a busy man, who has merely followed financial advice in making the investment; neither Shanghai nor cotton interests you, but only your dividends. Yet you become part of the force leading to massacres of innocent people, and your dividends would disappear if little children were not forced into unnatural and dangerous toil. You do not mind, because you have never seen the children, and an abstract stimulus cannot move you. That is the fundamental reason why large-scale industrialism is so cruel, and why oppression of subject races is tolerated. An education producing sensitiveness to abstract stimuli would make such things impossible.

Cognitive sensitiveness, which should also be included, is practically the same thing as a habit of observation, and this is more naturally considered in connection with intelligence. Aesthetic sensitiveness raises a number of problems which I do not wish to discuss at this stage. I will therefore pass on to the last of the four qualities we enumerated, namely, intelligence.

One of the great defects of traditional morality has been the low estimate it placed upon intelligence. The Greeks did not err in this respect, but the Church led men to think that nothing matters except virtue, and virtue consists in abstinence from a certain list of actions arbitrarily labelled "sin." So long as this attitude persists, it is impossible to make men realize that intelligence does more good than an artificial conventional "virtue." When I speak of intelligence, I include both actual knowledge and receptivity to knowledge. The two are, in fact, closely connected. Ignorant adults are unteachable; on such matters as hygiene or diet, for example, they are totally incapable of believing what science has to say. The more a man has learnt, the easier it is for him to learn still more—always assuming that he has not been taught in a spirit of dogmatism. Ignorant people have never been compelled to change their mental habits, and have stiffened into an unchangeable attitude. It is not only that they are credulous where they should be sceptical; it is just as much that they are incredulous where they should be receptive. No doubt the word "intelligence" properly signifies rather an aptitude for acquiring knowledge than knowledge already acquired; but I do not think this aptitude is acquired except by exercise, any more than the aptitude of a pianist or an acrobat. It is, of course, possible to impart information in ways that do not train intelligence; it is not only possible, but easy, and frequently done. But I do not believe that it is possible to train intelligence without imparting information, or at any rate causing knowledge to be acquired. And without intelligence our complex modern world cannot subsist; still less can it make progress. I regard the cultivation of intelligence, therefore, as one of the major purposes of education. This might seem a commonplace, but in fact it is not. The desire to instil what are regarded as correct beliefs has made educationists too often indifferent to the training of intelligence. To make this clear, it is necessary to define intelligence a little more closely, so as to discover the mental habits which it requires. For this purpose I shall consider only the aptitude for acquiring knowledge, not the store of actual knowledge which might legitimately be included in the definition of intelligence.

The instinctive foundation of the intellectual life is curiosity, which is found among animals in its elementary forms. Intelligence demands an alert curiosity, but it must be of a certain kind. The sort that leads village neighbours to try to peer through curtains after dark has no very high value. The wide-spread interest in gossip is inspired, not by a love of knowledge, but by malice: (no one gossips about other people's secret virtues, but only about their secret vices.) Accordingly most gossip is untrue, but care is taken not to verify it. Our neighbours' sins, like the consolations of religion, are so agreeable that we do not stop to scrutinize the evidence closely. Curiosity properly so called, on the other hand, is inspired by a genuine love of knowledge. You may see this impulse, in a moderately pure form, at work in a cat which has been brought to a strange room, and proceeds to smell every corner and every piece of furniture. You will see it also in children, who are passionately interested when a drawer or cupboard, usually closed, is open for their inspection. Animals, machines, thunderstorms, and all forms of manual work, arouse the curiosity of children, whose thirst for knowledge puts the most intelligent adult to shame. This impulse grows weaker with advancing years, until at last what is unfamiliar inspires only disgust, with no desire for a closer acquaintance. This is the stage at which people announce that the country is going to the dogs, and that "things are not what they were in my young days." The thing which is not the same as it was in that far-off time is the speaker's curiosity. And with the death of curiosity we may reckon that active intelligence, also, has died.

But although curiosity lessens in intensity and in extent after childhood, it may for a long time improve in quality. Curiosity about general propositions shows a higher level of intelligence than curiosity about particular facts; broadly speaking, the higher the order of generality the greater is the intelligence involved. (This rule, however, must not be taken too strictly.) Curiosity dissociated from personal advantage shows a higher development than curiosity connected (say) with a chance of food. The cat that sniffs in a new room is not a wholly disinterested scientific inquirer, but probably also wants to find out whether there are mice about. Perhaps it is not quite correct to say that curiosity is best when it is disinterested, but rather that it is best when the connection with other interests is not direct and obvious, but discoverable only by means of a certain degree of intelligence. This point, however, it is not necessary for us to decide.

If curiosity is to be fruitful, it must be associated with a certain technique for the acquisition of knowledge. There must be habits of observation, belief in the possibility of knowledge, patience and industry. These things will develop of themselves, given the original fund of curiosity and the proper intellectual education. But since our intellectual life is only a part of our activity, and since curiosity is perpetually coming into conflict with other passions, there is need of certain intellectual virtues, such as open-mindedness. We become impervious to new truth both from habit and from desire: we find it hard to disbelieve what we have emphatically believed for a number of years, and also what ministers to self-esteem or any other fundamental passion. Open-mindedness should therefore be one of the qualities that education aims at producing. At present, this is only done to a very limited extent, as is illustrated by the following paragraph from "The Daily Herald," July 31, 1925:

A special committee, appointed to inquire into the allegations of the subversion of children's minds in Bootle schools by their school teachers, has placed its findings before the Bootle Borough Council. The Committee was of opinion that the allegations were substantiated, but the Council deleted the word "substantiated", and stated that "the allegations gave cause for reasonable inquiry." A recommendation made by the Committee, and adopted by the Council, was that in future appointments of teachers, they shall undertake to train the scholars in habits of reverence towards God and religion, and of respect for the civil and religious institutions of the country.

Thus whatever may happen elsewhere, there is to be no open-mindedness in Bootle. It is hoped that the Borough Council will shortly send a deputation to Dayton, Tennessee, to obtain further light upon the best methods of carrying out their programme. But perhaps that is unnecessary. From the wording of the resolution, it would seem as if Bootle needed no instruction in obscurantism.

Courage is essential to intellectual probity, as well as to physical heroism. The real world it more unknown than we like to think; from the first day of life we practise precarious inductions, and confound our mental habits with laws of external nature. All sorts of intellectual systems—Christianity, Socialism, Patriotism, etc.—are ready, like orphan asylums, to give safety in return for servitude. A free mental life cannot be as warm and comfortable and sociable as a life enveloped in a creed: only a creed can give the feeling of a cosy fireside while the winter storms are raging without.

This brings us to a somewhat difficult question: to what extent should the good life be emancipated from the herd? I hesitate to use the phrase "herd instinct," because there are controversies as to its correctness. But, however interpreted, the phenomena which it describes are familiar. We like to stand well with those whom we feel to be the group with which we wish to co-operate—our family, our neighbours, our colleagues, our political party, or our nation. This is natural, because we cannot obtain any of the pleasures of life without cooperation. Moreover, emotions are infectious, especially when they are felt by many people at once. Very few people can be present at an excited meeting without getting excited: if they are opponents, their opposition becomes excited. And to most people such opposition is only possible if they can derive support from the thought of a different crowd in which they will win approbation. That is why the Communion of Saints has afforded such comfort to the persecuted. Are we to acquiesce in this desire for co-operation with a crowd, or shall our education try to weaken it? There are arguments on both sides, and the right answer must consist in finding a just proportion, not in a wholehearted decision for either party.

I think myself that the desire to please and to co-operate should be strong and normal, but should be capable of being overcome by other desires on certain important occasions. The desirability of a wish to please has already been considered in connection with sensitiveness. Without it, we should all be boors, and all social groups, from the family upwards, would be impossible. Education of young children would be very difficult if they did not desire the good opinion of their parents. The contagious character of emotions also has its uses, when the contagion is from a wiser person to a more foolish one. But in the case of panic fear and panic rage it is of course the very reverse of useful. Thus the question of emotional receptivity is by no means simple. Even in purely intellectual matters, the issue is not clear. The great discoverers have had to withstand the herd, and incur hostility by their independence. But the average man's opinions are much less foolish than they would be if he thought for himself: in science, at least, his respect for authority is on the whole beneficial.

I think that in the life of a man whose circumstances and talents are not very exceptional there should be a large sphere where what is vaguely termed "herd instinct" dominates, and a small sphere into which it does not penetrate. The small sphere should contain the region of his special competence. We think ill of a man who cannot admire a woman unless everybody else also admires her: we think that, in the choice of a wife, a man should be guided by his own independent feelings, not by a reflection of the feelings of his society. It is no matter if his judgments of people in general agree with those of his neighbours, but when he falls in love he ought to be guided by his own independent feelings. Much the same thing applies in other directions. A farmer should follow his own judgment as to the capacities of the fields which he cultivates himself, though his judgment should be formed after acquiring a knowledge of scientific agriculture. An economist should form an independent judgment on currency questions, but an ordinary mortal had better follow authority. Wherever there is special competence, there should be independence. But a man should not make himself into a kind of hedgehog, all bristles to keep the world at a distance. The bulk of our ordinary activities must be co-operative, and co-operation must have an instinctive basis. Nevertheless, we should all learn to be able to think for ourselves about matters that are particularly well known to us, and we ought all to have acquired the courage to proclaim unpopular opinions when we believe them to be important. The application of these broad principles in special cases may, of course, be difficult. But it will be less difficult than it is at present in a world where men commonly have the virtues we have been considering in this chapter. The persecuted saint, for instance, would not exist in such a world. The good man would have no occasion to bristle and become self-conscious; his goodness would result from following his impulses, and would be combined with instinctive happiness. His neighbours would not hate him, because they would not fear him: the hatred of pioneers is due to the terror they inspire, and this terror would not exist among men who had acquired courage. Only a man dominated by fear would join the Ku Klux Klan or the Fascisti. In a world of brave men, such persecuting organizations could not exist, and the good life would involve far less resistance to instinct than it does at present. The good world can only be created and sustained by fearless men, but the more they succeed in their task the fewer occasions there will be for the exercise of their courage.

A community of men and women possessing vitality, courage, sensitiveness, and intelligence, in the highest degree that education can produce, would be very different from anything that has hitherto existed. Very few people would be unhappy. The main causes of unhappiness at present are: ill-health, poverty, and an unsatisfactory sex-life. All of these would become very rare. Good health could be almost universal, and even old age could be postponed. Poverty, since the industrial revolution, is only due to collective stupidity. Sensitiveness would make people wish to abolish it, intelligence would show them the way, and courage would lead them to adopt it. (A timid person would rather remain miserable than do anything unusual.) Most people's sex-life, at present, is more or less unsatisfactory. This is partly due to bad education, partly to persecution by the authorities and Mrs. Grundy. A generation of women brought up without irrational sex fears would soon make an end of this. Fear has been thought the only way to make women "virtuous," and they have been deliberately taught to be cowards, both physically and mentally. Women in whom love is cramped encourage brutality and hypocrisy in their husbands, and distort the instincts of their children. One generation of fearless women could transform the world, by bringing into it a generation of fearless children, not contorted into unnatural shapes, but straight and candid, generous, affectionate, and free. Their ardour would sweep away the cruelty and pain which we endure because we are lazy, cowardly, hardhearted and stupid. It is education that gives us these bad qualities, and education that must give us the opposite virtues. Education is the key to the new world.

AIMS IN EDUCATION

John Dewey

1. The Nature of an Aim

The account of education given in our earlier chapters virtually anticipated the results reached in a discussion of the purport of education in a
democratic community. For it assumed that the aim of education is to
enable individuals to continue their education—or that the object and
reward of learning is continued capacity for growth. Now this idea cannot
be applied to *all* the members of a society except where intercourse of man
with man is mutual, and except where there is adequate provision for the
reconstruction of social habits and institutions by means of wide stimulation arising from equitably distributed interests. And this means a democratic society. In our search for aims in education, we are not concerned,
therefore, with finding an end outside of the educative process to which
education is subordinate. Our whole conception forbids. We are rather
concerned with the contrast which exists when aims belong within the
process in which they operate and when they are set up from without. And
the latter state of affairs must obtain when social relationships are not
equitably balanced. For in that case, some portions of the whole social
group will find their aims determined by an external dictation; their aims
will not arise from the free growth of their own experience, and their
nominal aims will be means to more ulterior ends of others rather than
truly their own.

Our first question is to define the nature of an aim so far as it falls
within an activity, instead of being furnished from without. We approach
the definition by a contrast of mere *results* with *ends.* Any exhibition of
energy has results. The wind blows about the sands of the desert; the
position of the grains is changed. Here is a result, an effect, but not an *end.*
For there is nothing in the outcome which completes or fulfills what went
before it. There is mere spatial redistribution. One state of affairs is just as
good as any other. Consequently there is no basis upon which to select
an earlier state of affairs as a beginning, a later as an end, and to consider
what intervenes as a process of transformation and realization.

Consider for example the activities of bees in contrast with the changes
in the sands when the wind blows them about. The results of the bees'
actions may be called ends not because they are designed or consciously
intended, but because they are true terminations or completions of what

has preceded. When the bees gather pollen and make wax and build cells, each step prepares the way for the next. When cells are built, the queen lays eggs in them; when eggs are laid, they are sealed and bees brood them and keep them at a temperature required to hatch them. When they are hatched, bees feed the young till they can take care of themselves. Now we are so familiar with such facts, that we are apt to dismiss them on the ground that life and instinct are a kind of miraculous thing anyway. Thus we fail to note what the essential characteristic of the event is; namely, the significance of the temporal place and order of each element; the way each prior event leads into its successor while the successor takes up what is furnished and utilizes it for some other stage, until we arrive at the end, which, as it were, summarizes and finishes off the process.

Since aims relate always to results, the first thing to look to when it is a question of aims, is whether the work assigned possesses intrinsic continuity. Or is it a mere serial aggregate of acts, first doing one thing and then another? To talk about an educational aim when approximately each act of a pupil is dictated by the teacher, when the only order in the sequence of his acts is that which comes from the assignment of lessons and the giving of directions by another, is to talk nonsense. It is equally fatal to an aim to permit capricious or discontinuous action in the name of spontaneous self-expression. An aim implies an orderly and ordered activity, one in which the order consists in the progressive completing of a process. Given an activity having a time span and cumulative growth within the time succession, an aim means foresight in advance of the end or possible termination. If bees anticipated the consequences of their activity, if they perceived their end in imaginative foresight, they would have the primary element in an aim. Hence it is nonsense to talk about the aim of education—or any other undertaking—where conditions do not permit of foresight of results, and do not stimulate a person to look ahead to see what the outcome of a given activity is to be.

In the next place the aim as a foreseen end gives direction to the activity; it is not an idle view of a mere spectator, but influences the steps taken to reach the end. The foresight functions in three ways. In the first place, it involves careful observation of the given conditions to see what are the means available for reaching the end, and to discover the hindrances in the way. In the second place, it suggests the proper order or sequence in the use of means. It facilitates an economical selection and arrangement. In the third place, it makes choice of alternatives possible. If we can predict the outcome of acting this way or that, we can then compare the value of the two courses of action; we can pass judgment upon their relative desirability. If we know that stagnant water breeds mosquitoes and that they are likely to carry disease, we can, disliking that anticipated result, take steps to avert it. Since we do not anticipate results as mere intellectual onlookers, but as persons concerned in the outcome, we are partakers in the process which produces the result. We intervene to bring about this result or that.

Of course these three points are closely connected with one another. We can definitely foresee results only as we make careful scrutiny of present conditions, and the importance of the outcome supplies the motive for observations. The more adequate our observations, the more varied is the scene of conditions and obstructions that presents itself, and the more numerous are the alternatives between which choice may be made. In turn, the more numerous the recognized possibilities of the situation, or alternatives of action, the more meaning does the chosen activity possess, and the more flexibily controllable is it. Where only a single outcome has been thought of, the mind has nothing else to think of; the meaning attaching to the act is limited. One only steams ahead toward the mark. Sometimes such a narrow course may be effective. But if unexpected difficulties offer themselves, one has not as many resources at command as if he had chosen the same line of action after a broader survey of the possibilities of the field. He cannot make needed readjustments readily.

The net conclusion is that acting with an aim is all one with acting intelligently. To foresee a terminus of an act is to have a basis upon which to observe, to select, and to order objects and our own capacities. To do these things means to have a mind—for mind is precisely intentional purposeful activity controlled by perception of facts and their relationships to one another. To have a mind to do a thing is to foresee a future possibility; it is to have a plan for its accomplishment; it is to note the means which make the plan capable of execution and the obstructions in the way,—or, if it is really a *mind* to do the thing and not a vague aspiration— it is to have a plan which takes account of resources and difficulties. Mind is capacity to refer present conditions to future results, and future consequences to present conditions. And these traits are just what is meant by having an aim or a purpose. A man is stupid or blind or unintelligent— lacking in mind—just in the degree in which in any activity he does not know what he is about, namely, the probable consequences of his acts. A man is imperfectly intelligent when he contents himself with looser guesses about the outcome than is needful, just taking a chance with his luck, or when he forms plans apart from study of the actual conditions, including his own capacities. Such relative absence of mind means to make our feelings the measure of what is to happen. To be intelligent we must "stop, look, listen" in making the plan of an activity.

To identify acting with an aim and intelligent activity is enough to show its value—its function in experience. We are only too given to making an entity out of the abstract noun "consciousness." We forget that it comes from the adjective "conscious." To be conscious is to be aware of what we are about; conscious signifies the deliberate, observant, planning traits of activity. Consciousness is nothing which we have which gazes idly on the scene around one or which has impressions made upon it by physical things; it is a name for the purposeful quality of an activity, for the fact that it is directed by an aim. Put the other way about, to have an aim is to act with meaning, not like an automatic machine; it is to *mean* to do something and to perceive the meaning of things in the light of that intent.

2. The Criteria of Good Aims

We may apply the results of our discussion to a consideration of the criteria involved in a correct establishing of aims. (1) The aim set up must be an outgrowth of existing conditions. It must be based upon a consideration of what is already going on; upon the resources and difficulties of the situation. Theories about the proper end of our activities—educational and moral theories—often violate this principle. They assume ends lying *outside* our activities; ends foreign to the concrete makeup of the situation; ends which issue from some outside source. Then the problem is to bring our activities to bear upon the realization of these externally supplied ends. They are something for which we *ought* to act. In any case such "aims" limit intelligence; they are not the expression of mind in foresight, observation, and choice of the better among alternative possibilities. They limit intelligence because, given ready-made, they must be imposed by some authority external to intelligence, leaving to the latter nothing but a mechanical choice of means.

(2) We have spoken as if aims could be completely formed prior to the attempt to realize them. This impression must now be qualified. The aim as it first emerges is a mere tentative sketch. The act of striving to realize it tests its worth. If it suffices to direct activity successfully, nothing more is required, since its whole function is to set a mark in advance; and at times a mere hint may suffice. But usually—at least in complicated situations—acting upon it brings to light conditions which had been overlooked. This calls for revision of the original aim; it has to be added to and subtracted from. An aim must, then, be *flexible*; it must be capable of alteration to meet circumstances. An end established externally to the process of action is always rigid. Being inserted or imposed from without, it is not supposed to have a working relationship to the concrete conditions of the situation. What happens in the course of action neither confirms, refutes, nor alters it. Such an end can only be insisted upon. The failure that results from its lack of adaptation is attributed simply to the

perverseness of conditions, not to the fact that the end is not reasonable under the circumstances. The value of a legitimate aim, on the contrary, lies in the fact that we can use it to change conditions. It is a method for dealing with conditions so as to effect desirable alterations in them. A farmer who should passively accept things just as he finds them would make as great a mistake as he who framed his plans in complete disregard of what soil, climate, etc., permit. One of the evils of an abstract or remote external aim in education is that its very inapplicability in practice is likely to react into a haphazard snatching at immediate conditions. A good aim surveys the present state of experience of pupils, and forming a tentative plan of treatment, keeps the plan constantly in view and yet modifies it as conditions develop. The aim, in short, is experimental, and hence constantly growing as it is tested in action.

(3) The aim must always represent a freeing of activities. The term *end in view* is suggestive, for it puts before the mind the termination or conclusion of some process. The only way in which we can define an activity is by putting before ourselves the objects in which it terminates— as one's aim in shooting is the target. But we must remember that the *object* is only a mark or sign by which the mind specifies the *activity* one desires to carry out. Strictly speaking, not the target but *hitting* the target is the end in view; one *takes* aim by means of the target, but also by the sight on the gun. The different objects which are thought of are means of *directing* the activity. Thus one aims at, say, a rabbit; what he wants is to shoot straight: a certain kind of activity. Or, if it is the rabbit he wants, it is not rabbit apart from his activity, but as a factor in activity; he wants to eat the rabbit, or to show it as evidence of his marksmanship—he wants to do something with it. The doing with the thing, not the thing in isolation, is his end. The object is but a phase of the active end,—continuing the activity successfully. This is what is meant by the phrase, used above, "freeing activity."

In contrast with fulfilling some process in order that activity may go on, stands the static character of an end which is imposed from without the activity. It is always conceived of as fixed; it is *something* to be attained and possessed. When one has such a notion, activity is a mere unavoidable means to something else; it is not significant or important on its own account. As compared with the end it is but a necessary evil; something which must be gone through before one can reach the object which is alone worth while. In other words, the external idea of the aim leads to a separation of means from end, while an end which grows up within an activity as plan for its direction is always both ends and means, the distinction being only one of convenience. Every means is a temporary end until we have attained it. Every end becomes a means of carrying activity further as soon as it is achieved. We call it end when it marks off the future direction of the activity in which we are engaged; means when it marks off the present direction. Every divorce of end from means diminishes by that much the significance of the activity and tends to reduce it to a drudgery from which one would escape if he could. A farmer has to use plants and animals to carry on his farming activities. It certainly makes a great difference to his life whether he is fond of them, or whether he regards them merely as means which he has to employ to get something else in which alone he is interested. In the former case, his entire course of activity is significant; each phase of it has its own value. He has the experience of realizing his end at every stage; the postponed aim, or end in view, being merely a sight ahead by which to keep his activity going fully and freely. For if he does not look ahead, he is more likely to find himself blocked. The aim is as definitely a *means* of action as is any other portion of an activity.

3. Applications in Education

There is nothing peculiar about educational aims. They are just like aims in any directed occupation. The educator, like the farmer, has certain things to do, certain resources with which to do, and certain obstacles with which to contend. The conditions with which the farmer deals, whether as obstacles or resources, have their own structure and operation independently of any purpose of his. Seeds sprout, rain falls, the sun shines, insects devour, blight comes, the seasons change. His aim is simply to utilize these various conditions; to make his activities and their energies work together, instead of against one another. It would be absurd if the farmer set up a purpose of farming, without any reference to these conditions of soil, climate, characteristic of plant growth, etc. His purpose is simply a foresight of the consequences of his energies connected with those of the things about him, a foresight used to direct his movements from day to day. Foresight of possible consequences leads to more careful and extensive observation of the nature and performances of the things he had to do with, and to laying out a plan—that is, of a certain order in the acts to be performed.

It is the same with the educator, whether parent or teacher. It is as absurd for the latter to set up his "own" aims as the proper objects of the growth of the children as it would be for the farmer to set up an ideal of farming irrespective of conditions. Aims mean acceptance of responsibility for the observations, anticipations, and arrangements required in carrying on a function—whether farming or educating. Any aim is of value so far as it assists observation, choice, and planning in carrying on activity from moment to moment and hour to hour; if it gets in the way of the individual's own common sense (as it will surely do if imposed from without or accepted on authority) it does harm.

And it is well to remind ourselves that education as such has no aims. Only persons, parents, and teachers, etc., have aims, not an abstract idea like education. And consequently their purposes are indefinitely varied, differing with different children, changing as children grow and with the growth of experience on the part of the one who teaches. Even the most valid aims which can be put in words will, as words, do more harm than good unless one recognizes that they are not aims, but rather suggestions to educators as to how to observe, how to look ahead, and how to choose in liberating and directing the energies of the concrete situations in which they find themselves. As a recent writer has said: "To lead this boy to read Scott's novels instead of old Sleuth's stories; to teach this girl to sew; to root out the habit of bullying from John's make-up; to prepare this class to study medicine,—these are samples of the millions of aims we have actually before us in the concrete work of education."

Bearing these qualifications in mind, we shall proceed to state some of the characteristics found in all good educational aims. (1) An educational aim must be founded upon the intrinsic activities and needs (including original instincts and acquired habits) of the given individual to be educated. The tendency of such an aim as preparation is, as we have seen, to omit existing powers, and find the aim in some remote accomplishment or responsibility. In general, there is a disposition to take considerations which are dear to the hearts of adults and set them up as ends irrespective of the capacities of those educated. There is also an inclination to propound aims which are so uniform as to neglect the specific powers and requirements of an individual, forgetting that all learning is something which happens to an individual at a given time and place. The larger range of perception of the adult is of great value in observing the abilities and weaknesses of the young, in deciding what they may amount to. Thus the artistic capacities of the adult exhibit what certain tendencies of the child are capable of; if we did not have the adult achievements we should be without assurance as to the significance of the drawing, reproducing, modeling, coloring activities of childhood. So if it were not for adult language, we should not be able to see the import of the babbling impulses of infancy. But it is one thing to use adult accomplishments as a context in which to place and survey the doings of childhood and youth; it is quite another to set them up as a fixed aim without regard to the concrete activities of those educated.

(2) An aim must be capable of translation into a method of coöperating with the activities of those undergoing instruction. It must suggest the kind

of environment needed to liberate and to organize *their* capacities. Unless it lends itself to the construction of specific procedures, and unless these procedures test, correct, and amplify the aim, the latter is worthless. Instead of helping the specific task of teaching, it prevents the use of ordinary judgment in observing and sizing up the situation. It operates to exclude recognition of everything except what squares up with the fixed end in view. Every rigid aim just because it is rigidly given seems to render it unnecessary to give careful attention to concrete conditions. Since it *must* apply anyhow, what is the use of noting details which do not count?

The vice of externally imposed ends has deep roots. Teachers receive them from superior authorities; these authorities accept them from what is current in the community. The teachers impose them upon children. As a first consequence, the intelligence of the teacher is not free; it is confined to receiving the aims laid down from above. Too rarely is the individual teacher so free from the dictation of authoritative supervisor, textbook on methods, prescribed course of study, etc., that he can let his mind come to close quarters with the pupil's mind and the subject matter. This distrust of the teacher's experience is then reflected in lack of confidence in the responses of pupils. The latter receive their aims through a double or treble external imposition, and are constantly confused by the conflict between the aims which are natural to their own experience at the time and those in which they are taught to acquiesce. Until the democratic criterion of the intrinsic significance of every growing experience is recognized, we shall be intellectually confused by the demand for adaptation to external aims.

(3) Educators have to be on their guard against ends that are alleged to be general and ultimate. Every activity, however specific, is, of course, general in its ramified connections, for it leads out indefinitely into other things. So far as a general idea makes us more alive to these connections, it cannot be too general. But "general" also means "abstract," or detached from all specific context. And such abstractness means remoteness, and throws us back, once more, upon teaching and learning as mere means of getting ready for an end disconnected from the means. That education is literally and all the time its own reward means that no alleged study or discipline is educative unless it is worth while in its own immediate having. A truly general aim broadens the outlook; it stimulates one to take more consequences (connections) into account. This means a wider and more flexible observation of means. The more interacting forces, for example, the farmer takes into account, the more varied will be his immediate resources. He will see a greater number of possible starting places, and a greater number of ways of getting at what he wants to do. The fuller one's conception of possible future achievements, the less his present activity

is tied down to a small number of alternatives. If one knew enough, one could start almost anywhere and sustain his activities continuously and fruitfully.

Understanding then the term general or comprehensive aim simply in the sense of a broad survey of the field of present activities, we shall take up some of the larger ends which have currency in the educational theories of the day, and consider what light they throw upon the immediate concrete and diversified aims which are always the educator's real concern. We premise (as indeed immediately follows from what has been said) that there is no need of making a choice among them or regarding them as competitors. When we come to act in a tangible way we have to select or choose a particular act at a particular time, but any number of comprehensive ends may exist without competition, since they mean simply different ways of looking at the same scene. One cannot climb a number of different mountains simultaneously, but the views had when different mountains are ascended supplement one another: they do not set up incompatible, competing worlds. Or, putting the matter in a slightly different way, one statement of an end may suggest certain questions and observations, and another statement another set of questions, calling for other observations. Then the more general ends we have, the better. One statement will emphasize what another slurs over. What a plurality of hypotheses does for the scientific investigator, a plurality of stated aims may do for the instructor.

Summary

An aim denotes the result of any natural process brought to consciousness and made a factor in determining present observation and choice of ways of acting. It signifies that an activity has become intelligent. Specifically it means foresight of the alternative consequences attendant upon acting in a given situation in different ways, and the use of what is anticipated to direct observation and experiment. A true aim is thus opposed at every point to an aim which is imposed upon a process of action from without. The latter is fixed and rigid; it is not a stimulus to intelligence in the given situation, but is an externally dictated order to do such and such things. Instead of connecting directly with present activities, it is remote, divorced from the means by which it is to be reached. Instead of suggesting a freer and better balanced activity, it is a limit set to activity. In education, the currency of these externally imposed aims is responsible for the emphasis put upon the notion of preparation for a remote future and for rendering the work of both teacher and pupil mechanical and slavish.

EDUCATION FOR PRIVACY

Marten ten Hoor

In view of the hundreds of conferences which have been held on liberal education, it would seem to be impossible to say anything new on the subject. Since there seems to be nothing new to say, one must, in order to be original, be contrary, eccentric or partisan. I have chosen to be partisan. The proposition to be defended is, frankly, a half-truth. If it can be established, there will be some cause for satisfaction; for the establishment of a half-truth is not a bad average in this complex and confused world. There is the justification, moreover, that the other, and possibly the better, half has in our day had practically all the attention.

Stated concretely, the proposition is this: Never in the history of the world have there been so many people occupied with the improvement of so few. To sharpen the point by a specific example: Never have there been so many people making a good living by showing the other fellow how to make a better one. If you are skeptical, I recommend that you try this exercise—add up, as of the current date, the social workers, planners and reformers; the college presidents, deans and professors; the editors of magazines, journals and newspapers (not forgetting college newspapers); almost everybody in Washington, D. C., during recent years; and the tens of thousands of miscellaneous social-minded folks who attend conferences, workshops and institutes organized for the improvement of the human race. Subtract that figure from the total population of this country, and compare this figure with a corresponding figure for, say, the year 1900. You will then see what I mean when I say that this is the era of undiscriminating allegiance to good causes. To come nearer home, compute the sum of all college and university presidents, deans and professors who have in the last five years attended meetings devoted to the improvement of education. Compare that figure with the number of those who remained on the campus working and you will find proof even *in academia*.

As further evidence, and as a striking symptom, there is the recent popularity of educational surveys. Most states and many institutions have experienced several. I have lived through eleven, without noticeable improvement in myself or my neighbors. Note the procedure and the technique, for there you will find the moral. The surveyors are always from another state or another institution. This is in accordance with the well-known principle that an expert is an ordinary person who is away from home. These outsiders are brought in because of their objectivity, objec-

ten Hoor, Marten. Education for privacy. *The American Scholar*, Winter, 1953–54, *23*, 27–42.

tivity being the capacity for discovering faults abroad which you cannot recognize at home. To be a good educational surveyor—or any kind of social analyst, for that matter—you must have a sharp eye for foreign motes but a dull one for domestic beams. You must be a contented extrovert, so that, after diagnosing the faults of others, you can continue to live in perfect comfort with your own.

I must confess that I view all this indiscriminate altruism with a jaundiced eye. It does seem to me that these days there are too many leaders and too few followers; too many preachers and too few sinners—self-conscious sinners, that is. If this were an illustrated article, I would insert at this point a wonderful cartoon I saw not long ago. A little boy was asking an obviously astounded and embarrassed father, "But if we're here to help others, what are the others here for?" Nobody has time these days to improve himself, so busy is he with attempts to improve his neighbor. There is something wrong with that equation. It seems to me that it is time to try to balance it. I suggest that this can be done by shifting some weight from one side to the other, by shifting the emphasis from social improvement to self-improvement. I suggest that over the door of every academic cubicle there should hang the sign which Thoreau had once over the door of his hut: "My destiny mended here, not yours." In short, I propose to make a plea for *education for privacy*.

Before undertaking to identify some of the elements of this type of education, I should like to offer some justification of my skepticism concerning the present emphasis on social-mindedness in education. To begin with, it is so easy to assume that your neighbor is much worse off than yourself. The universality of this tendency is undoubtedly accounted for psychologically by its attractive by-products. The assumption produces a feeling of comfort. If there is some slight suspicion that all is not well within, it is compensating to concentrate on the plight of one's neighbor. Since attention to him is distracting, it keeps the individual from worrying about himself. To do something about a neighbor's ignorance also makes one feel virtuous. This absorbing concern for the improvement of one's neighbor is undoubtedly a product of civilization. It is doubtful if primitive man worried much about it. The cannibal, in fact, represents the other extreme: he uses his neighbor solely for his own improvement.

In the second place, I doubt if the reformer always has the wisdom necessary to direct the lives of so many people—but this is certainly assumed. How many people are there who have demonstrated the capacity to prescribe for others? If an individual makes a mistake in trying to improve himself, this is not so serious; but consider the consequences if he has induced all his neighbors to do the same thing. History is filled with examples of self-confident leaders who led their followers straight to a common catastrophe. The fact is that we still know so little about human personality in the concrete. To be sure, there are excellent textbook pictures, with revealing analytical tables and graphs. But this is personality in the abstract. Any physician will tell you that he rarely finds a textbook picture in a patient. Not only is every human being a complex with variations, but there are the environment in which that complex functions and the accidental circumstances which confuse the vision and disrupt life.

Nor has the reformer too much reason for assuming that he has discerned the good life for his neighbors. Let us take as a familiar example the characteristic projection by parents into the lives of their children. This is something we can readily understand and, because it is suffused with parental affection, forgive. But how many parents are there who realize that each child is to some extent a new complex of elements and who can bring themselves to substitute that confounding reality for the fond subjective creation? Too often the recommendation of a way of life is nothing more than the advocacy of a personal preference.

From subjectivism in this sense of the term there is no complete escape. Even leadership is personalized in an individual. Hitler was an individual: he spun his fantastic and criminal notions out of his own warped private personality. It is therefore terribly important that everything shall be right in the reformer before he undertakes to reform others. "Nobody," says a character in Norman Douglas' *South Wind*, "has the right to call himself well disposed towards society until he has grasped the elementary fact that the only way to improve society is to improve oneself." And may I suggest in this connection that a major in the social sciences does not automatically qualify a student for social leadership?

Further reason for doubt is to be found in the characteristic reactions of the hypersocial-minded. They become so indignant when people resist their ministrations. They are so determinedly selfish in their unselfishness. Ideas, particularly ideas designed for the improvement of others, so quickly become inflated. In extreme cases, they devour themselves. How antagonistic even educators become over professional differences as to how the ignorant should be rendered less so! Note the bitterness between rival reform groups. Let us not forget that human beings have killed one another in the mass even on the authority of their religions. Note how political leaders fall out, quarrel, conspire, injure one another in their unselfish efforts to save the country. In the absence of sophistication and modesty, reform notions grow into delusions; their advocates become more and more autocratic; leadership becomes pathological; the desire to help one's fellow-men is transformed into fanaticism and tyranny—and societies become authoritarian.

Here lies the explanation of the tendency of hypersocial-mindedness to suppress individualism and to produce too much uniformity. There are good reasons for doubting the wisdom of this lack of interest in the individual as a unique personality. There is, to begin with, the obvious and inescapable fact that everybody is an individual. The higher the scale of life, the more individuals differ and the greater their potentialities for differing. Society must make provision for individual differences. Authoritarianisms of the type of national socialism and communism are primitivistic, for they propose to turn back the course of social change and to establish societies in which individuals shall have a status more closely resembling that of ants, bees, or even of atoms or electrons than of human personalities. They have forgotten, or propose to ignore, the incontrovertible fact that the great works of art, literature, music, philosophy, religion and science—that is, the world's great manifestations of excellence and leadership—were the products of intensely individual persons. Indeed, some of the world's great geniuses have been self-centered, unsocial and iconoclastic, with little or no interest in the improvement of their fellow-men.

But society can well afford that. A regimented society will not only suppress and possibly ultimately breed out these "exaggerated" individuals, but will generally discourage the manifestations of the adventurous and original spirit. Government and education designed to do this will bring about a tragic cultural impoverishment in human life; for individual differences enrich life, they stimulate the intelligence and the imagination, and they invite comparison and criticism. They keep the individual alive *as an individual*, and not merely as a bearer of the racial genius or a servant of the state.

It is true that modern life requires a certain amount of regimentation. Individuals obviously cannot be permitted to run amuck. At least the great majority of persons must adapt themselves to other persons. Mechanical contrivances, such as traffic lights, must replace individual judgment; laws are to some extent substitutes for individual choice. But let us not forget that it is not the basic purpose of these substitutes to repress individuality, but rather to make possible a more general and richer realization of individuality. It is not the purpose of social organization to reduce man to the subhuman, but to create more favorable opportunities for the realization of what is uniquely human.

The need of complex societies for a high degree of organization is one reason why so much attention is focused on the improvement of the other fellow. Especially in a democracy, where everyone is more or less free to advocate schemes for the improvement of society, lively and self-confident minds are inclined to expend their intellectual and emotional potential on reform movements. The attention of the reformer is consequently drawn away from contemplation of the state of his own soul. Since he is so happily exercised in improving others, the habit of self-examination gradually atrophies. How then can he be sure that he is the right person to prescribe for his neighbors? Should he not stop now and then to take an inventory of his resources? Does he in fact have these resources? It is because I have serious doubts of this sort, and because of the increasing neglect in education of attention to the accumulation of these resources, that I feel it time to make a plea for education for privacy.

What now are the essential elements of this education for privacy? In speaking of elements it is of course implied that the ideal construct of these elements constitutes an organized whole, a personality. It is this ideal at which we aim, though we know full well that in any concrete individual, no matter how well educated after the formula which we shall propose, one or the other desirable characteristic is certain to be under- or overemphasized.

The first requirement, clearly, is to learn how to think—not out loud or in print, but privately. The thinker himself, not his neighbor, is to be the beneficiary. To think does not mean to spend hours in idle daydreaming or in vagrant imaginings, or to make occasional impulsive sallies at ideas which happen to appear before the attention. The reference is certainly not to the semi-somnolent and comfortable ruminations which go on in the wandering mind of an inattentive student in the classroom. What is meant is systematic reflection, the constant purpose of which is to bring order out of the multiplicity and variety of things in which the human being is immersed.

To be sure, many people go through life with their senses alert, observing and savoring in generous measure the richness of the world about them. But what they experience they retain only in the form of materials for recollection. The mind gradually accumulates a rich inventory of goods, which can be brought out on display when there is social opportunity for it. But the relationship of these resources in the mind is one of mere contiguity, like that of goods in a department store. Experience has not resulted in an over-all understanding because it has not been systematically thought about. Such individuals

> . . . see all sights from pole to pole,
>   And glance, and nod, and bustle by,
> And never once possess [their] soul
>   Before [they] die.

To possess one's soul in an intellectual sense means to have found some answer, or partial answer, to the questions: What is the nature of this world in which I find myself, what is my place in it, and what must be my attitude toward it? The problem is one of intellectual and spiritual orientation.

The benefits of such intellectual and spiritual adaptation have been extolled by the wise men of all ages and all countries. A "view of life" prepares us for what life brings us, for what happens to us in our physical environment, and most important of all, for what people turn out to be and for what they do. To be spiritually and intellectually lost in the world, on the contrary, is to be unarmed and helpless. A disorganized mind is unprepared for reality and easily frustrated. The fate that awaits the individual so afflicted is to be always a stranger and a wanderer in the world. The "lost soul" of literature, the ultimate in tragic creation, suffers from this great spiritual illness.

It may be unfortunate, but it is a fact that the sharper and livelier the intelligence and the more sensitive the spirit, the more serious the danger of disorientation. The simple-minded find life simple. Plants find themselves easy to live with, no doubt; for it cannot be difficult to vegetate successfully. It is not likely that the cow's ruminations are philosophical. Man, for better or worse, is a rational animal. The more he thinks, the greater the need of organization among his ideas. The more subjects a student studies in college, the more extensive the potential disorder of his mind. It is not surprising that the scholarly mind, lost in a Babel of learning, seeks escape into a clearly defined specialty, and the practical mind, as soon as its owner has permission, into the comforts of a business, a profession, or domesticity. To be sure, we must integrate the curriculum. But what good is this if the professor's mind remains perched on its gaunt pinnacle or secluded in the laboratory?

The systematic way to the attainment of the organization of ideas is through philosophy and religion. It is true that the great intellectual constructions of the metaphysicians are not available to all men, and that even to the initiated they sometimes offer but poor comfort. Moreover, all of us have known individuals of great simplicity and humbleness of mind, quite untutored in dialectic, who somehow and in the simplest terms have securely located themselves in the cosmos. Especially in the realm of religious experience do we find examples of this. The spirit seems to have found peace in terms of some all-embracing conviction or great renunciation. But this is not often possible for the inquisitive and analytical mind. To cast all burdens upon the Lord in one grand resolve sometimes implies ignorance of the nature of those burdens. There is only consciousness of their oppressive weight, but no understanding of their nature or causes. To be sure, the critical intelligence may also come ultimately to make this renunciation, but it will not feel justified in doing so until it has reflected upon causes and relationships and seen the problem of human trouble and sorrow *whole*. The solution must be a conquest, not an escape.

For this, the mind certainly needs philosophy, sacred or secular. No learned profession, however, can offer the inquiring mind an official formula which every man need only apply in order to be permanently on understanding terms with the world. To be sure, there are systems of metaphysics, sacred and secular, from which the troubled spirit can choose a ready-made synthesis. But this does not make the chosen system of ideas an integral part of the inner personality. Intellectual orientation to the world must be something more than an acquisition; it must be an organic growth. The student should by all means seek out the great religious and philosophical thinkers, study their systems, and add their insights to his own. But in the last analysis he must work out his own solution, for such a solution must be the end product of his *own* reflection in the context of his *own* experience. Only through the alchemy of private reflection do philosophical ideas become private resources. Only then will they be available in time of crisis. When the normal course of existence is interrupted by conflict and frustration, it is a bit late to begin developing fundamental guiding ideas; that is the time to apply them.

A dramatic example of the saving grace of such resources is related by Admiral Byrd in his book on his expedition to the South Pole, entitled *Alone*. He had been left behind by the expedition in a dugout located several feet below the surface of the icecap. From this he periodically emerged through a vertical tunnel to make scientific observations. It happened that the heater in his subterranean shelter developed a leak of which he was not aware. Before he realized it, he had been dangerously poisoned and he became seriously ill. During his convalescence he found himself struggling to overcome not only the physical damage done to his body, but also a deep spiritual depression, an obstinate conviction of the meaninglessness of life, which threatened to overwhelm him. There was no physician or psychoanalyst or cleric available. His fellow-explorers would not return for months. He was absolutely *alone*. He had to guide himself out of this slough of despair. This he did, after many agonizing days, by steady thinking, by "digging down into" his intellectual resources. And it was then, to use his own homely but vivid phrase, that he "uncovered the pay-dirt of philosophy." He did not then collect the materials of his readjustment; he used them to recover his sanity. In this crisis, what would he have done without these resources?

But periods of crisis are not the only time when man needs an orderly mind. If a ship is to hold its course it needs a steady helm in good weather as well as in bad. I hasten to remark that this figure of speech has serious limitations, for a navigator has his chart prepared when he begins his voyage. Man, on the contrary, is faced with the problem of making a chart as he goes along. As a matter of fact, the plan of life is for every man to some extent an unconscious precipitate of his experience. We are not completely free agents: compulsion and fate, in the form of the physical world, our fellow-men and social institutions, push the individual this way and that. What happens to him and what he becomes are clearly the result of a complex of inner and outer compulsions, over many of which he has no control.

We are not here primarily concerned with action, however, but with interpretation. In philosophical reflection, the individual to some extent plays the part of the Greek chorus. He observes himself as actor in a cosmic setting. If he does so systematically, he will gradually discern not only his own role, but the direction of the whole drama. Only when he understands the meaning of the play can he orient himself in it. Such an understanding, vague and incomplete though it may be, will enable him to achieve his own view of life. If he is so fortunate as to see (what seems to him) the truth and to see it whole, he will thenceforth have a vision of the future as well as an understanding of the present and the past. If a rational man does not do that, why should he consider himself the crown of creation? If he does accomplish this, he can exult with the poet Dyer:

> My mind to me a kingdom is:
> Such present joys therein I find
> As far exceeds all earthly bliss
> .   .   .   .
> Look, what I lack my mind supplies
> Lo, thus I triumph like a king,
> Content with that my mind doth bring.

In education for privacy, however, more is involved than philosophical orientation to the cosmos. There is equally urgent need for education in the establishment and maintenance of moral harmony. From the days of primitive religion, through Greek tragedy, the Christian epic of sin and salvation, and modern psychology, Freudian and non-Freudian, to contemporary existentialism, there runs the theme of the uneasy conscience. The dramatic specter of moral guilt is the principal character in many of the greatest creations of literary genius. No matter what the learned explanation, the psychological state is one of inner moral disharmony. Though it may have outer causes, it is a private affliction and must be cured privately. In moments of despair or periods of cynicism we may doubt the existence or discernibility of moral meaning in the universe; but such a conclusion does not relieve the individual of the necessity for solving his personal moral problem. Even complete moral negativism, if not itself a moral philosophy, leaves the individual no recourse but to establish a private moral order in his life of action and reflection.

Here again, the more sensitive the individual, the greater the potentiality for disorganization. It is the sensitive who are the most deeply wounded by moral indifference, disorder and brutality. The predisposing causes of moral disorganization may be in the people and the things we love, in the institutions which demand that we conform to their customs and taboos, in the great world which so often mocks our need for moral significance and order. But a vision of the good life, the spirit must have; for devoid of it, the imagination is without moral perspective, conduct without guiding principles, and action without trustworthy habits. For an individual so unprepared for life, confusion will efface meaning and create frustration, with the onset in the case of the unusually sensitive spirit of pathological disturbances which may for a period or for a lifetime destroy happiness. Education for privacy must therefore include the education of the moral personality, the gradual acquisition by the self of moral resources. Here, too, there are available to the student in generous measure the works of the great philosophical and religious thinkers, for probably no one of the persistent problems of life has had more of their systematic and concentrated attention. It is relevant here to note that the previously discussed philosophical orientation to the world is sometimes the foundation for moral orientation.

A third requirement in the education of the personality is the development of emotional stability. Of all the immediate causes of unhappiness, emotional disorder is unquestionably the most serious and the most common. Currently there is a feeling that under the pressures of modern life its incidence is steadily increasing. Unfortunately, emotions are the component of the personality about which we know the least, as modern science has come to realize. Our ignorance is largely a consequence of the fact that traditionally the emotions have been considered to be effects rather than causes. Preoccupation with the flattering conviction that man is a rational animal has been attended with the assumption that therefore our emotions are under the domination of the reason. This assumption has been one of the basic tenets of formal education, though puzzled parents and self-conscious adults no doubt have all along had their suspicions. In our day, educators are being enlightened by psychology and the medical sciences on the subject of the devastating power of the emotions. Moreover, the modern conception of the integrated personality has redirected our approach to this subject, so that now we hypothesize and investigate in terms of interrelations and interactions. The simple classical vision of the reason enthroned in the psyche, making judgments, issuing commands, and directing the conscious life of the individual, is difficult to maintain in the face of the past record and the current spectacle of human behavior.

Let us grant that the contemporary individual lives in an age in which, as Goethe put it, "humanity twists and turns like a person on a sickbed trying to find a comfortable position." To offset this, however, he has the advantage of a better understanding of the compulsive and disruptive power of the emotions. He is aware of their insidious tendency to direct his thinking and affect his judgment. He knows that they feed on themselves and that, if they are of the destructive kind, they can bring him to the verge of despair. He knows that they can completely disorient him, isolating him from the friendship and sympathy of his fellow-men and estranging him from the beauty and utility of the world. He must learn that there is little he can do to remove the external causes, the irritants in his social and physical environment. In order to maintain or restore emotional stability *within* himself, he must learn to control the effects of these irritants *on* himself. Education of the emotions is education in self-control, in equanimity and serenity.

To these three objectives of education for privacy—the attainment of a philosophical point of view, a steady vision of the good life, and serenity of spirit—I should like to add one more: the individual should be able to live entertainingly with himself. He should accumulate resources on which he can draw when he is at leisure. The universal symptom of the absence of such resources is the homely but hapless state of boredom. It is an anomalous condition of the spirit, a state of indifference lying between the pain and pleasure. Neither the mind nor the hands can find anything interesting to do. In contrast with the other troubles of the spirit which have been mentioned, there is little excuse for this great emptiness. For there is a marvelous cure for boredom, universally available, readily tapped and virtually inexhaustible: the fine arts.

This claim hardly needs defense. Nor is it necessary to enumerate the arts and to identify their respective potentialities for beguiling the mind and the heart. For illustrative purposes, however, let us consider one form of art enjoyment which is available to virtually every normal human being, young or old, learned or simple, saint or sinner—reading. Its great virtue for education for privacy is that it is a strictly private experience. No other human being is necessary to the reader at the moment of reading. He can take his book with him to the jungle or the desert, on the ocean or the mountain top. He can select his company at will, and rid himself of it by a turn of the hand. It is potentially an inexhaustible resource: all ages of history; all countries; all varieties of human beings, and even of animals and plants and physical things; the entire range of human thoughts and feelings, hopes and fears, conquests and failures, victories and defeats; the real and the ideal—all are available at the turn of a page for the reader's contemplation and understanding.

When we measure the impoverishment of him to whom this world is literally and figuratively a closed book, whose ear is deaf to music and whose eye blind to the glories of painting and sculpture, we come to realize the responsibility of liberal education for instruction in the arts. I say instruction purposely, because I believe that the presentation of opportunities for enjoyment and training in appreciation are not enough: there should also be instruction and encouragement in the production of art. As even the bungling amateur knows, there is no greater source of pleasure than creative activity. The training of the most modest talent is an enrichment of a personality and develops another private resource for leisure hours. Even the unsuccessful attempt to create art, moreover, clarifies the understanding of art. To be sure, just as it is not necessary to trouble our friends with our thoughts, so it is not necessary to bore our friends with our productions. It is, after all, not the improvement of the neighbor but the improvement of oneself that is the immediate object of education for privacy.

An understanding of the world, a vision of the good life, serenity of spirit, appreciation and practice of the fine arts—these, then, are the elements of the integrated personality, the development of which is the immediate object of liberal education. These are the resources which are accumulated in the course of education for privacy. Why, now, is it so important for every individual to possess these resources? In the first place, simply because he is going to need them. We never know when we are going to lose our external resources, our public possessions. Without private resources the individual has nothing to turn to when disappointment, frustration, or misfortune become his lot. In the great depression which is still vivid in our memories, there were many individuals who possessed only external resources. When they lost these, life was over for them. They could not go on living with themselves because of their intellectual, moral, emotional, and artistic poverty. He who possessed these resources, however, could exclaim with Thoreau: "Oh, how I laugh when I think of my vague, indefinite riches! No run on the bank can drain it, for my wealth is not possession but enjoyment."

Resources of the spirit are like savings: they must be accumulated before they are needed. When they are needed, there is no substitute for them. Sooner or later, the individual faces the world alone, and that moment may overwhelm him if he has no resources within himself. Distraction helps but little and betrays us when we least expect it. We can escape our physical environment and our neighbors, but we cannot escape ourselves. Everyone with any maturity of experience and self-knowledge knows that the loneliest moments are sometimes experienced in the midst of the greatest crowds and the most elaborate entertainments. . . .

And now, in conclusion, I wish again to pay my respects to the other half-truth, the improvement of others, which was so cavalierly dismissed in the beginning of this essay. That objective together with the other objective, self-improvement, compose the whole truth, which is the grand objective of liberal education. Education for privacy and education for public service constitute education of the whole personality. He who is not educated for privacy is hardly fit to educate others. The blind cannot lead the blind. The man who is not at peace with himself cannot be trusted to lead his fellow-men in the ways of peace. The unbalanced leader is certain to unbalance the society in which he functions. Even the leader who is intent on the side of the good but who is a fanatic will stimulate fanaticism in his followers, arouse dogmatism and bigotry, and induce oppression and cruelty. When he is on the side of evil, he will lead his followers into such excesses and wickedness as will shame all humanity, and which even the innocent will wish to forget as soon as possible. Social pathology must in the last analysis be focused on the sickness of the individuals who compose the society. It is pure imagination, if not nonsense, to ascribe the ignorance, unbalance and wickedness of a collection of human beings to a mysterious social entity such as the group mind or the social organism. We might as well divorce the concept of an epidemic from the notion of the individuals who are ill, or ascribe hunger to a societal stomach. People mislead one another exactly as they infect one another. The psychopathic leader is potentially as dangerous as the carrier of an infectious disease.

The safe leader, in terms of the elements of education for privacy, is one who understands his place in the world and can thus envisage the place of his fellow-men; who can morally respect himself and can thus be respected by others; who has learned to control his emotions and can thus be trusted to exert control over others; who has learned to live in peace and contentment with himself and can thus with propiety urge others to do likewise.

We are living in a world and in a time when powerful leaders with millions of fanatical followers are committed to the forcible regimentation of their fellow-men, according to formulas which have no initial authority but that of their own private dogmatism. They not only refuse to recognize the right of private thought and personal conscience to be considered in the management of public affairs, but they have abolished the concept of the individual as a private personality and have reduced him to the level of the bee in the hive. To restore the individual to his former dignity as a human being is the urgent need of the day. This, in my opinion, should be the special objective of contemporary education.

But liberal education must so educate the individual that he is manifestly worthy of having his dignity recognized. If he wishes to lead his fellows, he must first learn to lead himself. Without education for privacy he will neither merit leadership nor learn to recognize it in others. He will strive in vain for happiness and success in private or public life until he has achieved understanding, goodness, serenity, and contentment within himself. That, according to my exegesis, is in this connection the meaning of the Biblical text: "For what is a man profited, if he shall gain the whole world, and lose his own soul?" It is surely what Thomas Hardy meant when he wrote:

> He who is with himself dissatisfied,
> Though all the world find satisfaction in him,
> Is like a rainbow-coloured bird gone blind,
> That gives delight it shares not.

Educational Evidence

ALBRECHT DÜRER, *St. Jerome in His Study*. The British Museum, London.

chapter 3

Measuring Models against Educational Evidence

Government is the potent, the omnipresent teacher. For good or for ill, it teaches the whole people by its example.

—Justice Louis D. Brandeis

What is Educational Evidence?

Educational evidence is empirical data we can use to help us judge whether or not we are moving toward an educational goal. The relationship between educational evidence and educational goals is a crucial one.

Educational evidence includes any information derived from controlled observation or experiment. When we use the term, "controlled observation" or "experiment," we imply that:

1. The information obtained is reasonably accurate as to its content and can be so checked. (NOT hearsay, NOT information unidentified as to its source, NOT global judgments)
2. The procedures are reliable, meaning they will give the same results if repeated under the same conditions. (NOT impressionistic information, reports, or media presentations)
3. The data have been systematically gathered through objective means, and therefore are independent of the views of those who collected the data. (NOT opinions, or anecdotal information unless systematically gathered; NOT utterances by authorities; NOT testimonials; NOT advertisements)

The essential point about empirical data derived from controlled observation and experiment is that the data are independent of the views of the person who collected the information. Objective data are used to test a hypothesis, not to support, substantiate, or prove a point of view. Data do not have opinions.

107

Educational evidence can include almost any piece of behavior. Behavior means any observable act, such as a spoken response, a written response, or any other observable physical act. Behavior is a very broad term, including items as diverse as the number of times a student blinks his eyes during a lecture, opinions expressed in a poll, pupil knowledge of the curriculum, and the number of squirms per minute that a young child makes in his seat. Empirical data can be obtained from controlled classroom observations when what is to be observed is carefully defined ahead of time and when there is adequate inter-rater agreement on the definition of what is to be observed, recorded, and counted.

Observation is a word that is often used quite loosely, often meaning "what I reported that I thought I saw," often from an observer who has entered the classroom with some biases. Objective observation in the classroom is an extremely difficult thing. There is much to watch; furthermore, it is often very hard for the observer to record behavior accurately as he is watching it. The use of acoustical tapes and videotapes solves some of these problems, but brings a new set of problems, such as the imperfections of recording, the selective recording of certain areas of the room, the effect that recording may have upon the teacher and the pupils, and then the final problem of transcribing and classifying all the material that is obtained.

In obtaining educational evidence, data are collected with a purpose in mind. The experimental design defines in advance what behavior is to be measured. The reader is probably familiar with the traditional research design requiring an experimental group and a control group. In traditional research design, the experimenter hopes to keep everything controlled except one or two variables which he varies systematically, and then measures the effects of the independent variable (what is manipulated) on the dependent variables (what is measured).

This classical model is often not useful in educational research because of the complications brought about by the nature of teachers, classrooms, pupils, and the educational needs of the school. It is almost impossible to install a laboratory research model in a school system without either distorting the behaviors of the teacher and pupils, or obtaining results distorted by such an artificial atmosphere that the results have little generality. However, the basic idea behind the classical experiment is one we want to retain, namely, to identify educational evidence that is free from bias, which means that we must pay careful attention to the control of the variables involved. Proper sampling is especially important as an antidote for biases and loose methodology.

Educational evidence does not include a number of things that are often used in arguments about education. It does not include anecdotal information, unless it is systematically gathered. It does not include hearsay. It does not include statements of opinion without accompanying information about the people sampled and how their opinions were solicited. It does not include information that is not identified as to source. It does not include reliance on authority or dogma. It does not include global judgments since we cannot identify what specific item the respondent may be answering.

If the teachers who created a new school program ask parents for reactions to the program, this would not be educational evidence. Why would it not? Opinions gathered about an educational program by those people who created or supported it are very likely not to be evidence because the developers are too likely to have their own vested interests in the outcome. That is one reason why evidence on the effectiveness of new educational programs should be collected by an objective person, someone separate from the program who does not have an axe to grind. In the same vein, we would be inclined to distrust evidence gathered by persons in authority from those working under them. A superintendent who asks his teachers if they are satisfied with the existing administrative structure, for example, is not likely to obtain unbiased responses. Given the realities of jobs, tenure, and promotions, it seems unlikely that subordinates are going to report that they are unhappy with the power structure.

We are unlikely to accept uncritically as educational evidence reactions from those who have special interest. Such an example would be the council of supervisory personnel in New York City who opposed abolishing the Board of Examiners' method for licensing city school personnel. It seems too likely that members of an ingroup, such as that of supervisory school personnel who reached their positions of authority through this particular method of selection, are going to support this method against any other. Such a group can hardly be without a vested interest.

We are going to ask of any data used to evaluate education whether or not the information was derived from controlled observation or experiment. If not, we may want to look at the information critically, making estimates as to its value, but not accepting it as educational evidence.

What is the role of opinion? Having said that the schools in this country are inevitably influenced by political considerations, surely we will admit that opinion also plays a role in what happens in schools and in the setting of their educational goals. Yes, this is true, and often opinions are held that are contrary to the available evidence. Sometimes we do so knowingly, often stubbornly, and often without analyzing our own opinions. But it is essential that we distinguish between evidence and opinion. Both have their rightful role in making judgments, but they are two rather different things. To say, "I feel somehow that . . ." or, "My personal reaction is . . ." is to express an opinion. But it is not the communication of educational evidence.

Judgment is the final step in making any decision. Judgment always involves some set of values, whether they are defined or not. Judgment has to play this role. Very often decisions must be based on inadequate evidence, but judgments have to be made. We would argue, however, that educational judgments should be based on as much educational evidence as possible, and, furthermore, that the underlying assumptions about the model of education one supports should be made perfectly clear.

A currently popular notion, for example, is that individualized instruction is good. What assumptions about an educational model are implied, but not made clear, in such an opinion? Some of the assumptions seem to be:

1. that individualized instruction will vary from pupil to pupil
2. that children differ from each other in their learning patterns
3. that children will profit from teaching geared to their learning style and pace
4. that children learn best on their own as individuals
5. that individualized programs of study are more interesting, appealing, motivating, or something else to pupils

Often implied as a corollary, is that teaching in the past has been too group-oriented and too lockstep, which explains why many children do not like school or do not do well in school.

Before endorsing the value that individualized instruction is a good thing, we should examine assumptions critically and ask for the educational evidence for each of these statements.

Educational Evidence for Educational Models and Goals

Let us approach the problem of developing the relevant educational evidence by taking a look at some of the models we have been discussing and asking ourselves: What educational evidence would indicate progress toward the goals of each model?

Chinese Model: The Tested Scholarly Officialdom Model

If we were to select people for the pre-1905 Chinese government on the basis of their ability to pass a scholarly examination, we would be assuming that passing the examination is related to the ability to make good governing decisions. This assumption would need testing. First, we would need to define good governing decisions. Then we would need to take a sample of those who had passed the examination, and a sample of those who had not passed it, and compare their performance in making good government decisions. If the scores failed to discriminate between these two groups of people, we would have to conclude that the examination bore very little relation to the desired behavior of making good governing decisions. We would have to conclude that the criteria were not relevant.

A better method would be to construct a criterion-referenced test from the very beginning. A criterion-referenced method is one based on criteria that can be demonstrated to be relevant to the desired behavior. We would start by identifying those behaviors that we want in our state officials. We would try to specify these in behavioral terms, that is, what such a person would actually be doing to demonstrate that he was behaving in the way we wished. We would:

1. name the behavior as explicitly as possible
2. state the conditions under which it should occur
3. state what the criteria would be for acceptable performance

For example, one such desirable behavior might be the handling of mail inquiries from citizens. We might postulate that good state officials should answer the mail (1) quickly, (2) courteously, and (3) with the requisite information. But we would have to spell out specifically what we meant by each of these requirements. For example, we might define answering mail quickly as answering it within two working days of the receipt of a letter 85 percent of the time. We would then need separate statements for (2) courteous behavior, and (3) the requisite information. We would want to define each behavioral objective separately and precisely so that each would be clearly understood. If we did this for each of the behaviors we wanted in the governing officials of the Chinese model, we would then have a behavioral test. We would hire or appoint those people who could behave these ways at the desired level of frequency and accuracy.

What has been described may seem like an outrageous suggestion because we are so accustomed to the notion that people are appointed or elected to governing positions because of a variety of circumstances not necessarily related to their ability to perform as governing officials. If we stop to think about this for a minute, we might speculate that in our own country we have fallen into the same contradictions as the Chinese model. Originally our public officials were elected by the people because they were known to have, or were thought to have, the competencies necessary for the job. In a relatively small rural society, it is likely that the competencies or incompetencies of the person running for office would be well known to those around him. In current elections where the size of the campaign budget and the use of media play such important roles, it is very hard for voters to know whether the face in the one minute commercial is likely to have the competencies desired in a governing official. Conceivably a breakdown in trust in a society may occur where people can no longer judge, on the basis of behavior or of evidence, the competence of the public candidate to represent them. Instead of asking our government candidates to take an examination on Confucian literature, we are asking them to do something perhaps even more irrelevant—to compete on television for popularity. Being successful in capturing the favorable interest of people in a brief commercial does not seem likely to be a valid criterion-referenced measure of good governing behavior.

When people are selected for a job or position, it is important that they be selected on the basis of their ability to perform the job for which they have been selected; otherwise there can be an erosion of faith in the process. In the Chinese model, there was obviously an assumption that the ability to be a scholar would carry with it those behaviors desired in governing officials. One could argue, logically, that probably there was a positive correlation, but that it was probably low. Such scholarship presumably required intelligence, scholarly integrity, a type of detachment, and perhaps less regard for worldly possessions (therefore, the candidate might be more immune to graft and corruption). All these are some of the positive correlates between scholarship and governmental performance. But scholars also can get so involved in their scholarship that they do not respond to the needs of citizens and can become quite remote from their concerns.

Athenian Model: Good and Noble Guardians

The Athenian model, like the Chinese model, involved that very difficult area of what it is to be a good public servant. This is a recurring problem for all of us if we think about education historically. Why is it that good public service is so highly desirable, but so hard to define? Let us take the other side of the Athenian model for a minute and explore the model's enjoyment of life, the cultivation of oneself. Theoretically, we could ask the students in the various Athenian schools whether they enjoyed life or not, and compare their answers with the answers of a group of people who did not attend the Athenian schools. We might find that 75 percent of the first group said that they enjoyed life, while only 25 percent of the second group gave such a report. Is that educational evidence? Even if the evidence was gathered objectively, we should be aware that other variables can confound the outcome. If we were to examine the group that attended the various Athenian schools, we would realize that this group is a very special sample of people. If we examine those who did not attend the Athenian schools, we would realize that many of this group probably were not admissible in the first place. We are dealing with two groups that not only differed in terms of whether they attended the Athenian schools or not, but they also differed in such characteristics as income, socioeconomic status, slave and free citizen status, and opportunity for enjoyment. What would have made one group happy and the other not may not have been the schooling, but the position in life that made schooling possible for one group and not for the other. The effects of schooling on happiness were therefore confounded with the status in Greek society of the two groups.

The Athenian model was also concerned with virtue. Perhaps it will seem foolish to raise the question of how to define virtue. Yet virtue is an important value, one we would like to see in most educational models. It is easy to define virtue by saying what it is not. Webster (1969) is helpful here, telling us that virtue means, "conforming to a standard of right." Notice the phrase, "conforming to a standard." We need only to define the standard. Theoretically, we could write a standard of morality, specifying how a virtuous person would behave in a variety of situations. We would set up a school containing such situations, and students would be tested and observed to see if they behaved virtuously a given percent of the time. We would keep a record of each graduate after he left the school to see if he behaved virtuously as a public servant, and dismiss from office those who did not. We might even do some retrospective research in which we found out the characteristics of (1) those graduates who were virtuous in school and stayed virtuous, as compared with, (2) those who went through school reasonably virtuous and then came to no good end. Then we could admit candidates to our school who looked as much as possible like (1) and least like (2).

Some readers might say that we cannot define virtue as an educational goal. But we develop complex codes of professional ethics, and codes of good practice. Do they work? We probably would agree that lawyers who had never been charged with unethical conduct probably behave more ethically than lawyers who had been charged one or more times. Could a moral code be written? Yes, a moral code could be written. Should it be written? As a matter of fact, there have been quite a few attempts historically to write a moral code. One superb teacher thought that people would find it easier to behave morally if the code were reduced to ten simple commandments.

In Athens in the fifth century B.C., there was a relatively small group of educated leaders who probably held in common a code of public morality. It is likely that deviants from this code would be known to the group. But virtue is harder to define and measure in a society such as ours, which is large, urban, postindustrial, scientific, and democratic.

The Spartan model is a somewhat easier model on which to gather evidence because the educational goal was stated in more behavioral terms. It is not so difficult to measure military competence as it is to measure virtue. Physical fitness is something that can be measured relatively easily. Courage is testable, at least in the Spartan society with its kinds of dangers. In preindustrial societies, where courage and ability to hunt were considered essential for survival and leadership, a very effective educational model existed. A boy was taught how to acquire these skills by his father or another adult male in a one-to-one tutoring situation. Courage was tested repeatedly, as were hunting and fishing skills.

Courage was viewed by most primitive societies as a critical trait for leadership. (It is one that Russell emphasized heavily in modern times.) Criterion-referenced measurement was used for assessing courage. At or about the time of puberty, rites of passage were held in which a young man's courage was behaviorally tested and he was observed to see how he reacted. A little torture tended to discriminate between the more and less courageous. Those who behaved bravely during these testing periods went into leadership groups and those who did not were scorned or not given posts of leadership importance. As Russell indicated, bravery helps one to be unselfish and more objective in making decisions, qualities that were very important to a leader in such a society.

Western Liberal Arts Model

Adler and Mayer (1958) stated that the western liberal arts model which existed for twenty-five centuries aimed at ". . . the cultivation of the individual's capacities for mental growth and moral development . . ." in order to prepare the leisured few for leadership roles in the vocations and public life. Now how would we collect evidence as to whether or not such a model was succeeding in its educational goals? First we would need to state our aims in more explicit terms. Note the important relationship between educational evidence and explicitness of the educational goal. *If a goal is stated vaguely, it is rarely measurable. If goals are unmeasureable, no evidence will be available.* If the goal is stated precisely, we can measure it and collect evidence as to whether or not we are getting there. Let us avoid the trap of thinking that when we are precise, we are talking only about minor or unimportant goals. This is a criticism often leveled at behavioral objectives by their critics. It is a good deal more difficult to be precise about grand goals, but just because it is a difficult task, we should not shun it and merely define trivia.

Let us take one important aspect of this western liberal arts model and see what we would need to do to obtain evidence. Let us limit ourselves to "the cultivation of the individual's capacities for mental growth." If we are going to develop a person's capacity, then we will need to measure his capacity before we start. After we finish, we need to measure what he has learned so we can see what development has taken place. But we do not know how to measure capacity. In human beings, we do not know how to measure the vessel that has not yet been developed. IQ tests measure how much a child knows at a certain age in comparison to what other children of that age know. But such tests do not tell us how much the child could learn, that is, his potential. We make the assumption that a child who has learned a lot relative to other children of that same age will probably continue to do so. This is the basis for the prediction that a child with a high IQ, for example, 130 at age eight, will maintain a similar rate of learning and so be viewed as "bright" when he is sixteen. But when he is eight, all we really know, the only educational evidence we really have, is that he knows a good deal more than other children his age. When we say, "knows," we are referring to the content of the typical IQ test which contains rather traditional school-related tasks. But our IQ tests do not tell us directly anything about what the child *could* know. They only tell us what he already knows relative to other children his age.

As for "mental growth" in this model, we would have to define what the capacity is that we would want to cultivate. Should it be reading or mathematics? Should it be exposure to a variety of stimuli? Should it be exposure to works that most people agree represent a high level of mental growth, such as the Great Books? Should we expose students to a diet of the best literature? But what would we then do about the best in mathematics or in science?

This western liberal arts model, we must remember, was quite an exclusive model and did not really have to produce evidence that it was working. As long as it was satisfactory to its clientele, which were the cultured and leisured few, it was acceptable. This is an important point for us to remember. When a selected clientele determines its own educational model through its own interest and needs, there is very little demand for any kind of outside evaluative evidence that the model is working. The contentment of the few with what they are doing is considered adequate. This is not the case in most countries today where there is a pressing need to determine what kinds of educational models produce what kinds of results. The need is pressing because education is being demanded by everybody, not just the few, and because it is expensive and requires more and more of the resources of every nation.

There is an alternative to the procedure of using developed capacity as part of a model. Granted that we cannot measure capacity very well, we could still measure children as they came into school and determine what they know in each of several areas. We then could ask the children to specify what they wanted to learn and what skills they wanted to master. We could test them over time and see how well they were reaching their own goals. This approach is quite feasible today and has a defensible rationale if we accept the notion that children at certain ages are the most competent judges of the skills and content they need to develop. This is a basic assumption underlying much independent study. We need to ask what relationships there are, if any, between a systematic acquisition of knowledge and skills and the eventual performance on some stated criterion. Will John be just as good a lawyer (whatever that means—we would need to develop criteria) if he pursues his own individual program of undergraduate study in college, which includes Chinese art, Swahili, African literature, and Russian history, as Robert who takes what some law school professors have decided is a systematic and cohesive undergraduate preparation for law school?

This illustrates one of the crucial questions we face in education today. Is it demonstrable that a prescribed and systematic course of instruction, devised by those presumed to have attained the desired performance level, produces people who perform better ultimately than those who take an individualized and often apparently unrelated course of study?

Most curricula have been organized to prepare people for some higher level of education or performance, and are presumed to have a rationale behind them, however imperfect it might be. Thorndike and Woodworth (1901) contested this very principle, as it was phrased in their time. A committee of the National Education Association (*Report of the Committee of Ten*, 1893) had drawn up a model for a high school curriculum in the 1890s. Its work grew out of a realization that national standards were needed because many children were attending high school and many were even going on to college. In its curriculum, the committee put a great deal of stress on the classical languages of Greek and Latin. The western liberal arts model was still very influential in American education in 1898, at a time when most youngsters did not attend or finish high school. Thorndike and Woodworth challenged the assumption that the study of Latin led to better use of English and that the study of mathematics led to a better sense of logic. In what we view as one of the great experiments in psychology, these investigators discovered that there was little or no transfer effect from one subject to the other because they lacked a sufficient number of what he called "identical elements."

In the 1970s, we again have very much the same problem that educators faced in 1900. We need sturdy educational evidence that preparation in

Curriculum A leads to better performance in Occupation A, or that there is a lack of sufficient identical elements between the curriculum and the occupation for such transfer to occur. If such preparatory curricula do not contribute to eventual performance, then we need to identify what, if anything, does. We might even question whether formal education, as we have known it, necessarily has any positive correlation with performance at the levels we need to specify in occupations.

American Model: The Democratic Universal Educational Model

The word, "democratic," appears again and again in discussion of the American model of education, as well it might. We often hear it said that graduates of our public school system should become good democratic citizens, an educational goal most would accept. But what is a "good democratic citizen"? What would a person have to do to convince most people that he was behaving like a good democratic citizen? How would we define how he would have to behave?

We might set up an experiment to find out whether or not direct teaching of democracy leads to democratic behavior in the pupils. Is it true that teaching children in grade school about democracy and how it works, and having them participate in it in the classroom, leads to more democratic behavior out of school or later in life? Is there any philosophical conflict between the democratic process in the school, and the process necessary for the acquisition of skills and content? When Dewey adopted the political model of democracy and made it a cornerstone of this educational philosophy (the adoption of political models into education is nothing new), what effect did it have upon the educational process? Because of their belief in democracy, do Americans tend to make an assumption that each person can plan his own education just as each person can vote as he wishes?

"Universal education" is part of the American model. Does that mean everyone should go to school, or that everyone should be educated? What does "educated" mean? If we measure education with an achievement test, everyone will not get the same score. Do we mean by universal education that everyone should perform at some minimum level? Or does universal education mean that everybody has the right to go to school as long as he wishes, regardless of his ability level, regardless of what he learns? Should we set a national educational goal such as a gross educational product, much as we do in the economy with its gross national product, and say that we want a specified percent of all our high school graduates to be able to do specified things at this level, and then keep increasing the level each year? This could be done and probably would achieve the results desired by some. But there would be many who would say that this plan conflicts with democratic notions about rights of choice in education. We can see that defining "democratic" and "universal" in the American model is not only difficult, but that the two goals may even be in conflict.

Rousseau Model: The Natural Child Model

Rousseau (1911) thought that children would develop naturally on their own. He recommended an educational system to cultivate the child, to observe him, to respect him, and to encourage him to grow in his own natural way. How would we obtain educational evidence to see whether Rousseau's model really worked? The moment we begin, we realize that we have an overwhelming problem in finding a group of "natural" children. Where are there children anywhere in the world who have not been exposed to some kind of education that somebody will claim is unnatural? What we would need would be an educationally "pure" group of children who had been encouraged to develop on their own, who had not had any undue influences. We could then compare these children with a group of children who had been educated along more traditional lines.

This same difficulty arises when we discuss individual children in our schools today. Some will claim that a child has not developed in a given way because of the negative influence of a classroom, a teacher, or the school atmosphere, thus implying that had the child been left alone or given encouragement to become more the person that he naturally could be, his development might have been different. This is a very difficult argument because we never have any basis for comparison. People do not grow up in this world without influence. They grow up interacting with all kinds of influences from their environment, some good, some bad, and some indifferent. When drugs came into widespread use in the 1950s in the treatment of mental illness, it became increasingly hard to find patients who had not been exposed to some form of drugs, yet such patients were very important as controls to see how effective drugs might be. "There are no drug virgins anymore," became a popular phrase among researchers. The same can be said about education: There are no educational virgins anymore. Any child born in the western world of natural intelligence and family background (and we would want these things to be natural for the purpose of our Rousseauean experiment) is bound to be affected by what goes on in his home, on television, on radio, on the street, even in the sky. The problem in developing evidence for the Rousseauean type of model is that it postulates how things would be if they were not the way they are. We cannot find the untouched, the unaffected, or the uninfluenced children who would make a valid experiment possible. The argument therefore merely opposes one set of opinions against another set without the use of any evidence.

The Gambetta Model: A National Revival Model with a Republican Twist

The Gambetta model is an interesting one to look at in the light of educational evidence. At least two aspects of the model lend themselves to our tests of evidence. One is the model's goal of increasing the supply of patriotic citizens; the other is the goal of increasing the accessibility of education on a merit basis. It may sound fantastic, but we could measure the supply of patriotic citizens by inventing several tests of patriotism, then seeing how many people qualify. Patriotism is considerably easier to define than virtue. If we want to know whether or not an educational system is becoming available to more people, we can conduct an annual educational census. We can find out whether or not the system operates on a merit basis by making public a comparison of the scores of those who passed the entrance examinations with those who did not. We could institute a procedure whereby all claims of favoritism or cheating could be publicly investigated. If we kept good records of the census and the examination scores, we would find out quite quickly whether or not we were making progress toward these two goals of Gambetta's model.

Russell: The Universally Desirable Character

Russell postulated four traits that he wanted his product to have: vitality, courage, sensitiveness, and intelligence. How could we develop educational evidence about these traits? How could we measure them? We could measure courage in kind of a rough, somewhat painful way as primitive societies have done. Vitality implies an active interest in life, and is theoretically measurable, but it certainly would not be easy and probably would entail considerable invasion of privacy. Sensitiveness is harder to measure. Intelligence can be measured in various ways, even though we may not agree on the particular measure. We could invent a number of indirect measures, such as personal inventories or attitude scales, to get at vitality and sensitiveness, but indirect measures do not tell us if people actually behave in a given way. (We took the position earlier that we wanted *behavioral* measures wherever possible.) We would need to develop students in Russell's model who would actually behave in a sensitive fashion, not merely reply to a questionnaire in a sensitive fashion. So we would have to develop standards for behavior that reflected sensitiveness, just as we had to invent measures for good civil servant behavior in the Chinese model.

Dewey: The Continuous Democratic Experimental Model

As we stated above in our discussion of Dewey's model, there seems to be a conflict between the model he espoused and the possibility of measurement. We would grant that continuous experimentation may indeed be a wonderful way for wonderful teachers to teach. If we could find a school where teachers engaged in continuous experimentation, we would measure some outcomes, including pupil achievement, democratic values, happiness, enjoyment, love of learning, and so on. Assuming we had an appropriate comparison group, we could find out whether the Dewey model more frequently resulted in the attainment of certain gains. The problem would remain that, if the teachers were continuously changing what they were trying to do, there would be almost no way to find out which kind of experimentation produced which kind of gains. Constant flux makes measurement almost impossible.

Dewey's stress on democracy presents us with a real challenge. We can measure how many people participate in a decision, but participation alone does not necessarily make a democracy. We might want to know about the quality of the involvement, the thoughtfulness of the decision, and the amount of information each person had. These are much more difficult matters. The figures are published on how many vote in an election; in many elections, voting by those eligible varies between 50 and 70 percent, sometimes going even lower. In some countries where there is only one choice on the ballot, 98 percent may participate, but one might question whether the participation was democratic.

If we cannot measure democracy effectively, it would be particularly difficult to measure the democracy in Dewey's model. Many high school student governments presumably are run on the democratic principle, but as we know, such student governments are often seen by the students as a mockery. Although students may participate in voting for the offices, they often feel that student governments have no power to make major decisions and have no real responsibility in school life. When teachers invite pupils to choose what they want to do, often there is very little real choice since the pupils know ahead of time that their choices lie among Project A, Project B, and Project C, and that if they proposed Project D, they would be dissuaded from it. There is often very little perceived choice even in the library, as far as pupils are concerned (White, 1968). In the library, a fourth grade child may be told he should not take out a particular book because it is on a sixth grade level and is too hard.

If our educational goal is a living democracy, then we may have to accept a classroom situation in which the aims change from hour to hour or from day to day depending upon the interests of the group. If our goal is educational more than political, we may be concerned that children learn certain content or skills, in some sequence, with some kind of measurement of their performance. We might become concerned if our pupils keep switching their goals around, particularly if at the end of the year they do not know how to define certain words, how to do certain mathematical operations, or how to write at a certain level of competence in English.

This hypothetical example suggests what may be an inevitable basic conflict between participatory democracy in the classroom and the setting of educational goals. The conflict lies not only in who is going to set the goal, but in the nature of the goal itself. If the goal is democratic participation, then there probably will be less concern with content and skills in the curriculum.

ten Hoor: The Education for Privacy Model

ten Hoor argued for self-improvement, which included the attainment of a philosophical orientation to the cosmos, a steady vision of the good life, serenity of emotions and spirit, and the ability to live entertainingly with oneself, which involves the appreciation and practice of the fine arts. How would we know whether we were approaching such educational goals? We might shudder at the prospect of trying to determine whether someone is "attaining a philosophical orientation toward the cosmos." We could ask them, but how would we know what to do with the answer? "A steady vision of the good life" presents another problem in measurement. Again, one could ask, but what does the answer mean? What about "serenity of emotions and of spirit" and "to live entertainingly with oneself"? The "appreciation and practice of the fine arts" is something we probably could determine because we could take direct measures of the performance of a person in the practice of the fine arts. We could give a test of appreciation, but, other than to accept his word for it, it would be very hard to find out if someone were living entertainingly with himself. We also again have the problem of protecting personal privacy, which haunts us every time we try to get at personal traits.

GENERALIZATIONS ABOUT MODELS AND EVIDENCE

What have we learned from this attempt to develop educational evidence for certain of our educational models? First, we have learned that it is easier to obtain measurements for some educational models than for others. Where a model sets a goal involving the availability of the educational system, we can collect educational evidence on that. We can find out, as in Gambetta's model, whether or not more people are going to school, for longer, and what their scores are when they pass examinations. When a model involves a loyal citizenry, we probably could devise measures for that, which might be costly, but nevertheless it could be done.

We might conclude: (1) When an educational model includes the responsiveness of the system or the behavioral characteristics of the product, we can find ways to develop educational evidence. (2) We can usually determine the predictive relationship between a test and the desired performance. In the Chinese model, for example, we could have determined whether or not the test of scholarship was an appropriate one for selecting prospects for displaying good governing behavior. (3) Where we find ourselves in most difficulty is in developing educational evidence for character traits such as nobility, virtue, vitality, or sensitiveness. We can measure those traits that are more obvious in behavior, such as physical courage, fitness, or endurance; but where educational models propose the development of what most of us would view as the finer aspects of man, the nobler side of man, the vision of the good life or of a true democracy, we find ourselves with fewer and fewer ways of developing firm educational evidence as to whether we are progressing towards such goals or not.

This last point raises the argument that many people have used against behavioral objectives. They claim, with some justice, that it is relatively easy to write behavioral objectives for minor goals while it is very hard to write them for overarching goals such as virtue and goodness of life. The response to this might well be that we have not tried very hard to develop behavioral objectives for noble educational goals. Since it is much easier to measure the little goals, we tend to do that.

Educational evidence, then, is much more likely to be found in those areas where educational goals have been spelled out explicitly. This, in turn, means such educational goals are likely to: (1) be circumscribed in their objectives, such as the training of a person to be a typist; (2) involve the countable use of a large system; or (3) prescribe the behavior of a person in a physically demonstrable situation. Explicit goals tend to be lacking in those areas we would term virtuous or noble, or aesthetic, or involving the cultivation of the self. Those areas that are most private to a person may nevertheless be the most direct route to a good, kind, and intelligent society. A public act is measurable. A private act is not measurable without involving an invasion of privacy. Much that could make a society a good one would have to come from the private life of its people.

We shall resolve our dilemma in this way in considering the contemporary educational issues we shall take up: We will seek educational evidence wherever it is available; where it is not available, we will search for it; where we must rely upon judgment, we shall label it judgment; and we will constantly discriminate between evidence and judgment.

REFERENCES

Adler, M. J., & Mayer, M. *The Revolution in Education*. Chicago: University of Chicago Press, 1958, 14–34.

Dewey, J. Aims in education. *Democracy in Education*. New York: Macmillan, 1964, 100–110.

Gambetta, L. Education for the peasantry in France. In W. J. Bryan (Ed.), *The World's Famous Orations*, Vol. 7. New York: Funk & Wagnalls, 1906, 58–60.

Report of the Committee of Ten on Secondary School Studies appointed at the meeting of the National Educational Association July 9, 1892. U. S. Bureau of Education. Washington, D. C.: U. S. Government Printing Office, 1893.

Rousseau, J. J. *Émile*. New York: Dutton, 1911, 29–35.

Russell, B. The aims of education. *Education and the Good Life*. New York: Boni & Liveright, 1926, 47–83.

ten Hoor, M. Education for privacy. *The American Scholar*. Winter 1953–54, **23**, 27–42.

Thorndike, E. L., & Woodworth, R. S. The influence of improvement in one mental function on the efficiency of other functions. *Psychological Review*. 1901, **8**, 247–261, 384–395, 556–564.

Webster's Seventh New Collegiate Dictionary. Springfield, Mass.: Merriam, 1969.

White, M. A. View from the pupil's desk. *Urban Review*. 1968, **5**, 5–7.

JAN STEEN, *The Music Master*. National Gallery of Art, London.

Weighing Educational Evidence: Some Pitfalls, Warnings, Traps, and Snares

. . . the basic proposition (is) that there can be no scholarly discussion of any broader matter until there is agreement—total, unqualified, and unconditional—on the ineluctable and binding quality of the data.
—Oscar Handlin. History: A Discipline in Crisis?
The American Scholar, Summer 1971, p. 463.

Our goal in this chapter is to illustrate criteria to be applied to educational evidence. This goal includes pointing out some of the possible errors of which the reader needs to be aware in the collection of evidence and in research methodology. It is hoped that the reader will be able to apply such criteria as yardsticks in evaluating educational evidence, particularly on those issues that are currently being debated.

Russell (1950) has offered some rules for avoiding foolish opinions and intellectual rubbish that make good sense. His rules can be applied equally well to education.

Rule 1: If it can be tested by observation, make the observation yourself. Russell illustrates his point with an example from Aristotle in which he says, "Aristotle could have avoided the mistake of thinking that women had fewer teeth than men by the simple device of asking his wife to keep her mouth open while he counted. He did not do so because he thought he knew." Educators, like Aristotle, make such statements as, "children love art class," and "boys like gym better than girls." Simple observation might help us determine that some children do indeed love art class, while others like not the art but the relative freedom of art class, and that some boys detest gym while some girls love it.

Rule 2: Be aware of your own biases.   Russell warns us that if a contrary opinion makes us angry, it is likely that a bias is being stepped upon. "The most savage controversies are those about matters as to which there is no good evidence either way." An example of this in education might be the eternal question of what constitutes good teaching. In practice, many may agree that Teacher A is an excellent teacher, while Teacher B is not, but when it comes to providing evidence as to the good teaching ability of Teacher A, it often is a matter of impression, student grapevine, parental reaction, or a pervasive reputation. It is quite hard to demonstrate what Teacher A does that constitutes good teaching, which is different from what Teacher B does that does not constitute good teaching. Most teacher organizations have resisted plans for giving merit increases for improved teaching, often because there is very little agreement as to what constitutes good teaching.

Rule 3: Seek out contrary opinion and experiences.   Russell urges us to read newspapers that have a point of view quite different from our own, or to imagine an argument with someone who holds an opposing view and to listen to that opposing view very carefully. If one thinks that independent learning is the true path for future education, it might be helpful to imagine a discussion with a proponent for directed learning and to hear what he might have to say in support of his viewpoint.

Rule 4: Beware of opinion that flatters your self-esteem.   In education, as in other fields, an opinion which enhances one's role is likely to be accepted more readily than one which detracts from one's role. Teachers, quite naturally, tend to support evidence that shows teaching has an effect. Likewise many teachers have rejected the findings of Coleman (1966) because they suggest that school characteristics have relatively little effect upon pupil achievement when compared with pupil background characteristics.

Rule 5: Beware of opinions coming from fear.   Russell urges us to face our fears honestly because fear, if unbridled, leads to superstitious beliefs. He stresses the importance of practicing courage of mind. When programmed learning and computerized instruction were first introduced as future developments for education, some teachers were concerned that they would be replaced by machines or programs. This seemed very unlikely in the eyes of those who advocated computer-assisted instruction, but the fear on the part of teachers was sufficient to make them doubt and distrust the innovations.

Rule 6: Beware of opinion based on the herd instinct.   Russell warns us that fear produces a ferocity towards nonherd members which leads to cruelty and persecution. Those who remember the Joseph McCarthy era in the 1950s will remember what opinion based on herd instinct can do in influencing people to turn upon their fellows.

To these six rules of Russell's for avoiding foolish opinions, we might add a few that have relevance for educational evidence today.

Rule 7: Beware of opinion based on status.   We may accept an opinion because it comes from a distinguished panel rather than examining the evidence for the opinion. An example of this is the projection published by the Educational Policies Commission (1937) that the United States population would reach 159 million by 1980 (See Readings: Section 2). Based on that prediction, developed by a very renowned institute, the commission projected a special role for rural schools. This commission failed to predict World War II, the baby boom, a population of well over 200 million by 1980, centralization of schools, and the resultant collapse of rural schools. Its projection in retrospect looks foolish, but in 1937, many people probably had faith in it. We might remember as we read reports from commissions and panels that they, too, can be wrong.

Rule 8: Beware of evidence developed by an agency with self-interest. This rule is akin to Russell's Rule 4 regarding opinion that is flattering to self-esteem. If a group is strongly opposed (or strongly favorable) to the introduction of a particular innovation in the schools, it is not hard for such a group to find some evidence to indicate that such an innovation would be a poor (or good) idea. Opponents (or proponents) of sex education in the schools are not the ideal people to look objectively at the effects of sex education programs. The publishers of a new series of reading texts, the author of a perceptual training program, or the advocates of a particular form of psychological counseling, may not bring the desired objectivity to evaluating the innovations they are proselytizing.

It is almost a universal rule of human nature that any group of people who have been admitted to status through a given set of rules will fight to maintain those rules. After all, those were the rules that defined their superior status, and they have a good deal of self-interest in not wanting to see them changed. Almost all boards that grant status or testify to competence tend to be conservative because the members who have been anointed have a deep investment in having been accredited by the traditional criteria. This situation also occurs when a university suggests new and more lenient admission requirements, as did the City University of New York in 1969 when it started a policy of open enrollment for its freshman class. The cry was heard that the City University's standards were going down, that the degrees would not have the same value as they used to, and that academic standards would disappear beneath a wave of academically inferior entrants. Those that raised this cry often were City University graduates whose educational status had been defined by existing standards. A corollary of this rule about status and self-interest might be that those who pass an examination successfully are more likely to defend its value.

Rule 9: Beware of evidence gathered by those either violently for or against a proposal.   This is not to say that a group violently for or against a proposal is necessarily wrong, for one group may be quite right and its evidence substantial. But those who have defined a position for themselves about a proposal may be collecting evidence in support of their position, rather than looking at the evidence objectively. Evidence may be used as a tool for reinforcing an opinion that has already been established, rather than letting the opinion flow from fact. In the middle 1960s, a program in early childhood education was started by Bereiter and Engelmann (1966) at the University of Illinois. Their program put heavy emphasis on the child's learning language and numbers through drills that had been carefully analyzed and prepared. The basic assumption of the program was that disadvantaged children had to improve at a vastly faster rate if they were to catch up with the middle-class child with whom they were going to compete in first grade. Few early childhood educators maintained an objective view of this program or were willing to wait for the evidence to form their opinion. The idea that four year olds were being drilled in language and numbers so offended many early childhood educators that the Bereiter program was denounced, even by those who had never visited the program nor read any data about its success or failure. In describing their program, the authors indicated that on one occasion they had shut a child in a closet temporarily in order to alter his behavior. This one incident was often cited by those who criticized the program as evidence that the authors were hostile and punished children.

This technique is similar to the ad hominem argument used to deride a person's theory. If all else fails, one can attack the theory from behind, by referring to the person himself, to some weakness or sin. In the 1940s, there was much controversy among psychologists about B. F. Skinner's (1938) theory of learning. Psychologists who opposed this theory noted that Skinner had constructed a total environment for his infant daughter similar to a Skinner box for training rats. This, critics implied, showed that Skinner was the kind of man who viewed children as rats. (Skinner may indeed have the view that rats and children are both worthy of objective study.) This ad hominem argument might have had a negative effect upon the views of Skinner among psychologists who placed a high value on warm human contact with children.

Rule 10: Postpone the gratification of having an opinion until you have examined the evidence. One can practice saying, "I have not formed an opinion yet because I have not read the evidence." Many people seem to think they should be armed with opinions on everything. One should always go to the actual data in its original source if one is interested in having an opinion formed solely by evidence. (As a guide to reading experimental evidence, see White and Duker "Some unprinciples of psychological research" in Readings: Section 2.)

An important recent illustration of the need to go to the evidence is provided by *Pygmalion in the Classroom* (Rosenthal and Jacobson, 1968). For his review of this book, R. L. Thorndike (1968) went to the data, with some surprising results. The thesis that Rosenthal and Jacobson supported in this book is that of the self-fulfilling prophecy effect in the classroom, in which teachers are said to perceive and react to pupil achievement in terms of teacher expectations. The experiment they conducted was essentially a simple one, in which a sample of normal children in grades one through six was given an initial intelligence test. The teachers were then told that certain children showed a great deal of academic promise based on this first test. In fact, however, the children with promise had been selected randomly from the list so that the information being given to the teachers was deliberately misleading. Upon retest in May, the experimental children in grades one and two appeared to make substantial gains as compared with their controls. This did not happen in grades three through six. As a result of these data, Rosenthal and Jacobson argued that the self-fulfilling prophecy was operating, particularly in grades one and two. In his review, which has been included among the readings in Section 3 of this book, Thorndike (1968) did what any serious student of education should do. He inspected the raw data. Thorndike pointed out that the initial test scores included a group of pupils with measured IQs of 31, some of 53, some of 47, and some a little higher. What such initial test scores should have indicated to the authors is that this particular test was not an appropriate one for normal children at this age, and that such data are worthless as a baseline. Thorndike remarked, "When the clock strikes thirteen, doubt is cast not only on the last stroke but all that have gone before." He concluded, ". . . that the basic data upon which the structure has been raised are so untrustworthy that any conclusions based upon them must be suspect."

This review illustrates the importance of looking at the raw data, particularly for an experiment that has been given such wide credence in educational thinking. As Thorndike says in his introduction, "In spite of anything I can say, I am sure it will become a classic—widely referred to and rarely examined critically. Alas, it is so defective technically that one can only regret that it ever got beyond the eyes of the original investigators! Though the volume may be an effective addition to educational propagandizing, it does nothing to raise the standards of educational research." What Thorndike suggests, unfortunately probably quite accurately, is that the educational public will absorb as true the thesis that children behave in the way that teachers expect them to behave, particularly academically. That this thesis has *not* been demonstrated in any way in Rosenthal and Jacobson's (1968) study will escape the attention of most people. Who will take the trouble to examine the evidence with sufficient care to detect the shortcomings in it?

The Role of Scientific Measurement in Educational Evidence

The example given above of the inaccuracies in the Rosenthal and Jacobson (1968) data also illustrates the importance of measurement and the impact, both positive and negative, it can have. Very few readers of *Pygmalion in the Classroom* are going to have the necessary skills for analyzing the test scores so as to find the glaring errors that Thorndike (1968) did. It is relatively easy to support an inaccurate thesis with numbers because technical skills are required for refutation. Because numbers are used inappropriately by some investigators, however, is not a reason for thinking that all numbers are suspect. Measurement in education is not precise; it is not adequately developed for many purposes; it always involves human judgment and possible error; it always needs to be inspected carefully before being accepted. With all its faults, however, measurement is still an immense improvement over personal anecdote and over opinions based upon faith.

Some who object to measurement in education claim it is a cold-blooded process that misses much that is of importance in the classroom and is unresponsive to the whole question of quality. It is interesting in this context that E. L. Thorndike, the father of the Thorndike who reviewed the Rosenthal book, has been inadequately quoted on this subject for many years. Perhaps you are familiar with E. L. Thorndike's phrase, "Whatever exists at all exists in some amount." The next sentence is usually left out. It reads, "To know it thoroughly involves knowing its quantity as well as its quality." The third sentence reads (and this was written in 1918, years before the current movement toward stating educational objectives in behavioral terms), "Education is concerned with changes in human beings; a change is a difference between two conditions; each of these conditions is known to us only by the products produced by it—things made, words spoken, acts performed, and the like." And the next sentences, "To measure any of these products means to define its amount in some way so that competent persons will know how large it is, better than they would without measurement. To measure a product well means so to define its amount that competent persons will know how large it is, with some precision, and that this knowledge may be conveniently recorded and used." (Thorndike, in Joncich, 1962)

Thorndike's statement could serve as the general credo of those who have been busy in the last decade trying to extend and improve measurements of educational products. The only way we can determine what education does is to concern ourselves with the changes it invokes in human beings, and that change has to be measured by the products of education. (See E. L. Thorndike's article in Readings: Section 2.)

The tradition that E. L. Thorndike introduced in education at the beginning of the twentieth century was the application of science to educational issues. He was concerned that changes in education be based upon empirical evidence rather than upon opinion or myths or folk tales. But he also pointed out that education was not like physics, from which much of our scientific methodology has been derived, because every educational measurement ". . . represents a highly partial and abstract treatment of the product . . . an educational product commonly invites hundreds of measurements. . . ." As he points out, in education, unlike physics, we cannot assume that four units of education are twice as much as two units of education because no such scale exists.

Does this mean that everything in education can be measured? No. Our educational measurement techniques are still very limited. We do not yet know how to measure many important aspects of education, which is a good reason for inventing some new ways. It is very hard, for example, to determine what educational condition makes pupils happier than another condition. It is very hard to measure what people feel inside. We can measure their behavior, their reports of how they feel, and the way they act. But what people report they feel, compared with what they actually feel, may be two quite different things.

Those who claim that measurement in education misses all that is important in the classroom must answer the question: How can anything that is so important in the classroom *not* have a product? If it does result in a product of any kind, it can be measured. E. L. Thorndike wrestled with this very problem for art by developing a set of criteria for the measurement of children's drawings. It is a laborious task, but one can develop a scale for such judgments by having a large group of teachers, or art critics, rate a large group of children's drawings according to criteria these judges develop.

With these warnings in mind about educational measurement—recognizing its imperfections, its misuse, the frailty of some of our instruments, and the lack of instruments in certain areas—we will turn our attention now to some of the pitfalls in gathering educational evidence. The ones to be discussed here are examples of those that an intelligent reader of educational research can identify for himself. Certain of these sources of bias were first identified by Campbell and Stanley (1963).

Sources of Bias in Educational Evidence

The examples of bias discussed below could mean that the results obtained in an educational experiment were not related to the particular innovation tested. These sources of bias can creep into any investigation, and so load the dice that a fair trial of the educational innovation is not carried out.

Subject Bias

1. *How were the subjects and schools chosen?* Did that choice bias the results? What hidden variables were at work when the experimental and control subjects were selected, assigned, volunteered, matched, or randomized? For example, assume we select two classrooms, assigning one as experimental and the other as control. Before we start, we have introduced many possible sources of error. Not only may the two classrooms differ on the very thing we wish to measure, such as educational achievement, but they may also differ on many other variables that could influence the outcome. The classrooms could differ on attitude or set toward the experiment, the amount of prior teaching the pupils have received, the backgrounds of the pupils, the amount of previous school testing practice, or variables related to being in that particular classroom in the first place, such as the type of academic schedule being carried by certain students or parent preference for a teacher. *Almost no classroom is created through randomization.* Most classes are put together with some rationale in mind about ability grouping, heterogeneity of pupils, schedule requirements, or teacher-pupil interaction. In choosing a class for investigation, it is essential to determine the characteristics of that class which makes it like, or different, from any other class.

In carrying out an investigation, we must ask whether we have unknowingly selected subjects who have special reactions or attitudes toward the innovation we wish to try out. Let us suppose that we want to try out a new teaching method. We attempt to get the cooperation of several schools in trying out this new method, and finally we find one that agrees to cooperate. What is different about this school that might affect our experimental results? Let us suppose that we had been studying a more sensitive issue, such as racial integration, and had been turned down by nineteen school systems, whereas the twentieth school system agreed to cooperate. Would it occur to us that there might be something quite different about that twentieth school system and its experience with integration that might introduce a bias into our study?

2. *To what influences were the subjects exposed other than this particular educational experiment?* Could artifacts or extraneous factors have influenced the results? Let us suppose that we have introduced a new text for one class in social studies, and have retained the old text in a control class. Let us further assume that we use pre- and posttests, that is, we test before and after we introduce the experiment. We find that the class using the new text has done better on our particular test. Before we leap to the conclusion that the new text is the experimental factor responsible for this improvement, we need to be certain that nothing else had been different for the two classes. If the class using the new text had also been taken on several field trips, for example, between the pre- and posttests, the field trips could have been the reason the scores had gone up, not the new text.

3. *Children change and grow over time naturally, so could the gains be due to their natural growth?* Let us assume that we have found a way to train kindergarten children on some perceptual tasks. We find that they have improved considerably over the school year on a perceptual test we have been using. We might be inclined to think that our particular perceptual training technique has been the magic ingredient. We should remember, however, that children in kindergarten mature naturally over time in a number of ways, including perceptual abilities, and that this natural growth might well be the basis for their increased scores. In order to test our training methods, we would need to compare the experimental group with a reasonably equivalent control group who had received no perceptual training to determine if their scores had also improved. If so, that would suggest that natural growth was the causal factor, not the training.

4. *How many of the original subjects still remained at the end of the experiment?* Could the results be biased by the loss of subjects? This is a special problem in any experiment that runs over a period of time. We very much need to know what works in education over a period of years, not just what works for a few weeks or months. About the only way we know how to do this is to measure children's behavior over a long period of time. Once we are committed to this longitudinal approach, we run into the very difficult problem of the loss of many of our subjects who move away and cannot be located. If we designed a study involving one hundred first grade children and their families in which we measured the effect of some innovation in first grade, we might need to measure them again in five years when they reach fifth grade, when we might well find only 50 percent of the original group remaining in the same school system. The other 50 percent, in the meantime, will have had all kinds of experiences in other school systems that would make it hard to judge the effect of the first

grade innovation. Furthermore, we can anticipate that some children will be absent on the day of testing, some will have incomplete record cards, others will have attended a different school in the interval between first and fifth grade, and some will have experienced substantial changes in their family situation. It is easy to understand why investigators hesitate to undertake longitudinal studies. People will simply not stand still over time. They tend to do such human things as radically change their life situations, while the conscientious investigator tries desperately to locate his original subjects.

5. *Did the subjects contaminate each other?*   Was the experimental treatment diffused? "Contaminate" seems like an odd word to use, but it is quite an accurate one in this context, meaning that the experimental treatment has been introduced inadvertently into the control group, so that we now have contamination between the two groups, and have lost a clean basis for comparison. One form of this contamination has been called "diffusion effect." Klaus and Gray (1968) (See Readings: Section II) originated this term to describe one form of contamination particularly likely to occur in educational experiments. These authors trained deprived children at a prekindergarten level, and then found that the gains for their experimental group over the control group were dwindling over time. When they analyzed the formal and informal contacts between the experimental and control families, they found that the experimental techniques they employed were being communicated to the families of the control children through friends and relatives, so that the control children were now receiving part of the experimental treatment. The dwindling differences between experimental and control groups may have been due to the diffusion gains of the control group, which was coming closer and closer to the performance of the experimental group, so that both groups were improving.

Contamination and diffusion are difficult problems in most educational investigations because children in school can spread a message through the school underground with all the speed of a brushfire. If we take children out of a classroom to question them, and then return them to the classroom, we will find that subsequent subjects have been given information, often distorted, but information that is likely to affect their responses.

Measurement Bias

In the above section, we discussed the biases that relate to the choice of subjects and groups of subjects. Now we need to talk about some of the problems that arise from measurement itself.

1. *Did measuring have an effect upon the results?*   What effect did administering the pretest have upon the posttest? In a typical educational investigation, we administer a pretest and a posttest to see if the experimental treatment has had an effect on the second set of scores. But in doing this, there is the possibility of a practice effect which could cause scores to increase on the second test. When the tests are widely separated over time, practice effect is less likely to occur. Younger children also appear to forget tests more quickly. A second concern is that giving a pretest could promote an expectation, or set, in pupils about what behavior is desired in our experiment, so that their attitudes and motivation could be altered in some way. *The moral is that the process of measuring change may change what is measured.* The alternative is not to measure, which we rejected earlier, but we cannot forget that whenever we measure, the act of measurement itself may be a source of bias.

2. *Were the measures appropriate?*   Were they stable over time? Obviously the investigator wants to use measures that are within the grasp of most subjects. We refer to tests as having a "ceiling" and a "floor," meaning that we want tests to be easy enough for most subjects to be able to score above zero (floor), but we want very few subjects to obtain the highest score possible (ceiling) on the test because that would not give the high scorers a chance to show what they really could do. In the Rosenthal and Jacobson (1968) study cited earlier, it was clear that certain of the normal first graders were not above the floor of the test since they received scores that put them at the mentally defective level. This test was obviously too hard for those children, and a more appropriate test should have been selected. The ideal test for most purposes is one that permits most of the children to perform somewhere between the floor and the ceiling so that they have sufficient range over which to demonstrate how they can perform.

Another question about appropriateness is whether or not the measure is the appropriate one for what we are trying to find out. If we are trying to measure the development of critical thinking in a social studies class, the test we use should obviously be a test of critical thinking. What would not be appropriate would be a test in which we ask the students to repeat information learned by rote.

The appropriateness of the measure, whether it is behavior in a real situation or a reaction to a paper and pencil test, is a crucial issue. If we wish to measure professional competence in students graduating from medical school, for example, a competence that certainly is of serious concern, we need measures that tap that professional competence, such as the ability to apply deductive reasoning and judgment to a situation involving a person's health, not rote memory of an anatomy chart. In an analysis of multiple-choice achievement tests used in medicine, Levine, McGuire, and Natress (1970) analyzed examinations in the speciality of orthopedics. They pointed out that certain of the items failed to tap the important areas of professional judgment essential for competence in orthopedic surgery.

All of our measures, like anything else that human beings create or use, have their frailties. Their accuracy may change over time. Let us assume we are interested in a certain class activity and have decided to use observers in the classroom to rate this activity. As time passes, the observers themselves become more sophisticated, more bored, or perhaps more involved, with the result that their ratings are not applied in the same way as they were at the beginning of the experiment. In educational research involving interviews, preventing interviews from changing over time is a serious problem. The interviewer may be making up his mind as the interview proceeds regarding what the outcome should be and may guide the interview subject into producing evidence to substantiate the conclusions he has already reached, perhaps unknowingly, in his mind.

The importance of careful interpretation of educational measures is illustrated in our use of achievement tests. As Beggs and Hieronymous (1968) pointed out, educational growth on standard achievement tests is not uniform throughout the year. There is less educational growth between October and January than there is during the rest of the year, probably because pupils are catching up from forgetting over the summer. Yet often educators will employ achievement test results as though a gain at one time of the year is equal to that of another.

3. *Did statistical regression play a role?*   If subjects for an educational investigation are chosen initially because they are an extreme group on some measure, such as very high achieving and very low achieving children, their scores on a second test are very likely to be closer to the mean (or average) than they were on the first test. This movement of scores from extreme positions toward the mean on later tests is termed "statistical regression." The more deviant the score, the more likely it contains a larger error of measurement. Let us assume that we have invented a new kind of remedial reading technique. We select a group that is low in reading according to a pretest and introduce our new reading technique. Predictably, when we retest our subjects some months later, we find that their scores on the posttest have risen, that is, have regressed toward the mean. Instead of assuming that our reading technique is responsible for this increase, we should take statistical regression into account, realizing that such changes were likely to happen as a function of the extreme scores on the first test. To guard against the effect, we could have used a control

group, also extreme, to whom the remedial reading technique was not introduced. Better yet, we should not have dealt only with extreme groups, but with a sample cutting across the whole range of ability.

The Experimenting Bias

1. *Just as the act of measuring can influence our results, so can the act of experimenting.* Schools in which we carry out an educational investigation are affected by that investigation in mysterious ways that we need to keep in mind. We must constantly ask ourselves whether the conditions necessary for the educational experiment have had an effect upon the results. This is particularly important with school children, because children form idiosyncratic views of what the investigator is trying to do. Such views are often very hard to unearth with young children, partly because they are children, and partly because school culture itself tends to place particular interpretations upon educational innovation and research. Children tend to interpret what happens in school in school terms. They tend to see strangers as teachers and questions as being related to their school work and to life in school. Children are curious and enjoy trying to guess what an investigator is up to, particularly if the investigator is mysterious about his purpose. If what the investigator says and what he does do not make sense to children, they will often invent their own rationales. When pupils are young, they try to produce what they think the investigator wants. By junior high school, they may be motivated to try to fool the investigator.

Teachers and administrators also have their own reactions to the conditions of an experiment. Teachers' reactions may relate to their perception of the central administrative support for the experiment. To the extent that an experiment interferes with a teacher's program for his class, the experiment will probably be resented, and understandably so. Teachers who care intensely about their teaching resent time being taken from it by other demands. Researchers must plan their studies carefully and work closely with teachers. Finally, there are a few teachers who resent any extra work put upon them by an experiment.

2. *From what setting were the pupils taken to carry out the experiment?* Could this affect their attitudes and performance? Elkind, Deblinger, and Adler (1970) have described this phenomenon as "context effect." When children were taken from interesting activities in a school especially designed to motivate them, they showed less interest in pursuing test questions than did those children who were taken from an ordinary classroom. Elkind, et al. thought those children in regular classrooms were bored and therefore anxious to come to the examiner's office, to answer questions, and to prolong their stay. In this particular experiment, the questions were related to tests of creativity. On some of the tasks, a child was given points

for the number of different answers he gave to such questions as, "What could _____ be used for?" A pupil could get a higher score on such a test if he were interested in prolonging the situation in order to avoid going back to a boring classroom.

This context effect can influence scores depending upon what activities the pupils are taken from or returning to. Anyone who has spent much time in a school is well aware of the context effect on an everyday basis. One would hesitate to take most elementary children out of a gym or recess period without weighing the consequences, particularly if his turn in a game were about to come up. Taking a child out of a classroom so that he misses taking a quiz tends to have quite a different context effect.

3. *Hawthorne effect.* The term "Hawthorne effect" was orginated in industrial studies carried out in the Hawthorne Western Electric Company plant by Roethlisberger and Dickson (1939). These authors were interested in factors affecting production. They found that there were production gains each time the level of illumination was changed, increased or decreased, in the work area. From this experience, the Hawthorne effect has come to mean that the act of experimenting itself can create a change in attitudes so that behavior changes. There has been some recent discussion that these original findings may not have been properly interpreted, so there is some doubt as to whether the Hawthorne effect was originally demonstrated. The term is in current use, however, and many teachers and administrators believe the phenomenon exists, and that changes in the educational environment will increase teaching or learning just because they are changes.

The Placebo effect is quite different from the Hawthorne effect. The Placebo effect is derived from drug research, in which the placebo (a pill that contains nothing more than inert matter of some kind) is made to taste like, look like, and feel like the presumably potent pill. It is necessary in most drug research studies to have people go through everything exactly as the experimental subjects do, except for taking the particular drug under study. When patients think they are getting a drug, and when they have heard about the drug's alleged effects, they are likely to report that they feel benefited in the anticipated direction and may even show expected side effects. In a study by Loranger, Prout, and White (1961), patients not only reported improvement when they were on the appropriate placebo, but showed side effects which, in some cases, were supported by laboratory analysis. Presumably the changes in blood composition were due to other concomitant conditions such as allergies, but had the potent drug been administered instead of the placebo, probably no one would have doubted that the side effects were attributable to the drug.

The Placebo effect in education has been tested in a number of studies.

Johnson and Foley (1969) reported that students performed better when they were told that a particular method of teaching being used with them had been proven successful.

4. *Anti-Hawthorne effect.*   Just as the act of experimenting can increase behavior, it is also true that experimenting can produce attitudes that decrease behavior. Teachers, in particular, can become very tired of continual changes in curriculum or materials, so that they may view another experiment as just another endless demand on their time. Their negative attitude in such a case could result in their not giving the new method a fair trial. If teachers think that the new materials or methods of instruction are not going to work, very likely they will not put sufficient effort into the trial, and, consequently, the innovation may not have the desired effect.

An Anti-Hawthorne effect is more likely to occur in a large school system where teachers may view educational experiments as forced on them by a central administration which is more remote than in a smaller system. In such conditions, teachers may develop an antiexperimental attitude, and may fail to give the treatment a fair test.

5. *Reverse Hawthorne effect.*   In the classical experiment, a new instructional method is assigned to an experimental group of teachers, while a control group is asked to continue with the traditional model of teaching. Zdep and Irvine (1970), who followed this design, have presented some data to suggest that a control teacher, if sufficiently motivated, can put so much extra effort into a traditional form of teaching that it outgains the experimental method. The motivation to improve instructional performance on the part of a control teacher can stem from a variety of sources, including a desire to show that the existing method is the best one, or from resentment at not being chosen as one of the experimental teachers.

6. *Was the treatment given a fair trial?*   Was there sufficient exposure? Was it intensive enough? Was it extensive enough? "Treatment" is a term used in experimental design in a somewhat different sense than its usual medical meaning. When we try something out to see if it works, we "treat" the experimental group in a way different from the control group. Treatment refers to the particular condition we assign to the experimental group. One of the most serious problems in educational research is our inability to be sure in a given experiment that the treatment was given a fair trial. Despite the best laid plans, the treatment may be neglected in classrooms when observers are not present. The particular materials one might be trying out may be used only during the observational period, rather than all day as had been planned. Unless the experimenter puts

video tape recorders in every classroom all day long and monitors them, it would be impossible to know whether or not the treatment has been given the intended trial. If a treatment is not given a long enough trial, or intensive enough exposure, negative results are likely to occur. In the long history of educational research, we cannot be sure which educational ideas did not work because they did not really have an effect, and which educational ideas did not work because they were never tried out systematically enough.

7. *Did overexposure influence the results?*   It may seem unlikely that there could be overexposure of a treatment when we have just been emphasizing the probabilities of underexposure. Both can happen. For example, we could introduce the use of classification as a way of getting children to think about the ecological problems of their environment. Let us assume that teachers find this an effective method, and consequently decide to try out classifying behavior in other areas of the curriculum, such as classifying books by topics, cultures by their climate, and arithmetic problems by their operations. A situation might develop in which pupils are not only classifying during their science period, but in mathematics, reading, and social studies. If we have a measure at the end of the experiment to see what effect classifying has had on their knowledge in science, we may be measuring not just that effect, but the overexposure of classifying behavior spread through the curriculum. It is very hard to prevent people from using anything new that they believe to be good.

8. *Does the treatment show improvement on the criterion measure?*   It is a very common problem in educational research to find studies that assume that improvement on A will have a facilitating effect on B, but, in many studies, this assumption is not tested. It is often taken for granted, for example, that training children to do better on a skill assumed to precede the criterion behavior will also improve their performance on the criterion behavior. An analogy would be the hypothesis that if we taught children who are poor runners how to walk better, they will also become better runners. This may not be true at all. Jensen and King (1970) trained children to trace, to match, and to rearrange figures in a variety of tasks. They found that such training was effective in improving children's performance on discrimination, but had no significant effect on their ability to read. Despite such evidence, it is often taken for granted that children who learn to discriminate better will also improve on the criterion behavior of reading. If doing A does not help children to do B, and B is our criterion measure, we are not going to be interested in improving A. The proof of the experimental pudding is in performance on B, on an educationally significant task.

REFERENCES

Beggs, D. L., & Hieronymous, A. Uniformity of growth in the basic skills throughout the school year and during the summer. *Journal of Educational Measurement*, 1968, **5**, 91–97.

Bereiter, C., & Engelmann, S. E. *Teaching Disadvantaged Children*. Englewood Cliffs, N. J.: Prentice-Hall, 1966.

Campbell, D. T., & Stanley, J. Experimental and quasi-experimental designs for research on teaching. In N. L. Gage (Ed.), *Handbook of Research on Teaching*. Chicago: Rand McNally, 1963, 171–246.

Coleman, J. S. *Equality of Educational Opportunity*. Washington, D. C.: National Center for Educational Statistics. U. S. Government Printing Office, 1966.

Educational Policies Commission. *The Effect of Population Changes on American Education*. Washington, D. C.: NES, 1938, 26–27, 32–33.

Elkind, D., Deblinger, J., & Adler, D. Motivation and creativity: The context effect. *American Educational Research Association Journal*, May 1970, **7**, No. 3, 351–357.

Jensen, N. J., & King, E. M. Effects of different kinds of visual-motor discrimination training on learning to read words. *Journal of Educational Psychology*, 1970, **61**, No. 2, 90–96.

Johnson, H. H., & Foley, J. M. Some effects of placebo and experiment conditions in research on methods of teaching. *Journal of Educational Psychology*, 1969, **60**, 6–10.

Klaus, R. A., & Gray, S. W. The early training project for disadvantaged children: A report after five years. *Monographs of the Society for Research in Child Development*, 1968, **33**, No. 4, No. 120.

Levine, H. G., McGuire, C. H., & Natress, L. W., Jr. The validity of multiple choice achievement tests as measures of competence in medicine. *American Educational Research Association Journal*, January 1970, **7**, 69–82.

Loranger, A., Prout, C. T., & White, M. A. The placebo effect in psychiatric drug research. *Journal of the American Medical Association*, June 1961.

Roethlisberger, F. J., & Dickson, W. J. *Management & the Worker*. Cambridge, Mass.: Harvard University Press, 1939.

Rosenthal, R., & Jacobson, L. *Pygmalion in the Classroom*. New York: Holt, Rinehart, and Winston, 1968.

Russell, B. An outline of intellectual rubbish. In *Unpopular Essays*. New York: Simon and Schuster, 1950, 103–111.

Skinner, B. F. *Behavior of Organisms*. New York: Appleton, 1938.

Thorndike, E. L. The nature, purposes, and general methods of measurements of educational products. In G. M. Joncich (Ed.), *Psychology and the Science of Education: Selected Writings of Edward L. Thorndike*. New York: Teachers College Press, 1962, 151–158.

Thorndike, R. L. Review of Rosenthal & Jacobson: *Pygmalion in the Classroom*. *American Educational Research Association Journal*, November 1968, **5**, No. 4, 708–711.

Zdep, S. M., & Irvine, S. H. A reverse Hawthorne effect in educational evaluation. *Journal of School Psychology*, 1970, **8**, No. 2, 89–95.

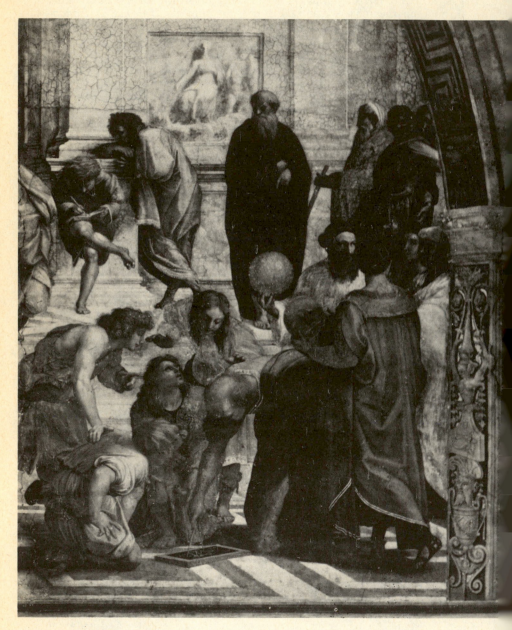

RAFAELLO SANZIO, *The School of Athens*, detail of geometrician and four students.
Stanza della Segnatura, Vatican. Courtesy Alinari.

chapter 5

Evaluating Educational Models

It is wrong always, everywhere and for everyone, to believe anything upon insufficient evidence.

—William Kingdon Clifford

Early Attempts at Educational Evaluation in the United States

Over three centuries of formal education in this country have left us with a rich legacy of noble goals. These goals have included: Jefferson's ideal of an educated citizenry based on ". . . the agencies and instruments for the cultivation of literacy and the advancement of science . . ." (Lee, 1961); Knox's plan for a national curriculum to produce a national citizenry (Messerli, 1967); Horace Mann's dream of universal education as the "great equalizer of human conditions, the balance wheel of social machinery and the creator of wealth undreamed of" (Cremin, 1961); Harris's formal educational system as preparatory to life (Cremin, 1961); and Dewey's vision of the school as the transformer of society, as a living instrument that would teach a new democracy resulting in "a larger society which is worthy, lovely and harmonious" (Dworkin, 1959). The nature of the school as an instrument for change lay in Dewey's concept of education as a "continuing restructuring of experience . . . the process and the goal of education are one and the same thing" (Dworkin, 1959). More recently, the public school has been seen as the agent for equal opportunity, particularly for minorities and disadvantaged pupils. Head Start, pre-kindergarten programs, and Follow Through assume the correction of educational inequity as a major goal.

History of Educational Evaluation

What attempts have we made to see if we have reached such noble goals? Let us take a brief look at our own history of educational evaluation.

Jefferson seems to have been the first to pose the question of educational measurement, which is not surprising for someone who had the scientific imagination to insist that Lewis and Clark make systematic biological observations in their search for the Northwest Passage. In 1779, Jefferson introduced a bill in the Virginia legislature which, in retrospect, may have been the prototype of today's Project Talent. He hoped to establish a system of selecting promising students and giving them free tuition. The best of these students would receive a free college education at William and Mary for three years, paid for by the state (Lee, 1961). The proposal was consistent with Jefferson's goal of identifying and training responsible leaders, and parallel to the practices of selection and cultivations associated with early scientific agriculture, of which he was a leader.

What was essential to Jefferson's proposal, as it is today in Project Talent, was the need to measure the ability of those pupils who would be chosen. In Jefferson's words, they were to be selected "after the most diligent and impartial examination and enquiry" (Lee, 1961). Jefferson did not specify how the measurement was to take place, except that the overseers were to carry out the examinations to identify those of "the best learning and most hopeful genius and disposition" (Lee, 1961).

There seems to have been little further concern with educational measurement until Harris championed a formal educational system, first as superintendent of the St. Louis public schools, and later as U. S. Commissioner of Education from 1889 to 1906. Harris's goals of formal education involved teaching the pupil what he was not likely to learn from his environment, a curriculum that presented a general view of the world in which the pupil would live and a moral but not religious education (Cremin, 1961). Given this model of formal education and too few teachers and educational facilities for the St. Louis pupil population of the 1870s, it is not surprising that Harris popularized the graded school. (We might remind ourselves that a national graded system is *only* one hundred years old.) The graded school was organized by years and quarter years of work. Pupils progressed, or did not progress, on the basis of frequent examination.

Here we have another instance, somewhat similar to that proposed by Jefferson, where measurement by examination is used as a selection device. In Jefferson's model, measurement was to be used for a talent search for granting scholarships to the best pupils from among all segments of society, in order to increase the reservoir of intelligent and responsible leadership for the larger society. In Harris's model, with too many pupils and too few teachers, the pupil population had to be restricted and examinations could be used to select *and* eliminate. Because of similar crowding in

Paris schools and thus the need for selection, Binet and Simon developed a test which developed into the IQ test. This test, a measure for predicting and selecting those pupils most likely to succeed in the existing school system, has performed its job very well.

At the beginning of the twentieth century, science and education had a rendezvous evidenced in educational measurement. The leader of this movement was E. L. Thorndike, who can be described as the first educational engineer. Thorndike searched for laws of learning. He also measured educational outcomes against processes, which marks the beginning of educational evaluation.

Many of Thorndike's laws of learning have been challenged, often on the ground that they ignored the complexity of learning common to pupils and classrooms. Many of his laws were derived from animal work and some felt the analogies were too simplistic. If we view his experiments as describing the very first stages of human learning, we may regard his emphasis on systematic conditions of learning as crucial.

There were many excursions into educational engineering in the 1920s and 1930s. In fact, some of the soundest work in educational evaluation stems from that period. The most ambitious of this work was the Eight Year Study (Chamberlin, 1942) which attempted to compare the subsequent college careers of graduates of a progressive high school curriculum versus a traditional high school curriculum. Thirty schools were selected and students from each type of curriculum were quite carefully matched. The experiment was a daring one, and in view of the methodology available in 1932, represented a highly commendable effort. The comparative follow-up study took eight years. It involved the cooperation of over three hundred colleges that had accepted students from these thirty progressive and traditional high schools, and required the evaluation of data from a vast array of measures on the 1475 pairs of students.

The results of the Eight Year Study showed that graduates of progressive schools did somewhat better than their matched partners on a variety of measures of college achievement and adjustment. Even though pairs were matched on as many background variables as possible, one could argue that the study did not take into account the possible selective factors that were operating when parents elected to send their children to what was then a rather radical schooling model. In 1932, this choice probably had a good deal of meaning in terms of parental value system, outlook on life, risk-taking, and educational philosophy. Such variables were hard to measure then and still are today. But we might predict as follows: Any educational innovations that appeal to participants who know they will have to compete later on traditional educational terms will be likely to attract participants who will perform well on traditional outcome measures. Their decision to take this step, in itself, identifies them as good educational risks for any educational experiment.

This possible confounding of treatment effect with a self-selecting educational population remains a persistent problem in educational evaluation. In the early days of Head Start, a national program at the pre-kindergarten level intended to aid disadvantaged children, for example, it was often observed that parents who were strongly oriented toward education were the first to enroll their children.

Beginning in the 1940s American education seems to have sought two partially conflicting national goals: that of scholarly competence on the one hand and of equality of education on the other. With their argument given increased impetus by Russian advances in technology, some urged a model of schooling that had academic competence as its goal, and, by implication at least, a high order of competence for the talented. This model has some parallels to Jefferson's model in that it was designed to produce a generation of gifted young people who would advance this country's technological capability. The curriculum revolution led by Bruner in the early 1960s was allied with the academic competence model. Proponents insisted that there was a structure to knowledge, which, if used for instructional purposes, could lead to earlier and higher levels of mastery of knowledge. At times Bruner's followers seemed to imply that any young pupil could conceptualize the knowledge in a field as defined by a university professor. Some even thought this was desirable.

Quite a different educational goal, one that emerged largely from the civil rights movement, is that the educational inequality that has existed for a long time in our public school system should be corrected. This is a noble goal, consistent with some earlier ones. What has not been clear is the best means for correcting the inequality, although integration has seemed the obvious beginning.

These two goals, one of scholarly competence and the other of educational equality, are conflicting in the sense that academic competence implies that some should perform better academically than others. Educational equality as a goal tends to emphasize equality over competence. Should any one group do better or worse than any other group in academic skills, those favoring educational equality could claim discrimination. The only school system that can completely escape the charge of discrimination is one that never measures or evaluates. To measure is to make discriminations. Measurement will inevitably turn up individual differences in achievement.

Recent Attempts at Educational Evaluation in the United States

This brief review of our history of educational models and their limited measurement suggests two major reasons for the impetus toward educational evaluation that occurred in the 1960s.

Elementary and Secondary Education Act

One was federal legislation and funding in response to the civil rights movement within the schools. As Stufflebeam (1968) pointed out, the billion or more dollars that poured into the public schools annually in the 1960s through the Elementary and Secondary Education Act (ESEA) was accompanied by the requirement that the schools make an annual evaluation report. Where public monies of this amount are going into education, it is reasonable to expect Congress to want an accounting of what these monies have accomplished.

Great strides had been made in the technological possibilities for educational evaluation as systematic management systems with computers were introduced. Systems analyses of various kinds and program planning and budgeting systems became popular as they were used in large governmental agencies. As the total federal budget became more limited, programs had to compete for funds on a very hardnosed basis. They were questioned by Federal officials and Congress as to their program objectives, costs, benefits, and alternatives. It was not long before educators became interested in more systematic methods of making decisions and tying courses of action of costs and benefits. It is part of our tradition that educators historically have looked to business practices as models (Callahan, 1962). Others may have developed this interest because of the cost benefit analysis used by funding agencies to evaluate the requests of school systems under the Elementary and Secondary Education Act. Behaviors that tend to produce funds are often imitated.

Coleman Report

A second source of impetus for further educational evaluation came from the fruits of evaluation itself. An example is the massive Coleman report, commissioned by Congress to evaluate the equality of educational opportunity (Coleman, 1966). This country had put a share of its resources to work to create equality of educational opportunity through a myriad of programs, some of them compensatory. The Coleman report identified the major variables in student achievement as what the student brought with him to school, which were his background factors. The major finding was that there was a ". . . relatively small amount of school-to-school variation that is not accounted for by differences in family background, indicating the small independent effect of variations in school facilities, curriculum and staff upon achievements" (p. 235).

Coleman's major finding has been seen as an enormous threat to education for it implies that schooling, in itself, does little other than permit, and possibly enhance, the pupil's own initial ability to achieve. This finding may be neither a tragedy nor a surprise, if we reconsider it, as we will below. These findings have been disputed at length, have been politically very unpopular, and have often been misquoted. Bowles and Levin (1968) have pointed out several deficiencies in the original data collection, such as the poor sample response from big cities, the heavy loading of "don't know" responses among lower achievers and younger pupils, and the lumping of school expenditures by district rather than by school.

Guba (1968), like many others in education, reacted to this conclusion as "simply incredible on its face . . . , that it makes no difference if a teacher is good or bad, whether good or poor materials are available, whether the school is a barn or a geodesic dome, students learn about the same (and not much at that!). Anyone who has spent any time at all in school knows that it is just not so; why then do our evaluative techniques not pick this up?" (p. 59). The result has been a hunt for the culprit, and one possible culprit is inadequate evaluation, as Guba suggests.

The question that Coleman's study provoked is, Does the critical role of pupil background drown out the influence of school characteristics in pupil achievement? Coleman's critics are quite correct in pointing out shortcomings in his data collection and analysis; but the burden of proof still lies with them to show that better data and analysis will not demonstrate once again that, given our current model of schooling and evaluation, pupil background will remain the major and, in fact, overwhelming factor in accounting for variance in pupil achievement. It does not seem surprising that variations in pupils' background circumstances, variations that are wide between groups and individuals, should prove to be the crucial variables in academic competence if we are still using the Harris model of a classification school system in which to compare rates of progress. This model allows little in the way of pupil variation except in rate of acquisition or movement forward according to the predetermined scheme of a common curriculum. How could one predict any other factor? We have no notion how individual pupils, or groups of pupils, would fare if they were in very different schools—some, let us imagine, in a Horace Mann school, and others in a school that has not yet been invented. Coleman used a measure of academic competence, administered once, and found that pupil outcomes were unequal, and related to their background.

Why should we expect a Harris model of a school system to correct for background inequalities when it is designed to do just the opposite?

Pupil background variables are also called pupil inputs in some studies, meaning those things that a pupil brings with him to school before the school has a chance to have an influence upon him. The Coleman study has been the most comprehensive so far, indicating that background variables of the pupils account for the major variance in pupil achievement. This relationship between pupil background and achievement seems inevitable as long as we retain a model of schooling that emphasizes individual pupil achievement measures under equal teaching exposure.

These findings have led to two types of intervention based on the assumption that this relationship of achievement to background variables is not desirable. The first has been an attempt to change the background variables before the child enters school. The second has been attempts to change the nature of the system of schooling. The first of these efforts has resulted in Head Start and other compensatory programs. Jensen (1969) reviewed these compensatory programs and reported that so far they have shown little evidence of their ability to modify scholastic achievement among disadvantaged pupils. Among the numerous respondents to Jensen's article, Hunt (1969) and others have argued that the evidence is not in yet as to the long-range effects of such compensatory programs, and that many of these programs were not adequately implemented. It appears to be fairly commonly held by those who advocate compensatory education that the key to changing scholastic achievement is to be found in affecting the parents of these pupils, particularly their attitudes and verbal interactions with their children.

The second type of intervention has been to recommend changing the nature of the system, a solution proposed by many critics of our schools. Within the framework of this discussion, the most salient issue has been the lack of clarity about what the outcome would be for any new school system. Until the outcome is specified, *and* the way it is to be measured is known, it is very hard to talk intelligently about alternative school systems. One could invent, for example, a school system whose goal was to improve the affective life of its pupils. (See Heath in Readings: Section 3.) One might even invent a measure of affective goodness that could be administered to such pupils. Given even these two somewhat radical departures, we would still be left with a measure of individual pupil affective growth. We would have essentially the same model of schooling, with affect as a new goal, but still a model of individual pupil achievement, of equivalent instruction exposure, of large-scale organization of instruction by teachers to pupils, and of accretion of affective goodness over time. This is the same problem that underlies much of the discussion about pupil attitudes. Those who have interpreted Coleman's findings to emphasize the importance of peer relationships have argued for a school that emphasizes "good" pupil attitudes. This would merely substitute the individual achievement of attitudes for traditional achievement, but we would retain the same basic model of schooling as we did with affective goodness.

If we are to change the nature of schooling, especially as a means of intervention for disadvantaged pupils, it is essential that the model itself change. We should be wary of substituting simply one form of individual pupil achievement for another under the same schooling conditions.

The time may have arrived for our nation to choose a different model of schooling—or more likely, different *models*—but unless we are aware of the crucial correspondence between a model of schooling and its model of evaluation, we are likely to become disillusioned with any new model. Our current disillusionment has led to a search for various educational culprits, which has been an erroneous search. The more appropriate response is to see our models of schooling and evaluation for what they are and to see how we need to change both models.

Behavior-oriented learning psychologists (Bloom, 1968; Carroll, 1963) have been among those arguing for more precise definitions of models and educational goals in behavioral terms. Since mastery of any given subject matter can be specified in fairly precise behavioral terms, it is therefore more subject to measurement. This could lead to a school in which each pupil can be expected to master some degree of proficiency in any given subject matter. This, in turn, would change drastically the nature of the school. As Carroll (1963) has ably argued, where (1) individual pupil achievement is the basic measure of the school, and (2) where the school is committed to uniform exposure to instruction, it is inevitable that pupils with higher IQ scores will achieve more, and pupils with lower IQ scores (that is, slower learning pupils) will achieve less in the same amount of time; and when all the achievement test scores are gathered together, the distribution will approach that of a normal curve.

It is critically important that this relationship be clearly understood. In general, pupils with higher IQ scores learn the same material faster than pupils with average or low IQ scores. IQ test scores predict rate of academic learning. If instructional time is held constant for all pupils, as is true in traditional high schools, for example, where exposure to a subject takes place four to five times per week for forty-five minutes, the outcome is fixed; that is, the faster learners will learn more than the slower learners during the same amount of instructional time, and consequently, the faster learners will achieve more and do better on achievement tests. It seems very unlikely that any foreseeable educational intervention or innovation will change this outcome in any substantial way *as long as the instructional time is held constant.*

Carroll proposed instead that the outcome measure should be that of mastery, and that the type of instruction and the time for it should be varied according to individual pupil characteristics. The outcome then would be, hopefully, that a majority of students would achieve a specified level of mastery; that there would be little or no correlation between aptitude and mastery measures; but time to mastery would still correlate with aptitude scores. This is an instance in which a model of educational evaluation could totally change the model of schooling.

Our present schools, however, are almost universally organized to give group instruction based on a uniform time schedule. This is an efficient way to run a large organization (the alternatives at first stagger the mind), but its very convenience in dealing with large numbers of pupils leads inevitably to the measurement of individual pupil achievement under conditions of standard exposure to instruction. It is critical that this relationship between measurement of educational outcomes and the organization of the school be kept in mind. No matter what ideal system of schooling is invented, if it relies upon standard time for instruction, it seems inevitable that the outcome measure is going to be pupil achievement distributed along a normal curve which will be positively correlated with the pupils' rate of learning as measured on some aptitude test. As long as the instructional time is held constant for all pupils, individual differences will increase and be related to the pupils' scores on intelligence tests, which predict rates of learning. This relationship between constant time and unequal achievement was pointed out over fifty years ago by E. L. Thorndike when he commented, "Equality of opportunity has no equalizing effect." The truth of this profound educational observation is very hard to accept for those who assume education should be an equalizing process.

Let us test this principle in the following example: Let us give all pupils in our elementary school equal opportunity to use the school library so that each pupil spends a specified number of hours per week in the school library. After a number of weeks, we will measure: (1) how much they have read, (2) how many new words they have learned, and (3) how much new general information they have acquired. (We will assume that we have the appropriate instruments for measuring these skills.) When we look at the results, we find that the scores of all the pupils, when they are put together, follow a normal distribution, with some at the top, some at the bottom, but most in the middle; furthermore, that the pupils who had scored higher on whatever earlier test of aptitude or relevant achievement had been given in the school were also likely to be those pupils who had read more, learned more new words, and picked up more new information. The earlier tests of aptitude could have included any of the standard group or individual intelligence tests, and the relevant achievement tests could have included tests of reading, vocabulary, general information, reasoning, and even mathematics.

This predicted outcome is unacceptable to many educators because it is contrary to their value system. It is ignored by almost every educational critic or reformer. Perhaps a different example will make the principle even clearer so that the reader can apply it in evaluating educational evidence. In this second example, we will give equal opportunity to all the boys in the tenth grade gym class to run around the outdoor track. Each boy will be permitted to run for five minutes in any running style he chooses. What will the outcome be? If we measure distance run, the faster runners will run farther in five minutes than will the slower runners. In effect, this is what most school achievement tests measure since they measure how far in the curriculum each child has gone in a standard amount of time.

For our third example, we will take one that is even closer to school and its remedial efforts. Imagine a consultant saying, "Remedial reading may help the slow readers somewhat, but the paradox about all educational remediation is that it would help the brighter pupils even more!" What would your reaction be to such a statement? Do you see that it is the same principle? If remedial reading were given to every child in a class, regardless of the child's reading ability, and if the remedial time were held constant, the better readers would read still better, and the slower readers would read better than they had, but not as well as the better readers. *Those who can learn faster will make more progress in a given period of learning time than will the slower learners.* That is the basic principle for us to keep in mind.

What could change this principle, which seems to doom slow learners to a life of coming in last? We could change our educational objective. Instead of measuring how far each pupil runs, we could make our objective that each pupil runs X yards during the course of his school experience and not care whether it takes him four minutes or five days. The objective would be that each child master a certain distance. This is the model of schooling that Carroll (1963) proposed. It would mean a school organized so that each pupil could spend different amounts of time to reach each mastery level.

The problem remains, however, even in the mastery model, of that old bugaboo of time. Granted a school where the mastery model was employed, and granted that each child took differing amounts of time to reach each level of mastery of each prescribed objective, the faster learning pupils would still reach these mastery levels sooner. So now what do they do with the remaining school time? If they spend the time in school, either they will learn other subjects or they will learn more advanced materials in the existing subjects. If faster learning pupils are dismissed earlier, for example, or go to school only four months a year instead of year-round, then schooling might become more equalizing. But it is hard to imagine that the parents of those faster learning pupils would accept such perceived discrimination without demanding or organizing an out-of-school school system where their children would continue to learn, and consequently, learn faster, and consequently achieve more, than slower learning pupils.

Most readers of Coleman's findings are unaware of, or disregard, this principle that achievement will vary by pupil ability if instructional time is held constant. The very title of Coleman's report, "Equality of Educational Opportunity," suggests that this principle was not taken into account in measuring achievement in our public school system, which is a classification model based on constant instructional time. Coleman's findings were completely predictable, as Thorndike indicated over fifty years ago.

The negative reaction to Coleman's findings has led to various hunts for the culprit in our school system. Some have selected as the culprit the resistance of the school system to innovation. Others have selected our techniques of educational evaluation, research in education, or the process of educational decision making. All agree that something must be wrong. The real wrong, from the point of view of educational evidence, has been our reluctance to analyze the model of schooling with its concomitant model of evaluation. The arguments will be discussed in the sections that follow.

Culprit: The School System

Sieber (1968) led an attack on the school system as the culprit, saying it is a "vulnerable formal organization with diffuse goals, whose functionaries are quasi-professionals, and which is devoted to processing people within its boundaries." He pointed out quite correctly that education in the United States has become a wholly public endeavor and that the schools are obliged to deal with a larger and larger percentage of the school age population from increasingly diversified backgrounds. From 1947 to 1964, the proportion of sixteen and seventeen year olds who were enrolled in public schools jumped from 68 percent to 88 percent (Sieber, 1968). Sieber believes that education as an institution is so highly bureaucratized and decentralized that it is difficult for it to adjust itself to these new demands.

It certainly can be argued that schools have an organization whose goal is to control the flow of students through its system. Student control itself is a highly important characteristic of the system, as Waller (1932) (see Readings: Section 2) pointed out forty years ago. The school organization in the classification model is based upon the premise that the school's job is to select some students to proceed up the vertical ladder and to terminate or slow down this process for others.

The regularities of the school system that impede change have been vividly documented by Sarason (1971) (see Readings: Section 2).

The reality of this model of schooling becomes apparent if we note the development of special education classes as one innovation that has been enthusiastically and rapidly adopted in school systems throughout the country. Why? Because such classes remove from the regular classroom groups of children seen as incompatible with their cohorts. We might speculate that school systems will adopt those innovations most readily which increase their ability to operate as a regulatory system for handling the flow of students. In turn, schools will be reluctant to adopt those innovations that are antiregulatory, such as truly individualized instruction, or, in fact, any innovation that would treat students as individuals rather than as units within a flow system.

Here we have the basic conflict. On the one hand, we are wrestling with a classification model of schooling organized to process groups of students at differential rates and using, quite properly, evaluation techniques to discriminate groups by differential learning rates. This model is faced in the 1970s with educating not just more pupils, but an almost universal pupil population rather than a selective one. Furthermore, it faces an increasingly educated clientele among its pupils and parents, a clientele which is demanding more educational freedom of choice and is rebelling against the classification model and its evaluative techniques which it associates with inequality and injustice.

This suggests that our earlier model of a school system as a selective one whose purpose is to organize a pyramid of pupils within limited educational opportunities, may no longer be the appropriate educational model. Education in the United States has now become a total population model. *We will no longer select a population to be educated. We will select those educational systems which, singly or in combination, can educate the entire range of our population.*

Culprit: Educational Evaluation

Those who have selected educational evaluation as the culprit view almost all educational tests as guilty. If the task were to select the fast from the slow learner, however, then it would make a good deal of sense to build a test whose items would make just that discrimination. The school intelligence and achievement tests that we have been using for over fifty years do this job quite well.

The issue here is whether or not this is what we want to measure. Glaser (1968a, 1968b), Glaser and Cox (1968) and Lindvall and Cox (1968) have been among the leaders who have argued for tests that measure how much the individual pupil has attained on criterion-referenced measures. Such measures depend upon an absolute standard of learning and give explicit information about what individuals can or cannot do subsequent to some sort of instructional exposure. Tyler (1967) goes even further, saying that we need tests to show what everyone can do, as well as what the top pupils can do. It might be very important in terms of human resources in this country for us to know what specific educational skills are at the command of all tenth graders. Tyler argues that "the task of the elementary school is now recognized as that of reaching all children, including the 15 to 20 percent who have not been making an appreciable progress in learning before."

Another so-called culprit in the evaluation fold has been that of curriculum evaluation. One group has criticized traditional curriculum evaluation procedures because they have failed to evaluate the central process, namely, what pupils have learned, at what level of mastery, and in what sequence. Gagné (1967) is one of those who has argued strongly in favor of trying out different sequences in a given curriculum to find out which contributes to mastery most effectively. Curriculum evaluation has encountered some very difficult methodological problems. Examples are the inability in actual practice to assign students or curricula randomly, or to change the sequence of teaching for purposes of experimental design, or to locate comparable control groups. (Those who report resistance of school personnel to taking a proper research attitude toward their teaching seem to forget that when university professors are asked to participate in similar scientific studies of their own teaching efforts, they often show even more reluctance. University faculty, in fact, can be charged with being less experimental in their teaching than are elementary and high school faculty.)

The methodological problems here are indeed most difficult. Often we find that students in experimental curricula do better on certain matters and less well on some other conventional ones (Herron, 1966). It is almost impossible to answer the question of which curriculum, old or new, is better, because determining what is better calls for a value judgment mixed with data. Which is better depends upon our educational goals, which are usually a matter of values. One might better try to answer the question of which curriculum achieves its own objectives most effectively, using data to answer that question, but reserving the ultimate question of value to one of value judgment. Another issue is whether or not varying the sequence and content of curricula is sufficient to alter student achievement, given the model of schooling and the means by which we have been measuring it.

Culprit: Educational Research

Many critics of the schools believe that our educational research efforts have been too pure, or too impure, or too applied, or not applied enough, or not sufficiently coordinated on target, or too organized—in any event, they claim those research efforts have not produced sturdy results as to what works in education. Indeed, they have not. If we take Stephens's (1967) review (See Readings: Section 2) of the nonimpact of educational research seriously, and it is this writer's view that we should; and if we heed a study by Dubin and Taveggia (Schutz, 1969) in which they reanalyzed the data of almost 100 comparative studies of different college teaching methods, reporting that: "We have found no shred of evidence to indicate any basis for preferring one teaching method over another as measured by the performance of students on course examinations"; and if we accept the essentially negative results of educational research that one form of instruction is superior to another; then we might be less harsh about the apparent reluctance of most school systems to adopt innovations. They might be right. Until there is strong evidence favoring a particular approach, the educational system is very likely to go on doing what it has done; namely, to adopt those changes that make its present job easier for it to accomplish.

Both Guba (1968) and Stufflebeam (1968) have called for new educational research designs, while criticizing experimental design for requiring conditions that they say cannot be met within the schools. The canons for educational research enunciated by Campbell and Stanley (1963) in their now classic article on quasi-experimental designs are, in fact, often unrealistic. For example, getting the cooperation of a school system or a building principal for a research venture is, in itself, a sampling process, not a random one, and often quite unrepresentative. If an investigator approaches fifteen systems and is told "No" only to find a sixteenth that is willing to have him investigate the relationship between X and Y, we might well ask how representative the sixteenth system is. Random selection of pupils or classrooms is almost impossible to achieve except in large city systems where a building can be assigned to Treatment X and another building to Treatment Y. Even when this is done, a host of problems may arise to invalidate the data collected in bureaucratic school systems where functionaries ordered to carry out a treatment can find thousands of ways to appear to cooperate, while they proceed to do exactly as they have always done. A lovely design of the type recommended by Campbell and Stanley may be workable in a large bureaucratic city or state system, but at the cost of contaminating treatments, that is, mixing in the effects of variables other than the treatment under study, and, more importantly, at the risk that the treatment is never adequately instituted. This may help to account for many nonsignificant findings in what appear to be well designed and controlled experiments. If the researcher proposes an elaborate design with many variables, he usually must obtain the cooperation of a large school system to carry it out. It then may be almost impossible for the experimenter to stay on top of his many treatments. He has no way of knowing, systematically, whether Teacher 26 was really teaching mathematics by Method X from 9:50 to 10:30, during the experimental period.

One alternative is to utilize simpler designs to pursue one variable in a large population so that the data may resist the complications of all those influences that operate in real school life. For example, we could determine quite accurately the developmental dentition patterns of school age children if we pursued a large enough sample. We could record what teeth developed, how often, and at what age, for thousands of school children. If we studied a large enough sample, of course, we would no longer have a sample, but the population itself.

A second alternative is to pursue the study of several variables in a school situation where the experimenter can stay in contact with all phases of the experiment, thus necessarily reducing the size of the sample but putting his scientific hopes into systematic control, observation, and recording. This is an expensive design, usually not possible for one investigator, for it takes a large staff to stay on top of the treatments for as few as thirty pupils. Even then, the experimenter worries about the interactive effects of the experiment, the experimenters, the observers, the pupils, and the school staff over time. Another worry is whether the sample, initially selected as representative of some population, has not become a special task force, representative of itself only, as a result of the research project. A third alternative is to experiment with one student, one class, or one school system to build a working model of whatever it is one wants to have happen in education, and then to see how well the model works.

Still another alternative is to consider the possibility that our experiments to date in education have not been educational experiments at all. Given a classification model of schooling which selects and processes cohorts or pupils according to their learning rates, and given approximately equal instructional exposure, the outcome is relatively fixed on any sort of achievement test. Most of the outcome has been accounted for by the method of pupil selection, teaching exposure, learning rates, and the model of evaluation, which so clearly mirror the model of schooling. The other variables, given the correspondence of these two models of schooling and evaluation, do not amount to educational peanuts, which is what our research has shown. Until we lift our eyes to the educational horizon, and see the model of schooling for what it is, we may not recognize that our experimental efforts have been pseudoscientific in the sense that the significant educational variables were already controlled by the classification model itself, namely, differing pupil learning rates and equal instructional exposure time.

Culprit: Educational Decision Making

From both industrial and governmental sources has come the suggestion that our school system would be improved if its process of decision making was more systematic. Much attention has been directed to how such systems work, but too little attention has been directed to the educational goals that such systems could help us reach.

A thoroughgoing application of systems analysis would cause the educator to face, more acutely than before, what it is he expects a system of schooling to do and how much he values the different things that he wants it to do. Value can be translated into people, money, and measures of pupils' progress towards a specified goal, but one can never get away from stating a purpose and putting a value on it.

This point is worth emphasizing. It may be a much simpler matter to weigh alternatives when the goal is specified, such as in the development of specific machinery or weaponry, than it is to weigh alternatives for an educational system where goals are viewed quite differently by different segments of the population and none of the goals are expressed in precise terms. Among the anticipated problems about which Hartley (1969) has warned us is that of "goal distortion," by which he means that organizations using a method like systems analysis may tend to place greater emphasis on goals that can be measured, and to neglect those that are harder to measure. If one adopts an accounting system of some kind, whether it be economic, political, knowledge accretion, or a form of systems analysis, it is very likely that whatever can be accounted for most easily by the system will get most of the system's attention. This is the charge that has been leveled at traditional achievement measures. Because they offer concrete data about how individual pupils are faring, the importance of such scores may be inflated to the neglect of other educational goals which are less easy to measure but just as important.

Let us return for a moment to Harris and the classification model that he helped to develop. His model has been described by Curti (1966) as a school system which justified the existing order, particularly capitalism, for Harris saw the school system as the servant of the established order. Harris also believed that one of the goals of the school would be to train the child to respect authority: "The school pupil simply gets used to established order and expects it and obeys it as a habit. He will maintain it as a sort of instinct in after life, whether he has ever learned the theory of it, or not" (p. 334). It is hard to evaluate how much Harris's model has influenced our present school system, but we recognize some aspects of an industrial model in its emphasis upon order, respect for authority, an organizational system built upon an efficient lockstep design, textbook teaching, and methods of organizing group instruction.

Harris's model could have been termed an industrial model instead of a classification one. An obvious historical analogy seems apparent between the way an educational system is organized and the concomitant organization of its parent society. It seems clear in retrospect that the Harris model of schooling was developed to meet much of the same needs as was the American industrial organization. Both were based on efficient processing of large numbers of units. The assumption that a school system should be run like a business has been a strong assumption in public education since the turn of the century (Callahan, 1962). Both organizations have accomplished their goals in the sense that they have delivered their projected outputs rather efficiently. It is the price of these outputs that now concerns us.

This classification model of schooling made excellent sense for the educational demands of the 1880s, and perhaps even into the 1940s, but the educational conditions of our society have changed radically. We need to consider this fact. We face these conflicting conditions: A demand for universal lifelong education which is already at hand; and a demand for a change in values, away from classification, conformity, and impersonalness, and toward individualization, freedom, and humanism. *It is ironic to recognize that only a highly successful model of schooling like Harris's classification model would be likely to produce a society so well educated as to demand this revolution in values.*

New Models of Education

The types of educational evaluation that are available to us at the present time have come from two sources: (1) that of experimental design which arose in agriculture where there was a need to compare the yield of seeds and soil, and (2) the need to use tests to compare draftees and students for a selection and classification process. If we step back and view educational evaluation with some perspective, it might occur to us that we probably have good evaluation techniques for measuring various educational applications to pupils, and that we also have good techniques for selecting and rejecting according to our historical model of schooling. But are these the appropriate evaluative models for the 1970s and 1980s?

We could substitute an evaluation model that stresses behavioral objectives. In theory, there seems little wrong with this approach and it is probably the direction in which a major part of evaluation will go. In practice, there are several things that make it quite difficult to achieve, not the least of which is that many important educational objectives are very hard to define in behavioral terms. This then leads us back into the same trap in which we end up measuring only what we can measure, and ignore what may be more important educational objectives, simply because they are not easily measured.

The overriding issue is the relationship between the model of schooling and the model of evaluation. If our current model is essentially a classification one, then it seems clear that both the model of schooling and the model of evaluation fit each other's needs very well indeed. Our overall educational objective has been to select and reject pupils for various stages of achievement within the broader educational system. This model has worked extremely well, and so have the corresponding measurement techniques, because they have selected and rejected pupils according to their school achievement.

In addition to a mastery model of education, a very persuasive argument for a different model of evaluation, that of the mastery of learning, has been put forward by Bloom (1968), Carroll (1963), Glaser (1968b), and Gagné (1967) which, if implemented, means a new model of evaluation based upon mastery in specified units. A mastery model of evaluation will require specified educational objectives, specified various routes to mastery, specified sequence, and specified measures of competency. In time, a mastery model of evaluation should permit far more individualization of the routes to mastery based upon learner characteristics and interests. The curriculum would have to undergo a logical analysis and evaluation which it has sadly lacked.

If we were not committed to a formal educational system and to the idea that only so many pupils can receive an education, there would be very little reason to have a sequential system of schooling, by grade or any other unit, or to have examinations to indicate passing of such units. This rather obvious point sometimes gets overlooked, as though we thought examinations, grades, and selection were inevitable components of every school system. They do not have to be. They depend upon the goals of the system. We need to remind ourselves that measurement will be tied to the educational goal. In fact, much of measurement is invented in response to the setting of goals. If, for example, we should decide that all pupils should receive X amount of education, and if the sequence of what they were taught did not make a substantial difference, we could have pupils of all ages and backgrounds taking a unit of learning together, much as we do in adult education. The nongraded school is an attempt in this direction, but it is only a limited attempt as long as the overall classification model is retained. Like many current and past educational innovations, it is likely to make little difference for it merely changes one of the many conditions within the same educational model. The view presented here is that such innovations will never produce meaningful improvement in learning as long as they are contained within the classification models of schooling and evaluation.

It seems unrealistic to retain a classification model of education in the United States into the 1970s and 1980s. We are faced with a new reality, that of extended education for all. We have rejected the old notion that only a few should be selected to go on to higher levels of education. We will have to provide for extended education for all along different routes. This has already raised the question of academic standards and what they mean, but specified mastery may be a more relevant standard than the awarding of a diploma. We have already entered the era when going to college will become an almost universal experience within our pupil population. If Trent and Medsker (1968) are correct, we can expect that an increasing proportion of our new population will have the attributes of college graduates, which include such characteristics as being more open-minded, flexible, autonomous, and intellectually receptive. This suggests that a changing model of education, in which further education becomes a more and more common experience, may be associated with certain acquired attitudes among its graduates. If so, this could have an enormous effect upon our society, as Aristotle long ago pointed out. A generation of educated youth has already demonstrated one of the effects of universal advanced education, namely, their intention to change the educational model itself.

If one substitutes the mastery model of evaluation for the classification model, there will still remain conflict over the criteria of mastery and who shall be judged as having achieved that mastery. Perhaps time may become the major basis of discrimination as was suggested earlier, in that nearly all will achieve mastery of a given skill or knowledge, but some may take longer to achieve it than others.

Some cherished notions are being challenged. Examples are the notion that it is society's role to select pupils for restricted higher levels of education, or that mass education is best accomplished through standardized instruction to pupils organized by learning rates and age. Once the classification model has succeeded historically—and it is only fair that we acknowledge that this model has been the most successful in man's history in providing more education to more people—once it has succeeded in this mission of producing an educated society, then that same educated society will demand a change in the model to a more individualized and civilized organization of schooling, with more access to higher levels. Once a critical mass of education is reached, the old relationship between schooling and society becomes reversed. In the past, the school selected those pupils for the higher steps of education. Now all of society demands the right to select its schooling from a variety of models.

We have entered the era of *pluralistic models of schooling* for a universal population target for which we will need pluralistic models of evaluation thoughtfully matched. With different models of schooling, we will need to evaluate how well each succeeds in reaching its specified goals for its target population, at what costs—educational, social, economic— and in terms of the values and outlooks that arise from each model.

REFERENCES

Bloom, B. Learning for mastery. *Evaluation Comment*. Los Angeles: UCLA Center for the Study of Evaluation of Instructional Programs, May 1968, **1,** No. 2.

Callahan, R. E. *Education and the Cult of Efficiency*. Chicago: University of Chicago Press, 1962.

Campbell, D. T., & Stanley, J. Experimental and quasi-experimental designs for research on teaching. In N. L. Gage (Ed.), *Handbook of Research on Teaching*. Chicago: Rand McNally, 1963, 171–246.

Carroll, J. A model of school learning. *Teachers College Record*. 1963, **64,** 723–733.

Chamberlin, D., Chamberlin, E. S., Drought, N. E., & Scott, W. E. *Did They Succeed in College?* New York: Harper & Row, 1942.

Coleman, J. S. *Equality of Educational Opportunity*, Washington, D. C.: National Center for Educational Statistics. U. S. Government Printing Office, 1966.

Cremin, L. *The Transformation of the School*. New York: Knopf, 1961.

Curti, M. *The Social Ideas of American Educators*. Totowa, New Jersey: Littlefield, Adams, and Co., 1966.

Gagné, R. M. Curriculum research and the promotion of learning. In R. W. Tyler, R. M. Gagné, & M. Scriven (Eds.), *Perspectives of Curriculum Evaluation*. Chicago: Rand McNally, 1967, 19–38.

Glaser, R. Adapting the elementary school curriculum to individual performance. In *Proceedings of the 1967 Invitational Conference on Testing Problems*. Princeton, N. J.: Educational Testing Service, 1968. (a)

Glaser, R. *Evaluation of Instruction and Changing Educational Models*. Reprint 46, Learning R & D Center, University of Pittsburgh, September 1968. (b)

Glaser, R., & Cox, R. D. Criteria-referenced testing for the measurement of educational outcomes. In R. Weisgerber (Ed.), *Instructional Process and Media Innovation.* Chicago: Rand McNally, 1968, 545–550.

Guba, E. G. Development, diffusion, and evaluation. In T. L. Eidell, & J. M. Kitchel (Eds.), *Knowledge Production and Utilization in Educational Administration.* Columbus, Ohio: University Council for Educational Administration, 1968, 37–63.

Hartley, J. J. Limitations of systems analysis. *Phi Delta Kappan,* May 1969, 515–519.

Herron, J. D. Evaluation of new curricula. *Journal of Research in Science Teaching,* 1966, **4,** 159–170.

Lee, G. C. (Ed.), *Crusade against ignorance: Thomas Jefferson on education.* New York: Teachers College Press, 1961.

Lindvall, C. M., & Cox, R. C. *Evaluation as a Tool in Curriculum Development: The IPI Evaluation Program.* Learning R & D Center, University of Pittsburgh, July 1968 (mimeo).

Messerli, J., The Columbian complex: The impulse to national consolidation. *History of Education Quarterly,* Winter 1967, 417–431.

Schutz, R. E. Methodological issues in curriculum research. *Review of Educational Research,* 1969, **39,** 359–366.

Sieber, S. D. Organizational influences on innovative roles. In T. L. Eidell & J. M. Kitchell (Eds.), *Knowledge Production and Utilization in Educational Administration.* Columbus, Ohio: University Council for Educational Administration, 1968, 121–142.

Stufflebeam, D. L. Evaluation as Enlightenment for Decision Making. Address delivered at Working Conference on Assessment Theory. Sarasota, Florida, January 19, 1968. Columbus, Ohio: Ohio State University Evaluation Center, 1968.

Thomas, J. A. Cost-benefit analysis and the evaluation of educational systems. *Proceedings of the 1968 Invitational Conference on Testing.* Princeton, N. J.: Educational Testing Service, 1969, 89–100.

Trent, J. W., & Medsker, L. L. *Beyond High School: A Psychosociological Study of 10,000 High School Graduates.* San Francisco: Jossey-Bass, 1968.

Waller, W. *The Sociology of Teaching.* New York: Wiley, 1932.

chapter 6

What Has Schooling in the United States Accomplished?

An unexciting truth may be eclipsed by a thrilling falsehood. A skillful appeal to passion is often too strong for the best of good resolutions.
—Aldous Huxley, *Brave New World Revisited.*

WINSLOW HOMER, *The Country School.*
The St. Louis Art Museum.

How could we tell if the school system in the United States were doing a good job? We might search for answers to a number of questions, such as:

1. In comparison with school systems in other countries, how effective has the United States school system been in lowering illiteracy rates?
2. What are the opportunities for further schooling for different segments of our population?
3. How equal is educational opportunity?
4. How costly is the system?
5. How do its dropout rates compare with those of other systems?
6. What is the relationship between educational attainment and social mobility?
7. How do the accomplishments of our school systems compare with their historical beginnings?
8. How does the United States system compare with other systems in performance?

In this chapter, we will look at some of the data on these questions.

Different school systems clearly try to achieve different goals, but one of the most common goals of an educational system is to have impact upon illiteracy. So we might start with that as our first question.

How Does the United States Illiteracy Rate Compare with Other Countries?

In Table 6–1, reported literacy rates are tabulated for forty countries. Self-reported literacy rates such as those in Table 6–1 may not be completely accurate because of inadequate and variable reporting methods, or because national pride may tend to inflate them. It seems a little unlikely, for example, that in several of these countries there is not a single soul who cannot read.

As one check on the reliability of these data, they were compared to illiteracy rates collected about 1960 for selected countries and published by the Educational, Scientific, and Cultural Organization of the United States (U. S. Bureau of the Census, *Pocket Data Book*, p. 162). For countries reported in both sources, agreement was quite close and there were no marked discrepancies.

By comparison, the United States is one of the most literate countries among those listed in Table 6–1, with a rate of 97.6 percent for its population aged fourteen years and over. It may surprise us that the United States is not the leader. Several countries listed in the full *Britannica* table (more lengthy than Table 6–1) report literacy rates higher than the United States. They are: Austria, Denmark, Finland, France, Iceland, Ireland, Liechtenstein, Netherlands, New Zealand, and Western Samoa. Probably the slight differences in percentages are not of practical significance, even assuming that they are accurate, but they tell us that there are other countries at least as literate as the United States.

We would have to conclude that the United States educational system, with its large and varied population and large geographical area, has reached a high level of literacy.

What Proportion of Our School Age Children Are Attending School?

In the United States in 1900, 72 percent of children between the ages of five and seventeen were enrolled in public elementary and secondary schools. By 1940, this percentage had risen to 84 percent. By 1968, it reached 87 percent (*Statistical Abstracts of the United States*, 1971, Table 171). Enrollment data for 1970 for public and private schools show that over 99 percent of children between the ages of seven and thirteen were enrolled in school, while percentages for five- and six-year-olds and fourteen- and fifteen-year-olds were above 85 percent and 98 percent respectively (*Statistical Abstracts of the United States*, 1971, Table 160). The answer is clear. Almost 90 percent of our children of elementary and secondary school age are attending public elementary and secondary

TABLE 6–1

Literacy Rates in Selected Countries

Country	Percent of Population Literate	Over Age
1. Afghanistan	20.	7 – 12
2. Argentina	91.5	—
3. Austria	100.	—
4. Barbados	96.	—
5. Burma	68.	—
6. Ceylon	71.9	—
7. Chad	14.	—
8. Chile	83.6	15
9. Colombia	72.9	15
10. Denmark	100.	8
11. Finland	100.	7
12. France	100.	7
13. Germany	100.	7
14. Hungary	96.6	7
15. Iceland	100.	—
16. India	30.	—
17. Iran	28.12	10
18. Ireland	100.	—
19. Italy	91.6	6
20. Jamaica	57.28	15
21. Jordan	42.	15
22. Kenya	48.	—
23. Korea, S.	93.3	11
24. Laos	19.4	—
25. Liberia	24.	—
26. Malaysia	54.6	—
27. Nepal	11.8	—
28. Netherlands	100.	—
29. New Caledonia	88.8	15
30. New Guinea	18.2	10
31. New Zealand	100.	—
32. Nicaragua	50.8	—
33. Pakistan	15.9	—
34. Peru	46.9	6
35. Philippines	72.	—
36. Portugal	59.7	—
37. Thailand	72.	—
38. Turkey	48.72	—
39. United States	97.6	14
40. Vietnam, S.	80.	—

Source: Abstracted from table on World Education, *Britannica Book of the Year*, 1971. Chicago: University of Chicago Press, 1971, p. 300.

schools—a total of 45 million in 1968—and almost all children are attending some kind of school.

Furthermore, children are getting more schooling. The average length of term has increased from 144 days in 1900 to 179 in 1968 (*Statistical Abstracts of the United States*, 1971, Table 171). Pupils also attend school much more regularly. In 1900, the average attendance was for only 99 of the 144 days in the term. By 1968, average attendance had reached 163 days. Over these years, the average pupil has gained 64 days of school exposure per year. This represents an increase of almost two-thirds over the figure for 1900.

If we look at the patterns of enrollment for white and nonwhite children in Table 6–2, we see that the percentage of nonwhite children in preschool programs is now higher than that of whites, which probably reflects the influence of Head Start and similar programs. In a report to Congress on Head Start activities (*Head Start Report*, 1969), enrollment data given for the 1967 full year programs indicate that 51 percent of the children were Negro, 24 percent were white, and other minorities made up the balance. Head Start has made preschool programs available to large numbers of children between four and six years old. In 1967 alone, 215,000 children were enrolled in the full year Head Start program, while an additional 466,000 were enrolled in the summer program (*Head Start Report*, 1969, p. 4). As can be seen in Table 6–2, nonwhite rates drop off faster than whites at the higher end of the age scale.

TABLE 6–2

Educational Enrollment of Whites and Nonwhites in U. S., October, 1968

Age in Years	Percent Whites	Percent Nonwhites
3–4	15.0	19.5
5–6	88.5	83.8
7–9	99.1	99.1
10–13	99.1	98.9
14–15	98.1	97.4
16–17	90.8	86.7
18–19	50.9	46.7
20–21	32.8	20.1
22–24	14.5	9.2
25–29	7.4	4.0
30–34	3.9	3.9

Source: *The New York Times*, January 12, 1970, p. 69.

We would have to conclude that the United States school system has developed schooling to the point where it reaches a very high proportion of its intended population. When we look at figures for other countries, we will judge whether or not this is a high or low enrollment percentage.

How Equal Is Educational Opportunity?

Let us start by asking whether there are any differences between males and females in educational rates. We may find the answer a bit more complicated than we anticipated. In 1960, white females twenty-five years old and older had obtained a slightly higher median number of school years completed (11.2) than had white males (10.7). By 1968, this had equalized and both are now completing 12.2 years of schooling (*Statistical Abstracts of the United States*, 1971, Table 162). So at first blush the answer seems to be that there is no difference in educational opportunity by sex. But let us look a little more closely at enrollment figures.

In 1970, in the age range 5–34 years, males had a higher percentage of school enrollment (62.4) than did females (55.5) (*Statistical Abstracts of the United States*, 1971, Table 154). If we trace this difference, displayed in Table 6–3, to its source, we find it arises chiefly in the college age group, ages 18–24 years. In the age range 18–24 years, 37 percent of the males were enrolled in school in 1970, while only 23 percent of the females were enrolled (*Statistical Abstracts of the United States*, 1971, Table 155). Although males and females graduate from high school at almost the same

TABLE 6–3

School Enrollment by Age and Sex
1970

| Age | Percent Enrolled | | |
	Male	Female	Total
5–6	87.6	89.1	88.3
7–9	99.3	99.3	99.3
10–13	98.8	99.5	99.2
14–15	98.2	98.0	98.1
16–17	91.3	88.6	90.0
18–19	54.4	41.6	47.7
20–24	29.3	15.2	21.5
25–29	11.0	4.3	7.5
30–34	5.3	3.1	4.2

Source: *Statistical Abstracts of the United States*, 1971, from Table 155.

rates, they do not attend college or graduate school at equal rates. In 1969, 58 percent of those receiving a bachelor's or first professional degree were men. In the same year, 63 percent of the master's degrees went to men, while 87 percent of the doctorates were awarded to men (United States Dept. of Commerce, *Pocket Data Book*, 1971, Table 222).

The disparities between men and women in degrees awarded increase markedly from bachelor's to master's to doctorates. At the doctorate level, where disparities are most extreme, the proportions of men and women vary tremendously from one field to another, but in almost all instances, men greatly outnumber women. Table 6–4 presents data on doctorates for 1969–1970 for major fields of study.

Table 6–4 was derived from a more elaborate table showing data for subspecialties as well as for major fields of study. In only three areas did

TABLE 6–4

Doctorate Degree Conferred by Higher Education Institutions in the United States and Outlying Areas, 1969–1970

Field of Study	Doctorates Awarded			Percent Female
	Men	*Women*	*Total*	
Agriculture	698	28	726	3.7
Biological Sciences	4,820	469	3,289	14.1
Business & Commerce	593	10	603	1.6
Computer Sci. & System Anal.	105	2	107	1.8
Education	4,698	1,196	5,894	20.3
Engineering	3,657	24	3,681	.7
English & Journalism	849	373	1,222	30.5
Fine & Applied Arts	592	142	734	19.3
Foreign Lang. & Lit.	581	293	874	33.5
Geography	140	5	145	3.5
Home Economics	33	83	116	71.6
Library Science	24	16	40	40.0
Mathematical Sciences	1,140	96	1,236	7.8
Philosophy	315	44	359	12.3
Physical Sciences	4,077	236	4,313	5.5
Psychology	1,296	372	1,668	22.3
Social Sciences	3,288	490	3,778	12.9

Source: Data computed from table in *World Almanac and Book of Facts*. Washington, D. C.: U. S. Office of Education, 1972, p. 335.

women equal or exceed men in doctorates awarded: (1) Early childhood education: 3 men, 10 women; (2) Nursing and/or public health nursing: 1 man, 10 women; (3) Home economics: 33 men, 83 women. When data on all areas are combined for 1969–1970, of 29,872 doctorates awarded, only 3980 (13.4 percent) were awarded to women.

Data for health professions, law, and architecture for 1969–1970 show comparable disparities. These are displayed in Table 6–5.

As might be expected, disparities in higher educational attainment between men and women are paralleled by disparities in employment levels and income. Murray (1970) presented some data comparing the professional attainment of women in the United States with that in other countries:

> Women in the professions in the United States compare unfavorably with their counterparts in other countries. In 1964, only 8 percent of the scientists, 6 percent of the physicians, 3 percent of the lawyers, and 1 percent of the engineers in the United States were women. In Denmark, 50 percent of all lawyers are women; in the Soviet Union, 36 percent; in Germany 33 percent; in France, 14 percent; and in Sweden, 6.1 percent. Women represent 32 percent of the pharmacists in the Soviet Union. They constitute 85 percent of the dentists in Finland and 24.4 percent of the dentists in Sweden (p. 526).

TABLE 6–5

Degrees Conferred in Architecture, Law, and Health Professions
by Higher Education Institutions in the United States
and Outlying Areas, 1969–1970

Field of Study	Bachelor's and First Professional Degrees Awarded			Percent Female
	Men	Women	Total	
Dentistry (D.D.S or D.M.D.)	3,712	36	3,748	1.0
Medicine (M.D.)	7,661	713	8,374	8.5
Nursing and/or Public Health Nursing	160	11,120	11,280	98.6
Pharmacy	3,690	853	4,543	18.8
Law	14,837	878	15,715	5.6
Architecture	3,698	204	3,902	5.2

Source: Data computed from table in *World Almanac and Book of Facts*. Washington, D. C.: U. S. Office of Education, 1972, p. 335.

Murray also reported that women in the United States are losing ground in academic professions: "In 1940, 28 percent of college faculty members were women. By 1960 the percentage had dropped to 22 percent. Although women constitute two-fifths of the faculties of teacher's colleges, they represent only one-tenth of the faculties of prestigious private universities" (p. 526). Furthermore, women in colleges and universities occupy lower ranks (generally not more than 10 percent hold the rank of full professor), are paid less than their male counterparts, infrequently hold department chairmanships, and seldom occupy administrative positions that carry policy-making responsibilities (Oltman, 1970). According to United States Department of Labor data (1971), marked salary differentials occur in all fields reported at all levels of employment:

> Women who work at full-time jobs the year round earn, on the average, only $3 for every $5 earned by similarly employed men. The ratio varies slightly from year to year, but the gap is greater than it was 15 years ago. From 64 percent in 1955, women's median wage or salary income as a proportion of men's fell to 61 percent by 1959 and 1960 and since then has fluctuated between 58 and 60 percent. Women's median earnings of $5,323 in 1970 were 59 percent of the $8,966 received by men (U. S. Dept. of Labor, 1971).

Median salaries of women scientists in 1970 ranged from $17,000 to $51,000 less than those of men in the same fields (United States Dept. of Labor, 1971).

If the United States report card on the equality of education receives a low grade for sexual equality, it also receives a low grade for other groups who have received more public attention. Nonwhite pupils still achieve less schooling than do white pupils, although both rates have risen remarkably in the past twenty-five years. Let us examine Table 6–6 carefully, noting first that for that group aged twenty-five years and over, who presumably have completed their education, the nonwhite group in 1969 achieved about two and a half years less schooling (median = 9.8 years) than did the total group (median = 12.1 years). Let us also notice that both groups increased in median years of schooling by almost three years during the twenty-two year period from 1947 to 1969. For the group aged 25–29 years, we notice immediately the increased educational attainment of both groups during the same period, with the larger gain of almost four years being achieved by the nonwhite group.

We note, then, two trends somewhat at odds with each other: (1) non-white students continue to achieve less education than do white students, yet (2) both groups have shown a considerable increase in schooling in the last twenty years.

Illiteracy rates (persons unable to read and write in any language) for

TABLE 6–6

White and Nonwhite Educational Rates

Age and Year	Median Years of School Completed	
Persons 25 years and over	*Total–all races*	*Negro and other (except white)*
1947	9.0	6.9
1957	10.6	7.7
1960	10.5	8.2
1965	11.8	9.0
1968	12.1	9.5
1969	12.1	9.8
Persons 25–29 years		
1947	12.0	8.4
1957	12.3	9.9
1960	12.3	10.8
1965	12.4	12.1
1968	12.5	12.2
1969	12.6	12.2

Source: *Statistical Abstracts of the United States*, 1970 (91st Edition). Washington, D. C.: U. S. Bureau of the Census, 1970, Table 159.

the decade between 1959 and 1969, which are shown in Table 6–7, exhibit similar trends for race. Between 1959 and 1969, illiteracy rates were cut in half for whites and nonwhites alike, but rates for nonwhites exceeded those for whites by amounts ranging from two- to eightfold depending on the age range involved. For both groups, illiteracy rates were highest in the older age ranges.

Data on employment and income for whites and nonwhites, like those for males and females, show inequalities that parallel those for education. In 1969, for example, although the median income in the United States for white families was $10,089, for the group classified "Negro and Other," the median was $6340 (*Statistical Abstracts of the United States*, 1971, Table 508). In 1969, 20.6 percent of white families had incomes of $15,000 or more, while only 7.2 percent of Negro families had incomes at this level. At the lower income levels, while 12.8 percent of white families had incomes in 1969 below $4000 per year, 31.5 percent of Negro families had incomes below $4000 (*Statistical Abstracts of the United States*, 1971, Table 505). Furthermore, increasing levels of education seemed to have higher payoff rates for white families than for Negroes and others. Data on

TABLE 6–7

Illiteracy Rates by Race
1959 and 1969

Age	1959 Percent Illiterate			1969 Percent Illiterate		
	Total	White	Negro & Other	Total	White	Negro & Other
Total, 14 and over	2.2	1.6	7.5	1.0	0.7	3.6
14–24 years	0.6	0.5	1.2	0.3	0.2	0.5
25–44 years	1.2	0.8	5.1	0.5	0.4	1.3
45–64 years	2.6	1.8	11.3	1.1	0.7	5.5
65 years and over	6.5	5.1	25.5	3.5	2.3	16.7

Source: *Statistical Abstracts of the United States,* 1971 (92nd Edition). Washington, D. C.: U. S. Bureau of the Census, 1971, Table 170.

education and income levels in Table 6–8 show incomes of families with white heads to be higher by $1000 to $3000 at the various educational levels. Several discrepancies are particularly glaring. The median income of families headed by a white with eight years of elementary school is only $200 less than that of families headed by a nonwhite with four years of high school. The median income of families headed by a white with 1–3 years of high school is $150 higher than that of families with a nonwhite head with 1–3 years of college.

Geography creates still other subgroups who do not receive equal educational opportunities. For example, in 1960, for students educated in Kentucky and South Carolina, the median number of years of school completed was only 8.7. At the other extreme, the median number of years of school completed was 12.2 years in Utah, and 12.1 years in Colorado, Wyoming, Nevada, Washington, California, and Alaska. If the student were nonwhite, he could hope that the dice of birth would land him in New Hampshire, where he would be likely to attain 11.7 years of schooling as compared with his less fortunate counterpart raised in South Carolina with a median schooling of 5.9 years (*Statistical Abstracts of the United States,* 1971, Table 166).

It is hard to believe that simply the state or region where one is educated could double the chances for schooling, and yet that is what such statistics tell us. This situation is partly due to the makeup of the state's population, as well as to its resources and school budgets. Money does not automatically mean more or better education, but there is a complex and positive

TABLE 6–8

Median Family Income By
Race and Education of Head, 1969

Years of School Completed by Head	Median Income	
	White	*Negro & Other*
Elementary School	6,769	4,754
Less than 8 years	5,799	4,351
8 years	7,651	5,927
High School	10,181	7,002
1–3 years	9,342	6,217
4 years	10,563	7,875
College	13,426	10,555
1–3 years	11,949	9,194
4 years or more	14,685	13,682
Total	10,089	6,340

Source: *Statistical Abstracts of the United States*, 1971 (92nd Edition). Washington, D. C.: U. S. Bureau of the Census, 1971, Table 508.

relationship between the resources of an area, the type of school system it supports, and the educational achievement of its pupil population. In the example given above, money is only partially related to median years of schooling by state. Colorado, for example, had an estimated school expenditure for 1971 of $780 per pupil, making it twenty-sixth in rank, while South Carolina was thirty-ninth with $656 and Kentucky was forty-sixth with $621. New York State, on the other hand, had the highest estimated expenditure per pupil, $1370, of any state except Alaska; even so New York does not lead the states in median school years completed (*Statistical Abstracts of the United States*, 1971, Table 186).

Years of schooling completed, however, does not tell us enough about the education a subgroup has received because we are well aware that different pupils get more, or less, from the same educational exposure. The reasons for this are complex, some still unknown, and all heatedly argued. (We will take up some of these reasons later in what we hope will be an enlightening manner when we discuss the Coleman report.) For our purposes here, let us simply note Table 6–9, taken from the same Coleman report, which shows that scores on this particular test varied for first grade pupils by race and ethnic group. These differences are somewhat more marked by twelfth grade, so that after twelve years of schooling, according

TABLE 6–9

Achievement Tests–Median Scores for Students in Grades 1
and 12 by Race or Ethnic Group, 1965[a]

Grade and Type of Test	White	Negro	Puerto Ricans	Indian Americans	Mexican Americans	Oriental Americans
Grade 1						
Nonverbal	54.1	43.4	45.8	53.0	50.1	56.6
Verbal	53.2	45.4	44.9	47.8	46.5	51.6
Grade 12						
Nonverbal	52.0	40.9	43.3	47.1	45.0	51.6
Verbal	52.1	40.9	43.1	43.7	43.8	49.6
Reading	51.9	42.2	42.6	44.3	44.2	48.8
Mathematics	51.8	41.8	43.7	45.9	45.5	51.3
General information	52.2	40.6	41.7	44.7	43.3	49.0
Five tests, average	52.0	41.1	43.1	45.1	44.4	50.1

[a] Estimates based on survey of public elementary and secondary schools. Represents results of standard achievement tests of such skills as reading, writing, calculating, and problem solving. Scores on each test were standardized so that the average over the national sample equaled 50 and the standard deviation equaled 10. This means that about 16 percent of all students would score below 40 and about 16 percent above 60.

Source: *Statistical Abstracts of the United States,* 1971 (92nd Edition). Washington, D. C.: U. S. Bureau of the Census, 1971, Table 182.

to these tests, Negro or Mexican American students presumably have achieved less educationally than their Oriental American or white schoolmates. Let us note, therefore, that differential educational performance is related to ethnic and racial identity among other things. We shall reserve until later the question of whether this differential rate is evidence that the school system is malfunctioning.

How Expensive Is the United States School System To Operate?

Is our school system receiving adequate financial support? Before we answer the question of how much we are spending, we should ask a prior question. How much does the United States have available to spend, compared to other regions of our world?

Table 6–10 may be surprising. It says, for example, that northern America and Oceania, a region that includes the United States, contain only 7.1 percent of the world's population, but that residents of this region

TABLE 6–10

Percent of World Population Distributed by National Average GNP Per Capita and Geographic Area, about 1958

GNP per capita (1958 U. S. dollars)	World Total	Northwestern Europe[a]	Southern and Eastern Europe	Northern America and Oceania	Latin America	Asia	Africa
Total	100.0	6.7	15.0	7.1	7.0	57.1	7.1
1,000 and over	13.3	6.2	0	7.1	0	0	0
575–999	8.9	0.4	8.1	0	0.3	0.1	0
350–574	6.1	0.1	3.9	0	1.4	0.1	0.6
200–349	13.3	0	2.9	0	4.3	5.7	0.5
100–199	6.6	0	0.1	0	0.8	3.8	1.9
Below 100	51.7	0	0	0	0.1	47.4	4.1

[a] Northwestern Europe comprises the U. K., France, F. R. G., Eire, the Low Countries, Scandinavia, and Switzerland; southern and eastern Europe, all the rest of Europe including all of Russia.

Source: Easterlin, R. A. "Economic Growth: Overview." In D. L. Sills (Ed.), *International Encyclopedia of the Social Sciences.* New York: Macmillan, 1968, Vol. 4, p. 405.

benefit from a per capita share of their gross national product (GNP) that is over $1000 per year per person. That does not seem like much money per person in United States terms.

But look closely again at Table 6–10 at the column labeled "Asia," and see that 47.4 percent of the people there have a share in their region's GNP of *below $100* per person per year. This table dramatically illustrates the differences in per capita wealth around the world, differences so great that it is almost impossible to comprehend what they mean. It is all too clear that those who live in northwestern Europe, northern America, and Oceania are financially blessed, whereas the residents of the rest of the world—and that represents 86 percent of the world's inhabitants—are by comparison financially underprivileged. Over one half of our neighbors on this planet have less than $100 per year in 1958 United States dollars as their share of their region's GNP.

The United States, by any comparison, is affluent and can afford to spend money on education if it so chooses. Has it so chosen? In 1920, United States expenditures for education totaled $64 for each of its 1 million pupils; in the school year of 1968–1969, this nation spent $834 on each of its 35 million pupils (Coombs, 1968). This represents an annual public school educational expenditure in 1968–1969 of about 30 billion United States dollars.

We made the point above, however, that our nation can afford a large educational investment because of the high per capita GNP. We might better ask: What percent of our GNP are we spending on education? How does this compare with other nations? Table 6–11 summarizes selected UNESCO (1969) data.

Our national educational investment compares favorably with that of other industrialized nations. More recent data for the United States indicate that total school expenditures represented 7.2 percent of the GNP in 1969 and 7.6 percent in 1970 (*Statistical Abstracts of the United States,* 1971, Table 150). Almost all national educational budgets have been growing, and many have doubled between 1955 and 1965.

Where does the money come from to support our public elementary and secondary schools in the United States? Since 1940, local revenues have declined. In 1970, they made up 40 percent of the funds for public schools; state contributions accounted for another 37 percent. Federal funds had risen to 10.5 percent by 1970, which seems a small proportion but actually represents a large share for school systems that traditionally have been fiercely local in character and opposed to federal support or control (*Statistical Abstracts of the United States,* 1970, Table 149).

What are those funds spent for? In 1968, the single largest item was for instruction, not surprisingly, which takes up about 55.7 percent of the public school budget. Despite concern of some taxpayers about adminis-

TABLE 6–11

Public Expenditures on Education
Percent of Gross National Product
Percent of Total Public Expenditures

	Canada	Denmark	France	West Germany	Italy	Japan	Netherlands	Sweden	United Kingdom	USSR	USA
1955[a]	—	3.1	—	—	—	—	3.7	—	—	5.8	3.3
	—	—	—	—	—	—		—	—	—	—
1963	5.5	5.1	3.4	3.1	4.8	4.6	5.7	6.7	4.8	6.4	4.8
	—	21.1	18.2	9.4	24.4	22.1	24.2	21.0	12.9	—	17.5
1964	5.5	5.3	3.4	3.2	4.9	4.5	6.1	6.7	4.8	6.5	5.1
	—	21.6	18.0	9.8	24.8	22.6	25.9	21.3	13.0	—	18.8
1965	6.3	5.7	4.1	3.4	5.2	4.4	6.3	7.0	5.1	7.3	5.3
	—	22.8	21.5	10.3	22.7	22.7	25.3	21.1	13.4	—	19.5
1966	7.2	6.3	4.2	3.5	4.7	4.4	6.6	7.8	5.3	7.4	5.3
	22.6	23.2	22.2	10.8	19.7	21.6	27.0	23.8	13.4	—	15.6
1967	8.1	6.1	3.6	3.6	5.2	4.2	—	8.1	5.6	7.2	5.6
	21.6	20.6	18.1	10.6	22.0	20.1	—	24.6	12.2	—	—

[a] First figure listed below each date is percent of GNP; second figure is percent of total public expenditures.

Source: UNESCO, *Statistical Yearbook*. Paris: United Nations Educational, Scientific, and Cultural Organization, 1969, Table 2.18, 387–422.

trative overhead, it is relatively low at 3.8 percent. The other large budget item is capital outlay at 12.9 percent for school buildings and equipment (*Statistical Abstracts of the United States*, 1970, Table 178).

Are we paying our teachers appropriate salaries? The answer depends on what we mean by appropriate. We are certainly paying them higher salaries than we did before. In 1848, in his Eleventh Annual Report of the Secretary of the Board of Education to the Massachusetts legislature, Horace Mann (Mann, *Annual Reports*, 1848) reported that the average monthly salary for male teachers in Massachusetts for 1846–1847, inclusive of their board, was $32.46. For female teachers, the average, inclusive of their board, was $13.60 (p. 26). Later in this report, in an impassioned plea for greater generosity in appropriations for education, Mann makes some familiar comparisons:

> Since the organization of the Federal government in 1789, the expense of our military and naval establishments and equipments, in round numbers, is seven hundred million dollars. Two of our ships of the line have cost more than two million dollars. The value of the arms accumulated; at one time, in the arsenal at Springfield, in this state, was two millions of dollars. The Military Academy at West Point, has cost more than four millions of dollars. In our town meetings, and in our school district meetings, wealthy and substantial men propose the grant of $15 for a school library, and of $30 for both library and apparatus; while, at West Point, they spend fifty dollars in a single lesson at target-firing. . . . The pupils at our Normal Schools, who are preparing to become teachers, must maintain themselves; the cadets at the academy receive $28 a month, during their entire term, as a compensation for being educated at public expense. Adding bounties and pensions to wages and rations, I suppose the cost of a common foot-soldier in the army cannot be less than $250 a year. The average cost of female teachers for the Public Schools of Massachusetts last year, was only $13.60 a month, inclusive of board; or at a rate which would give $163.20 for the year; but the average length of the schools was but for eight months, so that the cost of two common soldiers is nearly that of *five* female teachers. The annual salary of a colonel of dragoons in the United States army is $2,206; of a major general, $4,512; that of a captain of a ship of the line, when in service $4,500; and even when off duty, it is $2,500!! There are but seven towns in Massachusetts where any teacher of a Public School receives so high a salary as $1,000; and in four of these towns, one teacher only receives this sum (pp. 106–107).

Teachers' salaries have steadily increased since Mann's days. Elsbree (1939) reported that in the forty-seven years between 1890 and 1937, the average annual salary paid to teachers increased from $256 to $1325, which represents an increase of 418 percent. When the increase is translated into "real earnings" based on the purchasing power of the dollar from 1890–1899, however, the percentage increase is 277 percent (Elsbree, 1939, p. 434). Elsbree also reported comparisons for a number of occupations on average earnings in dollars per year for 1920–1936. Examples are: Medicine, $4850; Law, $4730; Dentistry, $4170; College teaching, $3050; Ministry, $1980; Skilled trades, $1430; Public school teaching, $1350; Nursing, $1310; Unskilled labor, $795; Farm labor, $485 (p. 437).

In 1969, when there were two and a quarter millions of teachers in the United States, the average salary for public school elementary teachers was $7476, and $8160 for secondary teachers (*Statistical Abstracts of the United States*, 1969). Since median income for all families in 1969 was $9433, teachers' salaries were well below this median.

By 1971, the average salary for public school elementary teachers was $9025, and $9540 for secondary teachers. The average salary for both groups combined was $9265. There was considerable spread from state to state in average salaries. At one extreme, the average for New York was $11,100 and for California $11,022. At the other extreme were Arkansas at $6668 and Mississippi at $6008 (*Statistical Abstracts of the United States*, 1971, Table 190). These figures are not particularly impressive when viewed in the light of the annual mean income of $12,532 reported four years earlier in 1967 for males with four years or more of college (*Statistical Abstracts of the United States*, 1971, Table 167). Since only 3.6 percent of teachers in 1970 had less than a bachelor's degree, while 30.6 percent had a master's degree or more, teachers compare favorably in educational level with the group involved in the 1967 mean income calculation of $12,532, but compare unfavorably in salaries. Since teaching is an occupation that continues to attract large numbers of women, however, the discrepancies partially reflect the usual sex differentials in salary. In any case, it seems safe to conclude that teachers seem underpaid in view of their education.

What have we learned about the financing of the United States school system? In comparison with other countries and their GNP, the United States spends generously on education and can well afford to do so. In 1971, total expenditures for education in the United States were expected to exceed 75 billion dollars, which represents 7.7 percent of the GNP (*Statistical Abstracts of the United States*, 1971, Table 150). The cost of educating one child has gone up at a very fast rate, however, and the problem of how to finance more and more education for more and more of our people is already upon us. This is a problem of critical proportions, not only for our country but perhaps even more for the developing countries whose resources are more limited.

How Do Our Dropout Rates Compare with Other Systems?

We learned earlier that well over 90 percent of our 5–17 year olds now attend school, which represents *the highest rate of attendance of any large society or nation, past or present*. The level and extent of education among our young people are unprecedented. This has implications that may be both bad and good, but no one can doubt that education has become the way of life in the United States for almost all of its young people. Those who drop out of high school tend to be male about twice as often as female and, contrary to what we may expect, include four times as many whites as Blacks (*Statistical Abstracts of the United States*, 1971, Table 169). Of course whites exceed Blacks in our nation by about sevenfold, and it is true that dropouts include a higher proportion of Blacks than their ratio in the nation. However, many people have the stereotype of a dropout as an unemployed Black teenager in an urban slum when a more accurate picture is of a white teenager, perhaps in a slum, but also in a rural area, and very likely to be employed, since 85 percent of all dropouts are engaged as wage earners. Black dropouts are considerably less likely to be employed than are whites. In 1970, for example, 19 percent of white dropouts were unemployed, compared with 31 percent of Black dropouts (*Statistical Abstracts of the United States*, 1971, Table 169).

Another way to look at dropout rates is to look at retention rates and ask: Are more of our pupils staying in school longer? One measure of this is to compute retention rates for each grade over a period of years. This measure is illustrated in Figure 6–1 which shows the striking increase in retention rates in thirty years. In 1961, the chances of a fifth grader entering college were *greater* than the chances that his parents in 1926 would graduate from high school! That is quite an educational leap in one generation.

We conclude that the United States school system has an impressive, and perhaps unsurpassed, record on retention and dropout rates, if the record is defined in terms of the proportion of eligible students retained in school.

What Is the Relationship between Education and Social Mobility?

This relationship implies a point of view that we should question, which is whether education necessarily should be a means for someone to rise in society, presumably through its effects on occupation and income. This assumption is commonly accepted among most contemporary schooling systems. Sometimes it is hard for us to imagine a different kind of school

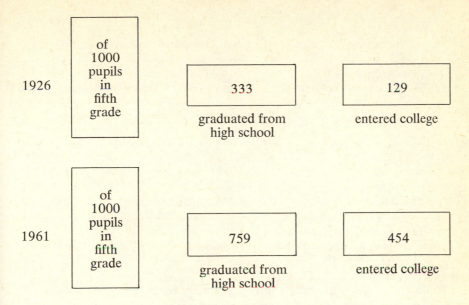

Figure 6-1

Retention Rates in U. S. Schools, 1926 and 1961. Source: After *Statistical Abstracts of the United States*, 1970 (91st Edition). Washington, D. C.: U. S. Bureau of the Census, 1970, Table 188.

system, one in which education takes place solely for the experience of learning something, or for indoctrination, but not in order to increase the student's income or occupational status.

Economists have recently become intrigued with the idea that education can be considered an investment in human capital that has its own rate of return. That return can be seen in Table 6-12 which shows a positive relationship between median income and years of schooling completed. In looking at Table 6-12, we realize that females and nonwhites do not seem to get equivalent monetary rewards for equivalent education, so that we will have to extend our thinking about equality of education to encompass those other variables that can be associated with education, such as income and occupation. Let us note here that if the argument is advanced that nonwhites receive less money for the same education because they achieve less well in school (reread Table 6-8), we would have to ask why this lower rate of return is also true of females who do as well or better than males in school achievement.

If anyone needs convincing about the close relationship between schooling and income in the United States today, a quick look at Table 6-13

TABLE 6–12

U. S. Income by Years of Schooling Completed and by Sex, 1967

Median Income (persons 25 years and older)	Years of School Completed			
	Elem. School *8 years*	*High School* *4 years*	*College* *1–3 yrs*	*4 years*
Male	$4,778	$7,244	$ 8,155	$10,000
Female	$1,379	$2,909	$ 3,083	$ 4,426
White families	$6,608	$8,962	$10,277	$12,770[a]
Nonwhite families	$4,897	$6,665	$ 8,189	$10,485[a]

[a] 4 years or more for family data.

Source: *Statistical Abstracts of the United States*, 1969 (90th Edition). Washington, D. C.: U. S. Bureau of the Census, 1969, pp. 108 & 325.

should do the job. This table shows a generally strong positive relationship between number of school years completed and income of male wage earners. The real difference in economic payoff appears to come in the

TABLE 6–13

Relationship between Education and Income
(based on 1969 data)

Median School Years Completed	Income Level	Percent of Male Earners
8.4	$ 1,500–1,999	3.4
8.6	$ 2,000–2,499	3.6
8.7	$ 2,500–2,999	3.0
9.2	$ 3,000–3,999	6.9
10.3	$ 4,000–4,999	7.2
11.6	$ 5,000–5,999	8.9
12.1	$ 6,000–6,999	9.6
12.3	$ 7,000–7,999	10.3
12.4	$ 8,000–9,999	15.2
12.8	$10,000–14,999	16.9
15.3	$15,000–24,999	5.6
16.3	$25,000 + over	1.8
		91.2

Source: After *New York Times Encyclopedia Almanac, 1972*. New York: The New York Times, 1971, p. 401.

year after high school, because it is at the point of 12.8 median school years completed that we see a jump in earnings. What seems critical now is post high school education. The big difference is between being a high school graduate only, and having one to two years in a senior, technical, or community college.

How Is the United States School System Performing Historically?

One way to evaluate any system is to ask the degree to which it has improved upon its own performance over time. It might be refreshing for us to remember, for example, that the almost universal school attendance that we find in this country has not always existed. There was a time when a large percentage of children in our country did not go to school. As a matter of fact, we may be surprised to learn that compulsory attendance in school in this country is only a little more than a hundred years old. As recently as World War I, there were still states in this country that did not require attendance. Even as late as 1928, some states required as little as three months of schooling per year, and several southern states did not require schooling past the fourteenth year.

If we ask how the United States schooling system has improved in raising its percentage of eligible students enrolled in school, the answer reflects an impressive success story. Look what it has accomplished in fifty years: In 1900, only 11.4 percent of our 14–17 year olds were in secondary school, but by 1950, 76.5 percent of them were so enrolled (*Encyclopedia International*, 1963). It might help to think about those figures for a minute. Is there any other school system in the world, past or present, that has made this quantum leap in terms of enrollment in only fifty years? And what about higher education? In 1900, if we had counted all the bachelor's degrees, all the first professional degrees, all the master's degrees, and all the doctor's degrees that were granted by institutions of higher education in this country, we would have a total of only 30,000 degrees. By 1950, this figure was 500,000. Our population has of course increased; however, over that particular fifty-year span, the college age group had not quite doubled, and yet the number of higher degrees had multiplied fifteen times. That is a sizable educational growth.

We have no choice but to conclude that the growth of the United States schooling system and its rates of educational participation have been exceeded nowhere. Although such widespread enrollment may not be proof of a good school system, in answer to our question about the history of performance of the United States school system, we must acknowledge that it demonstrates a remarkable and unparalleled record.

How Is the United States Schooling System Doing Compared with Those in the Rest of the World?

Compared with the other countries of the world, particularly the industrial countries with which the United States would most appropriately be compared, our schooling system is larger at every level. This largeness is not due simply to the size of our population, but to the proportion of our population enrolled in school. The numbers of students at the primary, secondary, and higher levels in the United States system dwarfs the numbers in comparable industrial countries, as indicated in Table 6–14. Our enrollments are increasing at a tremendous rate, as are those of other

TABLE 6–14

Recent and Projected Trends in Enrollment in Industrial Countries
(in thousands)

Country	Year	Primary	Secondary	Higher
France	1951	5,358	1,181	162
	1961	7,301	2,509	283
	1964	7,406	3,112	412
	1972	7,280	4,980	792
Netherlands	1950	1,615	325	30
	1960	1,915	655	40
	1965	1,965	725	65
	1970	2,105	760	80
	1975	2,375	805	110
Austria	1955	—	127	17
	1963	905	135	40
	1970	1,116	159	44
	1975	1,184	217	50
Ireland	1963–64	496	132	16
	1970–71	515	173	24
U. S. A.	1949	22,207	6,453	2,659
	1959	32,412	9,600	3,216
	1965	35,900	12,900	5,400
	1970	37,300	15,000	6,959
	1973	38,000	16,000	7,951

Source: Coombs, P. H. *The World Educational Crisis.* New York: Oxford University Press, 1968, p. 29.

TABLE 6–15

Estimated Percentage of Total Population of all Ages Enrolled in School,
Selected Areas, Since 1818 or Earliest Known Date Thereafter

	England and Wales	United States	Germany (later FRG)	Italy	Russia (later USSR)	Japan	Chile	India	Nigeria
1818	6								
1830	9	15	17	3					
1850	12	18	16	[b]	2				
1887	16	22	18	11	3	4[c]	4	2	
1928[a]	16	24	17	11	12	13	15[d]	4	1[d]
1954[a]	15	22	13	13	15	23	18	7	5

[a] Values for 1954 (and, to some extent, for 1928) for the most developed countries are biased downward relative to those for other times and places, because of the decline in ratio of school age to total population.
[b] Not available
[c] Around 1870
[d] 1938

Source: Easterlin, R. A. "Economic Growth: Overview." In D. L. Sills (Ed.), *International Encyclopedia of the Social Sciences*, Vol. 4. New York: Macmillan, 1968.

industrial countries. This is partly due to the population explosion following World War II, but it is also due to the higher and higher proportions
of young people who are enrolled in school. Our primary system seems to
be leveling off in terms of population growth, and almost every school-age
child in the United States already attends primary school. The larger
growth rates since 1949 have been in the secondary and higher levels.

Perhaps a better way to evaluate the comparative performance of the
United States system is to look at the percentage of the population of
all ages enrolled in school. This is shown in Table 6–15 for the selected
years 1818–1954. It may help us to gain better perspective on our study
of education to be reminded, as we are by this table, that 150 years ago
in what was then a highly civilized area, namely England and Wales, only
6 percent of the entire population were in school of any kind. In 1954, the
United States reached a total population enrollment rate of 22 percent. As
of 1970, this figure is probably 25 percent. What Table 6–15 says to us
about the United States schooling system is that it has had a sturdy history

TABLE 6–16

Estimated Primary School Dropouts in Certain Developing Countries

Countries	Grade I	Grade II	Percent Grade III	Grade IV	Grade V
Africa					
Cent. Afr. Rep.	21.8	11.7	9.6	7.1	8.0
Dahomey	24.5	12.8	10.7	11.0	5.7
Madagascar	18.1	10.6	13.6	23.4	9.2
Niger	12.6	4.8	12.0	5.0	11.9
Togo	3.1	1.9	1.0	2.0	10.9
Upper Volta	19.2	17.3	7.3	16.7	8.2
Asia					
Afghanistan	4.0	1.5	2.0	7.0	4.0
Ceylon: Urban	15.6	7.5	9.7	10.6	8.1
Rural	17.4	11.4	11.7	12.8	9.8
Philippines	9.2	6.8	7.6	10.0	8.5
Thailand	12.0	5.0	6.0	—	6.0
Latin America					
Argentina	13.4	5.6	7.6	10.0	10.1
Costa Rica	7.1	10.7	10.6	11.5	10.7

Source: Coombs, P. H. *The World Educational Crisis*. New York: Oxford University Press, 1968.

since 1830 in terms of the percentage of its population enrolled. In this particular table, Japan is the only country whose rate of participation appears to be higher, although this is a fairly recent phenomenon. The history of educational participation in the United States is not just good, it is better than that of any other country.

Earlier we discussed the dropout rate in this country. Within our school age population for elementary and secondary school, we are presently enrolling well over 90 percent of that population. It would not be fair to assume that the remaining children are necessarily dropouts. There are a number of children who do not attend school for physical, geographic, or mental reasons, so the actual percent of dropouts even at the high school level would be below 10 percent for any one year. The estimated dropout rates for certain developing countries are given in Table 6–16. We cannot make a direct comparison with the United States, of course, nor would it be fair in view of the differences in resources. From grades 1 through 5, the United States system does not experience dropouts except for the rare child who encounters severe difficulties and for whom no alternative schooling is available, or for seasonal dropouts for children of migratory workers. Table 6–16 tells a very sad story about the numbers of children among the developing countries who do not complete even the first grade. In Dahomey, for example, we can see that 25 percent of the children who start first grade do not complete it. In rural Ceylon, if we add up the percentages that drop out of each of the first five grades, we find that approximately 63 percent of Ceylon's pupils have dropped out by fifth grade. In comparison with these rates, the United States and all industrial countries show much higher rates of educational retention.

Although we might well congratulate ourselves on the success of our system in doing all this, a little humility is in order when we compare our resources with the limited resources of many of the developing countries which are being strained beyond measure to accommodate a rising population of school age children, increasing numbers of whom want more and more education. In most developing countries, the school age population between five and fourteen years is growing at an annual rate larger than that of the total population (Coombs, 1968). The educational aspirations of this group increase each year. Where there are limited enrollments in school, as in East Africa for example, the parents will spend $30 as a tuition investment. That $30 is being spent by parents who probably do not see more than $75 in cash over the entire year. The increased demand around the world for education, plus an increased educational population, has reached proportions in the developing countries that may lead to the new expression that their children will "learn" them out of house and home.

Summary: What Has the United States School System Accomplished?

The United States school system has performed impressively well in terms of delivering education to all. Its enrollment rates, retention rates, and opportunities for continued education are unequaled by any country, past or present. The only country whose performance approaches that of the United States in the recent past is Japan. Despite the fact that not all segments of the population achieve the same amount of schooling, it is still true that *there is no society anywhere that offers more of its people more education.* If that is a good school system, then the United States has a superb one. We have almost reached the presumed ideal of a universally educated society. Inequities exist nevertheless. Opportunities for education, and the returns from education, vary with race, sex, and geography.

REFERENCES

Coombs, P. H. *The World Educational Crisis.* New York: Oxford University Press, 1968.

Elsbree, W. S. *The American Teacher: Evaluation of a Profession in a Democracy.* New York: American Book Company, 1939.

Encyclopedia International. (1st ed.) New York: Grolier Inc., 1963.

Head Start Report. In President Nixon's Report to the Congress, February 19, 1969.

Mann, H. *Eleventh Annual Report of the Secretary of the Board of Education.* Boston: Dutton and Wentworth, State Printers, 1848.

Murray, P. The rights of women. In N. Dorsen (Ed.), *The Rights of Americans: What They Are—What They Should Be.* New York: Pantheon Books, 1970, 522–545.

New York Times Encyclopedia Almanac, 1972. New York: *The New York Times,* 1971.

Oltman, R. M. *Campus 1970: Where Do Women Stand?* Washington, D. C.: American Association of University Women, 1970.

Peterson, E. Working women. In R. J. Lifton (Ed.), *The Woman in America.* Boston: Houghton Mifflin, 1965, 144–172.

Pifer, A. Women in Higher Education. Speech delivered to the Southern Association of Colleges and Schools, Miami, Florida, November 29, 1971.

Rossi, A. S. Equality between the sexes: An immodest proposal. In R. J. Lifton (Ed.), *The Woman in America.* Boston: Houghton Mifflin, 1965, 98–144.

Statistical Abstracts of the United States, 1969 (90th edition). Washington, D. C.: U. S. Bureau of the Census, 1969.

Statistical Abstracts of the United States, 1970 (91st edition). Washington, D. C.: U. S. Bureau of the Census, 1970.

Statistical Abstracts of the United States, 1971 (92nd edition). Washington, D. C.: U. S. Bureau of the Census, 1971.

UNESCO, *Statistical Yearbook.* Paris: United Nations Educational, Scientific, and Cultural Organization, 1970.

U. S. Bureau of the Census, *Pocket Data Book, USA, 1971.* Washington, D. C.: U. S. Government Printing Office, 1971.

U. S. Department of Labor, Employment Standards Administration. *Fact Sheet on Earnings Gap,* 1971.

Readings
Section 2: Educational Evidence

Faith is always more aggressive than evidence.

—E. G. Boring

READINGS: SECTION 2

Educational Policies Commission. *The Effect of Population Changes on American Education.* Washington, D. C.: National Education Association, 1938, 26–27, 32–33.

White, M. A., & Duker, J. Some unprinciples of psychological research. *American Psychologist*, April 1971, **26,** No. 4, 397–399.

Thorndike, E. L. The nature, purposes, and general methods of measurements of educational products. In G. M. Joncich (Ed.), *Psychology and the Science of Education: Selected Writings of Edward L. Thorndike.* New York: Teachers College Press, 1962, 151–158.

Klaus, R. A., & Gray, S. W. The early training project for disadvantaged children: A report after five years. *Monographs of the Society for Research in Child Development*, 1968, **33,** No. 4, Serial No. 120, 1–3, 26–28, 54–55.

Sarason, S. *The Culture of the School and the Problem of Change.* Boston: Allyn and Bacon, 1971, 73–78, 83–87.

Stephens, J. M. *The Process of Schooling.* New York: Holt, Rinehart and Winston, 1967, 71–90.

Waller, W. *Sociology of Teaching.* New York: Wiley, 1932, 6–13.

THE EFFECT OF POPULATION CHANGES ON AMERICAN EDUCATION

Educational Policies Commission

Part II. Educational Implications of Population Trends

Summary of Part II

At the time the public schools were founded there were no effective methods by which predictions could be made with regard to the size of the task which would soon confront public education: the amount of money which would be required, the number of teachers to be trained, the number of schools that must be built in order to house the children of a nation that within a few years would reach from coast to coast. The need and desire for public education, rather than knowledge that the undertaking could be carried thru, motivated the launching of public schools. Today, if education is to realize the hopes of its founders, it is essential to give thought to its quantitative aspects. Information must be anticipated on the number of children to be educated in each locality and state, the amount of funds which will be needed, the number of teachers who must be trained, the amount of physical equipment which will be required. Such information needs to be interpreted so as to reveal the educational implications for each state and community. Five of the more general implications suggested by Part II are summarized below.

1. *Improvements and extension.* Decreasing numbers of children to be educated should be used as an opportunity to enrich and improve the educational program. Every effort should be made to bring into the schools those children who are now growing up without adequate schooling. The schools should play a crucial part in developing a universal civic intelligence required to meet the problems of an industrial democracy.

2. *School plant.* The location and design of new school buildings should be determined after careful studies of existing and probable future trends in the school population at the various educational levels. The growth of cities due to migration, rural resettlement projects, the movement of urban residences to the outlying sections, and the development of road systems facilitating transportation of rural pupils, as well as natural rates of increase or decrease in population, are among the factors to be considered.

Educational Policies Commission. *The Effect of Population Changes on American Education.* Washington, D. C.: National Education Association, 1938, 26–27, 32–33.

3. *Guidance and adjustment.*   Guidance services and other appropriate means should be used by the schools to adjust educational programs, not only to the great number of children who remain in one locality, but to those in a mobile population who change frequently from one school to another.

4. *Rural schools.*   The probability that the rural areas will be the reservoirs of the future population makes the improvement of rural education a national necessity. Rural education must offer opportunities suitable both for youth who will stay on the farm and for those who will migrate to the cities.

5. *Population facts in the curriculum.*   The facts with regard to the trends in the population of the United States should be presented at appropriate levels in the educational program, especially in connection with subjects such as the social studies, home economics, and vocational training.

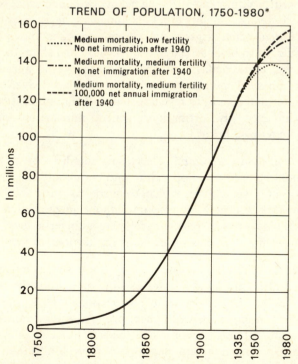

TREND OF POPULATION, 1750-1980*

.... Medium mortality, low fertility
No net immigration after 1940

_.._.. Medium mortality, medium fertility
No net immigration after 1940

----- Medium mortality, medium fertility
100,000 net annual immigration
after 1940

In millions

*Actual 1750-1930 as corrected from census figures by National Resources Committee's Committee on Population Problems.   Estimated 1935-1980 by Scripps Foundation for Research in Population Problems.   Nat. Educ. Assn.

SOME UNPRINCIPLES OF PSYCHOLOGICAL RESEARCH

Mary Alice White and Jan Duker

In these days of computer programs, multivariate analysis, and of an infinite number of journals to be read, we all suffer from the dangers of too much information, some of which contains errors of design or analysis, and almost none of which can we read as carefully as we should. To help the reader of the psychological research literature, we have prepared fictitious examples of certain errors as we perceive them. (Some of these are particularly familiar to us because they come from our own past work.)

Model 1. The Non-Sample Sample

Basic unprinciple: The sample of subjects represents only the universe of subjects conveniently available to the investigator, and is characterized by its non-generalizability.

Example: "A developmental study of Carlotta's theory of visual alertness was carried out among a group of nursery school children. The subjects consisted of the morning class (N = 11) in the University Experimental Nursery School. Seven of the children were Caucasian, 2 were Negro, one was Spanish-speaking, and one was Oriental. Their mean age was 45.2 months. Their mean IQ on the Schweppes Intelligence Scale was 132.7. Their parents were above average in mean years of schooling completed."

Model 2. It Is the Foam, Not the Brew, That Counts

Basic unprinciple: Although the major hypotheses are not supported, minor and serendipitous results are reported as major findings.

Example: "In a survey of 1637 high school students relating their school achievement, physical health, home conditions, aptitude test scores, attendance, extracurricular activities, and physical coordination (fine and gross) to their attitudes toward drugs, student government, sex education, parental influences, religion, and politics, 132 of the hypothesized relationships were not substantiated by the .05 level. Hypotheses 133 and 134, however, received partial support (although t-tests did not quite reach significance at the .10 level) in that the findings were in the hypothesized direction in 7 out of the 13 tests. The authors conclude, therefore, that students' overall adjustment in high school is positively related to their attitudes toward these current issues. Recommendations for altering these attitudes are described."

Model 3. Insignificant Significance

Basic unprinciple: Using a sufficiently large sample and/or a plethora of statistical tests, the results are interpreted as significant when the actual differences, in fact, are of no practical importance.

Example: "Half of the classes in a large suburban high school were given two months of training on the Geshwitzblink Optical Programmer, with the other half of the classes serving as controls. Pre and post testing was carried out with the National Reading Achievement battery. The gain scores for the experimental group (N = 492) averaged 7.2 points, whereas the control group (N = 536) gained only 6.3 points. The difference in the gain scores was significant at the .0000001 level. Suggestions for using the Geshwitzblink training program in other educational settings are made."

Model 4. The Progressive Raven; or One Swallow May Not Make a Summer, but It Sure Excites the Bird Watcher

Basic unprinciple: Investigator follows Unprinciple No. 2, and then proceeds to give progressively greater weight to selected trends as he reports his findings.

Example: (Investigator hypothesizes that third grade boys who develop school phobias will show more signs of dependency on the WART scale (Wenceslaus Anxiety Representation Taxonomy) than will controls. Subjects are carefully matched on the relevant variables; the WART protocols are scored by independent judges with high inter-rater agreement; and the data are analyzed with appropriate statistical techniques. The differences between groups do not reach the predetermined level of significance.)

Results section: "The differences between the experimental and control subjects did not reach significance at the .01 level. However, the data contain some interesting trends."

Discussion section: "The above mentioned trends in the data are in the predicted direction, indicating dependency in school phobia in boys of this age."

Summary section: "The data lend tentative support to the hypothesis that. . . ."

In paper read at subsequent meeting: "Data from my research support the conclusion that school phobics show more dependency than normal controls on such measures as the WART scale, indicating the interaction of dependency and parental response which is central to an understanding of this syndrome in children. I have termed this dependency. . . ."

Model 5. Peripatetic Passim, or, Something Happened on the Way to Class Today

Basic unprinciple: The investigator makes maximum use of the unusual, timely, or newsworthy situation with whatever is at hand.

Example: "A random sample of subway riders was tested during a prolonged service blackout to identify those personality characteristics associated with panic during enforced isolation. Analysis of handwriting samples and of figure drawings indicates that uneven line pressure and poorly articulated limbs are associated with verbal and motoric indices of panic. These results are interpreted somewhat guardedly because illumination was inadequate during part of the experiment."

Model 6. The Trojan Horse, or, Some of My Best Friends are Experimenters

Basic unprinciple: Install a set of experimental conditions within the ostensible experiment which will guarantee the desired outcome.

Example: The ostensible experiment: "The relationship between teacher attitude and pupil behavior was investigated among sixth grade boys. Using a scale of teacher attitudes toward selective behavior of boy pupils (STATSBOBP), it was found that changes in the scale scores correlated .72 with changes in the male pupils' behavior over a three month period. A specially constructed observational instrument was used to record the changes in the boys' behavior. Theoretical implications include the possible reciprocal relationship between teacher attitudes and pupil behavior."

The Trojan Horse: The experimenter has been a fifth-grade teacher in this particular school for thirteen years and is head of the building's teacher council. This year she is working for an advanced degree at a nearby university with a professor who is interested in teacher attitudes. She asked her close friends with whom she eats lunch regularly in the teachers' room, to volunteer their sixth grade classes for her experiment. After the initial scores were recorded, the teachers involved were most cooperative in reporting on the expected changes. They were also of considerable help in interpreting to some of the pupils why their teacher from the previous year spent time in their rooms marking down things about them when they behaved in certain ways. Everyone reported spontaneously on the improved behavior of those boys well known in the past for their misconduct.

Model 7. The Byzantine By-Pass, or Avoiding the Obvious

Basic unprinciple: In discussing experimental results, all simple, obvious, or parsimonious explanations are by-passed in favor of complex, obscure, and unlikely interpretations.

Example: "Pupil performance over age on the Conundrum Problem Solving Test was investigated. No marked differences between boys and girls were found in grades three through eight. However, those pupils who achieved higher scores on the mathematical achievement battery given two months earlier also received significantly higher scores on the Conundrum Test. A detailed analysis of both sets of scores for different ages and levels of ability suggests a pattern, probably developmental in nature, in which ability M (mathematical) develops ahead of ability C (conundrum) in a somewhat S-shaped curve. This developmental pattern is termed the Con-Math Profile. Applications to various cultures are made, indicating the role of the social order, geography, and climate in the growth pattern of the Profile. A special index was devised which indicates where a pupil is located on the Con-Math Profile as well as his potential."

A variation of the Byzantine By-Pass is found in Model 8 below.

Model 8. The Byzantine Rose

(The term, "rose," is used here in the sense of "a rose by any other name. . . .")

Basic unprinciple: The investigator develops a line of research which is quite narrow, using his own instruments, and then concludes that he has identified a new aspect of behavior which can only be measured by his original instruments.

Example: "In the series of experiments reported here, a new component of intelligence is identified, which the author has termed the Orpheic Deficit (after the Greek myth). The Orpheic Deficit was first identified through the use of instruments constructed by the author, the Zenobia Recall Scale, and the Zenobia Memory-for-Patterns Task. Children possessing the Orpheic Deficit show extreme difficulty on both the Zenobia Recall Scale and on the Zenobia Memory-for-Patterns Task. Their performance is characterized by an inability to recall pairs of words over time, and an inability to reproduce visual patterns, indicating that this deficit extends across sensory modalities. Those children who do well on these tasks show the ability to recall both verbal and visual stimuli over time. Low correlations between intelligence and Orpheic scores are reported for those children who scored two or more s.d.'s below the mean. The role of the Orpheic Deficit in learning, especially in school learning, is discussed and suggestions for instructional changes are made. Whether or not the Orpheic Deficit will hold up in the auditory sphere is discussed. Several suggestions are made for further research using the Zenobia Recall Scale and the Zenobia Memory-for-Patterns Task."

These eight models are intended to be suggestive and not exhaustive. The examples stem from our fields of interest because we are more familiar with that literature, but the examples should not be taken as a sign of special guilt for those areas. As a matter of fact, we would assert the generalization, one we happen to have termed the White-Duker Unhypothesis, that Unprinciples can be found in all areas of published psychology.

THE NATURE, PURPOSES, AND GENERAL METHODS OF MEASUREMENTS OF EDUCATIONAL PRODUCTS

Edward L. Thorndike

Whatever exists at all exists in some amount. To know it thoroughly involves knowing its quantity as well as its quality. Education is concerned with changes in human beings; a change is a difference between two conditions; each of these conditions is known to us only by the products produced by it—things made, words spoken, acts performed, and the like. To measure any of these products means to define its amount in some way so that competent persons will know how large it is, better than they would without measurement. To measure a product well means so to define its amount that competent persons will know how large it is, with some precision, and that this knowledge may be conveniently recorded and used. This is the general *Credo* of those who, in the last decade, have been busy trying to extend and improve measurements of educational products.

We have faith that whatever people now measure crudely by mere descriptive words, helped out by the comparative and superlative forms, can be measured more precisely and conveniently if ingenuity and labor are set at the task. We have faith also that the objective products produced, rather than the inner condition of the person whence they spring, are the proper point of attack for the measurer, at least in our day and generation.

This is obviously the same general creed as that of the physicist or chemist or physiologist engaged in quantitative thinking—the same, indeed, as that of modern science in general. And, in general, the nature of educational measurements is the same as that of all scientific measurements.

In detail, however, there are notable differences. An educational product, such as a composition written, a solution of a problem in arithmetic, an answer to a question about history, a drawing of a house or the performance of an errand, is commonly a complex of many sorts of things. The task of measuring it seems more like measuring a house or an elephant than it is like measuring a length or a volume or a weight. A complete measurement of, say, a composition might include an exact definition of its spelling, its usage of words, its usage of word forms, its wit, its good sense and so on and on; and each of these might again be subdivided into a score or more of component elements.

What we do, of course, is to make not such a complete measurement of the total fact, but to measure the amount of some feature, *e.g.*, the general merit of the composition or the richness of its vocabulary, just as physical science does not measure the elephant, but his height, or his weight, or his health, or his strength of pull. Every measurement represents a highly partial and abstract treatment of the product. This is not understood by some of our critics who object to tests and scales because of their limited point of view. The critic's real point should be that an educational product commonly invites hundreds of measurements, as we all well know. It should be noted also that single measurements are still in a sense complex, being comparable to volume, wattage or the opsonic index, rather than to length, weight or temperature.

In the second place, the zeroes of the scales for the educational measures and the equivalence of their units are only imperfectly known. As a consequence, we can add, subtract, multiply and divide educational quantities with much less surety and precision than is desirable. Indeed, in any given case, the sense in which one educational product is twice as good or as desirable as another, or in which one task is twice as hard as another, or in which one improvement is twice as great as another, is likely to be a rather intricate and subtle matter, involving presuppositions which must be kept in mind in any inferences from the comparison.

In some cases so little is known of units of amount that we do not even try to equate distances along the scale, but simply express relative size in terms of arbitrarily chosen units and reference points. This is the case, for example, with the most commonly used measurement in psychology and education, that due to applying the Binet-Simon tests.

Nobody need by disturbed at these unfavorable contrasts between measurements of educational products and measurements of mass, density, velocity, temperature, quantity of electricity, and the like. The zero of temperature was located only a few years ago, and the equality of the units of the temperature-scale rests upon rather intricate and subtle presuppositions. At least, I venture to assert that not one in four of, say, the judges of the supreme court, bishops of our churches, and governors of our states could tell clearly and adequately what these presuppositions are. Our measurements of educational products would not at present be entirely safe grounds on which to extol or condemn a system of teaching, reading or arithmetic, but many of them are far superior to the measurements whereby our courts of law decide that one trademark is an infringement on another. . . .

The purpose of measurements of educational products is in general to provide somebody with the knowledge that he needs of the amount of some thing, difference or relation. The "somebody" may be a scientific worker, a superintendent of schools, a teacher, a parent or a pupil. He may need a very precise or only an approximate measure, according to the magnitude of the difference which he has to determine. He may need it for guidance in many different sorts of decisions and actions.

Some of the most notable uses concern the values of studies in terms of the changes produced by them, the effects of different methods of teaching, and the effects of various features of a school system, such as the salary scale, the length of the school day and year, the system of examining and promoting pupils, or the size of class. There are many problems under each of these heads, and each of these problems is multifarious according to the nature, age, home life and the like of the pupils, and according to the general constitution of the educational enterprise, some small feature of which is being studied.

Another important group of uses concerns inventories of the achievements of certain total educational enterprises such as our educational surveys must become if they are to carry authority with scientific men. The total educational enterprise may be the work of a teacher, of a school, of an orphanage, or a prison, of a system of schools, or the like.

Another important group of users centers around the problem of giving the individual pupil the information about his own achievement and improvement which he needs as a motive and a guide. It is interesting to note that the first of the newer educational scales, which was expected to be used chiefly by scientific investigators of the teaching of handwriting, now hangs on the wall of thousands of classrooms as a means for pupils to measure themselves. There are many other purposes, and important ones, such as the detection and removal of gross prejudices on the part of teachers in their own evaluations of certain educational aims and products. These, however, cannot be described here.

The superintendents, supervisors, principals and teachers directly in charge of educational affairs have been so appreciative of educational measurements and so sincere in their desire to have tests and scales devised which they can themselves apply, that the tendency at present is very strong to provide means of measurement which are concerned somewhat closely with school achievements, and which can be used by teachers and others with little technical training. There is also a tendency, because of this need for a large number of measurements in the case of educational problems, to try to devise tests which can be scored by persons utterly devoid of judgment concerning the products in question.

It would ill become the present writer to protest against these two tendencies; and they are intrinsically healthy. There is, however, a real danger in sacrificing soundness and principle and precision of result to the demand that we measure matters of importance and measure them without requiring elaborate technique or much time of the measurer. The danger is that the attention of investigators will be distracted from the problems of pure measurement for measurement's sake, which are a chief source of progress in measuring anything. Perhaps not even one person in a million need feel this passion, but for that one to cherish it and serve it is far more important than for him to devise a test which thousands of teachers will employ. Opposition, neglect, and misunderstanding will be much less disastrous to the work of quantitative science in education than a vast output in mediocre tests for measuring this, that and the other school product, of which a large percent are fundamentally unsound.

We have seen that educational measurements vary from an assignment of a certain amount of some clearly defined thing, the zero, or "just not any," of which is fairly accurately known, to a mere assignment of a certain position in a series of products themselves only similarly defined. They vary also from measurements in the most unimpeachable of units, such as time, to measurements where the unit is "that difference in quality which 75 percent of a certain sort of observers succeed in observing" or is even more crudely and hypothetically defined. They include measures in the form of how well a certain task is performed, and of how hard a task can be performed with a certain degree of success. Consequently, the methods of devising and using educational measurements also vary widely—too widely for any unified exposition. What will be said about methods here will, in fact, comprise only certain recommendations and cautions which are likely to be often appropriate.

Consider first certain principles of method designed to ensure reliable measures, or at least measures whose degree of unreliability is known and can be allowed for. These are:

At least two specimens or samples should be taken of any fact about which a statement is to be made. If any individual's achievement in drawing is to be reported, use at least two drawings. If the achievement of a class in addition is to be reported, use at least two tests, preferably on two days. If the effect of a method is to be estimated, test the method with at least two classes taught by different teachers. If the quality of a specimen of handwriting is to be reported, have at least two judges rate it independently. It will often appear from the comparison of two samplings of a fact that many more samplings are needed to permit a statement that is precise enough for the purpose in view.

No fixed rules can be given, since the purpose in view determines the degree of precision that is required, but it may be noted that a test which gives, for a single pupil, an approximation so rough as to be almost useless, gives for a class of thirty-six a result which is six times as precise, and for a group of nine classes a result which is eighteen times as precise. Ten times as large a sampling of the product in question is required to measure a single pupil as to measure the average of a hundred pupils (to the same degree of precision). In general, eight tests of 15 minutes each are superior to four tests of 30 minutes each, and still more superior to two tests of 60 minutes each, since the accidents of particular temporary circumstances are thus reduced in influence.

Consider next certain principles of method that need to be observed if we are to secure measures whose significance is certain.

Great care should be taken in deciding anything about the fate of pupils, the value of methods, the achievement of school systems and the like from the scores made in a test, unless the significance of the test has been determined from its correlations. For example, it cannot be taken for granted that a high score in checking letters or numbers is significant of a high degree of accuracy and thoroughness in general. Letter-checking tests have been so used, but with very little justification. Courtis has given reason to believe that a test with stock problems from text-books in arithmetic may be a very inadequate test of ability to reason with quantitative facts and relations, this ability being in such a test complicated by, and perhaps even swamped by, the ability to understand the verbal description of the facts and relations.

A pupil's score in a test signifies first, such and such a particular achievement, and second, *only whatever has been demonstrated by actual correlations to be implied by it.* Nothing should be taken for granted.

The significance of one *ability* (A) for another (B), is given by the correlation coefficient γ_{AB} corrected for attenuation. The significance of a *particular test sampling* (A) for the ability (B) is given by the raw correlation coefficient γ_{AB}. Thus, arithmetical ability itself is significant to a high degree of promise of ability with algebra and geometry, but a five-minute test in arithmetic would be much less so.

It is unfortunately the case that we do not at present know at all well the significance of any school ability or of any of the tests which we have devised as convenient means of sampling abilities. We need not blame ourselves for this; the educational measurements now in use are much better than none at all. They do excellent service, provided inferences are made with proper caution. They will do still better service in proportion as the correlations of each are determined. This work is extremely laborious, but sound method requires it.

Consider next certain principles of method designed to free measurements from certain pernicious disturbing factors, notably unfair preparation for the test, inequalities in interest and effort, and inequalities in understanding what the task is.

The best protection against unfair preparation is the provision of many alternative tasks of demonstrated equality in difficulty. This again means extremely laborious and uninteresting work, which nevertheless requires expert talent. It should be subsidized.

There is and can be no absolute assurance of equality in interest and effort. Any educational product is a product of ability conditioned by interest. All that we can do is to choose such conditions for the test as are found to reduce inequalities in interest and effort to a minimum (that is, to show high correlations with the composite of results obtained with a sampling of all conditions likely to influence interest). There is reason to believe that, when the test is taken as a part of school work, the appeal to group competition, as in "We wish to find out whether you can do as well as the sixth-grade children in Boston did," and a promise to report the results to each individual, are useful. In the case of high-school and college students a small payment in money or release from tasks, together with the promise of a full report to each individual, seems a useful method.

Inequalities in understanding what the task is, may be reduced by a preliminary trial, identical in form with the test itself, but with very easy content, and by giving special tuition to any pupil who fails in this pre-liminary trial. Instructions should be in simple language and should always be accompanied by at least three concrete samples of the task.

One who is eager to find imperfections can find many in present measure-ments of educational products. Nor it is a hard task to make constructive suggestions for improvement. An intelligent student of education could probably in a single day note a score of sure ways of improving the scales and tests which we now use. That is really child's play. The hard thing is the actual expert work of remedying the imperfection, for this involves hundreds of hours of detailed expert planning, experimenting and com-puting. What is needed in educational measurement is not the utterance by onlookers of criticisms and suggestion with which the men actually at work with measurements are as familiar as they are with their own names, but expert assistance in overcoming the defect.

If those who object to quantitative thinking in education will set them-selves at work to understand it; if those who criticise its presuppositions and methods will do actual experimental work to improve its general logic and detailed procedure; if those who are now at work in devising and in using means of measurement will continue their work, the next decade will bring sure gains in both theory and practice. Of the gains made in the past decade, we may well be proud.

THE EARLY TRAINING PROJECT FOR DISADVANTAGED CHILDREN: A REPORT AFTER FIVE YEARS

Rupert A. Klaus and Susan W. Gray

Editors' note: What follows are excerpts from an extensive research report on the Early Training Project. These excerpts were selected to illustrate the use of empirical evidence in an intervention program in education. The reader should not evaluate the entire Early Training Project on the basis of these excerpts, and is referred to the original report for further reading. (See Klaus, R. A., & Gray, S. W. The early training project for disadvantaged children: A report after five years. *Monographs of the Society for Research in Child Development*, 1968, *33*, No. 4, Serial No. 120.) Copyright © 1968 by The Society for Research in Child Development, Inc.

The intervention program of the Early Training Project was based upon the fact that at the time we began, and indeed today, there is little clear evidence that, short of a complete change of milieu in infancy, it is possible to offset to any practical extent the progressive retardation with which we were concerned. We attempted, therefore, to develop an intervention "package," consisting of manipulations of those variables which, from research on social class, cognitive development, and motivation, seemed most likely to be influential in later school performance. At the same time, these were to be variables for which we could hope to effect some changes. We also tried to construct the package within a framework that could be employed on a wide scale, should our intervention program be successful.

Subjects

The experimental subjects and those of the local control group live in a city of 25,000 in the upper South. This town has a growing population, with little outward mobility. Its original economic base was agricultural, but since World War II there has been much development of light industry.

The children of the study are all Negro. At the time the subjects were originally selected, the schools were segregated. It seemed wise because of our need for continued school and community cooperation to work with either white or Negro children. We had reason to believe that in this particular setting there were greater chances of success with Negro families. Although there were many low-income whites in this city, most of their children at that time attended a school that was part of the county school system rather than the city system with which we had established over time on-going working relations.

A house-to-house census was made of all Negro children born in 1958 in this city. On the basis of this census, a group of 61 children were selected for our study according to the following criteria: (*a*) housing (points considered were whether the house was owned or rented, its general exterior and interior condition, the amount of crowding, and the "cultural" materials present, such as books, magazines, musical instruments, radio, and television); (*b*) education of parents; (*c*) occupations of parents.

By these criteria the families we selected were well below the usual cutting lines for poverty and its concomitant syndrome of living conditions. Income was low, although it was difficult to obtain more than rough estimates because of such factors as periods of unemployment and the inability of the parents to give any picture of their annual earnings. In 1964 we did obtain fairly accurate estimates of income from one of our workers who had been in each home weekly for a period of 2 years. For our first experimental group, to be explained later, the income was only slightly in excess of one thousand dollars—this for a family averaging seven members. In the second experimental group, the income was greater, but no more than two thousand dollars. Education tended to be somewhat higher than might be expected in terms of last grade completed in school, the mean level being eighth grade. It should be pointed out, however, that educational achievement was probably considerably lower. With one or two exceptions, all the mothers could read, but many probably fell below the functional literacy standard of fifth-grade reading ability. Occupations were either unskilled or semiskilled, and a few individuals were employed in more skilled trades such as concrete finishing, but their employment was seasonal.

From the group of 61 children so selected from our census pool, three groups were constituted by random assignment. This procedure was used rather than matching because of the limited number of potential subjects and the multiplicity of variables probably relevant for school performance. In addition, some of the information on variables of probable significance was not available until later in the study. Matching across groups also would have created problems if any attrition should occur, as well could happen in a 5-year study.

The first (T1) of the groups was to attend, over a period of 3 summers, a 10-week preschool particularly designed to attempt to offset the deficit usually observed in children from culturally deprived homes when they enter public school. In addition, this group was to have 3 years of weekly meetings with the home visitor during the parts of the year in which the school was not in session. The second group (T2) was to receive 2 summers of special experiences plus 2 years of meetings with the home visitor. A third group (T3) became our local control group. Because of the ghetto-like concentration of Negroes in this community, it was decided to introduce a fourth group (T4) which would also serve as a control group, but which was located in a similar city 60 miles away and hence would not have any interaction with the experimental groups. This second control group made possible some study of diffusion effects among children and parents living in proximity to the experimental children. Table 1 gives a layout of the general experimental design.

Attrition has been slight over the years of the study. At the beginning there were 22 children in T1, 21 children in T2, and 18 and 27 in T3 and T4, respectively. The number of the children who remained in the study through its 5 years is given in Table 2. This table shows MA's for the children who completed the program. It also indicates their performance at the inception of the intervention program in May 1962.

As may be seen from Table 2, randomization did not provide strict comparability of groups. The most conspicuous difference is the general advantage on performance enjoyed by the second experimental group.

TABLE 1

Layout of General Research Design

Treatments	T3 (3 Summer Schools)	T2 (2 Summer Schools)	T3 (Local Controls)	T4 (Distal Controls)
1st winter, 1961–62	(Criterion development, curriculum planning, general tooling up)			
1st summer, 1962	Pretest summer school; posttest	Prestest; posttest	Pretest; posttest	Pretest; posttest
2d winter, 1962–63	Home visitor contacts Pretest;	Pretest;		
2d summer, 1963	summer school; posttest	summer school; posttest	Pretest; posttest	Pretest; posttest
3d winter, 1963–64	Home visitor contacts Pretest	Home visitor contacts Pretest;		
3d summer, 1964	summer-school; posttest	summer school; posttest	Pretest; posttest	Pretest; posttest
4th winter, 1964–65	Home visitor contacts; follow-up tests	Home visitor contacts; follow-up tests	Follow-up tests	Follow-up tests
5th winter, 1965–66	Follow-up tests	Follow-up tests	Follow-up tests	Follow-up tests

TABLE 2

Status in May 1962 of Four Groups Used in Analysis in 1966

Tests	T1 (Exper.) ($N = 19$)	T2 (Exper.) ($N = 19$)	T3 (Local Control) ($N = 18$)	T4 (Distal Control) ($N = 24$)
CA (mo.)	45.0	46.0	47.0	45.0
Binet MA (mo.)	40.7	43.5	40.3	40.1
Binet IQ	87.6	92.5	85.4	86.9
PPVT MA (mo.)	30.0	30.6	29.4	32.0

Part of this is caused by the particular attrition that occurred: where N is only 20, the loss of one low-IQ child will slightly increase a mean IQ, and the loss of a superior child will depress it. Information collected over time on the families appears to indicate that, in general, the second group had a more favorable situation. For example, in T1 there were twice as many father-absent homes as there were in T2, and, as indicated earlier, the income of the T1 families was little more than half that of the T2 families. Since one of the purposes of our study was to compare the relative effectiveness of the longer experimental treatment received by the T1 group with the shorter period of the T2 group, this difference in initial status is unfortunate. It makes difficult any meaningful comparisons of the length of treatment. . . .

Stanford-Binet

The Stanford-Binet, Form L-M, was judged to be the most appropriate instrument to assess the children's intellectual functioning. Even with cultural limitations, it appears less biased for deprived children than other well-standardized tests. It has also been a highly useful predictor of future school performance. At the time of the first testing the children ranged in age from 3 years, 6 months, to 4 years, 5 months; at the final testing the range was from 7 years, 7 months, to 8 years, 6 months. The tests were administered at all pre- and posttest sessions indicated in Table 1, with the exception of May 1964. At that time the WISC was used in an attempt to avoid saturation with the Binet.

The analyses of the results were based on 19 subjects in T1, 19 in T2, 18 in T3, and 24 in T4. All of these children were present for the administration in 1966. During earlier administrations some children were not available for testing, and in a few of the first administrations tests were invalidated by breakdown of rapport. In these instances, the means of the available valid tests were assigned to the vacant cells. In all, 22 such assignments were made for the total 560 test scores, and the degrees of freedom in the analyses were adjusted accordingly.

Table 3 gives the treatment group IQ and MA means for the various test administrations, and Figure 1 provides a graphic representation of the MA means. The results of the seven administrations were subjected to a Lindquist (1953) Type I (treatment groups by test administration) analysis of variance. Both effects and the interaction yielded significant F ratios. To test for simple effects for groups at each administration, simple analyses of variance for groups at each administration were made using that data at that level only. Orthogonal comparisons of treatment group sums of scores were made to test for significant mean differences. The August 1962 and May 1963 comparisons were made testing the hypotheses T1 = T2 + T3 + T4, T2 = T3 + T4, and T3 = T4. All other comparisons were made testing the hypotheses T1 + T2 = T3 + T4, T1 = T2, and T3 = T4.

The results of the comparisons are shown in Table 4. For the May 1962 testing, the groups did not differ significantly. In August 1962, T1 was significantly above the combined performance of the other three groups, but there were no differences among the other three. In May 1963, T1 still showed the highest performance, but was not significantly different from the others combined. Beginning with August 1963, after both the training groups participated in the training activities, all subsequent comparisons led

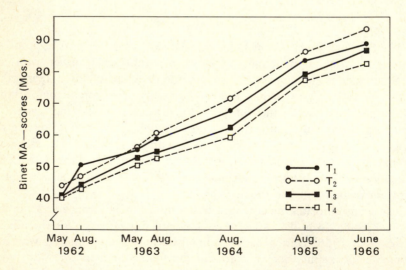

Figure 1   Mental ages for experimental and control groups on the Stanford-Binet.

to the conclusions that the performance of the combined treatment groups exceeded the performance of the combined control groups, and the two experimental groups did not differ significantly from each other, nor did the two control groups differ significantly from each other. . . .

TABLE 3

Mean Stanford-Binet MA and IQ Scores for the Four Treatment
Groups at Each Administration

Date of Administration	T1		T2		T3		T4	
	MA (mo.)	IQ	MA (mo.)	IQ	MA (mo.)	IQ	MA (mo.)	IQ
May 1962	40.7	87.6	43.8	92.5	40.3	85.4	40.3	86.9
August 1962	50.7	102.0	46.9	92.3	44.3	88.2	43.6	88.2
May 1963	55.6	96.4	56.0	94.8	53.2	89.6	50.7	87.4
August 1963	59.3	97.1	60.6	97.5	55.0	87.6	52.9	85.8
August 1964	68.0	95.8	71.6	96.6	62.3	82.9	59.6	80.8
August 1965	83.8	98.1	86.3	99.7	79.4	91.4	77.4	89.4
June 1966	88.7	91.2	93.4	96.0	86.8	87.9	82.8	84.8

THE CULTURE OF THE SCHOOL AND THE PROBLEM OF CHANGE

Seymour Sarason

. . . From a theoretical and practical standpoint—by which I mean theories of child development, intellectual growth, educational and learning theory, techniques of teaching, presentation and discussion of subject matter— the importance of question-asking has always been emphasized. It is surprising, therefore, that there have been very few studies focusing on this type of behavior. Susskind (1969) recently did a comprehensive review of the literature. He expresses surprise that a type of behavior considered by everyone to be of great importance has hardly been investigated. However, he points out that although the few studies vary greatly in investigative sophistication, they present a remarkably similar state of affairs. But before we summarize the findings, the reader may wish to try to answer Susskind's question:

> Before exploring the research literature we suggest that the reader attempt to estimate the rates of two classroom behaviors. Imagine yourself in a fifth grade, social studies classroom in a predominantly white, middle-class school. During a half-hour lesson, in which the teacher and the class talk to each other (there is no silent work), how many questions are asked (a) by the teacher, (b) by the students? How do the two rates correlate?[1]

The first two questions are deceptively simple because, as Susskind has made clear, there are different types of questions, and there are problems as to how questions (and which questions) are to be counted. For example, if the teacher asks the same question of five children should it be counted once or five times? Susskind has developed a comprehensive, workable set of categories, and the interested reader is referred to his work. We will now summarize the answers to the above questions in light of existing studies, including the very recent ones by Susskind, whose findings are very similar to those from older studies.

1. Across the different studies the range of rate of teacher questions per half-hour is from 45–150.
2. When asked, educators as well as other groups vastly underestimate the rate of teacher questions, the estimated range being 12–20 per half hour.

[1] E. C. Susskind, "Questioning and Curiosity in the Elementary School Classroom" (Doctoral dissertation, Yale University, 1969), p. 38.

3. From 67 to 95 percent of all teacher questions require "straight recall" from the student.
4. Children ask *fewer* than two questions per half hour. That is to say, during this time period two questions by children will have been asked.
5. The greater the tendency for a teacher to ask straight recall questions the fewer the questions initiated by children. This does not mean that children do not have time to ask questions. They do have time.
6. The more a teacher asks "personally relevant" questions the higher the rate of questioning on the part of children.
7. The rate of questions by children does not seem to vary with IQ level or with social-class background.

These statements derive from existing studies, but, as Susskind points out, scores of people have come to similar conclusions from informal observations.

We have here a clear behavioral regularity. How should we think about this? Is this behavioral regularity an intended outcome? Put in another way, this is the way things are; Is this the way things should be? I know of no psychological theory or theorist, particularly those who are or have been most influential on the educational scene, who would view this behavioral regularity as a desirable outcome, that is, as one kind of barometer indicating that an organized set of conceptions are being consistently implemented. In addition, I have never read of or spoken to curriculum specialists and reformers who would not view this behavioral regularity as evidence that their efforts were being neither understood nor implemented. Finally, the fact that teachers and other groups vastly underestimate the rate of teacher-questioning (in Susskind's study teachers were quite surprised when confronted with the rates obtained in *their* classrooms) suggests that this behavioral regularity is not an intended outcome according to some part of the thinking of teachers.[2]

We have, then, an outcome that practically nobody intends, a situation that would not be particularly upsetting were it not that practically everybody considers question asking on the part of teachers and children one of the most crucial means of maintaining interest, supporting curiosity, acquiring knowledge, and facilitating change and growth.

In Chapter 4, where we used the new math to illustrate the modal process of introducing change into the school culture, we emphasized the point that the curriculum reformers seemed quite aware that they wanted to do more than merely change textbooks; they realized that classrooms tended to be uninviting and uninspired places in which teachers were active and children passive. Their intended outcome was to change, among other

---

[2] Children are the one group who realistically estimate or know the behavioral regularity. My informal poll of scores of children leaves no doubt in my mind that they view the classroom as a place where teachers ask questions and children provide answers.

things, behavioral regularities such as the one we are here discussing. But this intended outcome was never systematically discussed (or even written about) or stated as a criterion by which the new curriculum was to be judged. Certainly the teachers who underwent retraining could not focus on this issue, if only because they were in the same passive role that characterized, and would continue to characterize, their own students.

For our purposes here the generalization that requires emphasis is that *any change in a programmatic regularity has as one of its intended outcomes some kind of change in existing behavioral regularities, and these behavioral regularities are among the most important criteria for judging the degree to which intended outcomes are being achieved.* At this point I am not interested in whether or not one likes or agrees with the programmatic change but rather in the fact that these changes require changes in some kind or kinds of behavioral regularities. It is almost always true that changes in the behavioral regularities will be assumed to be effected or mediated by internal emotional and cognitive processes and states, but the behavioral regularities remain as our most secure, albeit not infallible, criterion for judging what we have achieved. In fact (and the question-asking regularity is a good example), behavioral regularities are probably our best means for inferring internal cognitive and emotional states.

It is the rare observer of classrooms who has not inferred from the overt behavior of children and teachers that the great majority of children seem "inside" to be neither strongly interested in, curious about, nor feeling satisfaction in regard to what they are doing or what is going on. They are, in short, not having a particularly good time. But, someone can say, this is an inference, and it may frequently be a wrong one, which of course, is true. To what behavioral regularities can we look that could serve as a kind of check on these inferences?

One of them, of course, requires asking children to respond to relevant questions about what they are feeling, but this will be regarded as either too obvious or naive because of the frequently held assumption that what people, particularly children, report about what they feel should not be given much weight. But what if we were to look at the behavior of children in the hall *immediately* after they leave one classroom to go to another, as is the case in junior and senior high? How does one account for the noise level, the animated talking, running, and formation of groups, and the absence of talk about the intellectual substance of what they had just experienced? *Why is it that one of the most trouble-producing (from the standpoint of school personnel) times in the school day is when students are in the halls going from one room to another?* When the behavioral regularities in the hall are ascertained, I have no doubt that they will be found to be related to regularities in the classroom in a way that confirms inferences made about the internal states of children in the classroom.

But we cannot understand the question-asking regularity without briefly trying to understand what aspects of the school culture contribute to a state of affairs that few, if anyone, feel is the way things should be.

1. *Teachers tend to teach the way in which they themselves were taught.* I am not only referring to the public schooling of teachers but to their college experiences as well—and I am not restricting myself to schools of education. In general, the question-asking regularity we have described does not, in my experience, differ markedly from what goes on in college classrooms. The culture of the school should be expected to reflect aspects of other types of educational cultures from which the teachers have come. As suggested in Chapter 3, the university critic of the public schools frequently is unable to see that his criticisms may well be true of his own educational culture. It would indeed be strange if teachers did not teach the way they had been taught.

2. *In their professional training (courses, practice teaching) teachers are minimally exposed to theories about question-asking and the technical problems of question-asking and question-producing behavior—the relationship between theory and practice.* To the reader who may be surprised at this, I would suggest he consult the most frequently used books in educational psychology, learning, or child development courses. Such a reader may conclude either that it is not an important question or that the obvious is being overlooked.[3]

3. *Whatever educational help or consultation is available to the teacher (principal, supervisors, workshops, etc.) does not concern itself directly with the question-asking regularity.* Particularly in the earliest months and years of teaching the primary concern of everyone is "law and order," and the possibility that discipline may be related to, or can be affected by, the question-asking regularity is rarely recognized. The anxiety of the beginning teacher about maintaining discipline too frequently interferes with his sensitivity to, and desire to accommodate to, the questions and interests of his pupils.

4. *The predetermined curriculum that suggests that teachers cover a certain amount of material within certain time intervals with the expectation that their pupils as a group will perform at certain levels at certain times is responded to by teachers in a way as to make for the fantastic discrepancy between the rate of teacher and student questions.* This factor

---

[3] How the obvious can be overlooked can be illustrated (Sarason, Blatt, Davidson, 1962), by looking at a function that all teachers perform, are expected to perform, and must perform—talking to parents. Yet, I know of no teacher-training program (some may exist) that gives the prospective teacher five minutes of training in this function, a situation that can be justified only by assuming that God singled out teachers to have the special gift of how to talk to parents meaningfully and productively. Reality, as we shall see later, does not support this assumption.

touches on a very complicated state of affairs. From the standpoint of the teacher the curriculum is not a suggestion but a requirement, for if it is not met the principal and supervisors will consider the teaching inadequate. In addition, the teacher whom the pupils will have in the next year will consider them inadequately prepared. Therefore, the best and safest thing to do is to insure that the curriculum is covered, a view that reinforces the tendency to ask many "straight recall" questions.

From the administrator's standpoint the curriculum is only a guide, and the trouble arises because teachers are not "creative"; that is, the problem is not the curriculum but the teacher. As many administrative personnel have said, "We *tell* them to be creative but they still stick slavishly to the curriculum as if it were a bible." To which teachers reply, "What they want to know at the end of the year, and what I will be judged by, are the achievement test scores of my children."

Although both sides *correctly* perceive each other's behavioral regularity, the administrator feels unable to change the state of affairs—that is, he is of no help to the teacher—and the teacher continues to feel unfree to depart from the curriculum. In short, we are back to a familiar situation in which no one sees the universe of alternatives to current practices.

There are, of course, alternatives. For example, as Susskind's studies show, there is variation among teachers in the question-asking regularity; some teachers can utilize a curriculum without being a question-asking machine and without requiring pupils to respond primarily to "straight recall" questions. In addition, and a source of encouragement, Susskind obtained data suggesting that when a group of teachers were confronted with the question-asking regularities in their classroom, and this was discussed in terms of theory and intended outcomes, the teachers as a group were able to change the regularity. *But here one runs smack into the obstacle of another characteristic of the school culture: there are no vehicles of discussion, communication, or observation that allow for this kind of variation to be raised and productively used for purposes of help and change.* Faculty meetings, as teachers are acutely aware, are not noted for either their intellectual content or their sensitivity to issues that may be controversial or interpersonally conflictful. (As our man from outer space could well have discerned, the classroom, the PTA meeting, and the faculty meeting, are amazingly similar in the question-asking regularity.) We shall have more to say on these issues in Chapter 8.

For our purposes here what is most important is not the particular behavioral regularity or the factors that may account for it, but the obvious fact that within the school culture these regularities, which are in the nature of intended outcomes, are not recognized, and it is not traditional to have means for their recognition. What is not recognized or verbalized cannot be dealt with, and if it is important and not recognized, efforts to introduce substantive change, particularly in the classroom, result in the illusion of change. . . .

As I indicated earlier, discerning and examining regularities in relation to intended outcomes frequently lead one to questions, issues, or other observations that illuminate important aspects of the school culture. For example, in the process of doing this study—spending time in the elementary and junior high schools, talking to teachers, principals, and other administrative personnel—we became increasingly aware that junior high personnel view the new student in September rather differently than elementary school personnel did in the previous June. Whereas in June the elementary school viewed him as a *child*, in September the junior high viewed him as a *young adult*. These different views result in different expectations and are an important aspect of the discontinuity between the structure and organization of the two settings. I am, of course, suggesting that meeting these different expectations is frequently difficult for some children, even for many who manifested no problems in elementary school. (Anyone who has any knowledge of, or experience with, college freshmen will not be surprised by this explanation.)

There is another aspect to this problem that is illuminating of the school culture: *the differences in the ways in which pupils are viewed by elementary and junior high personnel are reflections of the differences in the ways in which these personnel view each other.* Many (by no means all) junior high school teachers view themselves as "specialists" in a particular subject matter, while they view the elementary school teacher as a somewhat superficial generalist—much like the differences between the general practitioner and specialist in medicine. Put in another way, the junior high teacher tends to view himself as "higher" and, therefore, better than the elementary school teacher.[4] Although less true today than in previous decades, there is still a tendency for junior and senior high personnel to receive higher salaries than those in the elementary schools. The fact that there are far more men teachers in the junior high school than in the elementary school is undoubtedly a reflection of the view that the elementary school pupil is a child (taken care of by child-care kinds of teachers) while the junior high school pupil (who two months before was in elementary school) is a beginning young adult. These differences in views and expectations sharpen the discontinuities between the two settings.

---

[4] This is, of course, identical to the situation in universities where those who teach only graduate courses tend to view themselves as doing a more important, more worthy, or more difficult task than the instructor who only teaches undergraduates. In the public schools, as well as the universities, it is as if the worth of a teacher is determined in part by the age of his students.

But why should social studies (in these two junior high schools, at least) be so difficult in the first year? We looked into the curriculum manual and guide (a heavy and imposing document of two hundred or more pages), talked to teachers, and sat in classrooms. I do not pretend to know and understand all the factors that would comprise an answer, but I can point to two related factors that seemed important. The first of these factors is that the student was frequently required to engage in projects for which he had to read in different sources, use the library (school and community), and organize readings and materials. Many of the pupils were simply not able to take on this kind of independent responsibility. The task was not made easier by the fact that the degree and content of direction given by the teacher seemed to assume an amount of previous experience with such a task that struck us as unrealistic.

Two years after the above observations I conducted a college senior seminar for the first time in my teaching life. Up to that time I had only taught graduate students. My attitude had been that parents who sent their sons to Yale had a right to expect that they would be given an excellent education, but it did not follow that I had to participate in that education. (Elementary school pupils = undergraduates; junior high school pupils = graduate students.) Midway through the seminar I was aware that I was frustrated and annoyed. Why do *they* know so little? Why is it that when I assign a paper, with a brief but commendably clear explanation of its purpose and scope, I get a barrage of questions (during and after class, in person and on the phone) about what I mean and want? Why are they so dependent and fearful of exercising independent judgment? Where have they been for three years? Who was spoon feeding them? The principle underlying these thoughts of a teacher is quite similar to that enunciated by Professor Higgins in *My Fair Lady* when he compares men and women and concludes "We are a marvelous sex!"

The second factor I can point to in regard to the social studies finding is that the pupils were required *to organize and write* papers and many of them clearly were inadequate to the task—and I must remind the reader that this population was discernibly above average in ability. This raised questions: In the last year (sixth grade) of elementary school how many times were pupils required to write a paper? How many times did a teacher sit down with a child and go over what he had written? My informal polling indicated that some teachers required as few as two "papers" and some required more than four.[5] Although I polled far more children than

---

[5] When my daughter was in the sixth grade in an elementary school (in an adjacent community) that had the best reputation of any school in our metropolitan area, she was required to write only *one* paper.

teachers, I did not hear of a single instance in which a teacher had sat down with a child to go over what he had written. When papers were returned to the children there were usually comments, pro and con, written on them, but the matter ended there.

At this point in our discussion it is not relevant to go into explanations of this state of affairs or to explore the universe of alternatives. I have used social studies for the purpose of illustrating how one regularity (i.e., interims)* leads one to another regularity (i.e., social studies), the examination of which can be extremely productive towards one's understanding of aspects of the school culture.[6]

The purposes of this chapter were to state and illustrate the following:

1. There are regularities of various kinds.

2. Existing programmatic and behavioral regularities should be described independent of one's own values or opinions.

3. Regularities exist because they are supposed to have intended outcomes.

4. There are at least two characteristics to intended outcomes: (1) aspects of them are discernible in overt behavior or interactions, and (2) they are justified by statements of value (i.e., what is good and what is bad).

5. There are frequent discrepancies between regularities and intended outcomes. Usually, no regularity is built into the school culture to facilitate the recognition of such discrepancies.

6. The significance of any regularity, particularly of the programmatic type, cannot be adequately comprehended apart from the universe of "regularity alternatives" of which the existing regularity is but one item. The failure to consider or recognize a universe of alternatives is one obstacle to change occurring from within the culture, and makes it likely that recognition of this universe of alternatives will await events and forces outside the culture.

7. Any attempt to introduce an important change in the school culture requires changing existing regularities to produce new intended outcomes. In practice, the regularities tend not to be changed and the intended out-

---

* Editor's note: An "interim" in the school system studied was a warning sent home that the student was doing failing work, or work significantly below expectations.

[6] The reader will recall that we and school personnel were surprised that mathematics did not produce the largest number of interims. One reason for this may be that mathematics teachers *expect* children to have difficulty and, therefore, either they proceed more slowly or they are more lenient in their grading and evaluations. I present this possible explanation in order to make the point that our understanding of the school culture requires that we try to understand why an expected regularity (or pattern of regularity) does not occur.

comes, therefore, cannot occur; that is, the more things change the more they remain the same.

8. It is probably true that the most important attempts to introduce change into the school culture *require* changing existing teacher-child regularities. When one examines the natural history of the change process it is precisely these regularities that remain untouched. . . .

THE PROCESS OF SCHOOLING

J. M. Stephens

Some years ago Wilson (1958) compared the achievement of grade-three pupils in two different cities. The schools in these two cities did not differ in the amount of time devoted to reading, spelling, or arithmetic. The pupils examined, moreover, were of comparable general ability. In administrative "advantages," however, the two cities differed markedly. In one city, all children had had the benefits of kindergarten education. In this city, the classes were also kept down to an average of thirty pupils each, and all teachers had received four years of training. In the other city, in contrast, none of the children had been to kindergarten, the classes averaged thirty-eight pupils, and the teachers had received only two years of training. When the pupils were compared on tests of arithmetic, spelling, and reading, there was no advantage whatever for the city with superior facilities. And differences that did appear regularly favored the city with larger classes, with the shorter period of teacher training, and with no kindergarten.

Wilson's study brings together a number of paradoxical results. But such results are by no means novel. For many years, as a matter of fact, scholars have noted a vast preponderance of such negative results. Within educational circles, this preponderance has been treated as a matter of common knowledge, calling for no documentation. A quarter of a century ago, for instance, Peters and Van Voorhis (1940, p. 476) state quite simply that the vast majority of educational experiments reveal differences which are not statistically significant. Almost two decades later, Nachman and Opochinsky (1958) make a similar comment and feel no need to supply evidence to support their remarks.

To say that many scholars comment on the impressive trend of negative results is not to say that the commentators necessarily accept this trend at its face value. More often than not, the commentator merely notes the trend and then goes on to show why it is misleading.

But no matter whether this trend of negative results will be viewed as common knowledge or as a surprising revelation, it should be brought together and given some documentary warrant. A complete documentation, as it happens, would be extremely unwieldy. The relevant studies run into the thousands, and, even then, no one could be sure of complete coverage. To keep the documentation within workable limits, I rely, wherever possible, on the conclusions of those who have summarized a number of investigations. When the summaries are very old, individual studies of more recent date are also added. The first summary to be reported is an ancient compilation of my own. The others, being put together by quite a variety of people, should be less contaminated by the specific biases or preconceived notions that I may bring to the task.

General Summaries

The early summary by the present writer (Stephens, 1933) included some two hundred investigations dealing with a variety of administrative factors. This survey reported only a slight relation between attendance and achievement. School cost and achievement were also unrelated when measurements were based on comparable pupils. In many investigations, but not all, size of school had little, if any, influence on attainment. Over two score investigations were unanimous in finding that pupils in large classes learned as much as their colleagues in small classes. A few investigations suggested that students who were prepared in "accredited" high schools got along no better in college than comparable students who were prepared in high schools which did not meet the accreditation standards. A sampling of the many experiments on methods of teaching revealed very little advantage for any one method. The methods which stressed visual aids or individual instruction seemed to have a slight but irregular advantage. Between the other methods, however, there was little to choose. One method was about as good as the other and no better.

A survey by Harris (1940), based on college performance, confirms the trend reported in 1933. Harris reports that attendance at a large high school or at an "accredited" high school is no dependable passport to success in college, and class size is immaterial. Harris failed to find any clear-cut advantages for any of the following procedures: sectioning students according to ability in language classes; giving weekly quizzes to motivate learning; replacing one class period by a program of independent reading; or substituting discussion or other methods of instruction for the lecture method.

During the early 1940s, Eaton and his associates (Eaton, 1942, 1944; Smith and Eaton, 1945) studied the general trends in achievement-test results of Indiana schools. These were based on mass tabulations involving 10,000 or 15,000 pupils and hundreds of schools. The results consist of raw trends with no attempt to hold any other factors constant when the influence of one factor is being considered.

According to these studies, achievement seemed to be unaffected by size of class, size of school, amount of time given to instruction, or by the administrative organization of the schools. In some of the reports, the length of the school year appeared to be related to achievement, but in other reports it was not.

Later general reviews of research on administrative factors (Ellis, 1960; Hatch and Bennet, 1960; Herrick, 1960) similarly report failure of such research to show a definite advantage for any one approach over another.

Summaries of Studies on Specific Administrative Factors

In presenting the conclusions based on the many summaries that are available, we include an occasional interpretative comment when it seems especially in order. For the most part, however, the interpretations are deferred to a later section.

Attendance

Summarizing the bulk of the evidence on attendance, accumulated during the first half of the century, Heck (1950) reports as follows: "While research at the moment is not conclusive, what there is tends to refute the too common assumption that absence results in a harmful effect upon scholarship as expressed by marks" (p. 920).

This conclusion clearly agrees with earlier summaries (Finch and Nemzek, 1940). When intelligence is held constant, the correlation between attendance and achievement clusters between .10 and .20, with occasional correlations reaching a value of .30.

Television

To what extent does the pupil's achievement come from the detailed, managed interaction between pupil and teacher? Does achievement fall off if the teacher becomes less able to adjust his deliberate efforts to each pupil's mastery of the subject?

The teacher on the television screen is completely oblivious to the status of each student in the subject being taught. Nor can this mechanical teacher modify his efforts to suit the varying needs of the pupil. Yet, from some hundreds of experiments (Schramm, 1962), we can detect no clear difference between the results achieved by instructional television and those from other procedures. Of the 393 investigations, 255 reported no significant difference. Of the remainder, 83 favored television, and 55 showed an advantage for the regular classroom. A later summary by Barrington (1965) covered some 30 investigations and revealed the same equivalence for television and classroom instruction. Schramm suggests that for the young children there is a slight benefit from instruction by television, and for college students there might be a slight handicap. But in no case can the difference be large, even if it exists at all.

In these experiments, of course, there are several factors at work. The television instructor can go to great trouble to prepare his lesson and can use close-up views and other materials not ordinarily available to the regular instructor. Perhaps these advantages cancel out the handicap arising from lack of individual attention.

But the solution cannot rest entirely in these additional facets that television can bring to instruction. Even when students listen to nothing more than a tape recording of a lecture, their achievement is no less than that of students listening to the lecture itself (Popham, 1962).

Independent Study and Correspondence Courses

In an early review of the efficacy of correspondence study at the college level, Bittner and Mallory (1933) found correspondence students somewhat ahead of students in the classroom. In a later review, Childs (1952) extends this same conclusion to secondary school pupils. Childs based this conclusion on eight separate experiments. Not all the reports favor the correspondence students, but the trend is clearly in that direction. The difference is very slight in any case and certainly cannot be interpreted as showing any definite advantage for the students in the classroom. The conclusions from these earlier reviews are borne out by isolated, later investigations (Child, 1954; Dysinger and Bridgman, 1957; Parsons, 1957).

Correspondence-school students are formally committed to a course of instruction but lack some features of the typical pupil-teacher interaction. In the same way, students taking a course by independent study are formally committed to a course but lack the classroom contact. When such independent study is elected on a voluntary basis, the students working on their own do just as well as those electing class attendance (Jensen, 1954; Milton, 1962).

With such self-selection of work, of course, it is always possible that it is the serious and motivated student who prefers independent work. This greater motivation, or interest, or seriousness of purpose, by the way, could also account for the fact that people lacking formal high school training frequently equal the typical high school students in college performance (Bent, 1946) or in performance on an objective test of General Educational Development (Leton, 1957).

In one investigation (Marr and others, 1960) the possibility of self-selection was eliminated. In this experiment students were arbitrarily assigned to one procedure or the other, and those assigned to receive one lecture per week excelled those not receiving the lecture. It would seem, then, that when interest and determination are held constant, class attendance will provide some additional help.

Size of Class

When teaching a small class, a teacher clearly comes to know more about the individual pupils in his charge (McKenna, 1957). But do pupils learn more from this increased attention on the part of the teacher? As indicated in earlier statements, this problem has been investigated as frequently as any in the entire educational literature (Fleming, 1959; Kidd, 1952; Powell, 1964). From several scores of investigations, the consensus is overwhelming. At all levels above the first few grades and in almost all subjects, the size of the class seems completely unrelated to the achievement of the pupils. If there is any advantage, it is in favor of large classes. Recent separate studies (De Cecco, 1964; Marklund, 1963; Eash and Bennett, 1964) confirm this historical consensus. Marklund, for instance, made some 281 separate, but not wholly independent, comparisons and found that 37 comparisons favored the large classes, and 22 favored the smaller class, whereas 222 showed no significant difference. Even in a subject such as fundamentals of speech, where one would ordinarily expect an advantage for smaller classes, there appears to be no loss when some of the instruction is given by mass lecture (Giffin and Bowers, 1962).

Against this overwhelming mass of negative results, some exceptions are to be noted. Powell (1964) mentions three studies, from the scores conducted, that seem to find an advantage for smaller classes. It is true, moreover, that students tend to prefer smaller classes (De Cecco, 1964). There are isolated reports that college students may give an instructor a more favorable rating when they encounter him in a small class (Powell, 1964). But this is by no means the prevailing trend of the most substantial investigations (Riley and others, 1950).

Individual consultations.   From earlier reports there was some evidence (reviewed by Hoehn and Saltz, 1956) that performance improves when each student is interviewed at length (thirty to sixty minutes) by a trained psychologist with a clinical bent. In their own investigation, Hoehn and Saltz arranged for individual conferences between students and instructors. The latter were not psychologists but regular classroom teachers who were given a brief orientation on how to interview. From a variety of approaches and from various amounts of interviewing, the investigators could find no difference in the performance of students interviewed and those not interviewed.

The consultations discussed so far have been one-shot affairs. As an extension of this sort of consultation, there is the tutorial system in which the student meets regularly with his instructor for discussion and guided reading. The results of the investigations in this area are in conflict. One early investigation (Greene, 1934) reported that such guided reading produced results superior to either a straight lecture course or a program of independent study. In a study conducted about the same time, Hartmann (1935) arranged that half the students should attend class three hours per week, whereas the other half should attend twice a week and spend the third hour in individual consultation with the instructor. The latter students fell behind the others. A later study (McKeachie and others, 1960) also found that students relying on extensive tutorial help fell behind those assigned to a conventional class.

Counseling

Students doing poorly in classwork are often referred to a specialized counselor for intensive help. The early investigations made use of students voluntarily seeking such help and, for this reason, it was difficult to eliminate the factor of motivation. Later investigators, however, have typically made sure that the counseling is applied to a random sample drawn from a pool of volunteers. In reviewing four such studies, Callis (1963) reports that two of them found no difference in the achievement of the counseled and uncounseled students. One reported an advantage for the counseled students, and one reported mixed results. Of two well controlled studies appearing too late for Callis' review, one (Shouksmith and Taylor, 1964) found an advantage for the counseled students, and one (Winborn and Schmidt, 1962) found that the students not counseled made a superior gain.

Instead of receiving individual counseling, students may be assigned to classes in "how to study." Here again, the evidence varies, but by and large such courses seem to help in student achievement (Entwisle, 1960).

Deliberate Intent to Influence

In a direct attempt to manipulate the intensity of the teacher's efforts, Tilton (1947) first selected thirty-seven pupils out of the total enrollment in six fourth-grade classes. He then asked the six teachers involved to concentrate especially on the three or four students selected by the experimenter from that teacher's class. The teacher was asked specifically to try to increase the performance of these pupils in arithmetic. The net effect was zero. Of the thirty-seven pupils selected, ten did show more gain than the pupils not selected. But some fell below the average gain, and the overall performance of the selected pupils was on a par with those not selected.

What happens when we try to increase the intensity of the educational forces by enlisting the aid of the home? From a group of high school students doing poorly in school (Schoenhard, 1958), some 158 were assigned to a home-visitation group, and 158 comparable students served as a control. Teachers visited the homes of the selected students and arranged for a series of follow-ups by telephone, letters, and consultations with students. In each of four grades, the two groups were compared at the end of four different intervals. Of these sixteen comparisons, ten favored the control, and six favored the home-visitation group. Only four of the differences were significant, however, and of these, two favored the home-visitation, and two favored the control.

Increasing the Student's Involvement

Along with our attempts to increase the amount of contact between teacher and pupil, we could employ devices to increase the student's application to his task. We could get him to become more involved in his subject, to study longer or harder or to avoid distractions.

Students learning by television may be tempted to adopt an extremely passive attitude and may be inclined to act as mere spectators. To overcome the possible disadvantages of this attitude, one group of investigators (Jacobs and others, 1963) encouraged the pupils in some fifteen fifth-grade classes to take an extremely active part. The students were asked direct questions about the television program. They were also urged to make written responses and to bring in illustrative material. These pupils achieved no more than comparable students not so stimulated. To a greater extent than the controls, the stimulated pupils came to dislike television instruction.

In contrast to these results, Gropper and Lumsdaine (1962) found superior performance on the part of students making active responses, provided the lesson itself was carefully programmed. When the responses were made to a regular unprogrammed lesson, no such advantage appeared.

Amount of Time Spent in Study

In an early summary, Strang (1937) reported six investigations showing almost no correlation between achievement and time spent in study. Here we face the possibility that dull students may study more and achieve less, and this factor might mask the advantage of increased study. This earlier summary is borne out by a more recent study at the college level (Jex and Merril, 1959). In contrast to these results, however, Ryans (1939) had found correlations of .20 to .40 between achievement on a brief assignment and time spent in study for that particular assignment.

Distraction

In general the influence of apparent distractions is almost negligible. College students earning money learn about as much as those not so distracted (Newman and Mooney, 1940; Trueblood, 1957). College students perform just as well when they engage freely in extracurricular activity as when these activities are curtailed (Brandbaugh and Maddox, 1936; Remmers, 1940). Younger pupils spending much time with television or radio do about as well in school as those of comparable intelligence who give little time to such entertainment (Heisler, 1948; Ricciuti, 1951; Thompson, 1964).

Size of School

In many general discussions, the small high school has been rather sweepingly condemned and its abolition recommended. Along with the general discussion there have been many investigations designed chiefly to see if a student's success in college is in any way affected by the size of the high school from which he comes. Although the research has received less publicity than the general discussions, a substantial body of data has been available for some time. In one of the pioneer compilations, Douglass (1931) summarized seven earlier studies and reported on one of his own. He concluded as follows: "In spite of the fact that all studies seem to show that in the smaller high schools will be found less experienced, more poorly trained, more poorly paid, and more heavily loaded teachers, inferior housing and equipment, more restricted curricular offerings, less well developed programs of guidance and counseling and other less desirable conditions, graduates of small schools should not be discriminated against as applicants for college entrance. Their achievement in college is in no material degree inferior to that of graduates from larger schools" (p. 57).

Some eighteen years later Garrett (1949) summarized another six studies and in these found no evidence for a relation between high school size and college achievement.

Ten years after Garrett's summary, Hoyt (1959) extended the summary to seventeen investigations and added one of his own. Of the seventeen earlier studies, five found no advantage for either large or small schools. The advantage lay with the large schools in six studies, with the smaller schools in three, and with medium sized schools in three. Hoyt's own study reported no significant difference in achievement between schools of different sizes.

The studies reported in these reviews vary in the extent to which they have controlled such factors as intelligence and home background. Most of them have made some efforts in this direction. Off hand, one would expect that failure to control such factors should lead to a spurious positive relation, since, by and large, background factors tend to be more favorable in the larger communities in which the larger schools are more likely to be found. In one recent study, (Street and others, 1962) we do find a positive relation between school size and attainment when intelligence and background factors are not taken into account. Conversely, Lathrop (1960), arranging for a meticulous control of both intelligence and type of high school program followed, found no relation between size of high school and college success. Studies attempting to control both intelligence and broad social background report mixed results. Kemp (1955) earlier noted an effect from school size, but Wiseman (1964) failed to duplicate this result.

In this discussion, of course, the emphasis has been upon academic achievement. The development of the "whole child" may be another matter, and in this area Barker and Gump (1964) suggest many advantages for the small high school.

Selection and Training of Teachers

Among the scores of studies dealing with teacher effectiveness, there are quite a few that try to relate the characteristics of the teacher to the achievement of the pupils being taught. To an overwhelming extent the results are negative. True, there is some suggestion that experience helps for a few years, but after those early years the older teacher is less effective (Ryans, 1960). In contrast to this suggestion of positive results, however, we find almost no relation between the academic gains of pupils and the qualities of the teacher that can be observed by principals or supervisors. Medley and Mitzel (1963), for instance, cite results from eight specific studies and refer in general terms to many others. They conclude that, "a reading of these studies reveals uniformly negative results" (p. 257).

Easing the Teacher's Load

Before the days of the modern ungraded classroom, the presence of two classes in a single room was considered an evil. Clearly such a mixed assignment seemed to impose more of a burden on the teacher and seemed to dilute the attention the teacher could give to any one class. The studies, however, have shown no harmful effect (Adams, 1953; Knight, 1938; Stephens and Lichtenstein, 1947). These studies were conducted before the ungraded school had been advocated. It is too soon to give any confident assessment of the ungraded school itself, but there is some evidence (Hopkins and others, 1965) that it is about as effective as the traditional procedures, but no better.

Offhand, one would suspect that team teaching would reduce the load for any given teacher. This is also a relatively recent innovation (Shaplia and Olds, 1964), and it is too soon to judge its effectiveness. The studies (Ginther and Shrayer, 1962; White, 1964; Zweibelson and others, 1965) emerging so far, however, suggest little, if any, consistent difference between the effectiveness of team teaching and the more traditional approaches. Lambert and his associates (1965) found team teaching to be somewhat less effective. In the Zweibelson report (1965), however, we find a favorable student attitude toward team teaching.

Ability Grouping

Homogeneous grouping should also permit the teacher to concentrate his efforts on a narrower range of problems Ekstrom (1961) reviewed some thirty investigations on the effectiveness of homogeneous grouping. She found no identifiable advantage or disadvantage for the procedure. In a later review, Pattinson (1963) reported a similar lack of difference. An extensive series of experiments from Stockholm (Marklund, 1963; Svensson, 1962) and one from Utah (Borg 1965) confirm this suggestion of comparable attainment under heterogeneous and homogeneous grouping.

Differences in Policy or General Approach

The violent argument about progressivism in the schools (Cremin, 1961) led to a variety of predictions and claims. On the one hand, we find "the critics" holding that progressivism would soon spell disaster for the schools, if it had not already done so. On the other hand, we note the innovators themselves suggesting that marked advantages should follow from the new approaches. Inevitably this has led to a flood of "then and now" studies in which the achievement of pupils at any one time is compared with performance in the schools of more recent date (Boss, 1940a, 1940b; Caldwell and Courtis, 1924; Gerberich, 1952; Gray, 1952; Harding, 1951; Leonard and Eurich, 1942; Muir, 1961; Wrightstone, 1951).

The many studies reported in these treatments vary tremendously in scope, in care, and certainly in outcome. The most frequent claim of the more comprehensive reviews is that of insignificant, or inconsequential, or inconsistent differences. A slight advantage for the older schools in one study seems promptly offset by an equally slight advantage for the modern schools appearing in another study. The great claim of the proponents of modern education is the progressive school *has held its own* in the matter of the three R's, and it has done this in spite of its concentration an a wider, real-life curriculum.

The outstanding result of the famous eight-year study (Chamberlin and others, 1942) is the rough academic equivalence of pupils from traditional and from progressive schools. In a careful analysis of this classical study and of ten other studies dealing with the same problem, Wallen and Travers (1963) report as follows: "In summary, the findings indicate no important differences in terms of subject matter mastery and a superiority of the progressive students in terms of the characteristics which the 'progressive school' seeks to develop" (p. 474). Here again, we find that there is at least no academic loss to be incurred when some of the school's attention is directed to real-life concerns.

The excitement and hopes once associated with the progressive movement have now been transferred to the new curriculums, especially to those in science and mathematics. So far we have only spotty evidence about the effectiveness of these innovations on which so much effort has been expended. The trends, however, both from the occasional summary (Brown and Abel, 1966; Burns and Dessart, 1966) and from isolated studies (Rainey, 1964; Lisonbee and Fullerton, 1964), again foreshadow the ancient refrain of no significant differences. Here again we detect the same bright spot: The new procedures result in no loss to the traditional material and may also induce some growth in topics not touched by the traditional curriculum.

Discussion versus Lecture

To many people it seems obvious that the discussion method should surpass the lecture. Yet summary after summary (see Stovall, 1958) can find no warrant for the assumption. Citing some sixteen studies, Wallen and Travers (1963) comment as follows: "With respect to immediate mastery of factual information, most studies find no significant differences between lecture and discussion methods" (p. 481). Along with this preponderance of negative results, they report four studies showing an advantage for the lecture and one favoring the discussion method. The matter of retention, as opposed to immediate mastery, has been investigated less frequently. Two studies of retention favor the discussion method, and one favors the lecture method.

McKeachie (1963), in a review of college teaching, also stresses the rough equivalence of lecture methods and discussion methods in inducing knowledge of subject matter. McKeachie does point out, however, that courses using a problem-solving, discussion approach may excel the lecture courses in producing skill in problem solving. The trends developed by these recent summaries are in line with those appearing earlier (Stovall, 1958).

Group-Centered versus Teacher-Centered

A discussion method need not be group centered, although many discussions do emphasize the goals and purposes of the class. The effect of this group-centered approach has been treated in a number of summaries (Anderson, 1959; Sears and Hilgard, 1964; Stern, 1963). Here again we find practically no differences in achievement. There may be a slight preponderance in favor of the teacher-centered methods, but the difference is very slight and by no means consistent.

Use of Frequent Quizzes

At the college level, students receiving frequent quizzes during the term learn about as much as those receiving only one midterm quiz, but they learn no more. This equivalence appeared in Noll's (1939) early summary of investigations and is borne out by recent isolated studies (Selakovitch, 1962; Standlee and Popham, 1960).

Programmed Instruction

It is too soon to sum up the evidence on programmed instruction. In the flood of reports (Lumsdaine, 1964) now appearing, however, there is much to suggest that this device is about on a par with other methods of individual study (Poppleton and Austwick, 1964; Owen and others, 1965). It may permit an average saving of time over straight classroom approaches, but its overall superiority to classroom teaching is by no means apparent (Feldhusen, 1963; Feldman, 1965).

Interpreting the Negative Results

Almost anyone familiar with the general literature will admit the vast number of negative results in the data from experiments. Not everyone, however, will agree on the interpretations. A great many rival hypotheses have been advanced, many of them suggesting that we should not take these results at their face value.

One Narrow Segment of Achievement

As one *ad hoc* explanation of negative results, it is pointed out that the experiments test only one narrow segment of achievement, namely those academic aspects of growth which are easy to test. The argument goes on to say that great changes in other aspects of achievement, especially in personality or character, might be discerned if these were tested.

Insensitivity

A second argument contends that our tests are not only too narrow in their scope, but they are relatively insensitive even in the area in which they do function. This argument implies that more sensitive measures might detect considerable growth which now escapes observation.

Poorly controlled investigations.   In the flood of investigations lying behind the various summaries, we will find much variation in rigor and in scientific care. Many of the investigations clearly failed to control factors that could have affected the results.

Overcontrolled investigations.   A fourth explanation attributes the lack of positive results not to lack of control but to "overcontrol." The educational investigator, in his zeal to become superscientific, has been held to control the investigation "to death," so to speak. In his effort to make sure that extraneous factors are held constant, he has held the whole growth process constant. It is often suggested, for instance, that the control of intelligence automatically restricts the differences that might be expected to appear in such a closely related thing as academic achievement. Consequently, it may often happen that a given pedagogical technique is really very superior, but it does not have enough freedom of movement to show itself.

Tests of significance.   Peters and Van Voorhis (1940) contend that, in judging whether or not significant positive results exist, we have used a criterion that is much too strict. Often we have refused to admit that a difference is significant unless we can be guaranteed odds of 1 to 100 or 3 to 1000. In the face of a handicap such as this, it is no wonder that many results have been negative. It is a wonder that any have ever been positive.

There is much force in these arguments which seek to explain negative results as error or artifact. Each of the arguments briefly mentioned may turn out to have a considerable amount of truth. It is true that tests of wider aspects of growth may show the results of pedagogical innovations even when no difference appears in the narrower field of scholastic growth. It is true that more sensitive instruments may show marked differences where our present instruments draw a blank. It is true, also, that due to the many possibilities of subtle interaction, the restriction of any extraneous factor may also result in the restriction of the factor under observation. And it is true that we have held our experiments to most exacting standards.

But for all their claims to plausibility as partial explanations, we should not push these arguments too far. It is always possible that the vast number of investigations have "just happened" to hit on the more intransigent areas of growth. It is also possible that they have just happened to miss the areas which would have shown the effects of the device being tested. But these possibilities are not very comforting. The argument implies that some systematic force has been at work to keep our sample a biased sample. The argument rests on the assumption that the unmeasured areas of character growth are more responsive to the devices being tested than the more measurable areas of academic achievement. Actually that assumption is very dubious, a point which will be developed at some length in Chapter 9.

The other four arguments are all confronted by one very serious obstacle. The fact is, insensitive as the tests may be and overcontrolled or under-controlled as some experiments probably are and exacting as the standards undoubtedly are, a great deal of growth does appear and does meet the standards. The investigations cited do not fail to reveal growth. They merely fail to reveal differences in growth attributable to the administra-tive variables. If we use other variables, such as background factors, moreover, marked differences in growth also come through. If the tests, and the designs, and the criteria of significance permit such differences to appear, it is difficult to see why they should not also permit differences in administrative factors to come through if these were present.

Inadequate Engagement of Basic Principles

In a more general explanation Wallen and Travers (1963) remind us that there are many forces (principles) at work to produce classroom achievement. These, they point out, have been imperfectly known. The experimenter, in groping in the dark, may so arrange his investigation that it happens to invoke one of these principles but fails to deal with the others. Even worse, a single innovation may engage one force so as to facilitate growth but may inadvertently act on another unknown force so as to inhibit growth.

Expectations from the Spontaneous Theory

The view put forward here is not unlike the suggestion of Wallen and Travers, with the exception that the spontaneous theory is intended pri-marily to explain what the school actually accomplishes. In providing a single, coherent theory to explain these positive accomplishments, we find the same theory automatically explains the flood of negative results as well. In considering the negative results, we merely have to remember the many forces that are at work to induce growth in almost any school situation. We should also remember that, in the typical comparison of two administrative devices, we have two groups which are comparable in the forces responsible for (say) 95 percent of the growth to be had and which differ only in the force that, at best, can affect only a small fraction of the growth.

The forces common to any two approaches are to be found both in the background factors and in the spontaneous tendencies that are always at work whenever the teacher is in the classroom. Suppose, for instance, that we are comparing two methods of teaching spelling to children in grade four. Through the forces of maturation, both groups are increasing in the ability to acquire skill in spelling. Both groups encounter spelling problems and opportunities in their experiences outside the school. Because of its reputation and the things it is known to stress, moreover, the school will further sensitize both groups to those spelling experiences encountered in the world at large.

As we turn to the different classrooms in which two different methods are being employed, we will still find much in common. In each class there is a teacher who knows how to spell and who spontaneously calls attention to matters pertaining to spelling. Both teachers are happy when the children spell correctly and are less happy when an error occurs. When the reason for the error can be formulated, each teacher spontaneously calls attention to this principle and to the results that follow when the principle is ignored.

With all these forces acting on both groups, we now arrange for some difference in the formal method of teaching. We cannot be sure, in the first place, that this difference in the formal approach will actually engage any of the basic primitive forces by which teaching is accomplished. But even if it does, this one slight change, imposed on the whole battery of powerful, prior forces, may have great difficulty in demonstrating its influence.

Our expectation of negative results is increased when we consider the very sequence in which different forces are applied. In a process such as educational growth, the first force to be applied is likely to have an unfair advantage. It can push the attainment of the children, through the easy portion of the curve of growth where a slight expenditure of energy brings about a considerable return in achievement. Each succeeding force that is applied must suffer an ever-increasing handicap. Administrative factors and pedagogical refinements, moreover, are notorious late-comers in this succession of forces. They are inevitably left to show their influence on that part of the curve where diminishing returns are the rule. In this part of the curve, the going is so heavy that a considerable effort will show only a limited increase in achievement, and a minor force will show nothing at all.

This impressive flood of negative results, although demanded by the spontaneous theory, cannot be used as proof of the theory. Negative results, however impressive, are notoriously unsatisfactory as proof of anything. What can we dependably conclude, for instance, from a sustained failure to observe a monster in Loch Ness? To explain such negative results, we can typically invoke the classical hypotheses of imprecision, excessive random error, and compensating interactions. We can also claim that we just did not try hard enough—that our doseages were inadequate, or our treatments were applied for too short a time. In the face of these inevitable rival hypotheses, any array of negative results could only be used to add to the plausibility of the theory. Failure to observe a pattern of negative results would have condemned it out of hand. That particular condemnation, of course, it has unquestionably escaped. But other and more telling tests are still to come.

SOCIOLOGY OF TEACHING

Willard W. Waller

The School as a Social Organism

The school is a unity of interacting personalities. The personalities of all who meet in the school are bound together in an organic relation. The life of the whole is in all its parts, yet the whole could not exist without any of its parts. The school is a social organism,[1] it is this first and most general aspect of the social life of the schools which we propose to deal with in this chapter. As a social organism the school shows an organismic interdependence of its parts; it is not possible to affect a part of it without affecting the whole. As a social organism the school displays a differentiation of parts and a specialization of function. The organism as an entirety is nourished by the community.

Changing the figure slightly, the school is a closed system of social interaction. Without pedantry, we may point out that this fact is of importance, for if we are to study the school as a social entity, we must be able to distinguish clearly between school and not-school. The school is in fact clearly differentiated from its social milieu. The existence of a school is established by the emergence of a characteristic mode of social interaction. A school exists wherever and whenever teachers and students meet for the purpose of giving and receiving instruction. The instruction which is given is usually formal classroom instruction, but this need not be true. The giving and receiving of instruction constitutes the nucleus of the school as we now think of it. About this nucleus are clustered a great many less relevant activities.

When we analyze existing schools, we find that they have the following characteristics which enable us to set them apart and study them as social unities:

1. They have a definite population.
2. They have a clearly defined political structure, arising from the mode of social interaction characteristic of the school, and influenced by numerous minor processes of interaction.
3. They represent the nexus of a compact network of social relationships.
4. They are pervaded by a we-feeling.
5. They have a culture that is definitely their own.

Waller, W. *Sociology of Teaching*. New York: Wiley, 1932, 6–13.

[1] We do not, of course, subscribe to the organismic fallacy, which Ward and others have so ably refuted. We have adopted the analogy here simply as a device of exposition. The school is like an organism; it is not a true organism.

Schools differ widely in the degree to which they show these traits and in the manner in which they are combined. Private boarding schools exemplify them all in the highest degree. They have a stable and homogeneous population; the original homogeneity, produced by economic and social selection, has been enhanced by intimate association and common experiences. They have a clear and explicit political organization, sometimes expressed in a book of rules and a long line of precedents. The persons of the school live very close to each other, and are bound each to each by an intricate maze of crisscrossing social relationships. Intimacy of association, stability of the group, the setting apart of the group by a distinctive dress and its isolation from other cultural influences, combine to make possible a strong feeling of unity in such a school; it has often been remarked that a private school has something of the solidarity of the family. The isolation of the school from the remainder of the community, and the richness of the life which its members lead in their close-packed association, make the culture developed in such a school pronounced and distinctive.

The private day school sometimes represents such a closed corporation, and shows up very clearly as a social unit. It may not, for the day school is sometimes nothing more than a painless substitute for public school for the children of wealthy parents. But in the ideal case the private day school may be a functioning unity much more clearly marked off from the rest of the world than is the public school.

The various kinds and conditions of public schools differ in the degree to which they are recognizable and delimitable social units. The one-room country school is obviously such a unit. So likewise is the great suburban high school, and the high school of the small city described in *Middletown*. Sometimes, however, the public school is so split into divergent social groups that the underlying unity is somewhat obscured. This is possible where the school population is drawn from several sources and where there is no school program capable of welding these groups together.

The school has, as we have said, a definite population, composed of those who are engaged in the giving or receiving of instruction, who "teach" or "are in school." It is a relatively stable population and one whose depletion and replacement occur slowly. Population movements go according to plan and can be predicted and charted in advance. A bimodal age distribution marks off teachers from students. This is the most significant cleavage in the school.

The young in the school population are likely to have been subjected to some sifting and sorting according to the economic status and social classification of their parents. The private schools select out a certain group, and there are specializations within the private schools, some being in fact reformatories for the children of the well-to-do, and some being very exacting as to the character and scholastic qualifications of their students. The public schools of the exclusive residence district are usually peopled by students of a limited range of social types. Slum schools are for slum children. Country schools serve the children of farmers. In undifferentiated residence districts and in small towns which have but one school the student population is least homogeneous and most representative of the entire community.

The teaching population is probably less differentiated. In part, this is because the variation from the teacher type must be limited if one is to teach successfully. There is nevertheless considerable variation in the training and ability of teachers from one school to another and one part of the country to another. Teachers the country over and in all schools tend to be predominantly selected from the rural districts and from the sons and daughters of the lower middle classes. The teaching population is in some schools more permanent than the student population. There is nevertheless a large turnover among the teachers.

The characteristic mode of social interaction of the school, an interaction centered about the giving and receiving of instruction, determines the political order of the school. The instruction which is given consists largely of facts and skills, and of other matter for which the spontaneous interests of students do not usually furnish a sufficient motivation. Yet teachers wish students to attain a certain mastery of these subjects, a much higher degree of mastery than they would attain, it is thought, if they were quite free in their choices. And teachers are responsible to the community for the mastery of these subjects by their students. The political organization of the school, therefore, is one which makes the teacher dominant, and it is the business of the teacher to use his dominance to further the process of teaching and learning which is central in the social interaction of the school.

Typically the school is organized on some variant of the autocratic principle. Details of organization show the greatest diversity. Intra-faculty relations greatly affect the relations between teachers and students. Where there is a favorable rapport between the teachers and the administrative authorities, this autocracy becomes an oligarchy with the teacher group as a solid and well-organized ruling class. It appears that the best practice extends the membership in this oligarchy as much as possible without making it unwieldy or losing control of it. In the most happily conducted institutions all the teachers and some of the leading students feel that they have a very real voice in the conduct of school affairs.

Where there is not a cordial rapport between school executives and teachers, control becomes more autocratic. A despotic system apparently becomes necessary when the teaching staff has increased in size beyond a certain limit. Weakness of the school executive may lead him to become arbitrary, or it may in the extreme case lead some other person to assume his authority. The relationship between students and teachers is in part determined by intra-faculty relationships; the social necessity of sub-ordination as a condition of student achievement, and the general tradition governing the attitudes of students and teachers toward each other, set the limits of variation. But this variation is never sufficient to destroy the fact that the schools are organized on the authority principle, with power theoretically vested in the school superintendent and radiating from him down to the lowest substitute teacher in the system. This authority which pervades the school furnishes the best practical means of distinguishing school from not-school. Where the authority of the faculty and school board extends is the school. If it covers children on the way to and from school, at school parties, and on trips, then those children are in school at such times.

The generalization that the schools have a despotic political structure seems to hold true for nearly all types of schools, and for all about equally, without very much difference in fact to correspond to radical differences in theory. Self-government is rarely real. Usually it is but a mask for the rule of the teacher oligarchy, in its most liberal form the rule of a student oligarchy carefully selected and supervised by the faculty. The experimental school which wishes to do away with authority continually finds that in order to maintain requisite standards of achievement in imparting certain basic skills it has to introduce some variant of the authority principle, or it finds that it must select and employ teachers who can be in fact despotic without seeming to be so. Experimental schools, too, have great difficulty in finding teachers who are quite free from the authoritarian bias of other schools and able to treat children as independent human beings. Military schools, standing apparently at the most rigid pole of authority, may learn to conceal their despotism, or, discipline established, may furnish moments of relaxation and intimate association between faculty and students, and they may delegate much power and responsibility to student officers; thus they may be not very much more arbitrary than schools quite differently organized, and sometimes they are very much less arbitrary than schools with a less rigid formal structure. The manifestations of the authority principle vary somewhat. The one-room country school must have a different social structure from the city high school with five thousand students, but the basic fact of authority, of dominance and subordination, remains a fact in both.

It is not enough to point out that the school is a despotism. It is a despotism in a state of perilous equilibrium. It is a despotism threatened from within and exposed to regulation and interference from without. It is a despotism capable of being overturned in a moment, exposed to the instant loss of its stability and its prestige. It is a despotism demanded by the community of parents, but specially limited by them as to the techniques which it may use for the maintenance of a stable social order. It is a despotism resting upon children, at once the most tractable and the most unstable members of the community.

There may be some who, seeing the solid brick of school buildings, the rows of nicely regimented children sitting stiff and well-behaved in the classroom or marching briskly through the halls, will doubt that the school is in a state of unstable equilibrium. A school may in fact maintain a high morale through a period of years, so that its record in the eyes of the community is marred by no untoward incident. But how many schools are there with a teaching body of more than—let us say—ten teachers, in which there is not one teacher who is in imminent danger of losing his position because of poor discipline? How many such schools in which no teacher's discipline has broken down within the last three years? How many school executives would dare to plan a great mass meeting of students at which no teachers would be present or easily available in case of disorder?

To understand this political structure of the school we must know that the school is organized on the authority principle and that that authority is constantly threatened. The authority of the school executives and the teachers is in unremitting danger from: (1) The students. (2) Parents. (3) The school board. (4) Each other. (5) Hangers-on and marginal members of the group. (6) Alumni. The members of these groups, since they threaten his authority, are to some extent the natural enemies of the person who represents and lives by authority. The difficulties of the teacher or school executive in maintaining authority are greatly increased by the low social standing of the teaching profession and its general disrepute in the community at large. There is a constant interaction between the elements of the authoritative system; the school is continually threatened because it is autocratic, and it has to be autocratic because it is threatened. The antagonistic forces are balanced in that ever-fickle equilibrium which is discipline.

Within the larger political order of the school are many subsidiary institutions designed to supplement, correct, or support the parent institution, drawing their life from it and contributing in turn to its continued existence. These institutions are less definitely a part of the political structure, and they mitigate somewhat the rigidity of that structure by furnishing to students an opportunity for a freer sort of social expression. These ancillary institutions are organizations of extra-curricular activities, and comprise such groups as debating societies, glee clubs, choral societies, literary societies, theatrical groups, athletic teams, the staff of a school paper, social clubs, honorary societies, fraternities, etc. They are never entirely spontaneous social groupings but have rather the character of planned organizations for which the major impetus comes from the faculty, generally from some one member of the faculty delegated to act as "faculty adviser." These "activities" are part of that culture which springs up in the school from the life of students or is created by teachers for the edification of students. Such groups are often hardly less pervaded by faculty control than classroom activities, and there seems a tendency for the work of such institutions to be taken over by the larger social structure, made into courses and incorporated into the curriculum. Perhaps the worst that can happen to such organizations, if they are viewed as opportunities for the spontaneous self-expression of students, is that they shall be made over into classes. But the school administrator often thinks differently; from his point of view, the worst that can happen to such groups is that they shall become live and spontaneous groups, for such groups have a way of declaring their independence, much to the detriment of school discipline.

The political order of the school is characterized by control on three levels. Roughly, these are:

1. Theoretical. The control of the school by the school board, board of trustees, etc.
2. Actual. The control of school affairs by school executives as exerted through the teaching force or directly.
3. Ultimate. The control of school affairs by students, government resting upon the consent, mostly silent, of the governed.

The school is the meeting-point of a large number of intertangled social relationships. These social relationships are the paths pursued by social interaction, the channels in which social influences run. The crisscrossing and interaction of these groups make the school what it is. The social relationships centering in the school may be analyzed in terms of the interacting groups in the school. The two most important groups are the teacher-group and the pupil-group, each of which has its own moral and ethical code and its customary attitudes toward members of the other groups. There is a marked tendency for these groups to turn into conflict groups. Within the teacher group are divisions according to rank and position, schismatic and conspirital groups, congenial groups, and cliques centering around different personalities. Within the student groups are various divisions representing groups in the larger community, unplanned primary groups stair-stepped according to age, cliques, political organizations, and specialized groups such as teams and gangs. The social influence of the school is a result of the action of such groups upon the individual and of the organization of individual lives out of the materials furnished by such groups.

A rough idea of some of the more important social relationships arising in the school may be derived from the following schema:

I.   Community-School relationships.
1.   Relation of community to school in general. (Mediated through tradition and the political order of the community.)
2.   Relation of community to students individually and in groups. The parental relation and the general relation of the elders of the community to the young.
3.   Relation of community to teachers.
4.   Relation of special groups in the community to the school. (The school board, parent-teacher clubs, alumni, self-constituted advisory groups, etc.)
5.   Relation of special individuals to the school. (Patrons, ex-teachers, patriarchs, hangers-on, etc.)
II. Pupil to pupil relationships as not affected by the presence of teachers.
1.   Pupil to pupil relationships.
2.   Pupil to pupil-group relationships.
3.   Pupil-group to pupil-group relationships.
III. Teacher-pupil relationships. (Including also pupil to pupil relationships as affected by the presence of teachers.)
1.   Teacher to pupil-group relationship. (The customary classroom situation.)
2.   Teacher to pupil relationship.
3.   Pupil to pupil relationship as affected by the presence of the teacher.
IV. Teacher to teacher relationships.
1.   Relation of teacher to teacher.
     a.   Teacher to teacher relationship as not affected by the presence of students.
     b.   Teacher to teacher relationship as affected by the presence of students.
2.   Relation of teacher to teacher groups.
3.   Relation of teacher groups to teacher groups.
4.   Relation of teaching force to administrative officers.

NOTE: All these relationships are reciprocal.

The school is further marked off from the world that surrounds it by the spirit which pervades it. Feeling makes the school a social unity. The *we*-feeling of the school is in part a spontaneous creation in the minds of those who identify themselves with the school and in part a carefully nurtured and sensitive growth. In this latter aspect it is regarded as more or less the property of the department of athletics. Certainly the spirit of the group reaches its highest point in those ecstatic ceremonials which attend athletic spectacles. The group spirit extends itself also to parents and alumni.

A separate culture, we have indicated, grows up within the school. This is a culture which is in part the creation of children of different age levels, arising from the breakdown of adult culture into simpler configurations or from the survival of an older culture in the play group of children, and in part devised by teachers in order to canalize the activities of children passing through certain ages. The whole complex set of ceremonies centering around the school may be considered a part of the culture indigenous to the school. "Activities," which many youngsters consider by far the most important part of school life, are culture patterns. The specialized culture of the young is very real and satisfying for those who live within it. And this specialized culture is perhaps the agency most effective in binding personalities together to form a school.

Contemporary Issues In Education **3]**

REMBRANDT VAN RIJN, *Boy Reading*. Kunsthistorisches Museum, Vienna.

7

Contemporary Issues in Learning

On a definition of education: The organized deliberate attempt to help people to become intelligent.

— R. M. Hutchins, *The Learning Society.*

What do we know about the factors that influence school learning? What is the evidence about the relationship between learning and such factors as intelligence, socioeconomic status, sex, and race?

Intelligence

One of the most obvious things that can be said about school learning is that it is related to the pupil's intelligence. The brighter the pupil, the more quickly he will learn generally, and the more he will know at each stage compared with the child who is less bright. But what is intelligence?

One common definition of intelligence is that it is the ability to deal with abstract symbols and relationships. But as Anastasi (1958) has pointed out, one pupil may be good at abstract verbal concepts and yet be poor at quantitative ones, or vice versa. A second definition is that intelligence is the ability to learn. This definition implies that all learning is similar, which hardly passes the test of common sense. We know that pupils have different abilities to learn depending upon what it is they are learning. Therefore, when we say intelligence is the ability to learn, we mean it in a very restrictive sense, namely, the ability of the child to learn those things most commonly asked of him in a traditional school. Terman, who, along with Merrill, developed the 1937 Stanford-Binet—the most widely used of all individual tests of intelligence and the standard against which other tests have been compared—defined it as follows: "An individual is intelligent in proportion as he is able to carry on abstract thinking" (Terman, in Tyler, 1969, p. 8).

Thurstone, who has written extensively about intelligence, gives a more complex definition: "Intelligence as judged in everyday life contains at least three psychologically differentiable components: (a) the capacity to inhibit an instinctive adjustment, (b) the capacity to redefine the inhibited instinctive adjustment in the light of imaginally experienced trial and error, (c) the volitional capacity to realize the modified instinctive adjustment into overt behavior to the advantage of the individual as a social animal. . ." (Thurstone, in Tyler, 1969, pp. 19–20). Thurstone labels these three phases of intelligence as inhibitive capacity, analytical capacity, and perseverance.

Still another definition of intelligence, a much-quoted one originated by Boring (Boring, in Tyler, 1969, p. 26), is that intelligence is what intelligence tests measure. Of all the definitions, this is probably the most accurate, if the least appealing. What do intelligence tests measure? In their manual for the 1937 Stanford-Binet, Terman and Merrill describe their widely used test as "a method of standardized interview which is highly interesting to the subject and calls forth his natural responses to an extraordinary variety of situations . . . . It is a method which, to paraphrase an oft-quoted statement by Galton, attempts to obtain a general knowledge of the capacities of a subject by the sinking of shafts at critical points" (p. 4). Most of our intelligence tests place heavy emphasis on verbal abilities and some emphasis on numerical skills. In a famous paper titled, "Three Faces of Intellect," Guilford (1959) pulled together the results of studies of the factors that make up intelligence into a theory about the structure of intellect. In 1959, when Guilford wrote his paper, fifty intellectual factors had been identified. Guilford believed that others would be discovered, perhaps as many as the 120 predicted in his model.

Our traditional intelligence tests are loaded with items requiring verbal ability. As Anastasi (1958) pointed out, the Stanford-Binet mental age score correlates .81 with the vocabulary subtest of the Stanford-Binet, telling us that ability to do well on the vocabulary subtest is highly related to the ability to do well on the Stanford-Binet as a whole. We might remember that Binet originally chose the items for his scale on the basis of their ability to predict what children could do in Paris classrooms around the turn of the century. Since Binet chose items representative of classroom demands, it is not surprising that vocabulary played such an important role. Binet was faced with a very important and practical problem, namely, to devise a test that would discriminate those children who could be expected to achieve normally in school from those who could not. Obviously the best predictor would be a sample of their school achievement behavior. If we wanted to distinguish fast runners from slow runners, we would follow the same principle of testing "close to the bone" and would sample running behaviors.

Correlational Evidence

At this point, we will discuss the meaning of correlations, because they are essential to understanding the evidence on learning. Correlations are used constantly in discussing current problems in our environment. We read of correlations each day when we read that the number of cigarettes smoked daily is positively correlated with the incidence of lung cancer. We are aware also that years of schooling is positively correlated with amount of income in the United States. The technicalities of how correlation coefficients are computed need not concern us here, but the meaning of the concept is very important. If Variable A is positively correlated with Variable B, we are saying that knowledge about A would permit us to predict B. The stronger (higher) the correlation between A and B, the more accurately we can predict B from knowledge of A. Positive correlations range from 0 to +1.00 (usually written without any plus sign, which is assumed in the absence of a minus sign) whereas negative correlations range from 0 to −1.00. In educational literature, it is rare to find correlations exceeding .80, or "point eight," because the research subjects (that is, human beings) do not usually produce perfect correlations. Finding two human characteristics that are perfectly correlated is a virtual impossibility; not even such variables as riches and degree of happiness, ability and achievement, love and consideration, or IQs of identical twins show this degree of relationship. Theoretically it is possible for A and B to be perfectly correlated, as in the case of the rise and fall of a column of mercury as temperatures go up and down. Assuming that the instrument is calibrated perfectly and is in perfect working order, we could say that the rise and fall of the mercury is perfectly correlated with the temperature. In practice, we assume that the behavior of the mercury *is* the temperature. If we had two identical thermometers in perfect working order, the readings on Thermometer A should correlate perfectly (+1.00) with the readings on Thermometer B. If we know the reading on Thermometer A, we can predict the reading on B with complete accuracy.

Intelligence, as measured on intelligence tests, is positively correlated with school learning. The correlations vary depending upon the measures of intelligence and school learning used. Typically they range between .30, point three, and .80, point eight (the second figure is assumed) with .50 being common. Negative correlations, expressed with a minus sign in front of them, mean that as Variable A goes up, Variable B goes down, as in a seesaw. Knowing that two factors are negatively correlated, we can predict that as Variable A goes up so many degrees, Variable B will go down so many degrees. One negative correlation seen commonly in education is that the length of the lecture is negatively correlated with the audience's attention. Instead of saying, "negatively correlated," sometimes we say, "inversely related," which means the same thing. From our common sense experience in schools, we could make many predictions about correlations. Among the things we might predict to be *positively correlated* would be:

1. school grades and good behavior
2. age of pupil and number of years of schooling
3. degree of excitement among pupils and closeness of holidays
4. tension among pupils and closeness of report cards

Among the *negative correlations* that we would predict might be:

1. number of days completed in the school term and neatness of book jackets
2. number of days completed in the school term and number of resolutions kept
3. age of the pupil and his naiveté about school authority
4. number of referrals for disciplinary attention and grades

Correlations between Intelligence and Learning

One point that is often overlooked in discussing standardized intelligence tests is that most intelligence tests used with children in this country correlate positively with the ability of children to succeed in our schools. This is an obvious but very important point. Knowing a child's score on a standard intelligence test permits us to make some fairly accurate predictions about his future school career. We may use that information in various ways, both good and bad, but the correlation does permit us to make a prediction about school performance from knowledge of test scores. This was precisely the problem that faced Binet in trying to make accurate and reliable predictions that would be used to select pupils likely to succeed in schools.

Let us assume that we have a school system that faces the problems Paris faced at the turn of the century, that is, we have a limited number of available seats and years of schooling, but lots of children who want an education. This situation is common in developing countries today where there may be a classroom seat for only one child in ten. Given this problem, someone has to decide who is going to be admitted to school. One way would be through a lottery, letting children take their fair chance. Assuming that intelligence in this hypothetical population is normally distributed, and assuming that the school system is run along traditional educational lines, we would predict that a certain percentage of the children selected by chance would not succeed in the school system. If the country is a poor one with limited resources, we might decide that the lottery is a pretty poor way to go about selecting students because it wastes time, money, and resources. Instead, we would rather select those students most likely to gain the most from the educational experience and who, in turn, would be likely to develop skills that would be useful to the country. If that were our objective, we might want to devise a test that would predict how well children would do in the school system, in which case we would hire a consultant of Dr. Binet's type to construct a test. Our test expert would take a sample of the tasks demanded in the existing classrooms and try out each item with children of varying ages to determine the average number of items passed at each age level. We could thus develop our own IQ test for our own country, culture, school system, and young people. With limited resources, we are almost obliged to employ some kind of predictive instrument so that those pupils with the best chance of succeeding are selected. The prediction obviously will never be perfect, but we want to maximize the accuracy of the prediction.

On the other hand, suppose that our school system follows a different model, one in which we believe every child should have as much education as he can possibly profit from, and in which there is a seat for every child. In this model, using tests to select children does not make very much sense. We might use tests to help each child develop his own educational program, but we would not eliminate a child from school on the grounds that there were not enough places in the schoolroom.

Those who criticize intelligence tests often miss the point that predictive instruments are extremely important to certain educational models. Such tests have a role to play and a service to perform. When the educational model is changed, the tests are quite likely to change. If we adopt a universal democratic educational model in which everyone goes to school to his learnable limit, we might want to employ criterion-referenced tests in which children are compared against a standard of performance rather than normative tests in which children are compared with other children.

Suppose we need to select students for certain educational endeavors? Then we may need measures to predict their learning abilities for these endeavors. In this area, our intelligence tests have done well. They have correlated highly with school success, so they have been valid predictors of school achievement. They predict well because their content resembles what is required in school, which in turn depends heavily upon verbal abilities. We could take the stand that verbal abilities should not matter that much, and perhaps they should not, but realistically, they are almost essential in contemporary life. Even a logger, for example, in a rural section of New England, finds that verbal abilities play a crucial role in his income. Unless he has the verbal abilities required for dealing with forms for contracts, insurance, taxes, and workmen's compensation, he is not in a position to employ other men and to expand his business. Without such verbal abilities, he is limited to functioning as a lone operator. As a lone operator under today's conditions in the logging industry, he will not make the income necessary to buy the expensive equipment. It is fairly predictable that he will end up working for someone else who has the requisite abilities for handling such a business. Obviously this need for verbal abilities discriminates against those people who lack them. In some of our subcultures, such as parts of New England, such abilities have not always been highly valued, whereas reticence and sparseness of expression have been.

To the extent our present culture changes, it will change the skills necessary for success, which, in turn, will change our definition of intelligence and our tests. If, for example, the culture of the future should emerge from the current youth culture, then a youth culture definition of intelligence would become standard and we might have tests for it. If the culture of the future puts a high premium on personal authenticity, warmth, idiosyncratic values and behaviors, or relevance to social problems, then tests may be developed to assess behaviors that will reflect the skills necessary for adaptability in such a culture if the situation requires some sort of predictive instrument. If we wished, we could have a test constructed today to predict success in a youth culture, just as is done for traditional schooling. As we ask our schools to perform tasks different from before, we may need to change our idea of what we want to predict. We may therefore need to change our instruments.

Just as intelligence and school achievement are positively correlated, so are intelligence and the educational level achieved. The higher one goes in education, the higher the average level of intelligence to be found there. Cronbach (1960, p. 174) developed some estimates a few years ago that reflect this relationship.

AVERAGE IQ	EDUCATIONAL LEVEL
100	average for total population
110	high school graduate
115	average of college freshmen in a four-year college
120	average of college graduates
130	average of Ph.D. degree recipients

In Cronbach's data, level of intelligence is expressed by the Intelligence Quotient (IQ). The IQ provides an index of how individuals compare in performance on test items with other individuals in their age group. If a nine-year-old child, for example, performs on an intelligence test at the same level as the nine year olds included in the standardization sample for the test, his IQ would be 100, which is average. On age scales such as the Stanford-Binet, IQs are calculated by dividing mental age as determined on the test by chronological age and multiplying by 100 ($\frac{MA}{CA} \times 100$). If a nine-year-old child obtained a mental age of twelve on the test, his IQ would be 133 ($\frac{12}{9} \times 100$), which falls in the superior range. If he obtained a mental age of six, his IQ would be 67 ($\frac{6}{9} \times 100$), which falls in the mentally retarded range.

Anastasi (1958) reports that in both world wars, there was a positive correlation of .30 between scores on army intelligence tests and highest grade reached in school. This finding could represent an egg and chicken dilemma, however, because the brightest students may elect to stay in school longer, or staying in school longer may tend to raise the IQ. We can be quite sure of the first statement, namely, that those who elect to stay in school longer tend to have higher IQs. But it also seems that staying in school is related to a gain in IQ. Husén is reported by Anastasi (1958) to have studied over 700 army inductees in Sweden for whom he was able to obtain third grade intelligence test scores. The changes in IQ since third grade in these young men were related to the amount of education they received. Those with most schooling had gained an average of 11 IQ points since third grade. The amount of schooling in this group correlated .80 with their most recent IQ scores, which in educational research, represents a strong positive correlation.

Socioeconomic Status

Socioeconomic status (called "SES") identifies a person's place on the social and economic scales of his society. In our type of society, the usual factors that identify a person's SES are his occupation, education, and income. The higher these three are, the higher is a person's SES. The relationship between SES and intelligence in our culture is a positive one, namely, the higher the SES, the higher the IQ. This states a positive relationship, but does not assign causes or explain why. There is enormous controversy in this area.

First, let us sample some of the evidence. The National Merit Scholarship test results which identified "talented" students in 1956 (White and Harris, 1961, p. 100) were embarrassing because 45 percent of all those identified came from the top SES class of professional and technical workers. On the nine classes by occupational level of their parents, the bottom level of laborers produced only .2 percent, or two-tenths of 1 percent, of talented people. This indicates that there is a positive relationship between the SES of a child's parents and the child's intelligence. Since intelligence and school learning are also positively related, we can make the following inference:

1. The higher the parental SES, the higher the child's IQ.
2. The higher the IQ, the faster the learning.
3. Therefore, the higher the SES, the faster the learning.

The positive association among these three factors (parental SES, the child's intelligence, and the child's ability to learn in school) is so strong that one can make quite reliable predictions about the school performance of youngsters coming to school for the first time without ever seeing the child or giving him a test. Correlations of around .50 between IQ of school-age children and education and income of parents have been reported in numerous studies (Bayley, in Mussen, 1970, p. 1187). There is an element of fatality and injustice about such correlations. Some feel that the child is unjustly influenced by his parents' socioeconomic status. This is probably true for every child since he is born into a set of circumstances, both genetic and environmental, over which he has no control and which do indeed affect him.

In an attempt to identify some of the specific background variables related to the development of cognitive and linguistic skills, Whiteman and Deutsch (1968) studied samples of 165 children in the fifth grade and 127 children in the first grade in twelve schools in New York City. Children were selected to provide variability in socioeconomic status (SES) and in race. Information on educational and occupational status of families was obtained by mail questionnaire or by interview in the event that the questionnaire was not returned. Lorge-Thorndike IQs varied systematically with SES. For the lowest SES level, SES I, the mean IQ for the first and fifth graders combined was 94; for SES II, 103; for SES III, 109. For Negroes, the mean IQ was 97; for Whites, 106. Achievement in the fifth-grade samples as measured by the Gates Reading Test was significantly related to general SES variables. Reading scores correlated .44 with the SES index, .45 with the education of the family's main supporter, and .35 with the occupation of the main supporter. Reading test scores also correlated (around .30) with housing condition, parental schooling desired for the child, and number of children under 18 (inverse relationship; —.29 correlation). These investigators believe that their results support the notion of a developmental sequence in which environmental conditions affect the development of certain abilities, and that these in turn affect achievement and sense of competence (Whiteman and Deutsch, 1968).

In 1942, Thorndike and Woodyard posed the question: What is the relationship between income and intelligence? Using scores on an intelligence test administered in sixth grade, and the per capita income in a sample of large cities, they found a correlation of .78 between intelligence test scores and per capita income (White and Harris, 1961, p. 101).

Data for 1968 (*The Chronicle of Higher Education*, November 23, 1970) indicate that the average or mean income in 1968 dollars is related to years of schooling completed by wage earners in the following way:

YEARS OF SCHOOLING	1968 DOLLARS
Elementary school, 8 years	$5,624
High school, 4 years	8,430
College, 1 to 3 years	9,692
College, 4 years	12,888

A college graduate has double the years of schooling of an elementary school graduate, but more than double the income.

Given our present society in which education plays an important role in SES mobility, it is to be expected that those who go up the SES ladder are also those who have gone up the educational ladder. In an agrarian society, this might not be true nor would it make sense. In a society where the level of occupational entry requires increasing educational skills, however, it is very likely that those who are most educated will be most rewarded in terms of income, social status, and occupational level.

Sex Differences

Girls and boys react very differently to school and learning. On our best-known intelligence tests, the items were discarded that originally discriminated between boys and girls, so it is hard to know from intelligence test items what things girls or boys do better at what age. Girls tend to excel boys in almost every aspect of language development. They talk earlier, reach maturity in articulation earlier, have larger vocabularies, and excel in reading speed and in such tests as analogies, sentence completion, opposites, and word fluency. Boys excel girls in tests of spatial and mechanical aptitude and numerical reasoning. Boys show much higher frequencies of language disorders such as reading problems, stuttering, and stammering (Anastasi, 1958, pp. 470–478).

Girls also tend to excel boys in academic achievement as a whole, most particularly in school subjects that depend on verbal abilities, perceptual speed and accuracy, and memory. Girls excel in the school progress indicators of promotion, acceleration, and low rates for repeating grades. They make better grades, even in academic areas such as science, arithmetic, and history in which achievement test results favor boys (Anastasi, 1958, pp. 492–494). The better showing in traditional schooling by girls seems to stem from several sources, among them superior linguistic abilities, neater handwriting stemming from greater developmental acceleration and manual dexterity in girls, and personality differences that lead girls to be more attentive, quieter, less distractible, and generally better suited than boys to the demands of traditional schooling.

Differences often level off somewhere in high school and girls do not go on to college as often as boys. This may be related to selective training of children in traditional sex role models, or it may be economic in that many families who have to make a financial choice will educate their son before they will educate a daughter. Most of the research literature suggests, however, that girls enjoy school more than boys, present fewer behavior problems, are less often discipline problems, and are more conforming than boys. Before we assume that these somewhat Pollyannish characteristics of girls reflect a lack of backbone, we should remember that girls mature more rapidly than boys physiologcally and neurologically, and that these differences affect performance in elementary school most strongly. Greater maturity means that girls can handle most of the daily school tasks more easily than boys. In his discussion of sex differences and psychopathology, Anthony (Anthony, in Mussen, 1970, pp. 722–723) describes the developmental rates as "markedly different." In development, girls are twelve months ahead of boys by age six, and eighteen months ahead by age nine. Anthony (1970) summarizes some interesting data on sex differences in school problems:

> During the first grade, the boy is referred eleven times as often as a girl for social and emotional immaturity, a syndrome characterized by a high rate of absenteeism, fatigability, inability to attend and concentrate, shyness, poor motivation for work, underweight, inability to follow directions, slow learning, infantile speech patterns, and problems in the visual-motor and visual-perception areas. As a school child, he is referred to the school clinic for stuttering (four to one), reading difficulty (five to one), speech, hearing and eye problems (four to one); and eventually to the psychiatric clinic for personality disorders (2.6 to 1), behavior problems (4.4 to 1), school failure (2.6 to 1), and delinquency (4.5 to 1).

Pupils who like school and behave appropriately in it tend to be those who are most strongly rewarded by it. Those rewarded by it are those who come with the requisite skills and attitudes, such as bright children, higher SES children, and a higher proportion of young girls than young boys.

We have so far reviewed quite briefly the evidence that there are positive associations between such variables as (1) intelligence, (2) socioeconomic status, and (3) sex, with learning in schools as measured by traditional tests and by traditional school achievement.

Aptitude-Treatment Interaction (ATI)

Now let us examine selected evidence on some current issues in learning. In doing so, let us bear in mind a new approach to the question of validity of educational measures. Validity tells us if the instrument measures what it purports to measure. In a recent review of this problem, Cronbach (1970) goes beyond this original criterion for validity, based on measurement principles, to indicate that we must consider the criterion of educational usefulness. He indicates that validity of an educational measure should include, first, its educational importance, and second, its usefulness for decision making. If, for example, we use a test to select students for an educational program, we should ask ourselves whether or not this instrument selects students who actually do better in this educational program than students selected by some other means. He also asks whether or not the interrelationship among aptitude, treatment, and interaction, actually works.

Behind the initials, ATI, which stand for aptitude-treatment interaction, looms a large question which has been concerning educational researchers for a long time. In a classical experiment, a treatment is administered to one sample of children while it is withheld from a second sample that serves as a control group. Pre- and posttests are administered and the treatment, which may be a specific educational approach or instructional method, either shows gains for the experimental group or does not. What has been lacking, according to many critics such as Cronbach, is a careful examination of the characteristics of the learners as they interact with the particular treatment. What this could mean is that a given teaching method may work extremely well for learners with the characteristics G, M, and Q, but it does not work with learners with the characteristics B, F, and T.

One of the most lucid discussions of aptitude-treatment interactions has been given by Glaser (1970). He believes that the abilities of the learner must be more carefully matched with the abilities required by the learning tasks at various stages of learning if instruction is to be properly individualized. He summarizes the few recent studies which have examined the relationships between abilities and success at various stages of learning. His conclusion has important implications for individualizing instruction.

> Analyses of the data . . . showed that the particular combinations of abilities that contribute to performance change as practice continues, and that the different abilities existing prior to entering a learning task influence learning at different learning stages. This implies

that individuals with different patterns of abilities require different learning experiences at different stages of learning (p. 25).

Glaser (1970) presents a model for individualizing instruction which he summarizes by listing six operational requirements (pp. 29–30):

1. The outcomes and subgoals of learning are specified in terms of observable learner performance and the conditions under which this performance is exercised.
2. Detailed diagnosis is made of the initial state of a learner entering a particular instructional situation.
3. Educational alternatives are provided which are adaptive to the classifications resulting from the initial student activity profiles.
4. As the student learns, his performance is monitored and continuously assessed at longer or shorter intervals appropriate to what is being taught.
5. Instruction and learning proceed in interrelated fashion, tracking the performance and selections of the student.
6. The instructional system collects information in order to improve itself, and inherent in the system's design is its capability for doing this.

This kind of research represents a new thrust, one that will take careful evaluation of learner characteristics on all the relevant dimensions, but it does speak to the attempt on the part of thoughtful educational researchers to match the individual characteristics of the learner with particular instructional strategies. This suggests that we are no longer looking for gross solutions, such as one curriculum or one instructional strategy, as being better than another, but we are asking: Which instructional strategy works best with what kinds of students?

Disadvantaged Learners

Probably the most vivid issue in learning today is what can be done to help disadvantaged children learn. This is an emotion-provoking subject about which most educators do not tend to be calm, cool, or inclined to collect evidence. A wide range of interventions have been tried, some in Head Start (Westinghouse Learning Corporation, 1969) and some outside of that particular program. They have yielded a variety of results that have been interpreted in a variety of ways by a variety of critics. Here we will be concerned primarily with one such intervention so that we may understand how to evaluate evidence from such intervention programs.

The Early Training Project and the DARCEE Project (Demonstration and Research Center in Early Education) at George Peabody College in Nashville, Tennessee were headed by Dr. Susan Gray. These works represent thoughtful attempts to utilize every possible approach to improve the school achievement of disadvantaged black pupils in this region of our country. Enormous efforts have been expended to help these children, including the use of home visitors, special materials, special instructional techniques to involve their parents and siblings, as well as the more traditional approaches of a summer school program and an increase in the breadth of their experiences. Such intervention programs are extremely costly in terms of manpower and money and consequently have been limited to quite small numbers. When we look at the results of the Early Training Project as reported by Klaus and Gray (1968) (see Readings: Section 2), we find that testing gains on the Stanford-Binet for the treatment groups are statistically significant, but the gains do not appear to be educationally significant. The two treatment groups gained 3.6 and 3.5 points on the Stanford-Binet over a period of four years, compared with the two control groups in which one gained 2.5 points and the other lost 2.1 points. We need to recall Cronbach's criteria of educational usefulness and importance, and admit that 3 or 4 points gain or loss by a group on the Stanford-Binet over four years is not a change of much educational significance. The standard error of measurement for the Stanford-Binet itself is about 5 points for this range of IQ, so that the changes reported are not as large as the possible error of the instrument. Generally we look for differences ascribed to any treatment that are considerably larger than the possible error of measurement. We have to conclude, despite all that is good about the Early Training Project, that the results as measured by the Stanford-Binet do not predict a major change in the educational achievement for these children.

It is very hard to draw a conclusion like the one above, because it involves disadvantaged children whom most educators want to see succeed in school more than they have. As students of education and as citizens, however, we need to look at the evidence objectively so that we can decide where to put our efforts.

One point of view that is often lacking in such a discussion is the historical one. Cohen (1970) reminds us of the history of immigrants in the United States schools (See Readings: Section 3). Contrary to the folklore that immigrants found schools a positive experience, he points out that most immigrants around the turn of the century were retarded in grade, and considered both dull and social problems. The exception were Jewish children who, in comparison with other minority groups, stayed in school longer and achieved better. Italian immigrant children were reported to have IQs in the neighborhood of 85, and were viewed as the low or disadvantaged group relative to other contemporary immigrant groups. It simply is not true that all groups of children who have entered our public schools have sailed through them with profit. Although black children are not immigrants in the usual sense, historically they have not been included in the mainstream of the predominant culture in this country. It can be argued that black pupils may behave like an immigrant group during the first stage of school integration. On the basis of that comparison, their school performance is not surprising and the future is optimistic. The IQs reported in Klaus and Gray (1968) are encouraging when compared with the IQs of Italian children in our public schools two generations ago.

This line of reasoning, however, does not assume instant change. St. John (1970) stresses that social class, over and above race, is a prime factor in school achievement. Since it is impossible so far to separate the effects of social class from race, we should be careful in interpreting results as being related to race alone. In studies comparing white and black groups, equal socioeconomic status cannot be assumed no matter what scale is used or how equal the numbers may look. A black father who works at the same occupation as a white father still does not command equivalent comparable SES factors, such as housing, income, or neighborhood resources. As the economic barriers are lowered, we can expect to see increasing equivalence between the SES status of blacks and whites. Currently, for example, when a child of a black mail carrier is compared with the child of a white mail carrier, this comparison is not simply a distinction based on race, but involves a whole host of social and cultural resources that are not equal between the two fathers or their families.

The Role of Genetics, Environment, and Education

Russell (1950) warned us that when a point of view upsets us very much, we can be sure that one of our biases is being stepped on. Let us look at one piece of evidence about inherited abilities that no one has objected to so far. Garron (1970) reviewed the evidence that certain kinds of problems in spatial and numerical abilities may be a syndrome based upon a sex-linked recessive pattern. This syndrome has been identified as Turner's syndrome. People with this particular genetic pattern show specific deficits, such as impaired spatial abilities (although their verbal abilities are not impaired), certain somatic abnormalities, and all have an X chromosome abnormality. As we do more research in this area, we are probably going to find that other specific learning deficits are related to particular genetic patterns. No one so far has objected to the evidence on Turner's syndrome, probably because it has not been associated with any one group. Where Turner's syndrome can be identified, it seems likely that one would be in a better position to try to help such children with their spatial abilities. One of the hopes of the geneticists is to identify inherited patterns of deficits so we can determine what methods work best if we are to improve the educational success of particular groups. With a child who has Turner's syndrome, for example, it would be cruel and foolish to think he simply was not trying on spatial tasks. We might well have to invent some learning aids for such a child to supply some missing spatial cues. If we were to find, for example, that American Indians as a group tended to have a genetic pattern that limited their verbal abilities in specific ways, we would want to learn how this pattern operated to modify instruction to meet the problem.

If we are going to be data-oriented, we are going to have to deal with the fact that currently black children as a group score below white children as a group on intelligence tests and school achievement tests. We should not conclude that all Negro children perform less well on intelligence tests than all white children, or that group differences will last forever. Based on the evidence, we will have to accept some genetic or hereditary role in intelligence, but how large a role is the matter under current debate. Jensen (1969) has estimated the genetic role to be a relatively large one. This line of reasoning is offensive to many people because they think it implies that blacks are genetically inferior, while others disagree with the size of Jensen's estimate or the way in which it was derived (Kagan, Hunt, Crow, Bereiter, Elkind, Cronbach, and Brazziel, 1969).

Until the geneticists can settle the question of how large is the role of heredity in human intelligence, two other factors which we know affect intelligence will continue to operate and probably in more positive ways. To the extent that a favorable environment can increase the growth of intelligence, such an environmental effect is likely to increase for minority children. Not only is more educational material becoming available through the media for young children, but more is being learned about nutrition which may change dietary habits which, in turn, may increase intelligence test scores and school achievement. More parents are aware of the importance of the early years for learning and are likely to take greater pains with their children's guided experiences, educational TV, toys, and games, which are thought to favor the growth of intelligence. At the same time, education is increasing for all, and probably it will increase somewhat faster in the future for minority students. If we extend Husén's finding above (Anastasi, 1958), that amount of education and intelligence test scores are positively related, then we would predict that the scores of minority children will rise as their education increases.

Organization of Schooling for Learning

Let us turn now to another area in education where the evidence exists but is not always taken seriously because it may interfere with some set opinions. If one considers the possibility of accelerating a bright child, for example, by skipping him from fourth to fifth grade, many concerns are expressed about what will happen to his social adjustment, about keeping up, and whether he is the right size for the next grade. There have been quite a number of investigations, including follow-up studies, about the effects of acceleration. A recent study by Klausmeier, Goodwin, and Ronda (1968) gives us still more evidence that accelerating bright pupils is to their advantage in terms of school achievement, and that they do indeed participate in school activities in normal ways.

Still another area in which strongly held opinions about schools are popular involves the advantages of centralizing schools, particularly in rural areas. One of the big arguments for centralizing schools has been that centralization cuts down costs and makes a much larger range of curriculum available to children. Whether or not it cuts down on costs in the long run is debatable, but one cannot disagree that it makes better science laboratories and a large range of choices in the curriculum possible. But it also means long bus rides, as one price. Students do not participate as much in school activities when they are in a large high school. Baird (1969) has corroborated such findings at the high school level, and in a college sample he found achievement negatively related to college size.

One of the questions we have not pursued strongly enough is the relationship between the size of the educational environment and the quality of life that goes on in it both for students and teachers. It seems likely that there must be appropriately sized units for various educational purposes. How desirable is it to have large high schools even though they may offer a wider range in the curriculum? One might argue that there are all kinds of negative effects from putting hundreds or thousands of people of this age together, for school becomes logistically similar to a large military machine. By concentrating educational production facilities in one area, perhaps imitating an industrial model again, we may have moved to the centralized high school without giving much thought to what it may have done to the quality of school life.

REFERENCES

Anastasi, A. *Differential Psychology*. (3d ed.) New York: Macmillan, 1958.

Anthony, E. J. The behavior disorders of childhood. In P. H. Mussen (Ed.), *Carmichael's Manual of Child Psychology*, Vol. 2. New York: Wiley, 1970, 667–764.

Baird, L. L. Big school, small school: A critical examination of the hypothesis. *Journal of Educational Psychology*, 1969, **60**, 253–260.

Bayley, N. Development of mental abilities. In P. H. Mussen (Ed.),

Carmichael's Manual of Child Psychology, Vol. 2. New York: Wiley, 1970, 1163–1209.

Cohen, D. K. Immigrants and the schools. *Review of Educational Research*, 1970, **40**, No. 1, 13–68.

Cronbach, L. J. *Essentials of Psychological Testing*. New York: Harper & Row, 1960.

Cronbach, L. J. Validation of educational measures. *Proceedings of the 1969 Invitational Conference on Testing Problems: Toward a Theory of Achievement Measurement*. Princeton, N. J.: Educational Testing Service, 1970, 35–52.

Garron, D. C. Sex-linked recessive inheritance of spatial and numerical abilities and Turner's syndrome. *Psychological Review*, 1970, **77**, 147–152.

Glaser, R. *Individual differences in learning*. Pittsburgh, Pa.: University of Pittsburgh Learning Research and Development Center, 1970.

Guilford, J. P. Three faces of intellect. *American Psychologist*, 1959, **14**, 469–479.

Jensen, A. R. How much can we boost IQ and scholastic achievement? *Harvard Educational Review*, 1969, **39**, No. 1, 1–123.

Kagan, J. S., McHunt, J. McV., Crow, J. F., Bereiter, C., Elkind, D., Cronbach, L. J., & Brazziel, W. F. How much can we boost IQ and scholastic achievement? A discussion. *Harvard Educational Review*, 1969, **39**, No. 2, 273–356.

Klaus, R. A., & Gray, S. W. The early training project for disadvantaged children: A report after five years. *Monographs of the Society for Research in Child Development*, 1968, **33**, No. 4.

Klausmeier, H. J., Goodwin, W. L., & Ronda, T. Effects of accelerating bright older elementary pupils—A second follow-up. *Journal of Educational Psychology*, 1968, **59**, 53–58.

Russell, B. An outline of intellectual rubbish. In *Unpopular Essays*. New York: Simon and Schuster, 1950, 103–111.

St. John, N. H. Desegregation and minority group performance. *Review of Educational Research*, 1970, **40**, No. 1, 111–134.

Terman, L. M., & Merrill, M. A. *Measuring intelligence*. New York: Houghton Mifflin, 1937.

The Chronicle of Higher Education. Washington, D. C., November 23, 1970, 7.

Tyler, L. E. (Ed.), *Intelligence: Some Recurring Issues*. New York: Van Nostrand Reinhold, 1969.

Westinghouse Learning Corporation, Ohio University. *The impact of Head Start: An evaluation of the effects of Head Start on children's cognitive and affective development*. Washington, D. C.: Clearing house for Federal Scientific and Technical Information, U. S. Dept. of Commerce, National Bureau of Standards, PB June 1969, 184–328.

White, M. A., & Harris, M. W. *The School Psychologist*. New York: Harper & Row, 1961.

Whiteman, M., & Deutsch, M. Social disadvantage related to intellective and language development. In M. Deutsch., I. Katz, & A. R. Jensen (Eds.), *Social Class, Race, and Psychological Development*. New York: Holt, Rinehart and Winston, 1968, 86–114.

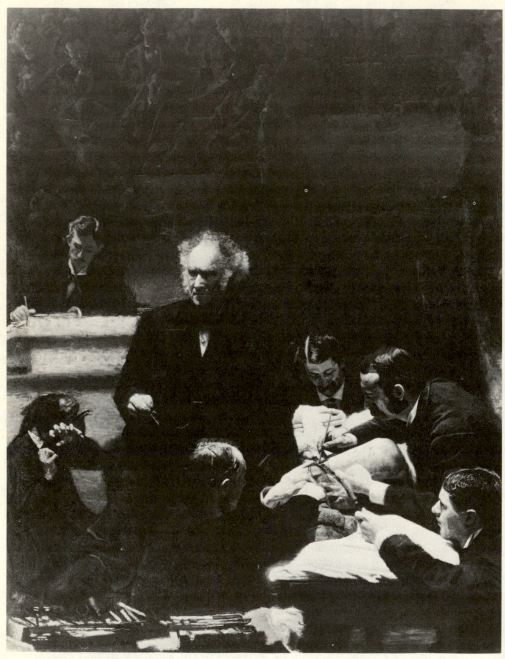

THOMAS EAKINS, *The Gross Clinic*. Courtesy of Jefferson Medical College of Thomas Jefferson University.

chapter 8

Contemporary Issues in Teaching

The soul of a child is like wax. Therefore he who directs the school directs the country's future.

—Bismarck

Who is the effective teacher? What is good teaching? This chapter will describe some of the approaches investigators have used in attempting to answer these two questions. In the past eight decades, they have attracted the attention of hundreds of investigators. They are important questions for parents, children, schools, and society. They have implications for how teachers are selected and educated and how they are recruited, assigned, and promoted by schools. It appears likely that no other characteristic of the school in the child's education is as important as the teacher. To the child and his parents, the teacher is the concrete representation of the school. During one year in school, the child will spend some 1000 hours with teachers, probably as much waking-time as he will spend with any other adult. If time spent in each other's company is any indicator, teachers have the potential for great impact on the child. The great mass of research on teaching and teacher effectiveness is further evidence of teachers' importance.

Since the research is so massive, even a comprehensive summary is outside the compass of this chapter. The first part of the chapter will focus on methodological problems, while a few representative studies will be summarized in the second section.

The Problem of the Criterion

Interest in teaching effectiveness has so dominated research on teaching that studies on teacher effectiveness occupy a central position in the research literature on teaching. This emphasis is reflected in the *Handbook of Research on Teaching* (Gage, 1963), the comprehensive volume that serves as the basic current reference on research in the field.

A problem which has been of greater concern than any other to the hundreds of researchers on teacher effectiveness is the identification of the criterion to be used in defining effectiveness. Researchers have been in general agreement on the definition of teaching. Gage's definition is probably representative:

> By teaching, we mean, for the present purpose of defining research on teaching, any interpersonal influence aimed at changing the ways in which other persons can or will behave. The restriction to "interpersonal" influence is intended to rule out physical (e.g., mechanical), physiological, or economic ways of influencing another's behavior such as pushing him, drugging him, or depriving him of a job. Rather the influence has to impinge on the other person through his perceptual and cognitive processes, i.e., through his ways of getting meaning out of the objects and events that his senses make him aware of (p. 96).

Investigators would generally agree to this, but agreement on the meaning of effectiveness has been far from general.

The emphasis on the evaluation of teaching effectiveness in the research on teaching has been traced to the beginning of this century when the efficiency movement in industry was at its peak (Davis, p. 43). In industry, in contrast to education, concrete, visible, and often countable criteria of efficiency are available. Efficiency experts could tally the number of pieces at a given quality standard that a worker could turn out in a unit of time, for example, and could use this tally as the criterion against which to evaluate workers. Researchers and factory owners could agree on this criterion. The effective worker is defined as the worker who can produce the most pieces with the fewest defects in the least amount of time. In evaluating teachers and teaching, however, researchers have found no such satisfactory solution to the criterion problem. They would like to find a criterion that can at least be measured consistently if not actually counted. The variables thought to be related to teaching effectiveness can then be measured and correlated with this criterion. In their search for criteria to use in the evaluation of teaching, researchers have turned to two general types. The first type is pupil achievement, commonly academic achievement. The second type utilizes judgments regarding some set of behaviors or characteristics against which the teacher's performance is compared. Both of these types of criteria have obvious deficiencies and have been criticized on a number of grounds.

Gage (pp. 116–120) describes the teacher's effect on his pupils' achievement of educational objectives of some kind as being the "ultimate criterion" of a teacher's effectiveness. The criterion that occupied top position in the hierarchy of criteria according to ultimacy formulated by the Committee on the Criteria of Teacher Effectiveness of the American Educational Research Association was "pupils' achievement and success in life." Gage (p. 117) presents an adaptation of this hierarchy which is useful in clarifying the relationship among various kinds of criteria on the dimension of ultimacy. In this hierarchy, teachers' characteristics are low in the hierarchy. The validity of each criterion in the hierarchy depends on its correlation with criteria higher in the list. Unless "teachers' intelligence," for example, bears some relationship to criteria at higher levels, it is useless as a criterion of teacher effectiveness.

Hierarchy of Criteria According to "Ultimacy"

Ultimate Criterion

Teachers' effect on:
    pupils' achievement and success in life
    pupils' achievement in subsequent schooling
    pupils' achievement of current educational objectives
    pupils' satisfaction with the teacher
    parents' satisfaction with the teacher
    superintendent's satisfaction with the teacher
Teachers' "values" or evaluative attitudes
Teachers' knowledge of educational psychology and mental hygiene
Teachers' emotional and social adjustment
Teachers' knowledge of methods of curriculum construction
Teachers' knowledge of subject matter
Teachers' interest in the subject matter
Teachers' grades in practice teaching courses
Teachers' grades in education courses
Teachers' intelligence

Research workers have disagreed among themselves on the position that criteria should have in a hierarchy of this kind. The widespread use of rating forms for evaluating teachers suggests that administrators in many school systems across the country might place the "superintendent's satisfaction with the teacher," for example, higher in this hierarchy than it actually appears. Although there is no tally available of the frequency with which the many investigators of teacher effectiveness have utilized various criteria, fewer investigators seem to have used the criterion of teachers' effect on pupil's achievement than have used other criteria. In one survey of the criteria employed in a very extensive research program on teacher effectiveness carried out at the University of Wisconsin over a period of several decades (Barr, 1961), ratings of various kinds were used with considerably greater frequency than were measures of pupil gain. This tally of the frequency with which various criteria of teacher effectiveness were used in the Wisconsin studies (Beecher, 1961, pp. 30–31) indicates that in-service ratings of one kind or another were used most frequently, combination criteria were second in frequency, and pupil gain scores were third. In this extended series of studies, therefore, the criterion of pupil achievement was not the most frequently used criterion. By frequency of use, ratings by administrators of various kinds seem to outrank other criteria.

A number of criticisms have been directed at both general types of criteria, that is, at the pupil achievement criteria of various kinds and at the teacher characteristics criteria. These will be summarized below.

Pupil Achievement Variables as Criteria

The criterion of achievement has been criticized because of the complexity of the variables involved, including complexities of definition, measurement, pupil-teacher-school interactions, and values. How is achievement to be defined and measured? Some investigators have responded to this question by defining achievement as being what achievement tests measure. Critics of this approach argue that it permits the test to dictate the curriculum and to determine who the good teacher is. Tests vary in the extent to which they assess various kinds of factual and conceptual knowledge. Tests tap only indirectly achievement variables related to habits of work, attitudes, and values. Achievement tests are not tailored to the goals of individual teachers or even to the goals of school or a school system. The kind of achievement most easily measured is subject matter knowledge of a factual kind. Nevertheless, the use of such scores does not free the investigator from measurement problems.

Problems in the use of pupil achievement variables as criteria of teacher effectiveness can perhaps best be illustrated by thinking about a hypothetical study in which an investigator is interested in identifying "the most effective" teachers. In an urban school system with one hundred elementary schools containing five hundred fifth grade classes, the investigator has to make a number of decisions with respect to the criterion of teacher effectiveness to be employed. He may be committed philosophically to the criterion of pupil achievement, but this commitment only focuses his questions more narrowly: How should pupil achievement be measured? If he utilizes standardized achievement tests, which tests should he use? In what subject matter areas should achievement be measured? Assuming that he will utilize gain scores and do pretest measurement at the beginning of the school year, when should the posttests be given? Since pupil gains on achievement typically do not progress at a constant rate, students will show greater gains some months than others. Amount of gain obtained will therefore vary according to the months in which the posttests are given. Should the investigator concern himself only with the achievement gains over one academic year or should he be concerned about longer-range objectives? What does he do about the variability from classroom to classroom, and from school to school, in initial pupil achievement level? What should he do about differences from classroom to classroom, and from school to school, in ability levels of pupils?

Assuming that for each of these questions the investigator reaches a satisfactory answer, it is still very likely that critics will object to his solutions on any number of grounds. Some will say that the investigator neglected whole areas relating to the impact the schools should have on the child. Those who maintain that the schools should promote positive mental health will object that the investigator did not measure changes in variables such as attitudes toward classmates, reactions to authority, self-confidence, self-concept, and a host of other variables. Those critics who are concerned with the differences among classrooms and schools will object on the grounds that pupil achievement was influenced by a whole complex of variables over which the investigator did not have adequate control, including home influences on learning, peer influences, effects of non-school experiences on the streets and in social groups, and a host of other variables. Critics of tests will have a great deal to say about the choice of instruments, the controls to assure strict adherence to standardized administration procedures, the statistical methods by which scores were combined and compared, and the relevance of the test to what is or should be taught in schools.

Teacher Characteristics as Criteria

The investigator who chooses this type of criterion for evaluating teacher effectiveness also faces a number of problems and possible criticisms. Studies that utilize this type of criterion typically rely on ratings of teacher characteristics or behaviors, or on devices that attempt to measure more directly characteristics of teachers such as personality traits, attitudes, and interests. The use of ratings may place the problem of the definition of effective teaching directly in the hands of the rater, or the investigator may ask raters to make judgments on a number of characteristics or behaviors he believes are related to effective teaching. In the first instance, the rater has a criterion of effectiveness in his head; in the second, the investigator determines the criterion in the use to which he puts the ratings. In either case, someone has to arrive at a conception of what effective teaching is, which involves preferences, attitudes, and values. Any two judges obviously might define effective teaching quite differently. Some judges might put the most emphasis on the teacher's ability to convey factual subject matter, while others might place most emphasis on the ability of the teacher to relate warmly and supportively to children. To a large extent, effective teaching lies in the eye of the beholder. The most compelling problem with the use of ratings lies in the lack of agreement from rater to rater. Ratings by principals may not agree with ratings by fellow teachers which in turn may not agree with ratings by pupils, parents, or teacher-training faculties. The measuring devices utilized present many problems, some of which will be detailed in the section on research using rating scales.

In many studies, attempts have been made to measure directly characteristics of teachers, including interests, personality traits, attitudes, and reaction tendencies. Such studies require that someone at some point make a judgment with respect to the relationship between such measures and being a good teacher. It is not necessarily the case that the warm, supportive teacher is the most effective teacher judging by other criteria such as pupil achievement. Data from some of these studies will be summarized in sections that follow.

As Biddle (1964, p. 21) points out, in the research literature the measuring technique has often been confused with the variable being measured, so that confusion has developed between variables related to effectiveness, that is, the dependent variables, and variables that serve as criteria of effectiveness. To be examined in this section are approaches to studying the variables that may correlate with teaching effectiveness, defined either by criteria of pupil gain or by judgments of experts.

Four approaches to measurement have been described by Biddle (pp. 21–31). More detailed descriptions of these approaches appear in various chapters of the comprehensive *The Handbook of Research on Teaching* (Medley and Mitzel, pp. 247–328; Remmers, pp. 329–378; Bloom, pp. 379–397; Stern, pp. 398–447; Getzels and Jackson, pp. 506–582).

Observation Techniques

Observation techniques require that investigators gather information through the direct observation of behavior. The direct observation of teachers and pupils in the classroom is an obvious, seemingly simple, approach to studying teaching effectiveness. As Medley and Mitzel (p. 247) point out, however, the typical study does not include any formal observation. These writers discuss a number of factors that seemingly account for the reluctance of most researchers to use direct observational techniques. Among the problems are the following: observations are costly in time, money, and skill required of observers; observations involve invasion of privacy that administrators and teachers resent and resist; the presence in the classroom of an observer is disturbing which results in behavior that cannot be regarded as typical of behavior that occurs when an observer is not present; the number of classrooms studied must be kept small in observational studies. In spite of these difficulties, however, the approach has been used in some of the studies on teacher effectiveness. Medley and Mitzel (p. 249) argue that observation is most useful in research on teacher effectiveness when it is used in an effort to increase understanding of the nature of effective teaching, and that it cannot be used in most instances to evaluate effects of teaching on pupils, the criterion of teacher effectiveness which these authors accept. They argue with supportive data that attempts to relate what goes on in the classroom to measures of pupil growth have not been successful.

Reliability.   Observational techniques are defined as "procedures which use systematic observations of classroom behavior to obtain reliable and valid measurements of differences in the typical behaviors which occur in different classrooms, or in different situations in the same classroom" (Medley and Mitzel, p. 250). In successive paragraphs, these authors discuss the requirements observational techniques should fulfill. As Medley and Mitzel define the term, reliability refers to the extent to which the average difference between two measurements obtained independently in the same classroom is smaller than the average difference between two measurements obtained in different classrooms. Unreliability in observations occurs when two measures of the same class differ too much, either because the behaviors are unstable or because the observers cannot agree. Unreliability also stems from classroom situations in which differences between classes are too small and exceed the sensitivity of the instrument.

Validity.   Medley and Mitzel (p. 250) define validity as follows: "A measure is valid to the extent that differences in scores yielded by it reflect actual differences in behavior—not differences in impressions made on different observers. For an observational scale to be valid for measuring behavior, it must provide an accurate record of behaviors which actually occurred, scored in such a way that the scores are reliable." There are three critical elements in this definition: observation of a representative sample of the behaviors to be measured; accurate recording of the observed behavior; scoring which reflects differences in behavior.

Observational techniques have been used in several studies in an attempt to identify the behaviors that distinguish ineffective teachers from effective teachers. It seems fair to state that this approach has not been very productive. Medley and Mitzel (p. 257) state this conclusion even more strongly: "No fallacy is more widely believed than the one which says that it is possible to judge a teacher's skill by watching him teach. It is difficult to find anyone, professional educator or layman, who does not think he himself, at least, can recognize good teaching when he sees it."

Medley and Mitzel do not believe that the data support the contention that observers can judge a teacher's skill by watching her teach. Their arguments are compelling. They quote conclusions (p. 258) from a number of studies in which ratings of effectiveness were compared with criteria of teacher effectiveness based on pupil learning, that is, on pupil achievement gain scores. Representative quotations follow ". . . no appreciable relationship exists between rating criteria and pupil achievement criteria," and "the criterion of pupil change apparently measures something different from that measured by teacher ratings."

Rating Forms

The rating method is probably the most common technique used in research on teacher effectiveness (Remmers, p. 329; Biddle and Ellena, p. 25). Researchers have asked judges to rate a wide range of variables including the teacher's classroom performance, personality characteristics, intellectual ability, and social skills. The judges used in rating studies have included supervisors, principals, superintendents, parents, other teachers, pupils, and the teacher himself. Since in the rating method the measuring device is the individual rater and not the form utilized, this kind of variability in rater use from study to study has had considerable effect on the results obtained. Remmers (1963, p. 329) quotes Good's definition of *rating* as follows: "An estimate, made according to some systematized procedure, of the degree to which an individual person or thing possesses any given characteristic; may be expressed qualitatively." *Rating scale* is defined (Remmers, 1963, p. 329) as, "a device used in evaluating products, attitudes, or other characteristics of instructors or learners."

Remmers (p. 330) suggests five criteria for the evaluation of rating scales as measuring devices:

1. *Objectivity*. Use of the instrument should yield variable, reproducible data not a function of the peculiar characteristics of the rater.

2. *Reliability*. It should yield the same values, within the limits of allowable error, under the same set of conditions. Since basically in ratings, the rater and not the record of his responses is the instrument, this criterion boils down to the accuracy of observations by the rater.

3. *Sensitivity*. It should yield as fine distinctions as are typically made in communicating about the object of investigation.

4. *Validity*. Its content, in this case the categories in the rating scale, should be relevant to a defined area of investigation and to some relevant behavioral science construct; if possible, the data should be covariant with some other, experimentally independent, index. These requirements correspond to the concepts of definitional, construct,

concurrent, and predictive validity (American Psychological Association, et al., 1954).

5. *Utility.* It should efficiently yield information relevant to contemporary theoretical and practical issues; i.e. it should not be so cumbersome and laborious as to preclude collection of data at reasonable rate.

Several types of rating scales have been used in research on teacher effectiveness. These include numerical rating scales, graphic rating scales, cumulated points rating scales, multiple-choice rating forms, check lists, and forced-choice rating scales. Remmers has described these devices in considerable detail (pp. 331–343). As Biddle states (Biddle and Ellena, p. 26), "Generally, the results of research using rating forms have been poor and contradictory." He credits these results to personal biasis on the part of judges, a lack of training for observation when ratings are based on observation, and a lack of first-hand information regarding the teacher or the classroom interaction. Other problems lie with the failure of many of the rating scales used in the studies of teacher effectiveness to conform to the standards of good measurement regarding reliability, validity, objectivity, sensitivity, and utility.

Ratings made of the same teachers by different judges—supervisors, principals, pupils—show little agreement among themselves. The supervisor of the teacher in training may have quite a different view of the teacher than the principal who rates her during her first, fifth, or tenth year on the job. Pupils may see the teacher in a still different light. Few relationships have been found between pupil gain factors and ratings. Schmid (1961) analyzed the results of seven of the Wisconsin studies on teacher effectiveness. He reached the following conclusion: "Pupil gain factors bear no relationship to rating factors" (Schmid, 1961, p. 69).

In spite of the generally discouraging findings, studies of teacher effectiveness using rating scales have proliferated. Biddle (p. 26) relates the proliferation to the continued prevalence of rating forms in school programs related to merit pay and promotion. Davis (p. 57) reports a study carried out in 1961 by the Research Division of the National Education Association on personnel practices of school superintendents. The questionnaire included a request for copies of forms used in evaluation of teachers. The questionnaires were sent to superintendents in 189 school systems in cities of 100,000. Forms were received from 81 systems. Some school districts used more than one form. Davis (p. 58) reports that "The first reaction was bewilderment at the infinite variety." Comparison of data from the 1961–1962 survey with data from a similar survey in 1955–1956 shows a marked increase in this six-year period in the percent of urban school districts in every population group that reported the rating of all teachers.

In 1955–1956, 39 percent of school districts over 100,000 in population reported that all teachers were rated. In 1961–1962, 58 percent reported that all teachers were rated. When comparisons were made between large and small school systems for the period 1961–1962, of districts reporting from large communities (100,000 to 499,999 in population), 56 percent reported that they rated all teachers, 37 percent reported that they rated some teachers, and only 6 percent reported that they rated no teachers. Of 186 small districts reporting (5000 to 9999 in population), the figures reported were 55 percent, 5 percent, and 32 percent respectively (Davis, p. 55). Data from the 1955–1956 study showed that in 37 percent of the districts, the principal was the only rater. Fifty percent of the largest districts (a half million or more) gave entire responsibility for rating to the principal. Of all districts reporting, 27 percent reported joint ratings by principal and supervisor. The bulk of the ratings, therefore, were carried out by the principal. Biddle (1964, p. 26) describes the rationale behind continued extensive use of rating scales as follows:

> Pressure is felt in many American communities to promote and raise the pay of only the best teachers. To those who are strongly committed to "quality" education, even a poor program of teacher evaluation seems better than no program at all. Probably the majority of educational administrators feel (with some justification) that they can identify the "best" and "worst" teachers. Many teachers themselves enjoy working in schools that provide "feedback" through the regular use of rating forms. Thus, despite doubt-casting evidence, there are strong pressures to keep rating instruments in the schools.

Remmers has summarized an extensive study by McCall (Remmers, p. 368) which casts considerable doubt on the ability of principals to identify the "best" and "worst" teachers. McCall carried out a three-year, statewide study for the State Department of Public Instruction in North Carolina. McCall used as the criterion of teacher effectiveness pupil gain variables as measured by a wide variety of tests. He defined good teachers as those who stimulated the most growth and poor teachers as those who stimulated the least growth. Remmers quotes his conclusions as follows: "Thus the principals tended to a very slight degree to call good teachers poor and poor teachers good (p. 23). . . . The rating of a teacher by her peers showed an index of validity of 11 percent. In short, there is a tendency for every adult associated with the teachers professionally to misjudge the teachers (p. 24). . . . All things considered, this research failed to find any system of measuring teacher merit which the writer is willing to recommend be adopted as a basis for paying the salaries of all teachers" (p. 366). In her report of the 1955–1956 study by NEA of the use of rating forms by school districts, Davis (p. 57) includes a table which shows the uses made of teacher ratings by percentage of 1064 districts using ratings. Uses reported were as follows: As a supervisory aid, 77 percent; in deciding on reappointment of teachers not on tenure, 71 percent; in recommending probationary teachers for permanent tenure, 56 percent; in selecting teachers for promotion, 36 percent; in paying regular increments on the salary schedule, 16 percent; in selecting teachers to receive super-maximum salaries, 7 percent.

There are few data in the rating studies on teacher effectiveness that would support use of such techniques in promoting, hiring, or paying teachers. Remmers (p. 367) quotes with approval and without amendment a report from the American Educational Research Association Committee on the Criteria of Teacher Effectiveness (1953): . . . "the present condition of research on teacher effectiveness holds little promise of yielding results commensurate with the needs of American education . . . after 40 years of research on teacher effectiveness . . . one can point to few outcomes that a superintendent of schools can safely employ in hiring a teacher or granting him tenure."

STUDIES OF TEACHING

There have been a number of observational studies of what occurs in classrooms. A thoroughgoing summary is well beyond the scope of this chapter, but one such study is worth dealing with in some detail so that we may become familiar with the evidence it has produced and the methodology involved. Bellack, et al. (1966) were interested in observing and analyzing precisely what occurred at a verbal level in the classroom. They selected a standard unit on trade and found fifteen teachers in tenth and twelfth grade classes in seven high schools in and around New York City who were willing to teach the unit and be tape-recorded. Among the many analyses of these data is one that simply refers to the percentage of verbal interaction for teachers and pupils. Using as a measure the number of lines transcribed, Bellack found that teachers had an average of 72 percent of the lines and the pupils had an average of 27 percent. This represents roughly a 3:1 ratio of teacher:pupil talking in favor of the teacher.

Bellack also identified a teaching cycle that seems to recur in systematic patterns. Fact stating and explaining occupied 50 to 60 percent of the total discourse. There have been many other studies using different techniques which seem to suggest that this ratio of teacher talk to pupil talk is quite stable over teachers, over time, and over subject matter. One of the curious things about education is how stable teaching behavior appears to be. Bellack's analysis of the classroom suggests a model of teaching in which four pedagogical approaches are identified: structuring, soliciting, responding, and reacting. This way of analyzing the verbal interactions of the classroom is useful in that it allows us to deal with such material in a conceptual way. But again what seems to be surprising is the finding that this model is quite stable despite the variety of differences in teacher personality and style, despite the efforts of teacher training institutions to change teaching behavior, despite all the writing and lecturing about theory and application in teaching.

If it is true that teaching behaviors follow a model rather regularly, whether it is the model described by Bellack or another one, it might be that teaching behavior in turn is shaped by the school system. This is partly what Sieber (1968) suggested when he wrote about the influences of the school and community which act to suppress innovation on the part of teachers. Sieber argues that the school system is in the unique position of having on the one hand to be a public performance and on the other to be a private one. The children come into the system each day and are instructed but then return to their families who in turn have considerable control over the system. Sieber argues that the school system is on the defensive and builds up unseen influences to make teachers conform and be supportive of each other for fear that any individual teacher could raise the demands made upon all by an innovative act which would be received favorably by the parents and pupils. This is much like the union attitude of not breaking the standard on the theory that anyone who would be more productive would endanger the performance demands for all others.

It would be even more interesting to analyze the positive and negative reinforcement system that comes to bear on young teachers when they enter a school system, to examine both the reinforcements that stem from pupils and those that stem from other teachers and the administration. (For an introduction to behavior modification as a teaching tool based on reinforcement theory, see Madsen and Madsen in Readings: Section 3.)

Another theory to explain what may be a remarkable consistency in teacher behavior from classroom to classroom, as well as in pupil behavior, is that the ways in which people can transmit knowledge and skills to each other may just be very limited. It may be that these ways have not changed dramatically over thousands of years with the exception of current technological developments such as television and computer assisted instruction. But when we rely in a classroom on what a teacher can say and do and what pupils can say and do, the number of channels open for transmission may be extremely limited and thus may lead to what may seem to be a ritualized arrangement, or conformity, or rigidity. It would be interesting to identify all the various ways of transmitting a skill or knowledge to another person. We might find that the ways are few. In any case, teachers do most of the talking. As Hudgins and Ahlbrand (1970) indicated in a study of seventh and ninth grade English classes, teachers spoke 83 percent of the time, which corresponds roughly to Bellack's measure by transcribed lines of 72 percent.

One of the most extensive studies of the characteristics of teachers was the massive Teacher Characteristic Study directed by Ryans (1960). In this eight-year study, extensive data were collected on some 6000 teachers in 1700 schools. For this study, which Ryans has summarized in detail (Ryans, in Biddle, 1964, pp. 67–100), a variety of data-gathering techniques were utilized including direct observation of teacher behavior in the classroom, questionnaires, tests and inventories, and background information surveys. The study involved more than six years of work and included some one hundred separate research projects. By means of carefully controlled classroom observation, some of the studies examined the nature of teacher behavior patterns in the classroom and their relationship to pupil behaviors. Three patterns of teacher behavior were derived from factor analysis of data from classroom observations: (1) understanding, friendly, warm as opposed to egocentric, aloof, restricted; (2) businesslike, systematic, responsible as opposed to unplanned, slipshod, evading; (3) imaginative, stimulating as opposed to routine, dull. On tests, elementary school teachers expressed more favorable attitudes toward pupils, teachers, and administrators than did secondary school teachers. Secondary teachers expressed more traditional attitudes than elementary teachers, who expressed more permissive attitudes.

Some twenty-five separate instruments were employed in the Ryans studies. From these, a 300-item omnibus self-report inventory was developed. Scores on the nine scales of this inventory were then related to a number of variables, including classroom behavier, early experience, age, sex, marital status, and size of school. In one study, responses on this inventory of two extreme groups of teachers were compared. The two groups were: (1) a higher group of teachers composed of the top 16 percent on the three dimensions cited earlier as judged by observers; and (2) a lower group of teachers composed of the bottom 16 percent on these three dimensions. Ryans listed a number of differences between the two groups (1960, pp. 397–398). Higher teachers were strongly interested in reading, music, painting, and the arts. They were generous in their evaluations of other people. They participated in social groups, enjoyed pupil relationships, and preferred nondirective classroom procedures. They were superior in emotional adjustment and in verbal intelligence. Lower teachers, on the other hand, tended to be less favorable toward pupils, to be more critical in their judgments of other people, and to prefer activities in which close personal contacts were minimized. They were lower in verbal intelligence and less satisfactory in emotional adjustment.

Numerous studies of teacher effectiveness were carried out at the University of Wisconsin between 1940 and 1960. Barr (1961) has summarized some seventy-five doctoral studies which made up this program of research. These studies, which varied markedly in focus and methodology, produced a mass of results and conclusions, only a few of which will be cited here: (1) In abilities, teachers showed much unevenness. They were high in some abilities and low in others. There appeared to be few multi-talented teachers. On the basis of the Wisconsin studies, Barr hypothesized that, "a good teacher is one that has one or more special talents and no deficiencies that the school, community or administration consider critical" (1961, p. 140). (2) Teacher acts have an appropriateness aspect. They are not bad or good in general, but must be seen in the light of situations, persons, and purposes. Therefore, teacher behaviors collected out of context should not be expected to distinguish good and poor teachers. (3) Since teaching does not take place in a vacuum, effectiveness does not reside in the teacher as such, but in the interrelationships among key aspects of the learning-teaching situation. (4) Certain broad categories of effectiveness seem to exist: a *cognitive category* composed of such characteristics as intelligence, subject matter, knowledge, and cultural background; an *affective category* composed of motivation, attitudes, value system; a *physical fitness category* composed of energy, drive, good health; a *personal fitness category* composed of such traits as cooperativeness, buoyancy, expressiveness, judgment, forcefulness, resourcefulness; a *professional competency category* made up of skills in communication and human relationships and manipulative and verbal skills associated with teaching. (5) "Efficiency ratings" may be heavily loaded with a compatibility component. (6) The constituents of teacher effectiveness may not be additive. New concepts of the structure of teaching ability may be necessary.

In recent years, descriptive studies have been used to develop normative data on teaching as it takes place in typical classrooms. In summarizing several studies, Rosenshine and Furst (in Smith, 1971, pp. 37–72), who decry our lack of knowledge about the relationships between teacher behavior and student growth, conclude:

> . . . there is very little difference in the interaction patterns which occur when teachers teach different subjects in elementary classrooms; that there is frequent use of teacher behaviors classified as "controlling"; and that a great deal of time is spent on managerial and administrative details. . . . Data from studies made of high school teaching show that teachers spend much of their time covering content

that requires but one common pattern of student thinking, fact stating or cognitive memory (p. 39).

Two recent trends in education may lead researchers and teacher trainers to focus more attention on the relationship between teacher class-room behavior and student gains, a relationship about which relatively little is known. One of these trends is accountability; the other is per-formance criteria. Under the demands of accountability, schools are asked to subject their operations to cost analysis and presumably will be inter-ested in including analysis of the costs of attaining certain educational outcomes. The emphasis on the use of performance criteria, that is, on the specific observables of teacher behavior, is related to the current em-phasis on behavioral objectives in instruction. If schools and teachers are to be held accountable for achieving specific behavioral objectives, the good teacher, the effective teacher, may be the teacher who helps the most children to reach the largest number of specified behavioral objectives in the shortest period of time. Evaluation of teacher effectiveness may then produce more clear-cut results than evaluation in the light of vague, tra-ditional objectives such as "individualizing instruction," "helping each child reach his potential," "educating the whole child," or even "pro-moting maximum achievement for every child."

REFERENCES

Barr, A. S. (Ed.) *The Measurement and Prediction of Teacher Effective-ness: A Summary of Investigations.* Madison: Dembar Publications, 1961.

Beecher, C. Data-gathering devices employed in the Wisconsin studies. In A. S. Barr (Ed.), *The Measurement and Prediction of Teacher Effectiveness: A Summary of Investigations.* Madison: Dembar Publica-tions, 1961, 30–47.

Bellack, A. A., Kliebard, H. M., Hyman, R. T., & Smith, F. L. *The Language of the Classroom.* New York: Teachers College Press, 1966.

Biddle, B. J. The integration of teacher effectiveness research. In B. J. Biddle & W. J. Ellena (Eds.), *Contemporary Research on Teacher Effectiveness.* New York: Holt, Rinehart and Winston, 1964, 1–40.

Biddle, B. J., & Ellena, W. J. (Eds.) *Contemporary Research on Teacher Effectiveness.* New York: Holt, Rinehart and Winston, 1964.

Bloom, B. S. Testing cognitive ability and achievement. In N. L. Gage (Ed.), *Handbook of Research on Teaching.* Chicago: Rand McNally, 1963, 379–397.

Bureau of Educational Personnel Development. *Do Teachers Make a Difference: A Report on Recent Research on Pupil Achievement.* Wash-ington, D. C.: U. S. Government Printing Office, 1970.

Davis, H. Evolution of current practices in evaluating teacher competence.

In B. J. Biddle & W. J. Ellena (Eds.), *Contemporary Research on Teacher Effectiveness*. New York: Holt, Rinehart and Winston, 1964, 41–66.

Dickinson, D. J. Changing behavior with behavioral techniques. *Journal of School Psychology*, 1968, **6,** 278–283.

Flanders, N. A. Teacher effectiveness. *Encyclopedia of Educational Research* (4th ed.) R. L. Ebel (Ed.) New York: Macmillan, 1969, 1423–1437.

Flook, A. J. M., & Saggar, U. Academic performance with, and without, knowledge of scores on tests of intelligence, aptitude, and personality. *Journal of Educational Psychology*, 1968, **59,** 395–401.

Gage, N. L. Paradigms for research on teaching. In N. L. Gage (Ed.), *Handbook of Research on Teaching*. Chicago: Rand McNally, 1963, 94–141.

Getzels, J. W., & Jackson, P. W. The teacher's personality and characteristics. In N. L. Gage (Ed.), *Handbook of Research on Teaching*. Chicago: Rand McNally, 1963, 506–582.

Hudgins, B. B., & Ahlbrand, W. P. Some properties of formal teacher and pupil classroom communication. *Psychology in the Schools*, 1970, **7,** No. 3, 265–269.

LeFevre, C. Teacher characteristics and careers. *Review of Educational Research*, October 1967, **37,** No. 4, 433–447.

Leveque, K. L., & Walker, R. E. Correlates of high school cheating behavior. *Psychology in the Schools*, 1970, **7,** No. 2, 159–164.

Madsen, C. H., Jr., & Madsen, C. K. *Teaching/Discipline: Behavioral Principles Toward a Positive Approach*. Boston: Allyn and Bacon, 1970.

Medley, D. M., & Mitzel, H. E. Measuring classroom behavior by systematic observation. In N. L. Gage (Ed.), *Handbook of Research on Teaching*. Chicago: Rand McNally, 1963, 247–328.

Morrison, A., & McIntire, D. *Teachers and Teaching*. Baltimore: Penguin Books, 1969.

Page, E. B. Teacher comments and student performance: A 74 classroom experiment in school motivation. *Journal of Educational Psychology*, 1958, **49,** 173–181.

Pi Lambda Theta. *The Evaluation of Teaching*. Washington, D. C.: Pi Lambda Theta, 1967.

Popham, W. J. Performance tests of teaching proficiency: Rationale development, and validation. *American Educational Research Association Journal*, January 1971, **8,** No. 1, 105–117.

Remmers, H. H. Rating methods in research on teaching. In N. L. Gage (Ed.), *Handbook of Research on Teaching*. Chicago: Rand McNally, 1963, 329–378.

Rosenshine, B. Enthusiastic teaching: A research review. *School Review*, August 1970, **78,** No. 4, 499–514.

Rosenshine, B., & Furst, N. Research in teacher performance criteria. In B. O. Smith (Ed.), *Research in Teacher Education*. Englewood Cliffs, N. J.: Prentice-Hall, 1971, 37–72.

Ryans, D. G. *Characteristics of Teachers*. Washington, D. C.: American Council on Education, 1960.

Ryans, D. G. The teacher characteristics study. In B. J. Biddle & W. J.

Ellena, (Eds.), *Contemporary Research on Teachers Effectiveness*. New York: Holt, Rinehart and Winston, 1964, 67–100.

Schmid, J. Factor analysis of the teaching complex. In A. S. Barr (Ed.), *The Measurement and Prediction of Teacher Effectiveness: A Summary of Investigations*. Madison: Dembar Publications, 1961, 58–69.

Scott, P. M., Burton, R. V., & Yassow, M. R. Social reinforcement under natural conditions. *Child Development*, 1967, **38**, 53–64.

Sieber, S. D. Organizational influences on innovative roles. In T. L. Eidell & J. M. Kitchess (Eds.), *Knowledge Production and Utilization in Educational Administration*. Columbus, Ohio: University Council for Educational Administration, 1968, 121–142.

Smith, B. O. (Ed.) *Research in Teacher Education*. Englewood Cliffs, N. J.: Prentice-Hall, 1971, 166.

Stern, G. G. Measuring non-cognitive variables in research on teaching. In N. L. Gage (Ed.), *Handbook of Research on Teaching*. Chicago: Rand McNally, 1963, 398–447.

Vance, B. J. Social learning theory and guidance in early childhood. In D. M. Gelfand (Ed.), *Social Learning in Childhood: Reading in Theory and Application*. Belmont, Calif.: Brooks Cole Publishing Company, 1969, 134–145.

White, K. Delay of test information feedback and learning in a conventional classroom. *Psychology in the Schools*, 1968, **5**, 78–81.

Worthen, B. R. Discovery and expository test presentation in elementary mathematics. *Journal of Educational Psychology*, 1968, **59**, Monograph Supplement No. 1, P. 2.

Yamamoto, K. Evaluating teacher effectiveness: A review of research. *Journal of School Psychology*, Winter 1963–64, **2**, No. 1, 60–71.

HENRY INMAN, *Dismissal of School on an October Afternoon*. Courtesy,
Museum of Fine Arts, Boston (M. and M. Karolik Collection).

chapter 9

Contemporary Issues
in the Curriculum

All who have meditated on the art of governing mankind have been convinced that the fate of empires depends on the education of youth. Educated men are as much superior to uneducated men as the living are to the dead.

—Aristotle: quoted by Diogenes Laertius

What shall be the criteria for inclusion in a curriculum? How can we determine if a curriculum is effective? What should the goals of a curriculum be?

History of Curriculum Development

If we review even superficially the history of curriculum making in this country, it becomes apparent that these questions still have not been answered and often are not even asked. The word "curriculum" means course, coming from the Latin, *curriculum*, meaning running or chariot. A curriculum is a course one runs.

The Committee of Ten on Secondary School Studies was appointed at a meeting of the National Education Association in 1892 and made its report the following year (*Report of the Committee of Ten*, 1893). The committee, formed to discuss "uniformity in school programmes and in requirements for college" was composed of ten distinguished representatives of colleges and secondary schools: Eliott of Harvard; Harris, Commissioner of Education for the United States; Angel of the University of Michigan; Tetlow from the Girls' Latin School in Boston; Taylor of Vassar; Robinson from Albany High School in New York; Baker of the University of Colorado; Jessey of the University of Missouri; McKensie from Law-

283

renceville School in New Jersey; and King of Oberlin. All were presidents of their educational units, headmasters, or principals. They represented selected public universities, distinguished private colleges for men and women, and leading high schools, predominately in the eastern and mid-western regions. The educators concerned with college admissions and the high school curriculum in 1892 represented the more selective high schools and colleges. In 1900, there was almost a 2:1 ratio in favor of attendance in a private college as opposed to a public one. By 1965, in contrast, the ratio was reversed in favor of the public college or university. In terms of numbers, 240,000 students were enrolled in higher education in 1900; by 1965, there were 5½ million, or an increase of twenty-two fold. As for high school, 630,000 students were in grades 9 through 12 in 1900; by 1965 there were over 13 million. Tremendous growth has taken place in our high school and college populations during this period, increasing by twenty to thirty times the numbers involved in 1900 (*Digest of Educational Statistics*, 1968).

The conference held by the Committee of Ten in 1892 was organized according to subject matter in the following order:

1. Latin
2. Greek
3. English
4. Other modern languages
5. Mathematics
6. Physics, Astronomy, Chemistry
7. Natural History, Biology, Botany, Zoology, and Physiology
8. History, Civil Government, and Political Economy
9. Geography, Geology, and Meteorology

What assumptions were inherent in the way this conference was organized? What model of education was assumed, if not stated? The first assumption was that the existing subjects should compose the curriculum, for there was no provision for subjects that were not already being taught. There was a clear emphasis on the classic western liberal arts model, with stress on Latin and Greek at the expense of more scientific subjects. Another assumption was that each subject was independent of the others, with no apparent concern for the overall curriculum reflected in the agenda.

The conference was to decide such questions as:

1. What is the best age, from six to eighteen years, for the introduction of a subject?
2. How many hours per week for how many years should subjects be taught?
3. How often should the subject be taught in high school?
4. What should be the content reserved for teaching at the high school level?

5. What should be college admissions level in the subject, and in what form? Should the examination consist of sight translation, a laboratory examination, or a written examination?
6. Should the subject be taught differently to those who are college bound, those who are bound for a scientific school, and those who are terminal high school students?
7. What is the best method of teaching the subject and the best method of testing for college admissions?

The questions assumed that the curriculum would be composed essentially of the same elements, and the major issue would be how much and when. We would predict that the primary outcome of the conference would be organizational and that subject matter specialists would press for greater emphasis on their areas. The recommendations that came out of the conference were indeed close to what we predicted. Almost all of the participants wanted the study of their subject to start earlier in the elementary grades. Languages, numbers, and geography had been in the elementary curriculum for a long time, and now the newer subjects wanted equal exposure. Advocates of mathematics, natural history, physics, and chemistry all felt that learning should have taken place at an earlier level that involved "observing, reflecting, and recording." The college history teachers who were present claimed that college students had "no habit of historical investigation." It is not surprising that the conference report included this interesting paragraph:

> It is inevitable, therefore, that specialists in any one of the subjects which are pursued in the high schools or college, should earnestly desire that the minds of young children be stored with some of the elementary facts and principles of their subject; and that all the mental habits, which the adult student will surely need, begin to be formed in the child's mind before the age of fourteen (*Report of the Committee of Ten*, 1893, p. 16).

Higher Teacher Mandate

This notion that the curriculum should be determined by the concerns of teachers higher in the educational system is a model for curriculum building which we will term *higher teacher mandate*. This model of curriculum building assumes that what a pupil needs to learn in elementary or secondary school is mandated by what a teacher at a higher level, usually in college, states a student should know before he enters the higher course. How the higher teacher determines what the student's entry skills need to be is rarely made explicit. We often do not even know if a student who had attained these skills many years earlier is aided at all in his attempts to learn the material at a higher level. It might well be that it is far more efficient, for example, to teach a student selected units in algebra for two weeks before he starts a statistics course than it is to have him take algebra for two years in high school some eight years before he enters the statistics course. Probably very little of the high school course remains available to the student when he starts on his statistics course.

Some teachers may decide that certain skills should already be present because they do not want to teach them. Other teachers may select as essential entry skills his own entry skills for teaching the subject, not for learning it. As a subject matter specialist, the teacher may have a very different goal in mind for himself within that subject than his students do, and he may therefore require a whole set of entry skills that are not necessary for the student. What is of even more concern, when we reflect upon this model, is the notable lack of data to tell us which prior skills are necessary for which objectives. Where are the data to tell us what is the appropriate sequence of learning for a desired end goal? This is an even more difficult question when the end goal is not stated, as it was not in the Report of the Committee of Ten, or when the end goal is merely assumed through some kind of expertise which we have called the higher teacher mandate. When high school curricula were being rewritten during the 1950s and 1960s, the higher teacher mandate apparently was operating again in a somewhat different guise, as we will discuss below.

Committee of Ten: Recommendations

The Committee of Ten did make one significant decision, one we did not predict, when it decided against tracking within subjects, but instead strongly recommended teaching the subjects in the same way to all students in the high school. The reason given is that the high school at that time did not exist to prepare "that insignificant percentage" who immediately went on to college. The main function of secondary schools, the committee stated, "is to prepare for the duties of life that small proportion . . . able to profit from education prolonged to the eighteenth year and who will not go on to further schooling." However, they wanted to make it possible that any graduate of a high school which followed the proposed curriculum would be able to apply to college and be considered for entrance at some time in his future. This equality of admissions would only be possible if subjects were taught the same way to all students, including those who did not think that they were going to be able to go on to college. This seems like a typically American decision because it has inherent in it a concern for the majority, a concern for equality of teaching and opportunity, and an attempt to keep open the gateway to mobility at some later stage if a youngster should find that he could go on to college after all.

As far as the particular subject matter was concerned, the committee made a number of decisions such as:

1. Latin was to be begun a year before Greek in the ninth grade.
2. Concrete geometry was to be taught in the fifth through eighth grades.
3. Biography and mythology in history were to be taught in the fifth and sixth grades.

We can only ask: Why? Why were these decisions made? From what criteria were they derived? On what data were they based?

A tenth grader who followed the suggestions of the Committee of Ten would have followed this curriculum, expressed as periods per week:

Latin	5
Greek	5
English	5 (Literature 3, Composition 2)
Algebra (or commercial math)	2½; Geometry 2½
English History	3
elective Modern Language	4
elective Modern Second Language	4
elective Astronomy	5

This reformation of 1893 was toward uniformity of the curriculum in what was to become a national trend for graduates of secondary schools to go on to college. It was obviously necessary to bring some order out of the chaos so that, no matter what high school they came from, students could expect a fair chance at college admissions. But one can also see some dangers in setting national standards of uniformity. One problem is that the curriculum became a catalog of subjects, with each of its inherents devoted to preserving and enlarging its part of the curriculum. Too little attention was given in these recommendations to the overall curriculum. We could predict that with each part of the curriculum devoted to its own ends and pressing for its share of time, a student would move from one subject matter to another, each compartmentalized and unrelated to the other. After a few years of this kind of high school curriculum, and assuming that the teaching was as mechanistic as some accounts report, we can understand more readily why Dewey's ideas must have sounded so refreshing. Dewey emphasized the importance of the learner as the basic unit, for example, and not the units of the curriculum. He also stressed an experimental approach to teaching and learning which must have been a welcome alternative to the complicated set of marching orders the mandated curriculum must have seemed.

Contemporary Curriculum Models

Bellack (1964) has pointed out that still a different model for the curriculum emerged during the 1930s and 1940s which emphasized the problems of youth. This was an attempt to link different subjects in terms of solving the practical problems faced by the students. It had at least one benefit, according to Bellack, in that it was based on an overall objective for selecting the curriculum.

Scholar's Mandate

In the 1950s still another model for curriculum emerged, this being the structure of knowledge that Bruner proposed. In the Bruner type of curriculum, the ingredients were to include the basic concepts and conceptual tools of the scholar. We earlier raised the question of whether the higher teacher mandate was not basic to the curricular revolution of the fifties. It might be more accurate to describe it as the *scholar's mandate* because this revolution assumed that what a scholar knew and was able to do should determine what was taught at the lower levels. We might ask why producing a scholar should be the behavioral objective, since few of the student population are going to become scholars. (There are even those who think that behaving like a scholar is not very desirable in any case.) Bruner and those who participated in this movement tended to be scholars, and quite naturally, teaching children how to behave like one seemed a desirable goal. We would have to concede that this model contained behavioral objectives, which were generally those of thinking and behaving like a scholar.

Bruner (1960) argued that concepts make experience more comprehensible because experience thereby becomes more economical and connected. The structure of knowledge, therefore, should be the proper emphasis in education. On the face of it, this seems reasonable, but it is peculiarly a scholar's way of dealing with experience because he is concerned with economical and connecting ways of looking at knowledge. Where are the data to tell us if this is best for everyone, or for a majority? Best for what? If one's life is meager in experience, quite routine, and at the level of mere existence as it is for over half of the world's population, thinking in this highly organized way might be disastrously barren, if not unbearable. Perhaps there is a richness in unorganized detail that serves a purpose in some styles of life. As Bellack emphasized, this spiraling curriculum that Bruner espoused was expected to enhance comprehension as pupils grew older and to emphasize patterns of advanced knowledge that would make the structure clearer and more organized. Bellack pointed out that the spiraling curriculum does not concern itself with the total curriculum.

The model of education that the curriculum revolution of the 1950s represented seems to be similar to the western liberal arts model (with a heavy dose of science added), but one in which each discipline pushed determinedly for its own skills, importance, and scholarly goals, without regard for the other disciplines, the curriculum as a whole, or, at times, the learner. We could picture a situation similar to what used to be rush week by the fraternities on the university campus. In this picture we have scholars from each discipline trying to persuade the learner to join his particular fraternity, and to make that commitment while he was still in elementary school, certainly by high school. This picture is overdrawn and not entirely fair to the curriculum revolutionaries of the fifties and sixties, for presumably much of what they intended to accomplish has been of worth in terms of the model they proposed. It is quite possible that the average pupil is gaining more mastery, and earlier, in certain subjects. The question remains unanswered as to the desirability or effectiveness of this earlier mastery.

Theoretical Curriculum Models

Let us now consider other notions regarding the goals of education that would determine the nature of the curriculum. Whitehead (1929) spoke about the rhythm of education, which he felt might serve as a basis for a curriculum model. He identified the stages of romance, precision, and finally, generalization, as being the three stages in the rhythm of education. The stage of romance is what he called the first unsystematic apprehension, an immediate cognizance of fact. The stage of precision concerns the grammar of language and science, the tools of analysis. The stage of generalization is essentially equivalent to synthesis. This is an appealing model aesthetically because it is simple and rather elegant. One could construct a curriculum on this basis in each subject matter area which would begin with storing of facts, then analyzing them, and then reaching synthesis. But we must ask: Does this cycle actually happen in learning? Does it happen frequently? If it does happen commonly, does it give the best results as determined by what criteria? Finally, what results do we want?

Spencer (1966) argued that the curriculum in the nineteenth century had been decided on the basis of custom, liking, or prejudice, whereas the criterion should be what things are really most worth learning. There is a limited time to learn, said Spencer, and we should weigh various alternative ways of spending that educational time. This was an enlightened view in that Spencer was weighing alternatives in education, something that has only recently come to the forefront as a result of program planning and budgeting systems. The standard that Spencer proposed is that something is worth learning if it prepares us for complete living more than something else does. By complete living, he included everything from self-preservation to leisure time, with self-preservation coming first. By putting leisure last of five activities, Spencer directly opposed the liberal arts model, which had as one of its goals education for leisure and the enjoyment of arts. Spencer wanted a very practical curriculum, practical in terms of its contributions to living fully throughout one's lifetime.

Before dismissing Spencer as being too utilitarian for our taste, let us recognize that if his standard were taken quite seriously, it might lead us to a fresh look at curriculum and education. If we asked ourselves the question of whether or not X helped more than Y to prepare us for complete living, we would then have to define complete living and how X contributed to it. This could include learning to drive a car, conceptualizing a field of knowledge, developing a set of values for oneself, living harmoniously with people, understanding the questions and answers of earlier philosophers, and comprehending the current technological revolution. Complete living need not be a course in dress-making, but could be what Spencer said, *complete living*. We would then have to order these components as Spencer attempted to do, according to some set of criteria which we would have to specify. Spencer's order was clear. He put self-preservation first; the means of living, second; the care of the family, third; citizenship to the state, fourth; and leisure, fifth. His values clearly involved the preservation of the race, family, and state, in that order.

Barr (1955) proposed that the curriculum shall be "the Great Conversation that we call civilization," and shall emphasize the classics, where "a few men have talked magnificently" and with great skill on the major problems of human experience. Life is short, and these things are the best civilization has produced, therefore the best is none too good for a man. Barr also seems, perhaps suprisingly, to have behavioral objectives. In his model, a student tries to comprehend the classics and in so doing, learns to practice the liberal arts himself. He practices the author's language, imagery, ideas, and questions. This exercise, Barr stated, "nurtures and disciplines and renders supple and subtle the minds of men." In contemporary terms, we would call this *modeling* or *imitation* since the student is learning to behave like the model of the classical writer. Barr (answering Russell's question) was quite clear as to what kind of man he wanted education to create: He wanted a man like the great classical writers. It would be hard to tell when Barr's behavioral objectives were met because great classical writers tend not to be identified immediately, so we would have to wait quite a long time, perhaps centuries before we could be sure about the product. We might agree with Barr that it would be good if more graduates of our schools became great classical writers. On the other hand, only a few are very likely to succeed, and education may not make them but only assists what are naturally gifted persons. If only a small proportion—a very small proportion—are going to be great classical writers, then how would this classical model work for the vast majority, who are less gifted? Barr probably would answer that it is better to have been exposed to a great classical writer, even if you cannot be one yourself, than not to be exposed. The answer, of course, would depend upon our objectives.

Curriculum and Models of Education

So the argument goes back and forth. Do we want students to become scholars? Great classical writers? To be prepared for the complete life? To be trained to learn in an effective way? The criteria for building a curriculum must derive from some model of education which either we assume implicitly or make explicit. These models, in turn, rest upon our values and assumptions about the kind of world and people we want to develop. We need to be clear about these ends if we want to stipulate what should be in a curriculum and how it should be organized.

Curriculum Evaluation

Once we decide to include Unit X in the curriculum, how can we tell if it is suitable, appropriate, effective, better than Y, timely, or in the right sequence? First, we would need to define what a student could do if he mastered Unit X that he could not do previously. We subscribe to the idea that we should be explicit about what Unit X is supposed to accomplish.

Let us consider the models of curriculum that we have reviewed. We discussed the *higher teacher mandate*, as we called it, of 1893; Dewey's *democratic experimental model*; the problems of youth dominant in the 1940s and 1950s; the structure of knowledge in the 1950s and 1960s that we have called the *scholar's mandate*; and now, in the 1970s, we seem to be entering into the individual curriculum which emphasizes that which is more personal, relevant, and idealistic. (See Hertzberg, "The Now Culture" and Heath, "Affective Curriculum" in Readings: Section 3.)

In comparing these different approaches to the curriculum, we need to keep in mind a number of questions: (1) What shall the desired product be? Do we want to turn out teachers, scholars, or practical men? (2) Is the curriculum appropriate and reasonable for its intended pupils? (3) Does the curriculum assume that the process imbedded in the curriculum is more significant than the content? This would be true for parts of the models proposed by both Dewey and Whitehead who felt that the activity of the classroom was more important than the actual material involved in the activity. (4) What *is* the curriculum? Is it the knowledge to be included? The skills? The process of learning? The instructional sequence? The end product in the form of a person?

The evaluation of curricula involves many problems. A particularly frustrating one involves the evaluation of a new curriculum. If we have introduced a truly new curriculum, traditional tests will not tap what we are trying to teach. We could invent a new test to tap what the new curriculum is supposed to teach, but then we cannot give the new test to pupils in the traditional curriculum. One attempt to resolve this problem is to give both the traditional and the experimental tests to both the traditional and experimental pupils. Presumably we will find differences between the two groups on the two tests. Then we have to apply our best judgment as to whether gains on the new test are worth the losses on the old test, a process which Scriven (1967) has described.

A second problem is whether or not the teacher actually implements the new curriculum as it was designed. Few new curricula contain statements as to the criteria for implementation. Curricula can consequently be adopted in hundreds of ways that may not be the intended ones and may not provide a fair trial for them.

Third, what variables shall we measure in our evaluation of a curriculum? In most evaluations, one has to select limited variables because of limited time and resources. We might choose to look at the ATI (an aptitude-treatment interaction) and determine which aspects of the curriculum worked best for what kinds of pupils with what kinds of aptitudes. We might obtain aptitude-treatment interaction (ATI) measurements on such question as: Have the pupils mastered the prerequisite skills before the new curriculum was introduced? What is the cost of this new curriculum, both direct and indirect? What was not taught because this curriculum was introduced? What was the wear and tear on the teachers, pupils, and administrators due to introducing this new curriculum?

Fourth, beyond statistical significance, we have to ask: What is the educational significance of this curriculum? Baker (1969) indicated a number of techniques available now for interpreting practical significance. We now can address ourselves to the question of how much practical gain would be involved in accomplishing this educational objective and at what educational costs.

Special Problems in Curriculum Evaluation

A question Gagné (1967) raised, which looks deceptively simple at first, is whether pupils taught a curriculum in an A, C, B order might end up with more proficiency than if taught in the A, B, C order. Some things may need to come before others for efficient learning. This is generally assumed throughout the curriculum but it has rarely been measured, so we lack firm data on which to make a judgment. One of the most obvious arguments that could be made, for example, is that the learning of another language should occur when children are more efficient language learners, probably somewhere early in elementary school. One could argue for a curriculum based on sequence in the curriculum which depended upon the learners' characteristics. If this argument were accepted, we might drop many things out of the elementary curriculum in order to put in the mastery of a second language which, if taught intensively and extensively, could be mastered much more easily at this age than at a later age.

If we decide to measure the effect of a particular curriculum, we need to measure when that effect takes place. Common sense tells us that not everything that has had effect in our education took place at the teaching moment. It may be, for example, that Curriculum A shows no particular effects on tests given right after its completion, but that four years later, or ten years later, students may show a positive or negative effect that can be traced to that particular curriculum.

One of the more troubling problems in evaluating curricula lies in determining whether or not the characteristics of the school organization were such that the full curricular change was ever implemented. Sieber (1968) strongly criticized the nature of the typical school organization that makes it almost impossible for the school to try out a new curriculum. He sees the school ". . . as a vulnerable formal organization with diffuse goals, whose functionaries are quasi-professionals, and which is devoted to processing people within its boundaries" (p. 122).

Finally, we may have to contemplate the revolutionary thought that the curriculum simply does not matter. Stephens (1967) (See Readings: Section 3) was very persuasive when he said that the forces that make education work are essentially primitive and pervasive ones, not responsive to experimental manipulation. He reviewed the literature extensively and reported the nonsignificant differences that most research on teaching has shown. According to Schutz (1969), Stephens's finding has been replicated at the college level by Dubin and Taveggia who found "no shred of evidence," based on student performance on course examinations, that one teaching method is superior to another. If this is true for teaching, it may be true for the curriculum also in the sense that what one learns in school may be the *techniques* of learning, not the content. How much of the curriculum content of your elementary and secondary school do you recall? We might guess 5 to 10 percent, at most. Perhaps the more important thing we learned is how to play with information, how to store it, how to organize it, how to retrieve it, how to put it in different combinations, and how to develop thinking and informational skills. Perhaps it does not matter so much what the actual content was compared to the practicing of such learning skills.

Criterion-Referenced Measurement in the Curriculum

Given all these problems, we still must attend to our original concern, namely, that the measures we shall use depend upon how the objectives were defined. If we argue that a curriculum is intended to produce mastery of some kind, as Carroll (1963) stated, then we have to spell out that mastery in criterion-referenced measures. In the past, we asked how fast something was learned, that is, how many trials did it take? If speed of learning is our educational objective, then we need to make that plain. We could measure performance after roughly equal pupil exposure, which is what almost every standard achievement test measures. Given equal exposure, that is, all pupils are exposed to roughly the same amount of teaching of a given subject, we could then measure all children at some point in time to find who learned the most. Given equal exposure, the child who needs fewer trials to learn tends to be the child who learns fastest and therefore the most. This type of measure is very useful for selecting people for certain purposes, but it may not be necessarily the only way, or the best way, to measure the effectiveness of the curriculum, particularly if the curriculum goals are specified with some precision. Although there are many arguments in favor of retaining normative-referenced measurements such as standardized achievement tests for certain purposes, it is also true that such measurement encourages vagueness in stating educational goals. Criterion-referenced measurement at least forces curriculum builders to specify what it is they are trying to accomplish, thereby helping us to understand the educational model they are assuming and the values the model implies.

Summary

It seems reasonable that the curriculum does make a good deal of difference, if only because it defines what the student will be exposed to, but the basis for this tentative conclusion is more one of reason than of evidence. It is certainly true that students taught Spanish know more Spanish than students who are not taught Spanish; that students taught science know more about science than students who are not exposed to a scientific subject in the curriculum. What we lack, however, are sufficiently clear definitions of the objectives so that we can measure the effectiveness of one curriculum versus the effectiveness of another curriculum in helping students to reach those objectives. We know almost nothing about what curricular combinations may be most effective, yet it seems reasonable that taking certain subjects together may be confusing, whereas other combinations may be more compatible and may promote learning more effectively. We know very little about sequence except to assume that Algebra I should precede Algebra II, yet surely there are many possible sequences for most subjects, and some may be more easily learned than others. Perhaps learning a sequence in history, for example, based not on chronology but on the occurrence of similar ideas, geography, diet, or language would assist the student to make more meaningful comparisons.

Until we define our educational objectives and experiment with different curricula and curricular sequences and combinations, we will not be able to support with educational evidence statements about which curriculum is more effective than another.

REFERENCES

Baker, R. L. Curriculum evaluation. *Review of Educational Research*, 1969, **39**, 283–292.

Barr, S. Liberal education: A common adventure. *The Antioch Review*, September 1955, **15,** No. 3, 300–312.

Bellack, A. A. The structure of knowledge and the structure of curriculum. In D. Huebner (Ed.), *A Reassessment of the Curriculum.* New York: Teachers College Press, 1964, 25–40.

Bruner, J. S. *The Process of Education.* Cambridge, Mass.: Harvard University Press, 1960.

Carroll, J. A model of school learning. *Teachers College Record*, 1963, **64,** 723–733.

Digest of Educational Statistics 1968. Washington, D. C.: Superintendent of Documents, 1968.

Gagné, R. M. Curricular research and the promotion of learning. In R. W. Tyler, R. M. Gagné, & M. Scriven (Eds.), *Perspectives of Curriculum Evaluation.* Chicago: Rand McNally, 1967, 19–38.

Report of the Committee of Ten on Secondary School Studies. Washington, D. C.: Superintendent of Documents, 1893.

Schutz, R. E. Methodological issues in curriculum research. *Review of Educational Research*, 1969, **39**, 359–366.

Scriven, M. The methodolgy of evaluation. In R. W. Tyler, R. M. Gagné, & M. Scriven (Eds.), *Perspectives of Curriculum Evaluation.* Chicago: Rand McNally, 1967, 19–38.

Sieber, S. D. Organizational influences on innovative roles. In T. L. Eidell & J. M. Kitchell (Eds.), *Knowledge Production and Utilization in Educational Administration.* Columbus, Ohio: University Council for Educational Administration, 1968, 121–142.

Spencer, H. What knowledge is of most worth? In A. M. Kazamias (Ed.), *Herbert Spencer on Education.* New York: Teachers College Press, 1966, 121–159.

Stephens, J. M. *The Process of Schooling.* New York: Holt, Rinehart and Winston, 1967.

Whitehead, A. N. The rhythm of education. In *The Aims of Education and Other Essays.* New York: Macmillan, 1929.

PABLO PICASSO, *Three Musicians.* Philadelphia Museum of Art: The A. E. Gallatin Collection.

chapter 10

Society and Schooling

To be educated is not to have arrived at a destination; it is to travel with a different view.

—R. S. Peters

The issues involved in the relationship between society and schooling lead to a number of questions that need to be asked despite our inadequacies in answering them. We need to ask:

1. How does society set its educational goals?
2. How does society evaluate its school system? What yardsticks does it use?
3. As we move into the future, will we need to change our models of schooling? Will we need to change our models of evaluation?
4. Will changes in society predict changes in schooling, or vice versa?

American Goals of Education

In the past, American society has set a number of goals for its schooling system. These have included: (1) education as a right of citizens, (2) education to prepare for participatory democracy, (3) education to add to national income, and (4) education for moral and religious goals.

Except for the idea that all citizens have the right to receive public education, none of these goals are unique to American society. This right has grown over time so that now the right to an education is viewed as protected by the Fourteenth Amendment. A recent lawsuit by the Pennsylvania Association for Retarded Children contents that "all children can benefit from some degree of education and that depriving them of an education is unconstitutional" (*New York Times*, October 8, 1971). When retarded children are evaluated as not being either educable or trainable, the suit charges that the system "arbitrarily and capriciously

297

discriminated against the excluded, classifying them as dependent and denying them rights to equal protection of the laws in violation of the fourteenth amendment." Even Horace Mann might be surprised at this idea of educational rights!

When the role of education in the United States was being formulated by our Founding Fathers, it is quite possible that their views on education were shaped by their own educational experiences. The forty-eight signers of the Declaration of Independence were educated largely in three ways: at Harvard, by private tutors, and by self-education. It is unlikely that one could have found such a group anywhere else, a group that had seized the opportunity to create a new society and whose membership came in almost equal numbers from three such different sources of education. Although the United States has moved to what is essentially a national public school system (granted that it is under local control), in the future we might turn again to the varieties of educational systems that our Founding Fathers experienced.

Let us compare the original goals our society held for its schooling with those it holds now, so we may gain perspective about current changes.

1. *Democratic right:* What began as an opportunity for many citizens in our country has become, in two hundred years, the educational right of all. This is indeed a new idea, one that presents many problems as it becomes mandatory rather than permissive.

2. *Political goals:* The original notion that schooling should prepare for citizenship is still probably held by most boards of education. But the notions of what appropriate citizenship should be are probably much more disparate than they were two hundred years ago.

3. *Economic goals:* The utilitarian training for the immediate future, which certainly was one characteristic of our early schools and the Yankee tradition, has grown to include the idea that schooling should involve utilitarian training for all, both for the highest and lowest levels of economic entry. This represents an enormous shift in what is being demanded of our schooling system. It was a far easier task to school pupils for the skills immediately useful and employable in the eighteenth century than it is to prepare all the nation's children, not only for job entry at or below the high school level, but for community college entry, college entry, and the possibility of graduate training.

One of the least commonly emphasized problems our schooling systems face today is the enormous range of vocational goals they are supposed to accomplish, with more and more breadth and depth of knowledge for each of these goals, with a higher level of competency being demanded by the receiving employer or institution. Surely it is far easier to prepare a class, even a class of sixty-five pupils, for the occupations of farmer, carpenter, blacksmith, and housewife, than it is to prepare a class of perhaps thirty pupils for a wide variety of occupations, ranging from that of waiter in a highly complex urban environment to that of graduate physicist.

4. *Moral and religious training:* In many minds, this is still a goal for American schooling, however, the more commonly held religious and moral views of the eighteenth and nineteenth centuries have undergone severe changes and emerged as the disparate, often not religious, much more pluralistic values of our society. In some school systems, teachers are not permitted to conduct prayers or to teach religious principles in any form, whereas in other systems, citizens demand that such teaching be increased. It has been observed by many contemporary social critics that religion as an institution has lost much of its meaning for many of our younger people, and that lack of a commonly held coherent value system characterizes much of our society. If this is so, it could make the task of the school for moral or religious training either infinitely complex or superficial and meaningless.

5. *Social goals:* We could not say that schooling did not have social goals when it originated in this country, because no doubt many of those entering school hoped to gain social mobility through education, as did their parents before them. But it is in a somewhat different sense that we now see our society, or segments of our society, not only expecting but demanding that schooling be the agent to solve current social problems. Looking back, it is hard to find another time in which education has been asked to do so much to change people's attitudes and behaviors regarding social problems as diverse as race relations, the role of women, the role of minorities, sexual behavior, drugs, conservation, and consumer education, to mention only a few. It is paradoxical that many in our society say, on the one hand, that the United States system of schooling is in crisis or is a failure, while at the same time many demand that schooling be instituted to cure our major social problems. If one believed the first, one would hardly recommend the second. Perhaps one reason that schooling is being asked to undertake major social reconstruction is that it is the only institution left in our society to which we can turn if we accept the opinion that the church and family have broken down as institutions for changing behavior.

6. *Personal goals:* Another new educational goal, as we interpret it, is the demand that education be devoted to personal development of the

pupil as a human and humane being concerned with his fellowman and open to trusting relationships that are meaningful to him and to experiences which give his life meaning. This goal bears considerable relationship to the original Greek model and the western liberal arts model in the sense that education then was seen as leading to personal development, to the use of leisure and the arts. But it is new that it is now being asked to occur on a universal basis for all pupils, and not for a select advantaged group. In one sense, the cry for education for personal development represents simply another social problem education is being asked to solve. The move toward individual dignity and expression and away from bureaucratic and indifferent treatment of people as groups is an indication that a severe social problem is being treated. Demands are being made for schooling to set such humaneness as its goal. Such demands carry implications for curriculum and instructional strategies.

It is clear then that the goals our society has held for its systems of schooling, however they have been defined historically, have changed considerably. The goals encompass a much larger scope, they include a variety of different goals that may even be in conflict with each other, and they are designed for a much wider audience which, in turn, presents new educational problems. The real revolution in the relationship between society and schooling lies in the change in expectations. Not only is our schooling system asked to do more and with widely differing goals, but it should do more for everyone.

Changes in the Nature of Schooling

As we cast a quick eye over the forms of schooling currently available, we are struck by a major change: Education no longer takes place exclusively in a formal school setting. It is true that informal education took place in rustic cabins two hundred years ago, but most education moved into a formal setting with the establishment of the public school system a little over one hundred years ago. Today the cycle is returning to a variety of schooling systems for providing an education.

One present alternative is an informal system that exists via television, radio, printed media, film, and other technological innovations. An example of how much pupils are exposed to the informal schooling system can easily be obtained by sampling a high school or elementary class at random, and asking pupils what television programs they had watched the evening before. Pupils are more likely to report the common experience of watching a particular television program than they are of having done the same assignment or read the same book. In addition to the educational network existing through the media, we also have competing schooling systems, both formal and informal, in the armed forces, industry, and adult education. With the advent of the open university model, we can expect to see these alternative schooling systems become even more available.

The importance of a variety of schooling systems, both formal and informal, is primarily that the school, as we have known it, no longer has the monopoly on the input of information or of values that it once did. We might even hypothesize that the competing sources of education, particularly the media, have more impact on the young in our society than does the formal school in terms of information and values, both of which the school was formerly expected to provide. (See Revel in Readings: Section 3.)

Changes in the Nature of Society

Many social critics have commented on major changes in our society, paramount among which is the postindustrialization of this country and its emergence into a new technological or technotronic era (Brzezinski, 1970). Among the many changes predicted are those in our technological environment which will require, in turn, changes in our value system toward a planetary consciousness. Whether or not these value changes will occur in time is the subject of a good deal of apprehension. (See "Recommended Readings on Future Schooling" at the end of this chapter.)

Another obvious change in our society over the past one hundred years is the concentration of people in centers of living and working which include both cities and their suburbs. In 1840, only 10 percent of our society lived in urban areas; by 1900, 40 percent lived there; and at the present time, depending upon how one defines an urban and suburban area, perhaps 80 percent of our population live in urbanized areas (Silberman, 1970).

It is also obvious that there has been a revolution in our thinking since the 1950s about the rights of individual human beings, about civil rights, racial rights, ethnic rights, and the rights of women. The revolution does not lie in the ideal that people should be treated justly and fairly, which is hardly new. The revolution is in our expectations that people should behave this way, and that if injustice occurs, redress should be sought through the courts, in some political form, or through the media. Some younger members of our society put great emphasis on not making value judgments about individual life styles. Some view this emphasis as leading toward a more humane and liberal attitude toward others, while others maintain that this is a movement toward a breakdown in morals, presaging a frightening return to more primitive and anarchical forms of living.

Almost every household in our society is hooked up to a technological educational system in which information of all kinds is brought into the home along with various sets of values, influence, and modeling. Someone remarked in the 1950s that the only experience all humans have in common is that they have all seen an airplane. Very shortly, all will have seen television. Of the two, television is much more likely to change their lives. It may be exaggerating only a little to say that the common school of the 1970s is the television tube.

The most serious problem that this new common school presents is that there is no effective board of education, which sets educational policy or control over what's programmed, responsible to the taxpayers of the community. Instead, the tube school, which has controlled indirectly the education of nearly all our children, is "almost exclusively the domain of private business and advertising (permitting) both standards of taste and the intellectual content of culture to be defined largely by a small group of entrepreneurs located in one metropolitan center" (Brzezinski, p. 269). (For an opposed view, refer to Revel in Readings: Section 3.) This absence of a responsible connection between society and a new form of schooling may be changed as part of the revolution in values. Just as the value is increasingly held that the physical environment cannot be exploited without responsible controls in the public interest, we predict that a similar movement will develop toward the public control of all media that influence the education of society's children.

Population Size

As we reach urbanization to a painful degree, we are experiencing the problems of size and density of population. For the first time in man's history, there really are no more earthly places to move. With the possible exception of space and the sea, there is no frontier to start over in, no far distant empire possessions where one could become a remittance man, no planetary closets, no planetary backyards, or even back-forties. It is becoming clear that we are going to have to learn to live, somehow, with each other within the confines of our planet.

Conservation and Pollution

Obviously allied to the population density problem and industrialization is the issue of the destruction of our resources that cannot be recovered, and the issue of pollution of our water, air, and earth.

Concomitant with the changes in our society is the increase in the size and density of our schooling system itself, which is a microcosm of what is happening in society. Not only has our school system grown as has our population, but it has grown much faster. In the last three decades of the nineteenth century, school enrollment in our society more than doubled.

The number of our high school students doubled again from 1900 to 1910, and doubled again from 1910 to 1920 (Silberman, 1970). School systems became larger and more complex as rural school systems became centralized. Some of the problems our schooling system currently faces most certainly are related to size and density, a source of many problems we have not recognized adequately.

Changes in Expectations

Beyond all the changes in our society and the rest of the world, it is our thesis that the real revolution has been in expectations. Not only has society changed in its expectations of what schooling should be able to do, and for whom, but there has been a revolution in expectations for each person's life on this planet. Individuals everywhere have become aware of what a better life could be, and have given up the assumption that their life has to be what it has been. The expectation has grown that a better life can be realized and should be now.

The yardsticks also have been revolutionized. We expect and measure by different psychological yardsticks than we did fifty or one hundred years ago. Most of the world wants to live better, wants to have more income, a better home, to eat and dress better, and to have more education for themselves and their children. Most people believe that it is possible to accomplish these goals and are no longer willing to wait.

To what extent are such expectancy yardsticks realistic? To what extent do they help us to measure what is actually happening?

Historical Comparisons as Yardsticks

If we review the period from 1945 to 1970 in the United States, we find that equal rights are now being practiced in almost all public places; that recruitment of minority students is occurring at all levels of education, although there is not yet full integration in public schooling; that minority candidates have been elected to every major public office including that of senator, mayor, and supreme court; and that Negro incomes are up 120 percent from 1950 to 1970 in comparison with white incomes, which rose 82 percent, although this still leaves the median Negro income at 60 percent of white income (Bendiner, 1970).

A common reaction is to say that this is not enough. By the yardstick of what one would have predicted in 1945, as Bendiner points out so well, these are major changes. If we are to play only the game of expectation, then clearly nothing will ever satisfy or succeed, because each gain that is made only increases expectation, thereby stretching the yardstick even more. We may say after each such gain that we are further and further from the heaven that has just been redefined.

The lack of any yardstick, except a vague historical one, is evident in what may have become the overwhelming issue in our society, that of the human environment. We may have reached a point in man's history where it is no longer true that war, politics, or economics are the paramount issues in the minds of most members of society. The human environment may be the overwhelming issue. The decline in quality of public life is obvious to all, but it is unmeasured. We do not know what this does to the behavior of people, to their values or attitudes, or what effect it has upon schooling. Some argue that more schooling is the cure for our urban problems. Banfield (1970) takes the provocative stance that more schooling may only make more problems for the city and its residents, not less (See Banfield in Readings: Section 3). It is hard for us to evaluate what disillusionment with a materialistic set of values may mean. It is hard to comprehend what the changing population of our cities may mean to public life. The population of our cities has remained essentially stable during the past twenty-five years, but the people have changed. The better off have moved outside the cities and the poor have moved in. Our larger cities are continually on the edge of crisis, as are all the public services. The quality of our human relationships may be deeply affected by the conditions stemming from such an environment. Relationships are altered by fear, distrust, noise, overcrowding, dirt, and inadequate services. For children raised in such an environment, how is their schooling affected? For people who teach in such an environment, how is their teaching affected? We need to remind ourselves constantly that urban schooling takes place in an environment that is often almost intolerable to human beings. Such an environment must have its effect, but one we have not begun to measure, except to apply the past as a nostalgic yardstick.

Expectations for Schooling

Against this background of changes in our society and yardsticks, what are some of society's expectations for formal schooling today? Among the expectations are these:

1. That all shall be educated with access to all parts of the system from the lowest to highest.
2. That all who desire education should be educated.
3. That education shall result in a better job, more money, more power, more social status, more choice, or a more human life. (The end product shall be the better life, although this is defined differently by different groups.)
4. Some segments of our society expect and demand that education be the corrector of society's wrongs.

5. Some see education as the humanizer, the place where humanity and feelings are cultivated with a permanent effect.
6. Some expect that schooling shall provide a liberal arts education for each person.

If education is to be the equalizer, the corrector of social injustice in our society, this is going to present us with some problems as far as a yardstick is concerned. If school is to be the equalizer, schools can no longer be competitive, nor can we measure pace or amount. This leaves us vague about the end product, except that it will be equal. Such a model assumes that all will be admitted, as in open enrollment, but what all will study and how effectively they will master their studies are unsettled questions. Will a degree no longer represent some understood competencies? Will there be any measure of what has been acquired, or will individual satisfaction be sufficient? The equalizing model has some unresolved problems if it proposes that the graduates of its particular system shall be admitted to the next higher level. If open enrollment in College A, for example, is expected also to mean admission to Graduate School B, then either Graduate School B will need to move toward open enrollment or College A will need to determine the competencies of its graduates in some manner acceptable to Graduate School B.

Education as the Humanizing Model

Let us explore one of these expectations, that of education as a humanizer, dealing with it as a model of schooling. The terms "radical romantics" or "romantic radicals" describe those who have advocated most strongly the humanizing education model. Among these advocates are Friedenberg, Holt, Kohl, Leonard, Postman, Maslow, Rogers, Heath (See Readings: Section 3) and Neill. Some of its followers claim that its founding father is Dewey, but this does not seem to be accurate. The basic assumption of those who want education to be a model of humanization seems to be that the child is naturally good, the assumption that Rousseau supported vigorously and Dewey supported partially. This assumption extends to the notion that the child is probably the best guide to his own education, and that he will select an educational structure that is meaningful to him based on his needs and interests. Such an assumption also rejects an external structure provided by an adult or teacher as inappropriate education for the child. In this humanizing model, high values are placed upon spontaneity, informality, warm and honest human relationships, feelings, and intuition. Negative values are placed upon reflection, formality, structure, ordering, objectivity, intellect, and measurement. (Attitudes certainly vary on each of these characteristics but these seem to be tenable generalizations.) Proponents of the humanizing model want a school that is spontaneous, informal, loving, and full of good feeling, centered around the child as the learner. This is an exaggeration but there is a suggestion here of a religion that worships the natural child.

Many of the adherents of this model feel that schooling somehow perverts the child or turns him into a callous and cynical person. Such proponents often seem to confuse schooling with experience. As children grow up in our society, they also simultaneously attend school. It is easy to confound these two influences. As children grow older, whether or not they are in school, they probably lose some of the bloom of their early trust and endearing qualities and become more cynical and less trusting as they gain experience. It would be interesting to study children in a society where they did not go to school to see if this same decrease in trust developed over time.

It is important to recognize that those who propose this model of schooling have decided what kind of person they want to produce, which Russell (1926) suggested as the first job in defining education. They are reasonably explicit about how they want this person to behave, that is, to be warm, honest, loving, spontaneous, trusting, and person-oriented. The kind of individual they wish to turn out may be designed to correct the current problems of the human environment. By the time he is produced, however, he may not be appropriate to the changed problems of that future society. One might even argue that society is forever reordering its school to correct the problems of today that may not exist when its pupils graduate.

The major problem with the proponents of this model of education is not that they are unwilling to say what kind of people they want, because they do, and this is to their credit, but that they never specify how they will know when they have achieved their goal. If they remain so anti-measurement (and measurement does not have to mean multiple-choice tests filled with petty items), how will they ever know what works? Certainly it is a very difficult task to know when one is helping to educate a humane person, but it is a noble task and one well worth trying to measure.

If the proponents of the humane model continue to reject measurement because they see it as antithetical to their set of values, we would predict another swing around on the progressive model, repeating Dewey's anti-measurement mistake and that of the people who followed him; and that this swing will be followed by a procognitive model; and thus, another cycle in educational fads. Unless the humanists can accept the need for measurement and research for humanistic goals, their romantic model is likely to end in disillusionment, as it did with the progressive movement.

A strong argument can be made that the overriding problem of society is also the overriding problem of education, which is the need to tame and civilize man before he destroys himself, to teach him how to inhabit the earth with other men in harmony with his physical and social environment. This is a humanistic goal in the sense that it would require a change in our values and behavior in a more humane direction. If it is worth educating for such a goal, surely it should be worth measuring to see if we are succeeding. If it is true that the overwhelming issues for the next generation will be those of taming man, of changing his values from those of aggression, competition, retribution, self-sufficiency, and fierce independence, toward cooperation, peaceful resolutions, mutual support of a system of justice, individual responsibility for both the individual and the group, and interdependence; and of accomplishing this change of values while still maintaining privacy, dignity, independence of thought, and rational processes—if these are the overwhelming issues for society, they certainly are the overwhelming educational issues, and we need to know when we are being effective.

Education of the Future

Compared with prior models of education, we could anticipate that one predominant model will still have its roots in Dewey's philosophy, which is "the growth of the learner." We can imagine the future as an international society consisting of many political systems, not just that of democracy. It may consist of highly technological countries as well as underdeveloped ones. It may include postindustrial states and preindustrial states. Probably such a society will consist of the widest range of man's scientific and technological repertoire that the world has ever known. Consequently, a premium may be put upon the ability of a person to continue his own education beyond formal school. Education may be considered successful in so far as it is followed by continued growth of the learner.

In a world where man will need to live with his fellowman, it will become necessary that no one group's interests supersede another's. The interests of all groups will have to be held in common in ways we do not yet know how to effect. If this is true, any model of schooling that is child-centered may be questioned as a way of preparing children to live in a society where every group's interests needs to be considered equally, a point Dewey stressed in his society-centered school (Mayhew and Edwards, 1966).

Predictions about United States Schooling in the Future

Let us try to estimate what schooling in our society may look like in the future, based upon our several assumptions about what the major problems are.

Education will be recognized as a necessary, basic, and continuous human function, not something restricted to the young, not something which terminates with a given age or degree. Schooling will become the basic social institution.

The varieties of educational systems, objectives, and techniques will be many. There will be formal and informal schooling; schooling which is done privately in the home and publicly in a public place; schooling which takes place from one person to another; and schooling which takes place between a technological apparatus and a group. There will be practice in real situations for certain training objectives, and there will be simulated practice. There will be schooling for short-term immediate goals and for long-term remote goals, some of them lifelong.

Schooling will be taught by people who are considered expert, but it will also be taught by peers, assistants, and the nonexperts (Gartner, Kohler, and Riessman, 1971). There will be utilitarian schooling and there will be schooling for self-development toward cultural goals. Many of these educational units will interlock in an overriding system in which a person can select pieces of schooling at different times in his life to arrive at a personal educational objective.

Experience will be redefined as an educational unit comparable to classroom education. Students will be able to go part-time or full-time, to start or stop, to make an individual educational plan or to follow an external goal.

For such a variety of schooling systems, it will be even more important that objectives be clearly defined and measures taken to find out whether or not those objectives are being reached.

We predict that schooling will be one of the two major forces that reshape our culture. The other force will be the media. It is ironic that at a time when there is a need for common values to unite our society, we no longer have a common schooling, and, in fact, schooling may become more and more diverse. Had we faced our current problems in the nineteenth century, we could have used the common school as one way of building a common culture. It should not surprise us, however, that as our society has fractionated, so has its schooling. Schooling not only reflects society's concerns but is a force in shaping those problems.

The media, in becoming the second schooling system, may have either undefined or undesirable objectives that will influence our values in a negative manner. Our schools in the past have been defined by the people in the community, whereas our concern with the media is that the people have almost no say about its educational message. As a result, we might predict the emergence of a citizen's culture in which the technology of society, including the media, will be put more at the service of society's interests.

We would predict the emergence of a model of schooling to reflect the need for the reformation of man. This model would look very different from the current humanistic model for it will be a model of the ideal earth society, in which all groups will be represented, including adults and older people, a model in which the school will be a living ecological unit, a human habitat where conflicts can be resolved rationally and where there is representation and resolution of all group interests. (Some of the communes appear to be experimenting in this direction.) It will be a model to train for living on this earth. Whether or not it will be a democratic model, as Dewey perceived it, is an unknown.

Educational Issues of the Future for Which We Need Evidence

Whether or not any of these predictions come true, we are still desperately in need of resolving certain educational issues that will be central to the construction of any new model of schooling. One of the most pervasive assumptions among those proposing a new model of schooling is that their model will have a lasting effect on their pupils in the desired directions. This is one of the most basic educational questions which is yet to be answered.

Hofstadter (1963) asked: Do we know whether an authoritarian classroom produces conformist pupils? We might ask: Does a highly socialized school produce socialized pupils? Does a humane school produce humane individuals? Does a democratic school atmosphere produce pupils who use democratic means? These were some of the assumptions that Dewey made. The assumptions made by Freudian theory as to the lasting influence of early childhood have been assumed to be true of schooling, but we do not have the evidence to tell whether this is so or not. There is a suggestion that religious schools do not tend to produce graduates who behave in a more religious fashion than those from equally religious families who do not attend religious schools, but it is hard to get reliable evidence on such a question. Russell (1926) assumed that a school system should be defined by the kind of person one wanted to turn out, and basic to this is his assumption that a school system determines what kind of person gets turned out. There is room for a lot of doubt that schooling systems, per se, have much influence on values or attitudes or modes of behavior.

Does the form of schooling influence the pupil's eventual character as much as his intellectual style or content? This is a more complicated version of the prior question. Let us assume that School A is authoritarian about its social roles, about its lack of choice in subject matter, about its discipline. Let us further assume that its teachers teach the classics, but do so with intellectual fervor and curiosity, and that they seek in their pupils a high level of critical ability and of individual critical evaluation of the classics. Let us assume even further that these teachers are reasonably successful in reaching their teaching goals. Now the question is: What is the effect, if any, upon pupils of the presumed authoritarian organization of the school versus the intellectual freedom of the style of teaching? Is the character influenced by one and the intellect by another? Or does a free intellect, an inquiring style, affect character? Can the character be conforming but the intellect independent? Does schooling influence values? How does schooling influence the future political and social styles of its pupils?

For what behavior is schooling a model? Is it primarily a model for future teaching and learning roles? It is reasonable to hypothesize that modeling is probably most effective in carrying over to those activities that are most similar to the activity in which the modeling took place. (This is simply a restatement of Thorndike's Law of Identical Elements applied to modeling.) In that case, one would expect a teacher to model for teaching. If this is true, one reason, which Silberman (1970) implied, why it is very hard to change the modes of teaching of people entering the profession, may be because they have been modeled by their own previous teachers.

Then what transfer of behavior, if any, takes place from school to broader social behavior? If we could find a way to ask and answer these questions, even partially, we could begin to identify those areas of behavior, attitudes, values, and character that schooling is most likely to influence, and then to devise a model based upon such evidence which might reach the desired effects. Up until now, a variety of educational models have developed without any dependable evidence that schooling, as we have known it, is likely to produce the desired effects. Given the appropriate evidence, the relevant educational factors (such as technique, style, content, experience, organization) could be identified which would be most likely to produce the desired outcome. For example, if the desired outcome is knowledge about X as measured by G, then we would be in a position to state that knowledge of X can be reached by any known method of teaching, in any classroom atmosphere, through any set of values, and through any intellectual style, provided that there is sufficient exposure to X, sufficient demonstration, and sufficient repeated evaluation of the knowledge desired. If, on the other hand, the desired outcome is an attitude to be developed toward other people, an attitude that puts a high value on responding to each person on the basis of how that person behaves and not to the group to which he belongs, we might find that no traditional form of schooling has been effective. We may find that such attitudes are most easily developed at home, or by selective models in adolescence, or by a single intensive experience, either positive or negative.

If we had evidence on these questions, we could then separate what education could do from what other agents of society might do better. We might discover that institutionalized schooling does little more than provide a relatively efficient way of transmitting knowledge to large groups. Some other means might be needed to achieve other educational outcomes. For example, a change in society's laws might change human behavior more directly. This is one interpretation of what happened in race relations in our society after the 1950s. By changing the law, behaviors were changed among people. It could be argued that education was of very little prior help in changing such attitudes and behavior.

To invent new models of schooling then, our strongest need is to find ways to conceptualize educational purposes and effectiveness. Our second need is to develop the relevant evidence as to what schooling can, and cannot, influence. The student of education, according to our view, will need two tools to help him evaluate these coming educational changes: (1) the ability to conceptualize education, and (2) the ability to apply educational evidence to the evaluation of future educational models.

(At the end of this chapter, the reader will find "Recommended Readings on Future Schooling." Such readings should help to extend the reader's ability to conceptualize education. The educational evidence may be lacking, but we hope that the reader will recognize when it is not present, and will be better able to evaluate what is present.)

REFERENCES

Banfield, E. C. *The Unheavenly City*. Boston: Little, Brown, 1970.

Bendiner, R. Great expectations, a quarter of a century later. *New York Times Magazine*. April 26, 1970, 36.

Brzezinski, Z. *Between Two Ages*. New York: Viking, 1970.

Gartner, A., Kohler, M., & Riessman, F. *Children Teach Children: Learning by Teaching*. New York: Harper & Row, 1971.

Hofstadter, R. The child and the world. *Anti-Intellectualism in American Life*. New York: Knopf, 1963, 359–392.

Mayhew, K. C., & Edwards, A. C. *The Dewey School*. New York: Atherton Press, 1966.

Russell, B. The aims of education. *Education and the Good Life*. New York: Boni & Liveright, 1926, 47–83.

Silberman, C. E. *Crisis in the Classroom: The Remaking of American Education*. New York: Random House, 1970.

RECOMMENDED READINGS ON FUTURE SCHOOLING

Bell, D. *The Reforming of General Education*. Garden City, N. Y.: Anchor Books, 1968.

Bremer, J., & von Moschziesker, M. *The School without Walls: Philadelphia's Parkway Program*. New York: Holt, Rinehart and Winston, 1971.

Brzezinski, Z. *Between Two Ages*. New York: Viking, 1970.

Chase, S. *The Most Probable World*. Baltimore, Md.: Penguin Books, 1969. (Begin with Chapter 15, "No path but knowledge," and "Epilogue.")

Fuller, R. B. *Education Automation*. Carbondale, Ill.: Southern Illinois University Press, Arcturus Books, 1964.

Galbraith, J. K. *The New Industrial State*. Boston: Houghton Mifflin, 1967. (Begin with Chapter 33, "Education and emancipation.")

Heath, D. H. *Humanizing Schools*. New York: Hayden, 1971.

Kahn, H., & Weiner, A. J. *The Year 2000*. New York: Macmillan, 1967.

Kerr, C. *The Uses of the University*. New York: Harper & Row, 1966. (Especially Chapter 3, "The future of the city of intellect.")

Kozol, J. *Free schools*. Boston: Houghton Mifflin, 1972.

Madsen, C. H., Jr., & Madsen, C. K. *Teaching/Discipline: Behavioral Principles toward a Positive Approach*. Boston: Allyn & Bacon, 1970.

Middleton, J. (Ed.) *From Child to Adult: Studies in the Anthropology of Education*. Garden City, N. Y.: Natural History Press, 1970.

Revel, J. F. *Without Marx or Jesus: The New American Revolution Has Begun*. Garden City, N. Y.: Doubleday, 1971.

Rossi, P. H., & Biddle, B. J. (Eds.) *The New Media and Education*. Garden City, N. Y.: Anchor Books, 1967.

Skinner, B. F. *Beyond Freedom and Dignity*. New York: Knopf, 1971.

Toffler, A. *Future Shock*. New York: Bantam Books, 1971.

Weber, L. *The English Infant School and Informal Education*. Englewood Cliffs, N. J.: Prentice-Hall, 1971.

Readings
Section 3: Contemporary Issues in Education

The best thing for being sad is to learn something. That is the only thing which the mind can never exhaust, never alienate, never be tortured by, never fear or distrust, and never dream of regretting.

—T. H. White in *The Once and Future King*

READINGS: SECTION 3

Cohen, D. K. Immigrants and the schools. *Review of Educational Research,* 1970, **40,** No. 1, 13–68.

Hertzberg, H. W. The now culture: Some implications for teacher training programs. *Social Education,* March 1970, **34,** No. 3, 271–279.

Thorndike, R. L. Review of Rosenthal & Jacobson, *Pygmalion in the Classroom. American Educational Research Journal,* November 1968, **5,** No. 4, 708–711.

Madsen, C. H., Jr., & Madsen, C. K. *Teaching/Discipline: Behavioral Principles toward a Positive Approach.* Boston: Allyn & Bacon, 1970, 23–31.

Heath, D. Affective education. *School Review,* May 1972, **80,** No. 3, 353–372.

Banfield, E. C. *The Unheavenly City: The Nature and the Future of Our Urban Crisis.* Boston: Little, Brown, 1970, Ch. 7.

Revel, J. F. *Without Marx or Jesus.* Garden City, N, Y.: Doubleday, 1971, 160–181.

IMMIGRANTS AND THE SCHOOLS

David K. Cohen

It is hard to imagine anything more characteristically American than faith in the efficacy of schooling. Particularly since the late nineteenth century, public education has been viewed as an antidote for the diminishing equality of opportunity generally thought to be associated with cities, industry, immigration, and hardening class structure. . . .

The thinking behind this involved a few key ideas. One was that cities typically attract domestic or foreign peasant immigrants; education could prevent their being constrained, *lumpen*, at the bottom of the heap by offering paths to occupational attainment based on merit. Allowing the able to work their way up might reduce social tension and avoid class warfare. A second was that providing minimal training to the poor would encourage punctuality, cleanliness, and respect, which would reduce crime and disorder; this would improve the quality of life for the laboring class and the quality of labor for the owning class. Finally, urban immigrants generally stood outside the mainstream of the national political culture; if the schools could teach them the language and the main features of the political system, the newcomers might then be expected to assume the responsibilities of citizenship.

These ideas form a rough general system—a popular ideology of social reform—which has increasingly dominated educational thought and practice since the turn of the century. Since it holds that schooling is the best remedy for inequalities of social and economic opportunity, the ideology assumes that adult social and economic status is determined on the basis of standards similar to those used to evaluate school performance: intelligence, order, discipline, and respect for authority. The ideology also implies that the desideratum of social reform is not the aggregate redistribution of social and economic status, but the maintenance of merit standards on the basis of which qualified individuals can effect a personal redistribution.

Finally, a view of history is involved. Schooling, it is assumed, "worked" for immigrants who arrived from Europe around the turn of the century, but has not had the same effect for Negroes (Weinberg, 1969, p. 28). The reasons advanced to support this account of events vary considerably. Some suggest that it was due to the fact that individual city schools were then politically and culturally more identified by (controlled by?) the immigrant groups they served, and some maintain that the quality of

Cohen, D. K. Immigrants and the Schools. *Review of Educational Research*, 1970, 40, No. 1, pp. 13–68. Copyright by American Educational Research Association, Washington, D.C.

teachers' commitment in the cities then was greater (Calhoun, 1969, p. 73). Still others argue that immigrants did not meet the racial bigotry which Negro children face in city schools today (Weinberg, 1969, p. 28). But whatever the reasons, it is widely believed that although public education provided the means by which southern and eastern Europeans moved into the social, cultural, and political mainstream, it is not currently performing the same service for Negroes.

An alternative view is that in many fundamental respects city schools related to working-class immigrants in much the same way as blacks. On this presumption, the educational problems which have erupted in city schools in the last decade—the cultural and linguistic content of curricula, the school staffs' ethnic and racial composition, the effectiveness of education for poor children—are recent variants of an old problem: the inability of public education to overcome the educational consequences of family poverty, and to recognize the legitimacy of working class and ethnic cultures.

The relative merits of these two interpretations of the educational experience of immigrant children can not be decided here. It is possible, however, to explore one particularly salient aspect of the issue—school performance. Did immigrant children do as well in school as native urban whites? Did they progress as far, achieve as well, and graduate as frequently? If so, one would be inclined to discount the idea that immigrants and Negroes fared similarly in city schools. If not, there would be a basis for further exploration of the similarities.

The earliest direct evidence on these questions arises from surveys of school retardation carried out at the turn of the century. The appearance of these studies coincides with the entrance of large numbers of immigrant children in city schools. Quite a few efforts were made in the first decade of the century (Corman, 1908; Falkner, 1908; Greenwood, 1908), but the first large-scale survey involving immigrants was published by Leonard Ayres (1909). It covered more than fifty American city school systems, in an effort to determine the extent of retardation.

Ayres found enormous variation among city school systems. Only 18% of all the students in Boston's public schools, but nearly 60% of those in Cincinnati's, were retarded; the average seems to have been around 30%. But such comparisons are valid only if the underlying phenomenon is the same in all cases. If cities followed dissimilar promotion practices, the variation among retardation rates would reflect these disparate practices and the results would not be comparable.

This problem seems to have escaped Ayres, for he presented no evidence on it; he did, however, conduct a depth study in New York City, and it seems reasonable to presume more uniform promotion policies in one city. He collected the records of 20,000 children from 15 public elementary schools. The analysis revealed that slightly more than 23% of all students were at least a year behind the expected grade for their age (Ayres, 1909, p. 107).

Ayres also pursued the relationship between nationality and retardation in this depth study. The results of computing retardation rates by national origin are displayed in Table 1 (Ayres, 1909, p. 45, Table 22). It reveals that retardation was twice as great for Irish and Italian children as for students of native or mixed parentage, but it shows even greater variation among immigrant groups themselves: children of German parents were less often retarded than any other group, including native white Americans. Although it is easy to imagine reasons for such variations—ethnic differences in duration of stay and language acquisition, or social class, or both, Ayres's data were not amenable to exploring these questions. The evidence tells us only that retardation was severe for some immigrant groups, mild for others, and on the whole somewhat higher for immigrants than for native Americans.

Another study of retardation in New York City secondary schools was carried out at about the same time by J. K. Van Denburgh (1911), a member of the Teachers College faculty. Although the extremely selective character of secondary education at the turn of the century means that the results must be approached with caution, the rank order of nationalities for high school completion is roughly the same as that for elementary school children. Van Denburgh's data (1911, p. 45) permit computation of retention rates (percent of those entering high school who graduated) for several nationality groups. The retention rates were .1% and 0% for Irish and Italian children, respectively, 10% for native whites, 10.8% for

TABLE 1

Grade Retardation in Fifteen New York City
Elementary Schools, by Nationality, 1908

Nationality	Per Cent Of Students Retarded At Least One Grade
German	16
American	19
Russian	23
English	24
Irish	29
Italian	36

those from Britain, 15% for those from Germany, and 16% for Russian children (who Van Denburgh and Ayres thought were almost exclusively Jewish).

These issues were explored in a larger and more precise study of schools and nationality carried out in 1908–09, and published by the U. S. Immigration Commission (1911). The survey covered all schools, students, and teachers in thirty cities (twenty of which were the country's largest in point of population), and produced information on 2,036,376 pupils. Its estimate of retardation was based on a less liberal definition of age-grade norms than Ayres's, and thus the results suggested a greater average retardation rate (36%) than given in the New York depth study (U. S. Immigration Commission, 1911, p. 31). Retardation for native American white children was 28% as against 40% for children of foreign-born parents. This considerable difference was accentuated when language variations were taken into account; children of immigrant parents from English-speaking countries were no more often retarded (27%) than children of native white parents, but more than 43% of immigrant children from non-English-speaking countries were retarded (U. S. Immigration Commission, Vol. I, p. 31). . . .

Research on the intelligence of immigrant children—most of which was undertaken in the decade following World War I—provides further indirect evidence on school retardation among immigrants. The studies involved a wide variety of tests and elementary schoolchildren of several ages and places; yet the rank order of nationalities did not vary. One study of New York City schoolchildren, for example, yielded the median IQ scores displayed in Table 2 (Murdoch, 1920). Another study of California fifth graders of about the same age range (Young, 1922) showed that the Median IQ for Native Whites was 110, and 85 for children of Italian-born parents.

Perusal of these studies reveals that the debate over immigrant intelligence parallels quite precisely the debate over Negro intelligence. One of the main issues was whether the differences were genetic or environmental; the other was whether the tests were culturally and linguistically biased

TABLE 2

Median IQ Scores for New York City Ten-Year-Olds, 1919

Nationality	Median IQ	N
Native White	108.5	48
Italian	84.3	28

against the immigrants. Although the measurement of intelligence and environment has improved somewhat since the 1920's, the terms of this discussion have changed not a bit. What happened was that immigration—and thus immigrant intelligence—ceased to be a relevant political concern.

Other studies report roughly similar findings in comparisons of these groups during the 1920s (Young, 1922; Brown, 1922; Pinter, 1923; Mead, 1927; Seago and Kolodin, 1925; Colvin and Allen, 1925; Pintner and Keller, 1922; Bingham, 1930). Although IQ is not the same thing as retardation, the two were not unrelated: research on New York City's elementary schools in 1930 found that the correlation between school average retardation and school average IQ was .698 (Maller, 1933).

Although much less research seems to have been carried out in secondary schools the IQ differences persisted at the high school level. One study (Feingold, 1924) of the Hartford, Connecticut high school in the early 1920s revealed the IQ differences displayed in Table 3. They are not as great as those for elementary schoolchildren, but this was probably due to the greater selectivity of secondary schools.

The Hartford research also illuminated the relation between ethnicity and high school selection. There appear to have been only small differences among ethnic groups in the likelihood of entering high school: the ethnic proportions within the freshman class correspond quite closely to the ethnic proportions in the entire city population. Jews were slightly over-represented in the freshman classes, and native whites slightly under-represented, but these differences were small. Staying power, however, was rather a different question. Table 4 presents the ratio between high school freshmen and juniors, for each ethnic group. Thus, the numbers in the last column can be read as probabilities—that is, as the number of chances in one hundred that a freshman from each of the groups had of reaching the junior year.

Over-all, the chances of students remaining in school until the junior

TABLE 3

Nationality and IQ, Hartford High School Freshman

Nationality	IQ	Nationality	IQ
Scotch and English	105	French	98
Native White	103	Irish	98
Jewish	103	Polish	97
German	103	Italian	97
Scandinavian	102		

TABLE 4

Nationality and High School Retention, Hartford, Conn.

Nationality	Freshmen	Juniors	Per Cent Juniors of Freshmen
Native White	892	572	64
Jewish	518	416	80
Irish	278	88	34
Italian	206	58	28
Scandinavian	114	56	48
Polish	90	22	24
German	86	40	44
English and Scotch	76	34	44
Total	2,260	886	38

year were slightly less than four in ten, but there was enormous variation by nationality. Polish and Italian students had about 2.5 chances in ten of remaining until the junior year, whereas native whites had over six chances in ten. The Irish were a bit below the average, the Germans were slightly above it. Jews who entered the freshman class had eight chances in ten of staying till their junior year, better than twice the city average. . . .

In summary, then, although the evidence I have presented is fragmentary and often non-comparable, it suggests that in the first generation, at least, children from many immigrant groups did not have an easy time in school. Pupils from these groups were more likely to be retarded than their native white schoolmates, more likely to make low scores on IQ tests, and they seem to have been a good deal less likely to remain in high school. It also appears that children of first-generation immigrants from these groups had as difficult a time in the 1920s or 1930s as their predecessors experienced during the first decade of the century.

It must be equally clear, however, that being the son or daughter of an immigrant did not in itself result in below-average educational attainment. Children whose parents emigrated from England, Scotland, Wales, Germany, and Scandinavia seem to have generally performed about as well in school as native whites; certainly their average performance never dropped much below that level. The children of Jewish immigrants typically achieved at or above the average for native whites. It was central and southern European non-Jewish immigrants—and, to a lesser extent, the Irish—who experienced really serious difficulty in school. On any index of educational attainment (whether it was retardation, achievement scores, IQ, or retention), children from these nationalities were a good deal worse off than native urban whites.

Perhaps the most interesting question this raises involves the origin of these ethnic differences: did they arise primarily from group differences in inherited social and economic attributes or were they chiefly the consequence of differences in culture and motivation? At first glance, the second seems a likely alternative; after all, the main over-achievers—the Jews—typically placed a great value on education. But there is more to it than that, for there is evidence which suggests that the rank order of intelligence among immigrant groups would correspond roughly to their rank order on an index of urbanization. This is clearest if one compares the Italians (most of whom emigrated from southern Italy) and the Poles with immigrants from Germany, or with the Jews. It is interesting to note, in this connection, that there were very great differences among the Jews according to nation of origin. The U. S. Immigration Commission (1911, Vol. I, p. 31) found that 37% of German Jewish children experienced school retardation, as against 41% for the Russian Jews, 52% of the Rumanian Jews, and 67% of the Polish Jews. These proportions closely resemble those for non-Jews of those nationalities. . . .

Another important issue concerns the schools' response to the immigrants. The arrival of large numbers of immigrant pupils coincided with the emergence of IQ and achievement testing, vocational guidance, and the movement to diversify instruction and curriculum in city schools. There is more than a little evidence that these practices were employed—if not conceived—as a way of providing the limited education schoolmen often thought suitable for children from the lower reaches of the social order. The tension this suggests also extended to the schools' culture: there is no evidence of any effort to employ the immigrants' language and culture as educational vehicles. I have been unable to find any hint that cultural diversity was entertained as a serious possibility; it appears that the WASP culture reigned supreme in urban public schools. In this connection, it is important to note that there appears to have been a substantial movement to create educational alternatives among some immigrant groups. For the Irish and Italians, of course, the Catholic parochial schools served this function, as did part-time religious schools for the Jews. There also were efforts—among the Bohemians, for example—to establish part-time "language schools" as a way of maintaining and transmitting the culture.

Finally, there is the question of schooling and social mobility. I have shown that there was a good deal of variability in immigrant children's educational attainment: some groups did as well or better than the average for native urban whites, and others much worse. But to show that the children of many immigrant groups had difficulty in school is not to show that education turned out to be a less effective way for them to climb the social and economic ladder. Almost all the results I have presented are based on evidence about the children of first generation immigrants, and it centers in the first two or three decades of the century. What data I have found on exposure to the urban American culture and society suggests that it coincided with drastically reduced educational differences between immigrants and native whites. Furthermore, the Duncans (1968) have presented evidence that education may have been no less important for the children of immigrants than for native whites, in accounting for differences in occupational attainment.

This, however, is another part of the story, and like the other questions I have raised, it requires more attention than is possible here.

THE NOW CULTURE: SOME IMPLICATIONS FOR TEACHER TRAINING

Hazel W. Hertzberg

. . . Today the study of the remote in place or in time seems to many students—as well as to teachers, parents, and administrators—an exercise in futility, even when it comes labeled as "new." There is some justice in this attack. The model of the child to which the new social studies is addressed was largely a cognitive one. He was thought of essentially as a mind, a miniature university scholar, working with the kinds of concepts and ideas familiar to the advanced researcher, eager in the pursuit of his discoveries, working alone rather than in groups. He was the middle-class, suburban, high IQ student of the fifties.

The upheavals churning up in the world outside the classroom—the emergence of the "third world," the crises of the cities, the agony of the blacks, the uprising of the poor, the eruption of war and violence—all these subjects which were to engage the passionate attention of students in the sixties were just the subjects about which the new social studies had little to say. Faced with demands for curricula and materials in these areas, many schools responded with instant social studies, with curricula hastily put together using little or none of the careful selection and testing of materials nor of the approaches characteristic of the new social studies. Today there are probably at least as many classrooms in which instant social studies are being taught as those using the new social studies.

But beyond the question of subject matter, the new social studies largely neglected the student himself other than his cognitive dimensions. Their model of the student is no longer adequate, if indeed it ever was. In ways largely unanticipated by the creators of the new social studies, the values assumed by them as central—intellectual curiosity, a careful weighing of cause and effect, commitment to the pursuit of truth or truths as defined by the scholarly disciplines, the intellectual excitement of the lonely scholar —were being rejected by students, and by many of the younger or more activist prospective teachers who by rights should be the standard bearers of the new social studies. And the academy itself from which the new social studies were generated is rent today by conflicts almost unimaginable when the massive efforts at reform were begun. The world into which the new social studies are emerging is a very different one from that in which they are conceived.

This picture of the plight of the new social studies is of course over-

Hertzberg, H. W. The now culture: Some implications for teacher training programs. *Social Education*, March 1970, *34*, No. 3, 271–279. Reprinted with permission of the National Council for the Social Studies and Hazel W. Hertzberg.

drawn and to it there are numerous exceptions. Nor do I mean to imply that the new social studies are valueless; on the contrary the values they project are desperately needed. Neither the traditional rote learning which takes place in far too many social studies classrooms, nor the exigencies of the instant social studies, is adequate to the situation in which we now find ourselves. *But if the new social studies, or any successive movements for rational reform, are to have the impact they deserve, they must be modified to take account of a factor largely neglected: the sub-culture of students themselves. And the training of teachers of the social studies must be structured so that a continuing analysis of this culture becomes a central element. For what we are faced with is no less than the emergence of a new and seemingly permanent sub-culture, attached to but distinct from the dominant culture; a sub-culture whose preoccupation is with nowness, whose homeland is education, and whose constituency is the young.*

The emergence of the now culture obviously has far-reaching implications for education, and especially for our sector of education which deals directly with society: with analyses of the remote in time and space, with definitions of the present, and with the possible shape of the future. If we are to create ways of educating teachers which will enable them to deal both rationally and sympathetically with students who are the product of the now culture, to say nothing of achieving some detachment themselves about their own relationship to it, we have first to begin to identify and analyze it.

Analysis of the Now Culture

So complex and bewildering a phenomenon is not susceptible of easy analysis. We will not fully understand it until we analyze it from a number of perspectives. Here I will attempt to suggest some ways of looking at this new sub-culture: its conceptions of time, its location in space, and its relationships to the social sciences and history. Then, assuming that this analysis has some validity, and realizing that it is by no means complete, I will suggest some ways in which teacher training programs might be restructured to take account of it.

1. Time and Change

First, the now culture involves new conceptions of time and change which differ dramatically from two fundamental temporal conceptions which, with many variations, have characterized most of the thousands of cultures in which man has lived.

In traditional tribally or rurally based societies, men perceive themselves as moving through a cycle of time in which past, present, and future blend together. The present is thought of as a necessary and desirable repetition of the past. Concepts of temporal duration are usually quite limited, for the time beyond that of a few generations back melts together. Accounts of the past are embodied in myth and legend. Typically the people believe that through ritual they can ensure re-creation of the present in the image of the past. If formal education exists at all, it is usually directed to acquiring command over the religious rituals believed to be essential to the continuation of the society. The life pattern of the individual follows that of his forebearers, and he expects that his children's lives will be much like his own. Training for the limited array of traditional occupations in which people expect to engage is achieved through observation or other informal arrangements or through a system of apprenticeship. In such cultures the future of the culture as a whole and of the individuals who comprise it are well defined. The cyclical rhythms of nature with which the people are in intimate contact undergird their conceptions of time. In such cultures, men deal with changes by attempting to incorporate them into traditional ways and by reinforcing the identity and continuity of past, present, and future.

The progressive model of time, characteristic of urbanizing and industrializing cultures, is quite different. The present is defined as different from though not detached from the past. Change is generally conceived of as necessary and good and is equated with progress. The past is thought of as of much longer duration than is the case in traditional societies. The record of the past is contained in history, which is analytical, comparative, and subject to interpretation. Myth and legend do not disappear but rather are fragmented, some elements being incorporated into history, some into religious and other institutions, some continuing on a folk level. Time is thought of as moving forward. The future is conceived of as different from and better than the past. The individual does not simply repeat the past pattern of life but assumes that his life will be an improvement on that of his father's, and that in turn his children's lives will be different from, and better than, his own. He plans present conduct to ensure future success. Education becomes much more widespread, more formal, and of longer duration and is thought of as an essential prerequisite for the proliferation of occupations and differing life styles now available. The direct contact of man with nature is more tenuous but a substantial portion of the population still works either in agriculture or as artisans dealing directly with natural materials. Such cultures deal with change by projecting their bonds with the future and by comparing the present favorably with the past.

The now culture model of time bears certain resemblances to both of the other temporal conceptions. In its intense preoccupation with the present it has some of the characteristics of the traditional model but unlike the latter it does not conceive of the present as a desirable and necessary repetition of the past. On the contrary, the past is believed to be so different as to be irrelevant. Yet its poignant yearnings for the security of traditional societies may be seen in its panoply of heroes, many of whom come from traditional societies or from groups outside the mainstream of modern industrial life. If it rejects history, it recreates myth and mythical figures, casting the past as a timeless struggle between good and evil. It partakes of the progressive model of expectation of success, but telescopes the progressive hopes of a better future for society and for the individual into a demand that these dreams be translated intact into reality now. Men have ever dreamed of perfection. Traditional societies often locate perfection in a vague hereafter; progressive societies shift the locale to earth but consign it to an indeterminate future. But in the now culture, perfection is to be achieved here and now. It does not attempt to incorporate changes into traditional patterns by reaffirming its identity with the past, as in the traditional model, nor does it regard change as a step towards a better future, as in the progressive model. Rather it demands instant and immediate satisfaction, regardless of the connection of change with past patterns or the effect of change on the future.

As the life pattern of individuals in traditional societies undergirds their focus on the present as a recapitulation of the past and that of individuals in progressive societies undergirds their focus on the future as an improvement over the present, so that of the now culture epitomizes the concentration on the moment as the only reality, detached from the irrelevant past. The ideal life stage of the now culture begins somewhere around the time when children enter junior high school and ends somewhere around thirty. It is to this vague life stage that older and younger people try to conform. But no one seems to know where the locus of age is, for there is a series of under-thirty generations. Nor is it very clear where adolescence or youth begins and ends. In reality we seem to be producing a new generation every three or four years characterized by a sense of estrangement from the generations above and below it in age and a feeling that one is already growing old and is separated from youth. In this strange dislocation, people in their mid-twenties are already complaining of aging and of their psychic distance from what is new and emerging.

In the now culture's intense focus on youth there is little conception of a life cycle which includes the very young or the "mature" or "old." Childhood is sometimes thought of as beautiful or innocent; age is almost universally dreaded or condemned. In keeping with its temporal conceptions, the now culture conceives of one large and amorphous life stage rather than a series of life stages each with its own rewards, duties, pains and satisfactions.

Now culture people continually proclaim their allegiance to the moment by a constant redefinition of what is new. Characteristically they do so by means which are easily changed. They take up and discard fashions—including hair styles and buttons—language, causes, heroes and anti-heroes, styles of behavior and music. Through such means they attempt to create instant identities, to place themselves firmly at the center of an ever-changing now, to feel themselves secure in a world of flux.

The pathology of the now culture is the culture of drugs. Whether or not mind-expanding drugs are harmful to the individual, they have in common the quality of distorting time and space and producing an intense feeling of nowness. Since their use is illegal, drugs also tend to separate the individual from society, or at least its juridical and police functions. It is significant, however, that the use of the most popular mind-expanding drug has become to an important extent socialized. Often marijuana is taken in a semi-ritualized fashion, thus providing the individual with a social as well as a purely personal experience. Here, as in many other instances, the now culture creates its own rituals and informal institutions.

2. Location of the Now Culture

Secondly, the now culture has its location in the schools and colleges. Educational institutions seem to be the most stable and enduring ones with which the young are involved, and those with which they have the most continuous contact. In traditional societies, formal education is either non-existent or ancillary to other social institutions. In progressive societies, education for most people is of relatively brief duration and tends to be vocationally oriented; people acquire the basic skills needed for successful functioning in the outside world and somewhere in their teens are graduated to the world of work. But in contemporary society formal education occupies the first two decades and often the third decade of life as well. A decisive shift in balance has taken place: what was once essentially peripheral and preparatory has become (at least from the perspective of those involved in it) central and permanent.

Other social institutions and identifications—family, church, political party, neighborhood, ethnic groups—seem fragile by comparison with educational institutions. The family is not perceived as a basic and enduring unit of society, but as a more temporary arrangement, or series of arrangements. Traditional religious institutions have little appeal and their attempts to be "relevant" frequently alienate the old while only momentarily holding the young. Traditional political loyalties are exceedingly tenuous. The neighborhood and community are not places to strike roots. People expect to move from place to place, from group to group, and to shift allegiances and loyalties. Diminution of prejudice and expanding opportunities have weakened ethnic allegiances as the memories of past disabilities fade. A sense of national community or of patriotism becomes largely irrelevant, downright embarrassing, or a positive evil.

But participation in education is compulsory up to the middle-teens. Thereafter a massive series of societal pressures, including the "necessity" for keeping the young out of the job market, the social prestige attached to education, the training requirements for specialized jobs, the draft, and parental willingness and ability to support their offspring, keep the young as perpetual students. Even those who leave are defined in relation to education—as "dropouts."

As might be expected, the leaders and articulators of the now culture are frequently drawn from the educated, suburban, upwardly mobile middle class, from just those sectors of American life in which ties of family, church, political party, community and ethnicity are most brittle and whose aspirations for education—and the financial capacity for acquiring it—are greatest. Often they are musicians who play and sing of the concerns of the now culture, helping to set its fashions and styles of behavior, providing through all-enveloping sound a timeless moment, or shifting series of moments. Into educational institutions today are poured the energies, hopes, and definitions of identity once dispersed and channeled into a range of other institutions, all of which had traditional bonds with the past and characteristic visions of the future. It is small wonder that students are asking the educational enterprise to serve as surrogate for these other human institutions which they believe have failed them or which often seem only tangential to their main occupation. . . .

Students also seek within educational institutions or on their borders the temporary equivalents of family, community, and church. They have themselves created with considerable ingenuity a variety of arrangements to carry out the functions once performed by these institutions. The commune often serves as temporary family and community. The mass meeting often bears a stronger resemblance to a religious revival than to an old-fashioned political gathering. What is said is relatively unimportant. The critical aspect is the ritual—the songs, the skits, the cheers and jeers and, most important, the intense identification with the group, the surge of emotion, the sense of being absolved from guilt, of being saved, the division of the world into the elect and the damned.

One form of organization which education is often asked to employ is the "T group" or sensitivity training, a technique which originated in education. While sensitivity training antedates the now culture, its present popularity is probably due to its consonance with now culture ideas. It is, in fact, an almost perfect vehicle for this culture and it represents also an attempt to solve some of its most difficult problems. The "T group" normally holds in abeyance both the past and the future and concentrates on the immediate in time and space. People develop very strong loyalties to the group itself and frequently strong hostilities to those outside it. The "T group" may become surrogate family and community, but it has none of the legal or social ties which bind members of families and communities together. Through a "T group" persons who have been strangers only a short time previously may quickly learn a great deal about each other as well as about themselves. They may just as quickly move on and lose contact with each other. The kind of mutual responsibilities developed in a "T group" are therefore quite different from those of family or community where the bonds are more formal and durable.

Most—although not all—of the equivalents which students either develop themselves or ask of educational institutions are characteristically now-centered. Ideally, they provide temporary shelter and temporary commitment and ideally they are non-bureaucratic. They are not thought of as permanent arrangements in which individuals will develop a complex set of long-term obligations. When the latter are involved, as in changes in student government, students frequently lose interest, become bored with the minutiae of day-to-day operations, or develop intense factions around conflicting sets of demands. For however immersed students are in the now and the here, they know also that their stay must eventually come to an end, that the "real" world lies elsewhere. But for faculty and administration, whose commitments are more permanent, and for whom education is *their* real world, the situation often looks quite dismaying. They will be around to pick up the pieces. . . .

The concentration of the now culture in education has had further effects in furnishing its adherents with a set of attitudes and ideas characteristic of the educational enterprise. Education deals not with things but with their symbols. Its characteristic outputs are words and ideas. It is thought of and conceives itself to be a place where student and scholar grapple in comparative isolation with a vast array of conflicting ideas and words, where they are subjected to discussion and analysis. Critics have traditionally accused educators of living in an ivory tower, by which they mean that ideas in the academy are frequently irrelevant to or unconnected with life in the "real" world outside and that academics lack a sense of the nitty-gritty of ordinary life. There is obviously some truth in this accusation. Yet some isolation from and protection from the pressures of society are essential in education, especially in the case of unpopular or new ideas. But the price paid for this protection has sometimes been high. For academic dealers in ideas sometimes become their captives and reify the models they create. Moreover, the academic concentration on words often results in the neglect of other aspects of human experience and needs (a condition, incidentally, of which professors in colleges and universities are often hardly aware, but of which teachers in the schools are much more cognizant). When a significant portion of the population spends several decades in educational institutions, when they are largely insulated both from the "real" world of men and the underlying world of nature, when they deal in words and ideas but not in their effects, and when their senses other than visual and auditory are almost entirely neglected, it is not surprising that they cry out for "relevance" and "experience," and at the same time deal with that relevance and experience in terms which often reveal a confusion between the idea and the possibility or the effect of its translation into practice. . . .

To now culture people, history often seems to be a prison. By its insistence on comparison, it seems to them to deny the uniqueness of their own passionate experience. It seems to tell them that everything has happened before, that the more things change, the more they remain the same. It insists that the present is a product of the past, affirming the very link which they want to break. It is the disciplinary equivalent of their parents, speaking of other times when things were different.

To the extent that now culture people are willing to consider history at all, their uses of history are quite different from those of the professional historian. The now culture sees history as a gigantic morality play, a struggle between the forces of good and the forces of evil. On these the now student sits in judgment, enshrining those heroes or movements in the past which he believes to be good and casting into outer darkness those he believes to be evil. This view of history bears a marked resemblance to the history often taught in the schools, but with the good and evil forces inverted. Perhaps the now culture is turning against history a now version of the model they learned in school, shorn of the thousands of "facts" which usually envelop it.

But even in those social science disciplines which are relatively ahistorical, there are problems. Each investigates a whole range of phenomena which necessarily lie outside the area of immediate now culture concern. Each deals with cause and effect and the consequences and testing of ideas in a variety of situations. In each, one must take account of contradictory evidence. Each stresses (or should stress) probabilities rather than certainties, relativities rather than absolutes. To the extent that either history or the social sciences are presented as simple, given truths, they are welcomed—provided that they reinforce current now culture notions. But to the extent that they question these notions, or contradict them, or to the extent that they reveal doubts and uncertainties, they are rejected.

Many of the characteristics which make history and the social sciences unpalatable to the now culture are of course shared by other academic disciplines. The difference lies in their perceived relationship to society. Students do not expect of biology or mathematics the conceptual tools for analysing their own relationship to society or for attacking the social evils which they so passionately abhor. It is in our disciplines that they expect to find "answers," and our disciplines which they attack so bitterly when they fail to find the kinds of answers they seek.

The forces which are producing the now culture are neither transient nor ephemeral. They lie in a matrix of affluence, urbanization, social and geographic mobility, the acceleration rate of technological change, the breakdown of traditional institutions, increasing population, and—perhaps most important of all—instant communication. Nor is the now culture confined to the United States alone, although it is most highly developed here. It is already appearing in other societies in a similar stage of development. In the United States the Vietnam war and the civil rights and black revolutions have shaped many of its major concerns but it would have developed in any case. The conceptions of time which it holds and its locus in education will not, I believe, change radically in the foreseeable future. What will change, often with bewildering speed, are the loci of its interests.

The idea of the now culture is, like the idea of culture itself, a creation of the human mind, a model which corresponds only roughly to the rich complexity of the reality it seeks to organize into comprehensible patterns. I have sought only to outline what seem to me to be some of its characteristics most relevant to our own field of interest, fully cognizant of the fact that the same data are susceptible of other interpretations and emphases. Certainly we need more adequate conceptual tools with which to analyse our situation. If we do not develop them, we will view the behavior of students only as individual aberrations rather than as manifestations of much broader social patterns. . . .

REVIEW OF ROSENTHAL AND JACOBSON

Robert L. Thorndike

The enterprise which represents the core of this document, and presumably the excuse for its publication, has received widespread advance publicity. In spite of anything I can say, I am sure it will become a classic— widely referred to and rarely examined critically. Alas, it is so defective technically that one can only regret that it ever got beyond the eyes of the original investigators! Though the volume may be an effective addition to educational propagandizing, it does nothing to raise the standards of educational research.

Though it may make for a dull review, I feel I must dissect the study to point out some basic defects in its data that make its conclusions (though they may possibly be true) in no sense adequately supported by the data. The general reasonableness of the "self-fulfilling prophecy effect" is not at issue, nor is the reported background of previous anecdote, observation, and research. The one point at which this review is directed is the adequacy of procedures (of data gathering and data analysis) and the appropriateness of the conclusions drawn from the study that constitutes the middle third of the book.

Before we can dig beneath the surface, we must outline briefly on a surface level what was done and what was reportedly found. In May, 1964, the SRA-published Tests of General Ability (TOGA) were administered by the classroom teachers to all pupils in kindergarten and all six grades of a school. The test had been presented to the teachers as a test that ". . . will allow us to predict which youngsters are most likely to show an academic spurt." The following September each teacher was given a list of names of pupils (actually selected by a table of random numbers) who were alleged to be the ones likely to show a spurt.

The children were tested again in January 1965, May 1965, and May 1966. The authors assert that the results support the proposition that the teachers' expectancies influenced the mental development of the children.

The main results of testing in May 1965 (from the authors' Table 7-1) are as follows:

Thorndike, R. L. Review of Rosenthal and Jacobson. *Pygmalion in the Classroom. American Educational Research Journal*, November 1968, *5*, No. 4, 708–711. Copyright by American Educational Research Association, Washington, D.C.

| | Control | | | Experimental | |
Grade	N	Gain	N	Gain	Difference
1	48	+12.0	7	+27.4	15.4
2	47	+ 7.0	12	+16.5	9.5
3	40	+ 5.0	14	+ 5.0	0
4	49	+ 2.2	12	+ 5.6	3.4
5	26	+17.5	9	+17.4	−0.1
6	45	+10.7	11	+10.0	−0.7

Thus, to all intents and purposes, the alleged effect of the "prophecy" appears in 19 children in grades 1 and 2. If we are to trust the results, and the large edifice of further analysis and speculation built upon them, the findings for these two grades must be unimpeachable. Let us examine them.

TOGA has two subtests, one consisting of oral vocabulary and one of multi-mental ("which one doesn't belong") items. For the K-2 level of the test, the one used in the pretesting and posttesting of grades 1 and 2, the two parts of the test contain respectively 35 and 28 items. Let us look first at the pretest data for six classrooms, three tested in kindergarten and three in the first grade. The results, from Appendix A-2 and A-3 were (expressed in numbers that are always spoken of by the authors as "IQs"):

| | Experimental | | | | Control | | |
Class	N	Mean Verbal "IQ"	Mean Reasoning "IQ"	N	Mean Verbal "IQ"	Mean Reasoning "IQ"
1A	3	102.00	84.67	19	119.47	91.32
1B	4	116.25	54.00	16	104.25	47.19
1C	2	67.50	55.50	19	95.68	30.79
2A	6	114.33	112.50	19	111.53	100.95
2B	3	103.67	102.33	16	96.50	80.56
2C	5	90.20	77.40	14	82.21	73.93

On the Reasoning Test, one class of 19 pupils is reported to have a mean "IQ" of 31! They just barely appear to make the grade as imbeciles! And yet these pretest data were used blithely by the authors without even a reference to these fantastic results!

If these pretest data show anything, they show that the testing was utterly worthless and meaningless. The means and standard deviations for the total first and second grade classes were (calculated by combining sub-groups):

	First Grade		Second Grade	
	Mean	*S. D.*	*Mean*	*S. D.*
Verbal	105.7	21.2	99.4	16.1
Reasoning	58.0	36.8	89.1	21.6

What kind of a test, or what kind of testing is it that gives a mean "IQ" of 58 for the total entering first grade of a rather run-of-the-mill school?

Unfortunately, nowhere in the whole volume do the authors give any data expressed in raw scores. Neither do they give the ages of their groups. So it takes a little impressionistic estimating to try to reconstruct the picture. However, it would not be far off to assume an average age of 6.0 for May of a kindergarten year. An "IQ" of 58 would then mean a "mental age" of 3.5. So we go to the norms tables of TOGA to find the raw score that would correspond to a "mental age" of 3.5. Alas, the norms do not go down that far! It is not possible to tell what the authors did, but finding that a raw score of 8 corresponds to an "M.A." of 5.3, we can take a shot at extrapolating downward. We come out with a raw score of approximately 2! Random marking would give 5 or 6 right!

We can only conclude that the pretest on the so-called Reasoning Test at this age is worthless. And in the words of a European colleague, "When the clock strikes thirteen, doubt is cast not only on the last stroke but on all that have gone before."

Another look at one of the Appendix tables (A-6) shows that the 6 pupils in class 2A who had been picked to be "spurters" have a reported mean and standard deviation of posttest "IQ" of 150.17 and 40.17 respectively. This looks a little high! What does it mean in raw score terms? Again, we must turn detective with somewhat inadequate clues. Not knowing pupil ages, let us assume 7½ as probably on the low side for May in the second grade. An "IQ" of 150 implies, then, a mean "M.A." of 11¼. Back to our TOGA norms to find the corresponding raw score. Alas, the highest entry is 10.0 for a raw score of 26! We must once more extrapolate, and the best we can do from the existing data is to get 28+. (Remember, there are only 28 items in this sub-test.) The mean of 6 represents a perfect score! But the standard deviation is 40 "IQ" points. What of those who fall above the mean?

When the clock strikes 14, we throw away the clock!

In conclusion, then, the indications are that the basic data upon which this structure has been raised are so untrustworthy that any conclusions based upon them must be suspect. The conclusions may be correct, but if so it must be considered a fortunate coincidence.

TEACHING/DISCIPLINE

Charles H. Madsen, Jr. and Clifford K. Madsen

What Is the Payoff?

A traditional viewpoint prevalent in education is to focus upon many antecedent events (reinforcement history) leading toward a particular behavioral goal, rather than to focus upon the manipulation and control of the present environment. This procedure of looking backward is both unproductive and unnecessary, especially when it absolves the responsibility of solving the current problem. When the teacher wants to change a specific inappropriate behavior, the teacher must first *find the payoff* and eliminate it if possible. *Behavior that goes unrewarded will extinguish.* The teacher must watch the student carefully to determine the payoff. The teacher must also recognize individual differences; the payoff is often different for each child. For example, students A, B, and C talk in class. After many warnings the teacher finally sends them to the principal's office. This is just exactly what student A wanted; he finally managed to goad the teacher into "punishing" him. Student B just liked to make the teacher angry. Every time she got stern it just "broke him up." He knew he was bothering her, and he enjoyed her distress—"Wow! She gave me such *stern* looks." Student C did not care about the teacher or the principal. He did care about students A and B. Every time he talked, they listened. On the way to the principal's office, student A filled the others in. "Listen, the principal sits you down and comes on with all this 'You've got to be a good boy' stuff. Man, the last time I was in there I really had him snowed. Besides, he never checks to see if you go back to the class, so we're out for the day." When students A, B, and C return to class, they will continue to talk—even more.

Teachers who have simple monolithic explanations for all maladaptive behaviors will be generally ineffective. "All those children need is a little love." "The thing they need is a good hard paddling." "Get them out in the world; then you'll see how they do." "They need a decent place to live." "They need someone who truly understands them." The problem with this type of analysis is that it is not differentiated. There are some children who may fit one, none, or all of the above categories, plus countless others. The one thing that children exhibiting inappropriate responses *do* need is a teacher who can find the payoff. What is keeping the behavior alive? If the payoff can be found and completely eliminated, then the behavior will gradually extinguish—*if consistency is maintained*.

One significant result of eliminating the payoff is that the undesired behavior will get initially worse before it gets better. The teacher must remember that the student has learned a behavior to get what he wants. When the "reward" is abolished, he tries even harder (i.e., the inappropriate behavior increases) before he comes to realize that there is no payoff. After this initial surge the behavior will extinguish. This initial rise is extremely important to remember. Many people give up during the storm before the calm. "Oh, I've tried ignoring, but the baby cried even louder."—Of course.

Finding the payoff can be difficult, and sometimes the payoff comes from a source that the teacher cannot control (parents, peers etc.). Nevertheless, many problems can be solved by cutting out the "reward." *What is the payoff?—That which keeps the behavior alive. . . .*

What Constitutes Reward?

After the teacher determines the payoff and eliminates it, the teacher will soon observe a decrease in undesirable behavior. Sometimes this alone is all that is needed. Yet more often the teacher must control other stimuli (i.e., structure contingencies) in order to discipline. It is better to start with just one behavior and not try to eliminate everything simultaneously, unless the teacher has a great deal of help and can initially devote all the time just to social behavioral problems. If many maladaptive behaviors are prevalent throughout the classroom, the teacher is advised to establish a hierarchy and start with the deviant behavior that most interferes with learning. It is also advisable to make up a set of easily understood rules for the classroom. In making up the contingencies (i.e., structuring the rewards) the new payoff for *desirable* behavior (following the rules) must be known, tangible, and close enough to the student's own behavioral responses to motivate the student to seek it. Initially it is better to give too much reward than not enough. The idea is to get the students winning as soon as possible. For general classroom control in the elementary grades, various "token systems" are highly effective; group activities and peer group approval are also effective for the junior high and high school years. Token systems come closest to representing our social monetary system. Correct responses earn "tokens" that are exchanged for tangible goods (e.g., toys or classroom materials which do not need to be expensive): Rewards earned for tokens should have marked values (i.e., colored paper —30 points, ruler—50 points, glider plane—80 points) so that students can receive tangible credit for following the rules (written on the board and explained daily). Each child can have a small notebook on the upper left corner of his desk, and at appropriate intervals the teacher marks the student's points. The teacher may start the morning by holding up the rewards and asking the children which one they are working toward. Then the teacher may go over the rules: We sit quietly during individual study. We raise our hand before we talk. We stay at our own desk unless given permission by the teacher, etc. At opportune times the teacher circulates, writing down the points. The very act of recording may be used as an effective control. Sometimes the teacher will want to *catch a child being good* and reward him with points instantaneously.

In the initial stages of control it is important to have the child achieve success quickly, after which the time between behavior and reward may be stretched for longer periods while pairing with appropriate personal responses from the teacher (praising, smiling, touching). In time the personal approval of the teacher or even self-approval will probably be all that is needed for proper motivation. This is certainly what every teacher desires, but in order to achieve this level of sophistication, one must start where the child is. Some children enter school with response expectations amenable to smiling, pleasing the teacher, being obedient, etc. Others have to learn appropriate responses through more tangible rewards.

One extremely effective technique for small children is the use of food (M & M's, juice, flavored cereal). The teacher may start the very first class with an M & M party. While the children are eating, the teacher says, "We will have another M & M party if everyone is quiet while I count to ten." (The teacher counts aloud quickly, making sure they win.) After giving the candy the teacher says, "If everyone is quiet for five minutes we will have another party, but if someone talks we will not get to have one." Now the teacher sits back and waits; in all probability someone will talk, whereupon the teacher says, "Oh, I'm *very sorry*. Mary talked before our time was up; now we will not get to have a party. Maybe tomorrow we may have one if everyone is quiet." (Some children will think this is not "fair.") *Because the teacher does not get angry at Mary, Mary cannot give her problem to the teacher*. Mary receives the disapproval of the group so there is no payoff from the other children. Instead of interacting directly with Mary, it may be better to use vicarious reinforcement and modeling. To use this technique the teacher chooses one of the most well-behaved children and says, "I surely like the way Sheila is sitting so quietly. If everyone behaved like Sheila, we could have our party." Sometimes the teacher may wish to give rewards to those children who were quiet and not give anything to those who were not. (Mary may not think this is fair.)

The use of group approval-disapproval is very effective, particularly with older students. When activities are given or denied, contingent upon the behavior of all students, the students themselves will take the responsibility for discipline; and discipline will start to evolve from within the group. *Peer approval* is extremely important to older students. This is precisely the reason for such high *esprit de corps* in many student organizations, such as band, athletics, social clubs, gangs, etc. When teacher and students are taught to cut out the payoff for an individual's deviant responses, the student's maladaptive behavior extinguishes. Some students are indeed embarrassed after receiving such responses from the teacher or their peers—so be it.

Rewards the teacher can use contingently include: (1) words (spoken and written—rules), (2) expressions (facial—bodily), (3) closeness (nearness—touching), (4) activities and privileges (social—individual), and (5) things (materials—food—playthings—awards). Other than subject matter itself, these categories constitute the *entire resources* the teacher has for structuring. The teacher should develop them well. (See lists on pages 116–131.) *What constitutes reward?—That which the student will work toward....*

Can Contingencies be Structured?

The basic premise of reinforcement teaching is to arrange the stimuli of the external world to shape the behavior of the students—to structure the environment so that the student receives approval-disapproval reinforcements contingent upon appropriate/inappropriate behavior. Therefore, *reinforcement teaching is the structure of approval and disapproval reinforcers, in time, to shape desired behavior toward specific goals.* Experimentation in learning demonstrates that: (a) If a student knows specifically what is expected of him, and (b) he wants to do it, then (c) he probably will. The necessity for specific measurable goals (expectations for students) has already been mentioned. The crux of the problem rests with (b): arranging the contingencies of reinforcement so that a student will want to do what the teacher expects.

Five techniques used in structuring contingencies are:

1. *Approval* (rewards)
2. *Withholding of approval—withholding rewards* (hope)
3. *Disapproval* (punishment)
4. *Threat of disapproval* (fear)
5. *Ignoring* (not attending in any manner)

1. Approval is easily understood. Approval is anything that is generally related with *happiness*, such as food, candy, smiling, touching, attention, praise, proximity, clothes, cars, etc. The teacher must be sure, however,

that what the teacher believes is functioning as a positive reinforcer is truly positive (some children don't like ice cream).

2. Withholding of approval (withholding rewards) is used when the positive reinforcer has previously been established. Withholding the positive reinforcer probably functions to produce "hope for the attainment of a reward the next time—if the behavior is improved." In a way this procedure acts as "punishment," although with greater effect and less wear and tear on everyone concerned. "I'm so sorry you didn't finish on time. Now we cannot go out to play. Perhaps tomorrow you will finish on time. Then you may play."

3. Disapproval is also easily understood. Disapproval is generally synonymous with *unhappiness*, such as frowning, getting yelled at, being frightened, put in isolation, embarrassed, being made to do an unpleasant task, etc. The teacher must also be careful here not to ascribe monolithic judgment concerning what constitutes disapproval. Maladaptive children often exhibit many perverted associations. "I like to get spanked." "I enjoy making the teacher angry." Extreme disapproval (corporal punishment) should be used very sparingly, if at all.

4. Threat of disapproval (fear). This also should be rare; yet it is profoundly effective once the knowledge of disapproval is established. This procedure leads to a way of behaving to avoid disapproval (unpleasant stimuli): "I am careful when crossing the road to avoid getting killed"; "I don't play with guns because I could get shot"; "I study so I won't fail"; "I act appropriately in class so as to avoid the disapproval of the teacher," etc. While fear is an extremely effective suppressant, it does little in establishing the joy of learning. Children who are completely negatively motivated usually are tense, unenthusiastic, quiet, shy, passive, and generally fearful. Some of these children do eventually succeed, although this negatively motivated "success" usually comes at the high price of guilt, compulsiveness, generalized anxiety, and, perhaps later, even ulcers.

5. Ignore—just that—ignore. . . .

The teacher is advised, if at all possible, to use primarily approval, withholding of approval, and ignoring in controlling behavior. There is some indication that these "positive approaches" may be more effective, but more important, *much less damage can be done than through the use of punishments*. This does *not* mean the teacher should be permissive. It indicates that as the teacher structures the child's environment contingent on appropriate behaviors, the teacher should diligently try to do so through the use of "positive" techniques and structuring incompatible responses. Alternately, there are times when punishment might need to be used. Some maladaptive behaviors of children are much worse than the punishment it could take to eliminate them. *Can contingencies be structured?—They must!*

AFFECTIVE EDUCATION

Douglas Heath

. . . just what do we mean by affective education? The phrase has been applied to a variety of contemporary trends, some of which have their roots deep in the history of American tradition. Four inter-related educational trends now in process capture its spirit.

First, affective education is the education of affects, or feelings and emotions. Educators have been educating affects since the Athenians first insisted every youth learn to play the lyre. Music teachers have tried to nurture musical sensitivity and appreciative feelings for years. Curricular pilot studies are now underway to sensitize students in more systematic ways to rhythmic, artistic, and dance patterns in order to cultivate artistic judgment. But I have yet to discover any adequate rationale for identifying the specific types of feelings to be nurtured and refined. Psychology is of little help. It has no adequate theory of emotion. Emotion does have many functions. It stirs and incites us. Simulation games are frequently used in the classroom to involve emotionally a youth so he will become interested in more academic topics. Emotion has an expressive function. Its expression reduces tensions. The rigorous athletic programs of some boarding schools are frequently defended because they "drain off" urgent sexual and aggressive impulses. Emotions also direct behavior. Our values and convictions are relatively stable emotionalized preferences and beliefs that guide behavior. . . .

A second focus of affective education is to make the learning process less abstract and deductive and more concretely experiential and inductive. Field trips to the zoo, the integrated day or British-infant school model, or, for adolescents, apprenticeship types of experiences or a semester abroad seek to take advantage of more inductive experiential forms of learning. These approaches aren't new. Their renaissance is due to the increasing didactic abstractness of the teacher-dominated classroom and of formalistic teaching methods that accompany a too verbal curriculum. Such experiential learning takes much more teaching skill than most of us are aware. . . .

A third related meaning of affective education is to make learning a more organismic experience rather than only cerebral exercise. Learning doesn't stick if it is only verbal, not integrated into action. . . . Too much academic learning is primarily visual and aural. The progressive loss of enthusiasm and joy in our schools as students move from kindergarten through college is due in part to the enforced constriction of physical movement (students must sit for hours), of vocal activity (students must be quiet), and of other sensory modalities. The integrated day program does have releasing effects and its principles already are seeping into the secondary school. It recovers what Dewey and Whitehead always insisted upon. We do not know if we have learned something until we act upon what we have learned. And when we act, we act as a thinking, feeling, sensing, deciding organism. . . .

The fourth and last meaning of affective education is the belated recognition that man is fundamentally a social being whose humanity needs to be nurtured and educed and that we don't help him become more human using inhuman or impersonal methods of learning. While TV and computer-assisted instruction have a place, the central arena for growth is the interaction of a student with another human being. It is not just that by listening, discussing, arguing, criticizing, and telling some other responding person that is the primary spur to intellectual development—an insight we have been ignoring in our schools; it is that such experiences also humanize a person. . . . Affective education insists we reorder our goals to recognize the centrality of a human and humane learning environment. Affective education also means we teachers learn *how* to help children communicate; *how* to work out personal problems that block their development; *how* to reflect about their own relationships with others. Most of us really don't help any of our students learn these skills of being and doing in our classrooms.

Given such reasonable and hopeful shifts in emphases in our schools, why is affective education a potentially dangerous innovation? It is potentially dangerous for several reasons. By releasing and cultivating emotional involvement, confronting values, providing youth with experiences that involve their feelings, many teachers will discover they themselves also become more emotionally involved in their teaching. Affective education cannot be effective if a teacher doesn't allow himself to become vulnerable to his own feelings. And that will require greater maturity of us. . . .

Those who work with children may not encounter the intensity and indiscriminate expression of feelings that teachers unexpectedly meet when they initiate more experiential forms of education with older students. Adolescents have been so emotionally suppressed in the classroom for years that some literally just cannot contain their own explosiveness when no longer protected by traditional aseptic classroom rituals. So the first danger is that teachers will find their ability to deal maturely with their own feelings challenged.

A second danger results from the depth of the estrangement of some youth from their own impulses and feelings. When given the opportunity to participate experientially they find the arousal of their own feelings to be so seductively integrating that they resist any effort to take an objective, logical, rational, evaluative attitude toward their experience. Affective education risks intensifying anti-intellectualism—hopefully only temporarily until its cathartic effect has been diminished.

A third danger, particularly for adolescents, though the seeds for it are sown when younger, is that affective education may accentuate the potential for narcissism that is already quite strong in today's students. My own studies with American students, confirmed by studies with Italians and Turks, suggests that too developed an aesthetic attitude, as we see in psychedelia, in an adolescent may be symptomatic of an excessive self-centeredness and preoccupation with the subjective at the expense of forming skills and attitudes that tie him to reality or to others. The consequence is that an education that accentuates the immersion of the self in feelings, that justifies beauty as the only criterion of worth, that stimulates self-sufficiency may have immaturing effects—unless we locate such education within a more powerfully social and caring context.

A fourth related danger is that stimulating aesthetic expression without encouraging the development of skills to transform its subjectivism into some socially communicable form, risks intensifying an already strong trend toward dilettantism. Too many of today's youth believe emotional expressiveness is creative. They ignore that creativity involves not only accessibility to aesthetic impulses, but also disciplined craftsmanship in communicating such impulses and insight in some form. Affective education demands much maturity of students for it requires them to master skills for integrating potentially disturbing feelings and conflicts. This is a much more demanding educational task than to master skills for handling nonpersonal, nondisruptive information. But my evidence, at any rate, is very clear. A characteristic of maturity is the ability to use one's logical ordered thought processes to resolve personally disruptive and emotional situations. . . .

Another related danger is that affective education when injudiciously introduced could confirm students' impressions that freedom means the absence of restraint to be able to be whatever one's emotional impulses dictate—Summerhillian style. . . . Genuine freedom comes from acquiring the attitudes, motives, and skills that increase one's options for making choices—an insight many youth today reject because to acquire such skills requires the patience, tolerance for frustration, and persistence after excellence that deny them the pleasures they associate with freedom from expectations.

The final potential danger is that affective education, however we define it, becomes a substitute for academic excellence as *the* goal of education. Both academic and affective development are partial goals. In reacting against the sterility of academicism, we risk plunging into the fecundity of an undisciplined aestheticism that is nonintegrative of a youth's intellectual talents.

Our goal should be to further the educability of a youth, that is, help him learn those attitudes, motives, and skills to be open to continued experiencing and growth. Educability is not equivalent to high academic aptitude or an A average, nor with a dilettantish abandonment to every impulse that emerges into consciousness. The primary determinants of educability are the qualities that make for emotional maturity. . . .

To educate for educability then means travelling two routes: creating a loving relationship with our students and cultivating a religiously reverent receptivity to the inward presence that is integrated with communicable skills.

So how does a youth mature and how do we help him develop a disciplined aestheticism as exemplified in meditation?

Growth is initiated when we confront a problem, when we are frustrated, bewildered, and unsure about how to proceed. Such frustration spurs us to reflect, to inquire, to think. . . .

The evidence is clear: mature persons are more understanding of others, more accurately understand themselves, and are able to reflect more adequately about problems . . . educators must begin to educate affectively with elementary school children. How do we help a first and second grader keep open to his own feelings and impulses and learn how to differentiate between and then symbolize the inchoate feelings he has? We begin by teaching him to learn how to listen more carefully outwardly and then help him transfer those skills to learning how to listen inwardly. Well how? Some teachers take their children for silent walks in nearby woods or streets where they each sit quietly to listen and remember as many different sounds as they can hear. Of course we stay within the concentration span of small children. If being quiet is too challenging, begin then visually by asking each child to discover on a walk as many different colors as he can, and then describe them. The principle is to sensitize a child in various sensory modalities to his external world. Then some morning begin with a quiet time in the classroom. Darken the room. Have each child put his head in his arms and close his eyes. Then ask him to imagine a TV screen and turn on Channel 5 to see what is going on. Many children won't see anything. We may be surprised how much TV has emptied the imaginative capacity of our youth. So we might make up a four or five line vivid story asking the children to imagine a picture for the story. We might even initiate short guided meditation periods on certain themes or take the children on an imaginal trip inside their bodies, helping them to become aware of what their hungry stomach or cramped tense left ankle is feeling, or we could play music that induces certain moods and have the children try to describe their feelings. We need to help students of all ages learn to differentiate and then label their feelings if they are later to gain intellectual control over them. As a student progresses from elementary to secondary school we could, in our meditative curricular plan, begin to use Zen and yoga principles to teach him how to shut out distractions, that is, concentrate his consciousness, or how to empty his conscious mind to become more open to the imaginal richness that constantly goes on at the periphery of consciousness. Within a few years, schools and colleges will be offering courses on meditation. Fanciful? Not at all. One of the exciting frontiers of psychological research is the demonstration that man can secure much greater access to and control over his consciousness through meditation than most of us have thought possible.

What are the values we will be teaching? We will be teaching openness and honesty; we will be teaching a youth the skills of being true to his own feeling experience.

The second facet of maturing is that as we search for ways to solve a problem through reflection, we learn how to take symbolically another person's point of view and so break out of our self-centeredness. We come to understand a problem, another person, even ourselves, from a multiplicity of perspectives. Some philosophers identify this development to be at the heart of becoming educated. For its consequence is the transcendence of the self and the development of a sense of shared humanness. In furthering this more allocentric skill, I would help my students learn how to listen to and anticipate another's experiences. Once a class had been together for some time, we could use many games to cultivate this skill. Jimmy could try to act like Jane in certain situations; Susie could predict what Margie's reaction would be. We could use role-playing and psychodrama techniques to help students learn how we, the teacher, feel, or to learn how students perceive us as a teacher; we could take the role of Susie and act out how we see her acting. Boys could take the role of girls and have the girls decide how accurately the boys experienced being a girl. But we don't really learn how another person feels unless we learn to listen *with* him. So I would create ways to teach my first graders to listen to other children—a noble and basic educable skill most of us never systematically try to cultivate. In small circles during our meditative time, I would encourage each child to say only a word or two to describe his image or feeling of the moment. Then we could play a game of recalling exactly what every other child in the circle said. I might utter the words of one child to discover who could identify who said it. Or the children might pair up to share a dream they had had the night before and then try to repeat it to the other. As the children became more comfortable speaking spontaneously about their own images and feelings, I would have longer unprogrammed and undirected meditative periods in which a child or teacher could spontaneously share with the others some thought or feeling. Of course, we wouldn't force a child to participate or punish him if his imaginal life was very barren or he didn't want to share.

The values we would be teaching? Understanding, acceptance, tolerance, respect, and caring—basic allocentric values that are intrinsic to developing an educable attitude.

The third dimension that defines maturing is that as we identify different possible attributes of a problem, different perspectives and alternative solutions, we begin to put them together into some feasible relationship. We begin the process of linking, combining, fitting together, and integrating to find the most economical, simple, harmonious solution. A more mature person thinks relationally, is more consistent, has "himself together," and so can act spontaneously. Much of formal education is devoted to helping a youth create relationships, identify similarities from dissimilarities, become more consistent between what he says and does. The depth of our mutuality, our sense of we-ness, manifests the degree to which we have developed integrative interpersonal skills. In our meditative group, I would encourage students, by personal example, to learn how to combine their feelings and images with other modalities of expression. . . .

The values we would be teaching are harder to define for they involve the wholeness, the harmonizing, the relatedness of living. Consistency, flexibility, integrity, and perhaps even grace and harmony are surely involved. . . .

How do we create more stable and autonomous meditative skills? When we begin to shift our sensitizing experiences with the external to the internal world we enhance the process of stabilization. That is, we help students become independent of external stimulation for maintaining their ability to concentrate. We might play a game with our students by deliberately creating distractions during our meditation period to teach them to ignore them. . . .

To encourage the autonomy of the skills of meditation I would begin at different times of the week, like during regular class time, when tension or an argument was in the making or we were blocked by a problem, to introduce quiet meditative times. . . .

And the values we would be teaching? Persistence, steadfastness, independence, and courage.

The values of honesty, understanding, caring, integrity, steadfastness, and courage are intrinsic to developing an educable attitude. If the most brilliant academician is dishonest, or intolerant, or unsympathetic to contradictory viewpoints, or cheats, or is inconsistent, or doesn't stand up for what he believes, how successful have we his teachers been?

If we decide to help a youth learn how to integrate his feelings and values with his intellect, then we will not shy from questions like these:

What is our school doing that inhibits, suppresses, blocks the development of honesty, understanding, caring, integrity, steadfastness, and courage in our students? What are we doing to cultivate such values? A maturing youth has energy free for enthusiasms, curiosity, and joyful commitment. Are our eleventh graders as enthusiastic, curious, and joyful in our classrooms as are the first graders? If not, why not? What have we been doing to make them less mature and so less educable?

What is our school doing to help our students become more accessible to their inner world—to their feelings, impulses and imaginations—the first stage in nurturing creativity? What systematic curricular plan do we have for helping students escape the narcissism latent in such accessibility to the personally subjective? How do we help them put their inner words into some more social, communicable form—the second stage of becoming creative?

Do we really educate for educability? Or are we blindly following the ritual of a narrow academicism preparing our students only for college and graduate school? Or are we cavalierly playing emotional games with them? We need to educate a youth, not just his head or just his heart. The promise of affective education is that it will stimulate us to recover the person lost amongst our abstractions; its danger is that it may devalue man's most promising adaptive and educable skill: a disciplined intellect. . . .

THE UNHEAVENLY CITY: THE NATURE AND THE FUTURE OF OUR URBAN CRISIS

Edward C. Banfield

Editors' note: Because of space limitations, Banfield's point of view is given limited development in this edited selection. The student is urged to read in full Banfield's reasons and evidence for concluding that improved schooling is not a solution to the problems of urban America. See Edward C. Banfield. *The Unheavenly City: The Nature and the Future of Our Urban Crisis.* Boston: Little, Brown, 1970, Ch. 7. Professor Banfield is Henry Lee Shattuck Professor of Urban Government at Harvard University.

The most widely recommended "solution" to the problems of the city is more and better schooling. There is almost nothing that someone does not hope to achieve by this means. City planners see it as a necessary and perhaps sufficient condition for bringing the middle class back into the city from the suburbs. Almost everyone (except economists) thinks that the unschooled will be unemployable in the automated society of the future and—a *non sequitur*—that schooling will prevent unemployment. Since it can be shown statistically that the least schooled have the lowest incomes, schooling is also thought to be a cure for poverty and thus, indirectly, for the slum and the "ghetto." A proper system of education, the HARYOU manual says, is "an inescapable foundation for the reality of respect and self-respect . . . and the basis for the type of vocational and academic adjustment essential for an effective life. . . ."

Education is, of course, a good thing, and no society can have too much of it. What must be questioned, however, is whether "schooling" and "education" necessarily imply one another and, more particularly, whether the kind of schooling possible under existing circumstances—for instance, the intelligence of children, their class culture, the state of the art of teaching, the character of the teaching profession, and so on—is capable of producing the desired effects. The view to be taken in this chapter is that the possibilities for improving the city by reforming its schools are sharply limited. Even if the schools were to do much better those things that it is possible for them to do, the result would hardly change the main features of the situation in the city. Nothing that can be done in the schools of the central city can significantly affect the movement of the well-off to the suburbs or reduce the amount of poverty or teen-age unemployment. Nothing done in them can provide that "inescapable foundation of respect and self-respect" which HARYOU thinks would reduce racial unrest and social disorganization in general. On the contrary, the reforms that would probably be made in the name of "education"—especially requiring more children to spend more time in school—may be expected to produce results exactly the opposite of those intended; that is, they will very likely hasten the movement of the well-off from the city, increase unemployment and poverty, widen the chasms of class and race, and plunge deeper into apathy, or stir into fiercer anger, those already angry or apathetic. . . .

That, on the average, high school graduates earn more than dropouts does not necessarily mean that they earn more *because of anything that they learned in high school* (although of course it may mean that). Their greater earnings may be attributable partly or wholly to their greater quickness of mind. Suppose that all those who now graduate (average IQ 112) became dropouts instead and that all those who now drop out (average IQ 98) became graduates. If this happened, one might find twenty or thirty years hence that dropouts had higher incomes than graduates. Of course, it would be a mistake to attribute their success to their having dropped out.

The higher earnings of graduates may also be attributable in part (conceivably entirely) to their class culture. Perhaps class characteristics (for example, willingness or ability to defer gratification, accept discipline, and behave in ways acceptable to middle-class people) rather than what such youths learn in high school account for their greater employability later. Suppose, again, that middle- and upper-class children left school and lower- and working-class ones got diplomas. In this case, too, the dropouts might have higher average incomes later on.

Still another possibility is that employers attach more importance than they should to the number of years a person has spent in school and perhaps also to the value to them of what he has learned there. . . .

In times of slack employment especially, employers are likely to give an automatic preference to graduates. Even if the work (e.g., wrapping packages) could be done as well by a dropout, the employer will probably prefer a graduate if he can have him at the same wage as the dropout. . . .

A distinction should be made between a "trained" worker and an "educated" one. The trained worker has learned how to perform certain tasks of more or less complexity—to operate a machine, say, or to keep accounts. Training may mean acquiring certain manual dexterities, mastering some body of facts, or learning to apply a set of rules or to exercise discretion within some given limits. The educated worker, by contrast, (1) possesses the kind of general knowledge, especially of reading and mathematics, that will enable him to solve various new problems, and (2) has certain traits of character—especially motivation to achieve, ability to accept the discipline of a work situation, willingness to take the initiative and to accept responsibility, and ability to deal fairly with employers, fellow-employees, and others.

Training may be given entirely in school or on the job. Education, on the other hand, cannot be wholly acquired in either place. Some of what it takes to make a worker educated (especially in reading and mathematical knowledge) can only be learned from books and is usually best learned in school—or perhaps one should say would be best learned there if the school were, in fact, a place where boys and girls generally tried to learn; but the traits of character that are equally a part of education are not learned in school—or at any rate not there more than elsewhere. For the most part, they are acquired in childhood as part of one's culture.

The lower-class person cannot as a rule be given much training because he will not accept it. He lives for the moment, and learning to perform a task is a way of providing for the future. If the training process is accompanied by immediate rewards to the trainee—if it is "fun" or if he is paid while learning—the lower-class person *may* accept training. But even if he does, his earning power will not be much increased, because his class outlook and style of life will generally make him an unreliable and otherwise undesirable employee. Besides, the ability to perform tasks (that is, to do what he has been trained to do) is seldom a very rare or valuable commodity. He *would* increase his earning power greatly if he became educated (as opposed to trained); to have in high degree and in combination both general education and the traits of character mentioned above is rare and valuable. Unfortunately, however, the lower-class person acquires in childhood an outlook and style of life completely antithetical to education.

The lower-class person presents the extreme case: it is all but impossible to increase his employability by training. With the lower working class the difficulties are the same in kind but less in degree. There are also many persons who, because of racial prejudice or other externally imposed handicaps, are taken to be lower or lower working class when in fact they are not. Their abilities, motivation, and traits of character are such that they can be trained to perform tasks and sometimes educated to hold down skilled jobs. Most such people would find ways of getting the training or education somehow even if there were no schools, but not all of them would, and in any case there is much to be said for any measures that will help them. That the general problem of the low-capability worker can be solved in this way is too much to hope for, however.

Much more might be accomplished by altering jobs to fit the limitations of workers than vice versa. The principle of specialization could be applied so as to make the low-intelligence and even the lower-class worker much more employable than he is at present. Cutting meat, for example, need not involve dealing with customers: the two activities could be organized as separate jobs. If employers would program work for low-capability workers in the manner that they program it for computers, the workers' job opportunities would be vastly increased. They are not likely to do so, however, so long as minimum-wage laws, union practices, and social prejudices compel them to pay more for low-value labor than it is worth. Instead, they will do the opposite—find ways to replace low-capacity workers with high-capacity ones and with machines.

To say that the school cannot change the child's class culture is to deny that it can serve what many believe to be its principal purpose. The schools, many people think, exist to liberate the child from the confines—moral and emotional as well as intellectual—of his earliest environment and to open higher horizons for him. No child is more in need of liberation than the lower-class one, and therefore it is thought that the schools are—or at any rate should be—instrumentalities for drawing this child into the larger, freer, more productive world of normal culture as well as for encouraging and facilitating the movement of the working-class child into the middle class and the middle-class child into the upper class. This seems to be what is meant when it is said that schooling provides an "inescapable foundation for the reality of respect and self-respect . . . and the basis for the type of vocational and academic adjustment essential for an effective life." This is why it is generally held that, both from the standpoint of the individual and of the society, it is impossible to have too much schooling. And this is why the inability of the schools to prepare thousands of boys and girls for skilled (or even semiskilled) work and for responsible citizenship and adulthood is counted against them as a failure and is taken as a portent of social decay and collapse.

This idea of what the schools should do contrasts strangely with the account sociologists give of what they do in fact. According to this account, the school does not liberate the child from his class culture but instead confines him in it even more securely—it thickens the walls that separate him from the rest of society. The child has absorbed the elements of his class culture long before reaching school; what the school does is to "socialize" him into it more fully and to make him more aware of the differences that separate him and his kind from others. The child has "picked up" from parents and playmates an outline map of his universe, and the main features of it—the continents, so to speak—cannot be changed by anything that is said or done in school. At best, teachers can only help the child to fill in certain empty spaces on the map he brings with him to school. If the map is extremely crude or wildly inaccurate, teachers and textbooks can be of little help. Nor can they help very much if it is drawn in symbols that are incomprehensible to them. (Working-class Italian-American children studied by Gans in Boston's West End were not adept at manipulating concepts or at handling the reasoning processes in texts and lessons; instead, they were sensitive to people, used words not as concepts but to impress people, and stressed the anecdotal and the episodic—all of which led to learning difficulties in school.) In extreme cases (that is, those presented by lower-class children) not much filling-in of the map is possible, and the little that is possible must take place in the street rather than in the school.

How, it may be asked, can this claim that the school furthers the socialization of a child into his class culture be reconciled with the familiar fact that in America the schools are and always have been a principal vehicle of upward mobility? The answer is that the children who are stimulated into mobility in school are ones whose initial class culture permits or encourages —perhaps even demands—mobility. The more nearly upper class the child's initial culture, the more susceptible he is to being "set in motion" by the school. At the other end of the continuum, the lower-class child's culture does not even recognize—much less value—the possibility of rising or, rather, of doing those things, all of which require some sacrifice of present for future gratification, without which rising is impossible. The lower-class child's conceptual universe lacks the dimension of time; in such a universe it would never occur to anyone to try to change things.

The circumstances that prevent the lower-class child (and in lesser degree the lower-working-class one as well) from learning in school the traits of character that contribute to education also prevent him from learning adequately how to read, write, and compute. The inadequacy of his preparation in the earliest years imposes a handicap that schools cannot overcome later on. By the age of fourteen, according to Basil Bernstein, many such children are "unteachable." Keeping them in school does not add to their knowledge; it only damages their self-respect, which is already small. For the child whose class culture *does* encourage upward mobility, schooling very often has the broadening and liberating effects that it is supposed to have. But even for these children, ". . . education is but one of many factors influencing mobility, and it may be far from a dominant factor."

Class-cultural factors largely account for the conspicuous difference between the slum and the suburban school. Each school has a class character imposed upon it by the social setting in which it exists; this, and not staff inefficiency, racial discrimination, or inequitable provision of resources, is the *main* reason for the virtues of one and the defects of the other. The implication is one that reformers find hard to accept—to wit, that no matter how able, dedicated, and hardworking the teachers, no matter how ample the facilities of the school or how well-designed its curriculum, no matter how free the atmosphere of the school from racial or other prejudice, the performance of pupils at the lower end of the class-cultural scale will always fall short not only of that of pupils at the upper end of the scale, but also of what is necessary to make them educated workers. . . .

These and other studies lead one to conclude that if the teachers, facilities, and curricula of all slum schools were exactly as good as those of the very best suburban ones, and if all schools were integrated, there would be almost as many low achievers as there are now.

If the view that has been taken here is correct, the principal difficulty is that the school is future-oriented, whereas the lower-class (or "disadvantaged") pupil is present-oriented. "The school," writes Bernstein, "is an institution where every item in the present is finely linked to a distant future, and in consequence there is no serious clash of expectations between the school and the middle-class child." The lower-class child, by contrast,

> is concerned mainly with the present; his social structure, unlike that of the middle-class child, provides little incentive or purposeful support to make the methods and ends of the school personally meaningful. The problems of discipline and classroom control result not from isolated points of resistance or conflict but from the attempt to reorient a whole pattern of perception with its emotional counterpart. . . .

The implication is that the school must adapt to the mentality of the lower-class child if it is to be of use to him. . . .

The trouble with this idea, however, is that a lower-class education is a contradiction in terms; lower-class culture is the attitudes and behavior patterns of people who have not been educated at all. To be sure, a child "learns" this culture in the sense that he learns to be improvident, undisciplined, and so on. But what he learns is not knowledge that could be taught in school even if everyone agreed that it should be. No one would write it down in books (for to do so would require a large measure of "middle-class" knowledge), no one would teach it (a lower-class teacher would not come to work regularly and would not have anything to teach in a classroom if he did), and no one would learn it (for the lower-class pupil is poorly disposed toward learning anything).

Giving a "lower-class education" can only mean giving no education at all, and this, one would suppose, can be done better on the street than in school. If, for example, it is pointless to try to teach the child correct English, it is pointless to try to teach him English at all. The only system that will not favor the child at the upper end of the class-cultural scale is one that frees the lower-class child from having to go to school at all. *All* education favors the middle- and upper-class child, because to be middle- or upper-class is to have qualities that make one particularly educable. . . .

There are at least three compelling reasons for getting nonlearners out of school. The first is to stop what one educator has called the process of "anti-education" in school and thus to prevent further injury to the nonlearners' self-respect and further lessening of their regard for the institutions of the society. As matters now stand, the pretense of the school—one that must be ridiculous to boys who will be manual workers and to girls who will soon start having babies—that it and it alone offers "opportunity" is surely one cause of youth unrest. The boy who knows that he has learned nothing since the eighth grade but that he must nevertheless sit in boredom, frustration, and embarrassment until he is sixteen or seventeen (in a few states, eighteen), when finally he will be labeled "dropout," must be profoundly disaffected by the experience. . . .

The frustration, anger, and contempt for authority engendered by the school may possibly enter into the personality of the individual, coloring his attitudes in adulthood and leading him to take a cynical and resentful view of the society and all its works. Conceivably, the practice of forcing the incapable and unwilling to waste their adolescent years in schoolrooms further weakens the already tenuous attachment of the lower classes to social institutions. The discovery that the school consists largely of cant and pretense may prepare the way for the discovery that the police and the courts, for example, do too. . . .

A second reason for getting nonlearners out of the school is—paradoxical though it may seem—to give them opportunities and incentives to learn. Not everything worth learning must be (or indeed can be) learned from books and teachers, and not everyone—not even everyone with a first-rate mind—learns better from books and teachers than from other sources. Educators tend to overlook this, since they have a professional interest in booklearning and have been self-selected into their occupation on the basis of an aptitude for it. . . . Even a few troublemakers can distract and intimidate a whole class of serious students and wear almost any teacher down to the breaking point. In one slum school it was found that even the best teachers had to devote half the school day to discipline and to organizational detail. . . .

An able pupil under the present system is usually ready for college after the tenth or the eleventh grade. (In one experiment, such "dropouts" did as well or better in college than classmates who spent four years in high school; moreover, "their interest in their studies is often greater than that of their contemporaries who have been exposed to the boredom which frequently accompanies high school education.") The system should be changed to speed up the process of education. It is evident from European practice, as well as from that of the better schools in this country, that with proper curricula and teaching methods almost as much can be learned in a nine-year school as in the present twelve-year one. Fritz Machlup, whose conclusion this is, has remarked, "Most people *can* learn what they ever learn in school in eight years, and if they are kept there for ten, twelve, fourteen, or sixteen years they will merely learn it more slowly. . . ."

If large numbers of boys and girls are to be let out of school after eight grades, which in most cases would be at the age of fourteen, the question arises of how their time is to be occupied. One could argue that, even if they learn nothing in school, it is, on the whole, better to keep them there than to let them lie around in idleness or roam the streets. The young require a certain amount of looking after. Who is to look after them if not teachers?

In principle, the answer to this question is easy. At whatever age they finish school, boys and girls should go to work. The discipline of the job will more than take the place of that of the school.

WITHOUT MARX OR JESUS

Jacques-François Revel

. . . There is a chasm between developed countries and underdeveloped countries; and there is another chasm between informed countries and underinformed countries. Two different kinds of men are being created. The first information revolution was that which established freedom of the press and of written communication. Only a limited number of countries have, thus far, been affected by that revolution. The second information revolution established the freedom of the audiovisual media; and it has affected an even smaller number of countries. The power of the audivisual media, which results from that freedom, is the only effective counterbalance to the quasi omnipotence of the Executive branch, the only source of energy which nourishes and buttresses the traditional means of parliamentary control. And that power must be complete or it cannot exist. Except for the necessity of protecting the rights of individuals to legal recourse against the media—rights which should be ample—and for insisting on the "equal-time" provisions of the law, which are imperative, any restriction, whether overt or secret, that is imposed upon the information media under the pretext of preventing abuses, is the equivalent of prescribing suicide as a cure for the common cold. Information must not be editorialized or moralized except to the extent that information itself is capable of having an editorial or moral impact. And the first prerequisite of freedom of information, like any other freedom, is abundance of information.

Frenchmen, when discussing television, often ask one another, "Did you see the program last night?" They do not ask, "What did you watch last night?" Most often, there is only *one* program; and sometimes there is not even that. In the United States, the chance of two viewers watching the same program is statistically small. In the larger cities, for example, there are eight or ten channels from which to choose. The term "American media" therefore signifies diversity. When, at eight o'clock in the evening, one can choose between a panel discussion on the pill, a detailed analysis of the Supreme Court and of the ways in which a citizen can appeal to it, a one-hour coverage of school desegregation in Mississippi, a course in dietetics, and, of course, old movies, game shows, situation comedies, and variety shows, then one is hardly a "slave to television." Indeed, it is more like being turned loose in a library.

In New York, there are programs for deaf-mutes, in which sign language is used. There is a preschool program, *Sesame Street,* on the so-called educational network, which give some indication of what television could mean to elementary education. This educational network was begun during a strike at the commercial networks, and received immediate financial aid from the Ford Foundation and from private contributors. No commercial advertising is permitted. It is an outstanding illustration of what private initiative can do when a system is flexible and free from monopolies. . . .

When something happens in America, the media cover every detail of the event: a Mafia scandal in New Jersey, with political implications; illegal betting on football games; the financial wheeling and dealing of a former secretary to the Senate Majority. There is never any "Mr. X." Names are given, and photographs, and details about the crime, and the amounts of money involved. On the series of programs about the F.B.I. that I mentioned earlier, for instance, former agents of that agency appeared in person to explain and criticize certain operations in which the rights of citizens had clearly been violated.

Though the television networks depend on commercial advertising as their source of revenue, they still retain a certain independence with respect to their sponsors. One indication of this is the fact that, even when cigarette commercials were allowed on television (they have been prohibited as of January 1, 1971), the networks also carried special programs that were designed to point out the dangers of smoking. (This is inconceivable in France, since the sale of tobacco is a state monopoly.) Another proof is the rise to prominence of Ralph Nader, the young lawyer who is known in Europe chiefly for his book *Unsafe at Any Speed,* and for his confrontation with General Motors. Since then, he has turned his attention to other subjects also, ranging from the intrigues of insurance companies to the ingredients of hot dogs, and his efforts have, on several occasions, resulted in congressional legislation. When Nader has something important to say about a particular product, or about an industry, he is accorded wide attention on the television networks, and most often appears on Walter Cronkite's celebrated newscast on C.B.S. When it happens that what Nader is going to say would offend a sponsor, the network informs the sponsor of the substance of Nader's report; then, if the sponsor wishes to withdraw, he is free to go in peace. Even so, there is a long waiting list of sponsors for Mr. Cronkite's half-hour program. In that sense, and contrary to what is generally believed, sponsors need C.B.S. more than C.B.S. needs sponsors.

In addition to product commercials, American television also carries various announcements and messages designed to inform viewers about their rights. One nonproduct commercial, for example, explains the existence of an antidiscrimination housing law, and gives a Washington telephone number that anyone can call for free legal advice on problems in that area.

Certainly, without television no one would ever have suspected the amount of opposition to the Vietnam war that exists in America. Neither French nor British imperialism, in its heyday, was ever challenged from within to the degree that American imperialism is being contested by Americans.

We often hear people say that, even if the above description of the availability of information in America is correct, all that information serves little purpose. American public opinion is still dominated by emotion and self-interest. However, the recent history of the United States proves just the opposite. We tend too much to ignore the fact that, for the first time in the history of the world, a foreign war—especially a colonial expedition or a war that is supposed to be in the interests of national security—has been strongly opposed within the country waging that war. Usually, all struggles for freedom or justice take place at the domestic level, and are carried on for the benefit of the people in the country where they are happening. And, generally, even the lower classes share in the imperialistic ambitions of the governing class, especially when it is a matter of a colonial war. One of the most persistent lessons of history has been that the countries most on guard against abuses at home are the ones who most lack a critical or moral sense when it comes to abuses committed against other peoples. The transition from internal democracy to external democracy, or at least to a preoccupation with external democracy, represents a giant step—a step that the United States has been the first to take. That Americans were able to make that transition is due to the freedom of information in their country. It means that there has been real progress toward the abolition of the right to perpetrate crimes in the name of foreign policy. Neither Athenian imperialism nor the colonial adventures of the English, French, and Dutch ever met with substantial opposition. Opposition, if it existed at all, was confined to a few intellectual circles among the privileged elite; that is, to those who were sufficiently well informed to be conscious of the atrocities committed for the sake of conquest. Popular sentiment was in no way engaged when it was a question of exploiting and exterminating foreigners. The French Communist Party, recognizing this fact, blinked at the French government's resumption of control over its colonial empire immediately after the Second World War. In the years following 1947—the year in which the communist ministers were forced to resign from the government —its opposition, however ineffective, to the wars in Indochina, Madagascar, and North Africa, centered around the more general conflict of the cold war. There was never any protest of sufficient breadth or weight to influence the course of events, or any internal protest against the injustices resulting from foreign policy.

There has never been, in any country, any dissent of sufficient breadth or weight to influence the course of events, or any internal protest against the injustices resulting from foreign policy. The moratoriums and other antiwar demonstrations in the United States are the first mass phenomena of this kind; and they are all the more significant since the participants are people of all ages and of all social classes. During the French war in Algeria, there were protests in France, but they came only from the extreme Left; or rather, they came from newspapers of the extreme Left and center-Left, and never succeeded in winning the support of the people—let alone of the middle class. Even young people, except for a number of students, did not rebel. Resistance to the draft was negligible, and public opinion strongly disapproved of draft evasion (of which there were not more than a few dozen cases). In the United States, however, there are tens of thousands of draft evaders; and, instead of being condemned, they are encouraged and aided. Any inquiry in Canada or Sweden will indicate the extent, and the degree of organization, of American draft evasion and army desertion since 1964. It has become a commonplace occurrence for a young man to return his draft card to his local draft board, or even for small stacks of the cards to be burned in the streets, as the owners of the cards look on.

Never before has the "sacred ego" of a nation become a subject of political controversy; and especially not in a nation that stands at the apex of its power. The consequences of this development are incalculable, for the criticism of imperialism and nationalism is taking place, for the first time, at the very source of imperialism and nationalism, and it is being spoken by those who are in a position to do something about it. Other kinds of criticism are, for practical purposes, useless. One is always opposed to the imperialism of other people; and those other people could not care less. The hard thing is to be opposed to one's own imperialism. The whole world was against British imperialism during the Boer War, and against French imperialism during the Algerian war; and the only effect that opposition had was to exasperate the chauvinists of both countries, except in the case of a few fringe groups without power or support.

We have not yet discussed the question of whether this massive, internal, and non-elitist opposition to patriotic imperialism is the result of the accessibility of information. The unprecedented power and style of opposition in America seems to result both from the free flow of information and from the factors that made that free flow possible. At the root of American democracy is the idea that everyone has the right to improve his situation, but that no one has the right to take unfair advantage in doing so. This attitude has been incorporated into the legal system, in the form of the antitrust laws—which are far from being the joke that Europeans think they are. It also involves the conviction that neither the state, nor special-interest groups, nor institutions—however praiseworthy their goals—nor industry, nor the army, nor anyone or anything else has the right to refuse to explain its actions or to withhold information. This is particularly true in the case of groups or individuals whose activities are suspected of being detrimental, not only to the common good (a term which, of itself, means nothing), but also to the well-being of this or that group of citizens. Americans, in keeping with this principle, have never permitted newspapers to be closed down by the government, or books to be censored either directly or indirectly. Today, not even films are censored, except in a single state; and, in the latter case, the censorship is not political.

The federal structure of the United States, its legislative diversity, and the lack of uniformity in moral climate in different parts of the country, all offer infinitely more numerous means of fighting oppression and intolerance than are available in countries with strongly centralized governments. A legal argument to the effect that something is "harmful to the morale of the armed services" (an argument used in France even in peacetime, and most recently used to refer to journalists of the Left), is unheard of in the United States. A short time ago, following the success of the film *M.A.S.H.*, one legislator was inspired to introduce a bill forbidding the use of the American uniform in movies or plays that openly ridiculed the armed services. The bill was not taken seriously even at the congressional committee level.

This climate makes it possible for Americans to produce and distribute such films as *Dr. Strangelove, M.A.S.H.*, and *Catch-22*, in which war, militarism, chaplains, and the arbitrary and whimsical nature of decisions at the highest level are satirized with that same freedom from compromise that one finds in the tales of Voltaire. It would be impossible for such films to get beyond the script stage in almost any other country in the world, including more than half of the countries of Europe—and especially France. Eight years after the end of the Algerian war, G. Pontecorvo's *La Bataille d'Alger* (The Battle of Algiers), which won a Golden Lion at the 1965 Venice Film Festival, was ordered withdrawn from circulation within forty-eight hours; and the staff of the Premier himself contacted the French television network and forbade it to show a short clip that had been scheduled. It would also be impossible, in most of the world and especially in France, for anyone to make and distribute films on domestic policies, such as *Medium Cool* or *The Strawberry Statement*, which respectively depict, without understatement, the unleasing of police brutality, and recent instances of police brutality at the 1968 Democratic National Convention in Chicago and in handling students who had occupied a university campus. It is puzzling to see some French critics either treating these films with contempt, or else discussing them as though they were perfectly ordinary, everyday movies. Surely they must know it would be difficult, if not impossible, for a French producer to make a similar film, or even a watered-down version, on the events, say, of May 1968. . . .

This simple distinction between the two kinds of information serves as a line of demarcation between two kinds of civilization. And, to me, it seems that only one of those civilizations has a future. The other seems destined to sink into a maelstrom of errors—errors that will never be recognized until it is too late, until the price of error has been paid and it is too late to do anything about it. . .

It seems impossible that freedom of information is unable to change anything in a society that is exposed to front-page pictures in newspapers and magazines of atrocities committed by the American army in Vietnam, or to direct television coverage of the results of those atrocities, or to interviews with the soldiers, subordinate officers, and generals who have been indicted and handed over to courts-martial for war crimes. What is certain, however, is that never before has there been, in any country, either detailed information on crimes against humanity, or prosecution of those responsible for those crimes. It is not impossible that, somehow, the availability of information is what has made America the exception to that rule. . . .

When we say that the perception of truth by ever increasing numbers of people can have no beneficial effect on the course of history, what we are really saying is that revolution is impossible. Personally, I believe the opposite: that only the free flow of information, which has become politically so efficacious since the beginning of the age of mass media, can effect that synthesis of social revolution and democratic freedoms which has had so many false starts in the past century. . . .

The information revolution is both a political revolution and an intellectual revolution. It calls into question both power and culture. It challenges the distinction between governors and governed, between intelligentsia and masses. No one can claim to be a revolutionary who wants to abolish the political revolution and support the intellectual revolution.

The mass media, above all, have proved to be a means not only of transmission, but also of causing people to act on an event, and no longer by propaganda, but through the information itself. This situation, commonplace as it is in the United States, was experienced by the French only for a few weeks in May 1968. On that occasion, the media were part of the events covered, and they affected those events. In the United States, television produces a constant rubbing-of-elbow among communities which, without television, might never meet, but which, through television, know one another with some intimacy. Direct coverage of a black riot or of police intervention on a campus not only allows the population as a whole to become better "informed" and to "reflect" on that information—which is the classic concept of information—but it also transforms the spectator into an actor; it makes him more than the product of his own personal experience; it incorporates him into the event. . . .

Index